Shojo Beat

OTOMEN

Story & Art by
Aya Kanno

Volume
FIVE

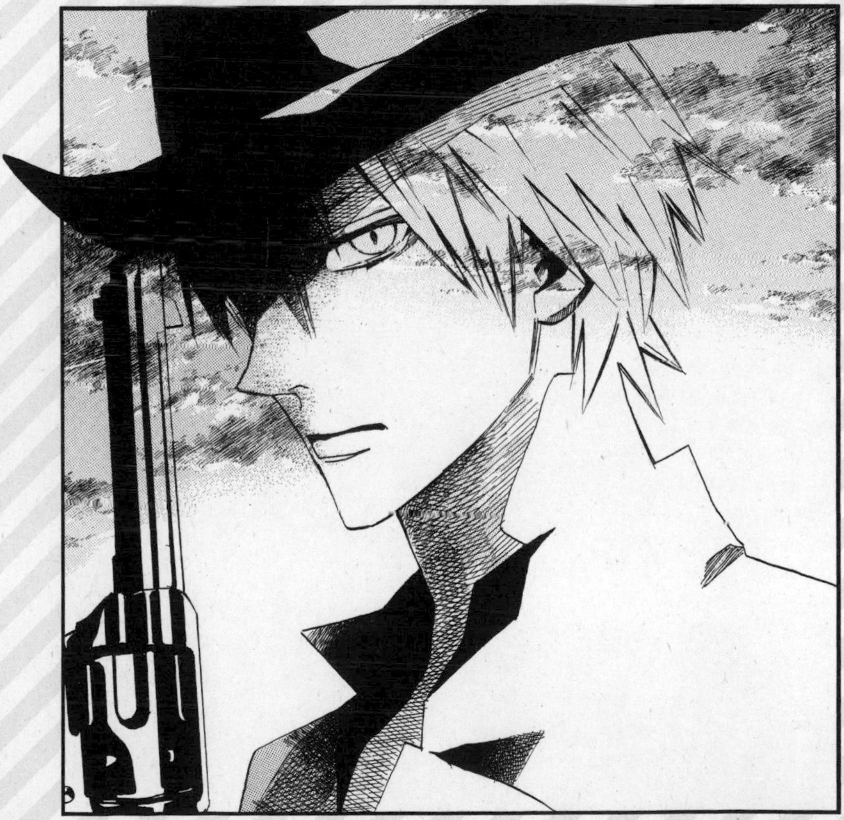

OTOMEN CHARACTERS & STORY

What is an OTOMEN?

O•to•men *[OH-toe-men]*

1) A young man with girlish interests and thoughts.

2) A young man who has talent for cooking, needlework and general housework.

3) A manly young man with a girlish heart.

Asuka Masamune

The captain of Ginyuri Academy High School's kendo team. He is handsome, studious and (to the casual observer) the perfect high school student. But he is actually an *otomen*, a man with a girlish heart. He loves cute things ♥, and he has a natural talent for cooking, needlework and general housekeeping. He's even a big fan of the shojo manga *Love Chick*.

STORY

Asuka Masamune, the kendo captain, is actually an *otomen* (a girlish guy)—a man who likes cute things, housework and shojo manga. When he was young, his father left home to become a woman. His mother was traumatized, and ever since then, he has kept his girlish interests a secret. However, things change when he meets Juta, a guy who is using Asuka as the basis for the female character in the shojo manga he is writing (←top secret). Asuka also starts having feelings for a tomboy girl who is good at martial arts. Because of this, he's slowly reverting to his true *otomen* self!

Ryo Miyakozuka

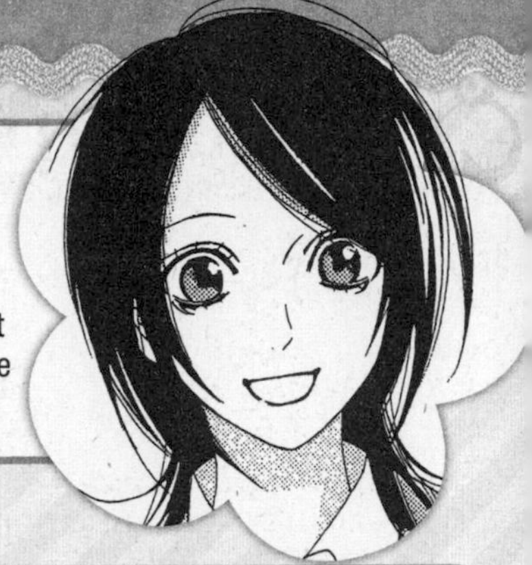

Asuka's classmate for whom he has feelings. She has studied martial arts under her father ever since she was little, and she is very good at it. On the other hand, her housekeeping skills are disastrous. She's a very eccentric beauty.

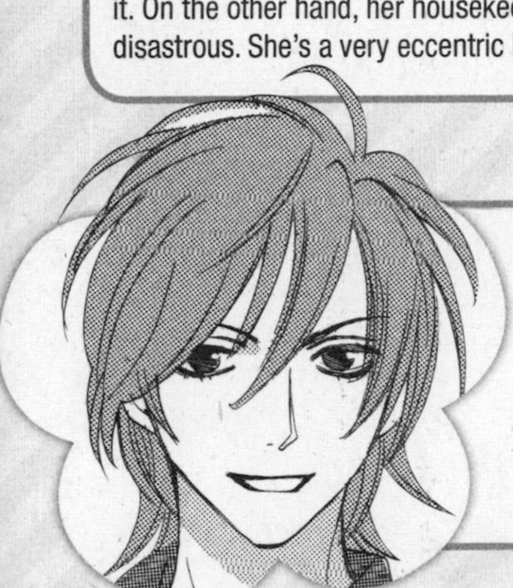

Juta Tachibana

Asuka's classmate. He's flirtatious, but he's actually the popular shojo manga artist Jewel Sachihana. He is using Asuka and Ryo as character concepts in his manga *Love Chick*, which is being published in the shojo magazine *Hana to Mame*. His personal life is a mystery!

Yamato Ariake

Underclassman at Asuka's school. He looks like a girl, but he admires manliness and has long, delusional fantasies about being manly…

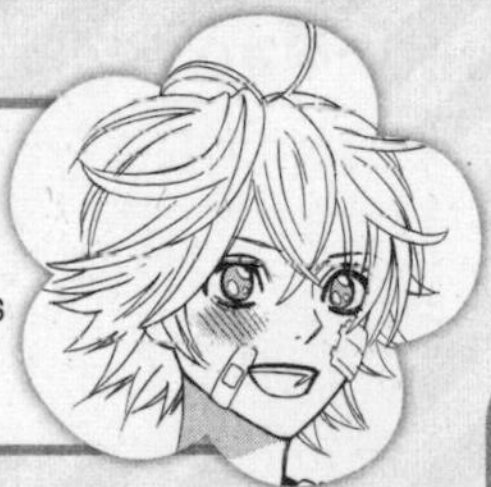

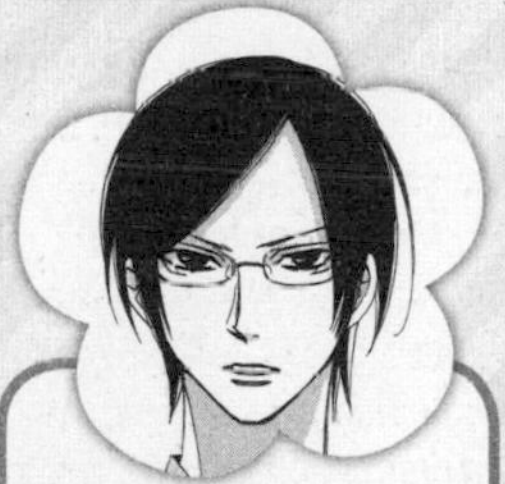

Hajime Tonomine

The captain of Kinbara High School's kendo team, he sees Asuka as his lifelong rival. He is the strong and silent type but is actually an *otomen* who is good with makeup. A *Tsun-sama.*

("Tsun-sama" © Juta Tachibana.)

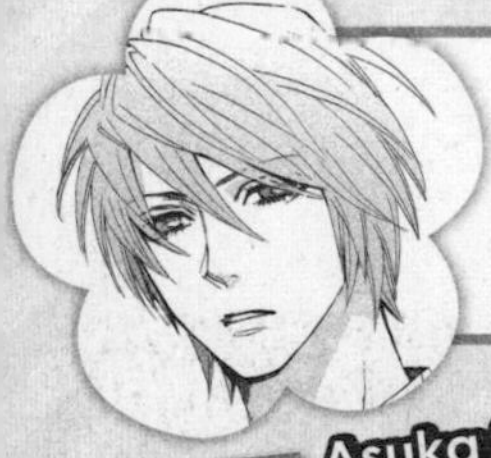

Kitora Kurokawa

Asuka's classmate. He is obsessed with the beauty of flowers. He is an *otomen* who refers to himself as the Flower Evangelist.

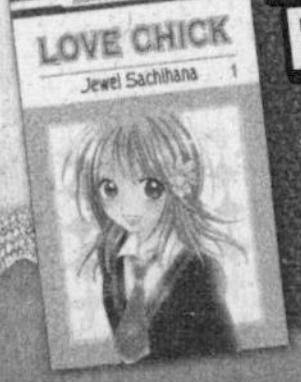
HANA TO MAME COMICS
LOVE CHICK
Jewel Sachihana 1

Asuka is also a BIG FAN!

Hana to Mame Comics

LOVE CHICK by Jewel Sachihana

(Now serialized in *Hana to Mame*)

The very popular shojo comic that Juta writes (under the pen name Jewel Sachihana).

OTOMEN volume 5
CONTENTS

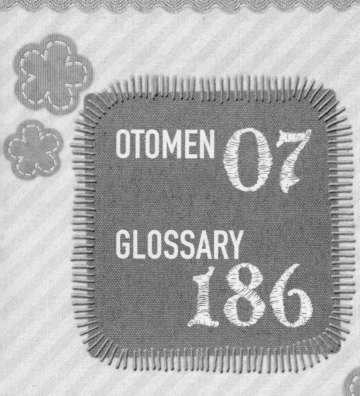

OTOMEN 07

GLOSSARY 186

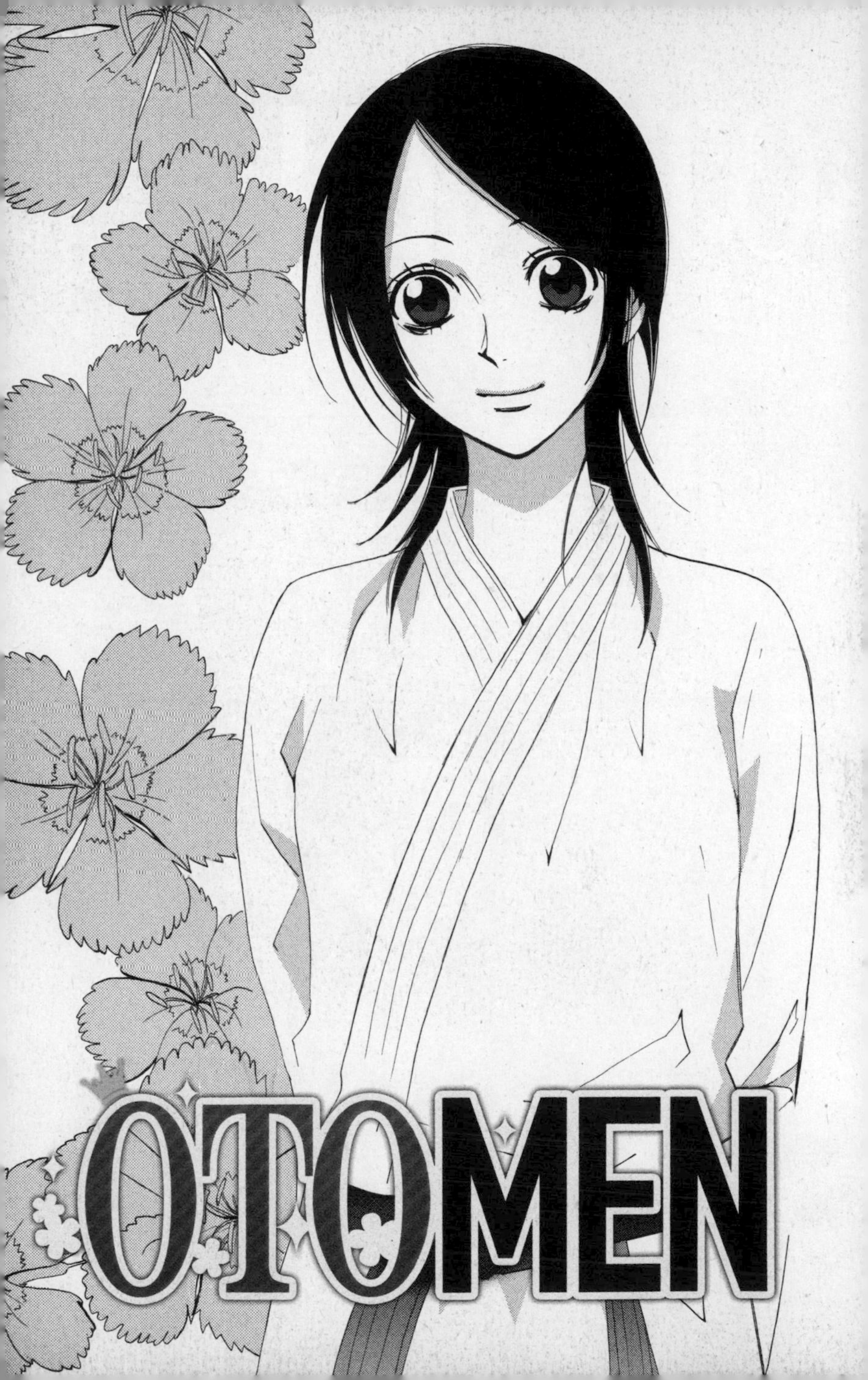
OTOMEN

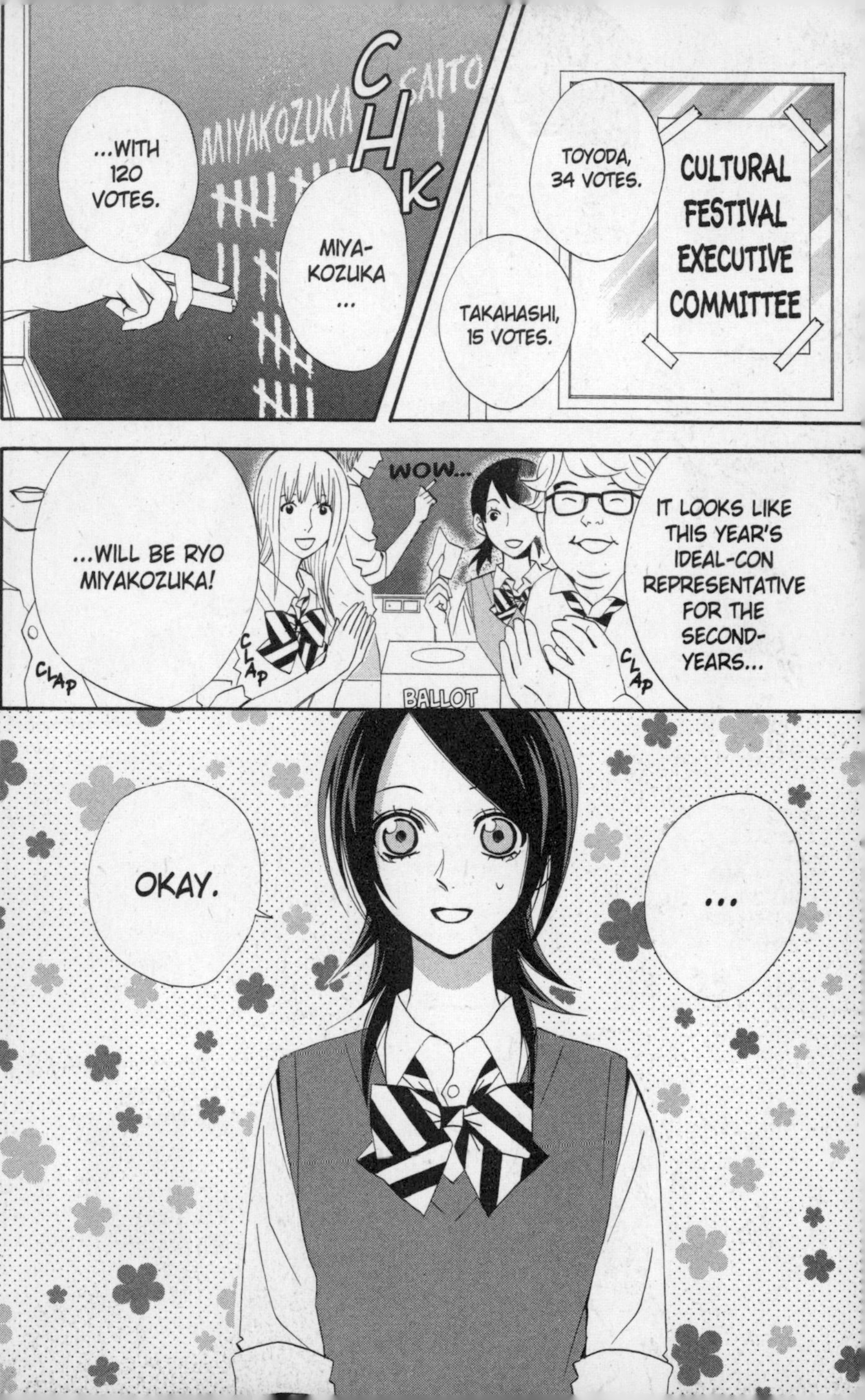
CULTURAL FESTIVAL EXECUTIVE COMMITTEE
TOYODA, 34 VOTES.
TAKAHASHI, 15 VOTES.
SAITO
CHK
MIYA-KOZUKA...
MIYAKOZUKA
...WITH 120 VOTES.
IT LOOKS LIKE THIS YEAR'S IDEAL-CON REPRESENTATIVE FOR THE SECOND-YEARS...
CLAP
WOW...
BALLOT
CLAP
...WILL BE RYO MIYAKOZUKA!
CLAP
...
OKAY.

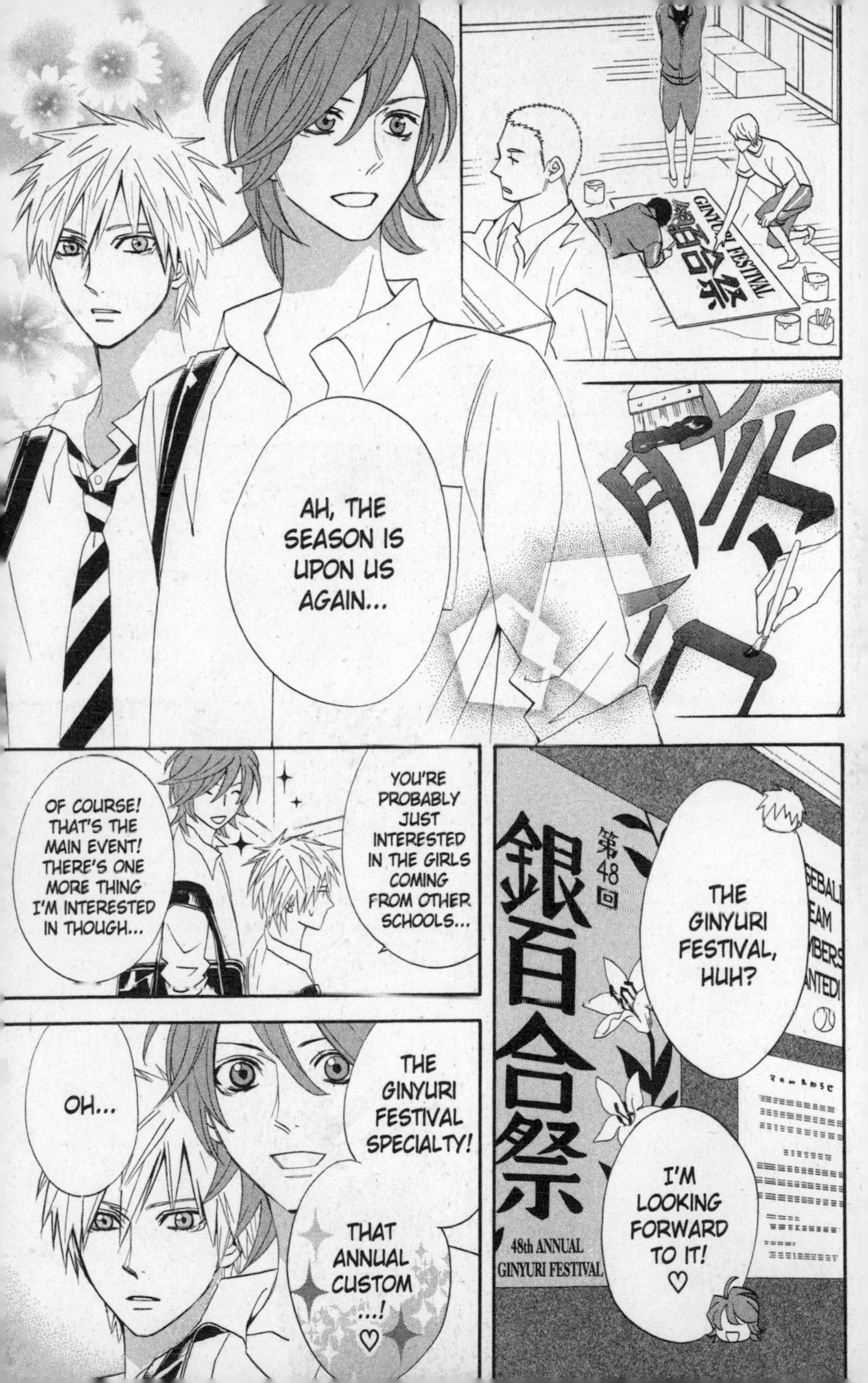
GINYURI FESTIVAL
AH, THE SEASON IS UPON US AGAIN...
第48回 銀百合祭
48th ANNUAL GINYURI FESTIVAL
THE GINYURI FESTIVAL, HUH?
I'M LOOKING FORWARD TO IT! ♡
YOU'RE PROBABLY JUST INTERESTED IN THE GIRLS COMING FROM OTHER SCHOOLS...
OF COURSE! THAT'S THE MAIN EVENT! THERE'S ONE MORE THING I'M INTERESTED IN THOUGH...
THE GINYURI FESTIVAL SPECIALTY!
THAT ANNUAL CUSTOM ...! ♡
OH...

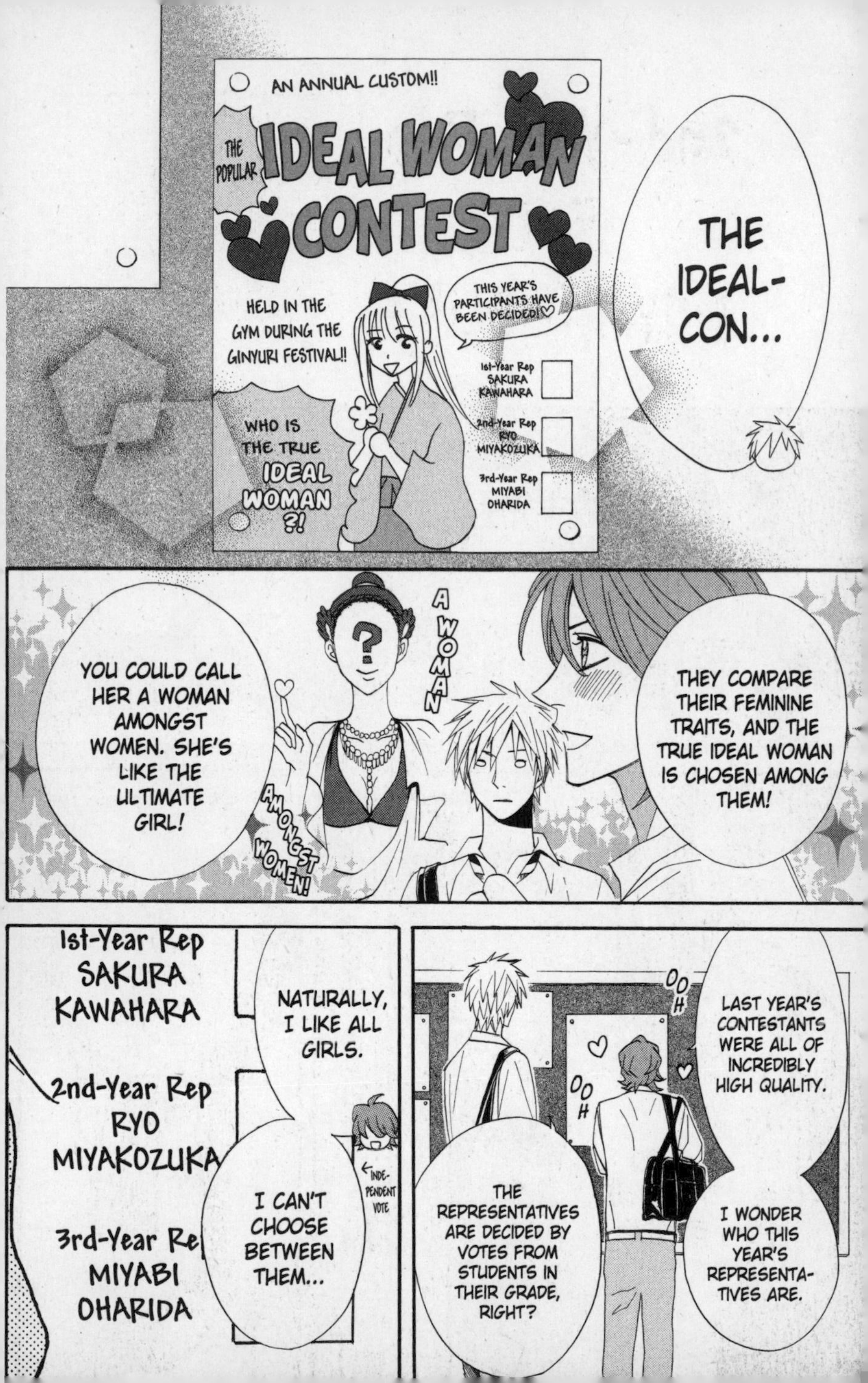
THE IDEAL-CON...
AN ANNUAL CUSTOM!!
THE POPULAR IDEAL WOMAN CONTEST
THIS YEAR'S PARTICIPANTS HAVE BEEN DECIDED!♡
HELD IN THE GYM DURING THE GINYURI FESTIVAL!!
WHO IS THE TRUE IDEAL WOMAN ?!
1st-Year Rep SAKURA KAWAHARA
2nd-Year Rep RYO MIYAKOZUKA
3rd-Year Rep MIYABI OHARIDA
THEY COMPARE THEIR FEMININE TRAITS, AND THE TRUE IDEAL WOMAN IS CHOSEN AMONG THEM!
A WOMAN
YOU COULD CALL HER A WOMAN AMONGST WOMEN. SHE'S LIKE THE ULTIMATE GIRL!
AMONGST WOMEN!
LAST YEAR'S CONTESTANTS WERE ALL OF INCREDIBLY HIGH QUALITY.
OOH
OOH
I WONDER WHO THIS YEAR'S REPRESENTA-TIVES ARE.
THE REPRESENTATIVES ARE DECIDED BY VOTES FROM STUDENTS IN THEIR GRADE, RIGHT?
NATURALLY, I LIKE ALL GIRLS.
I CAN'T CHOOSE BETWEEN THEM...
← INDE-PENDENT VOTE
1st-Year Rep SAKURA KAWAHARA
2nd-Year Rep RYO MIYAKOZUKA
3rd-Year Rep MIYABI OHARIDA

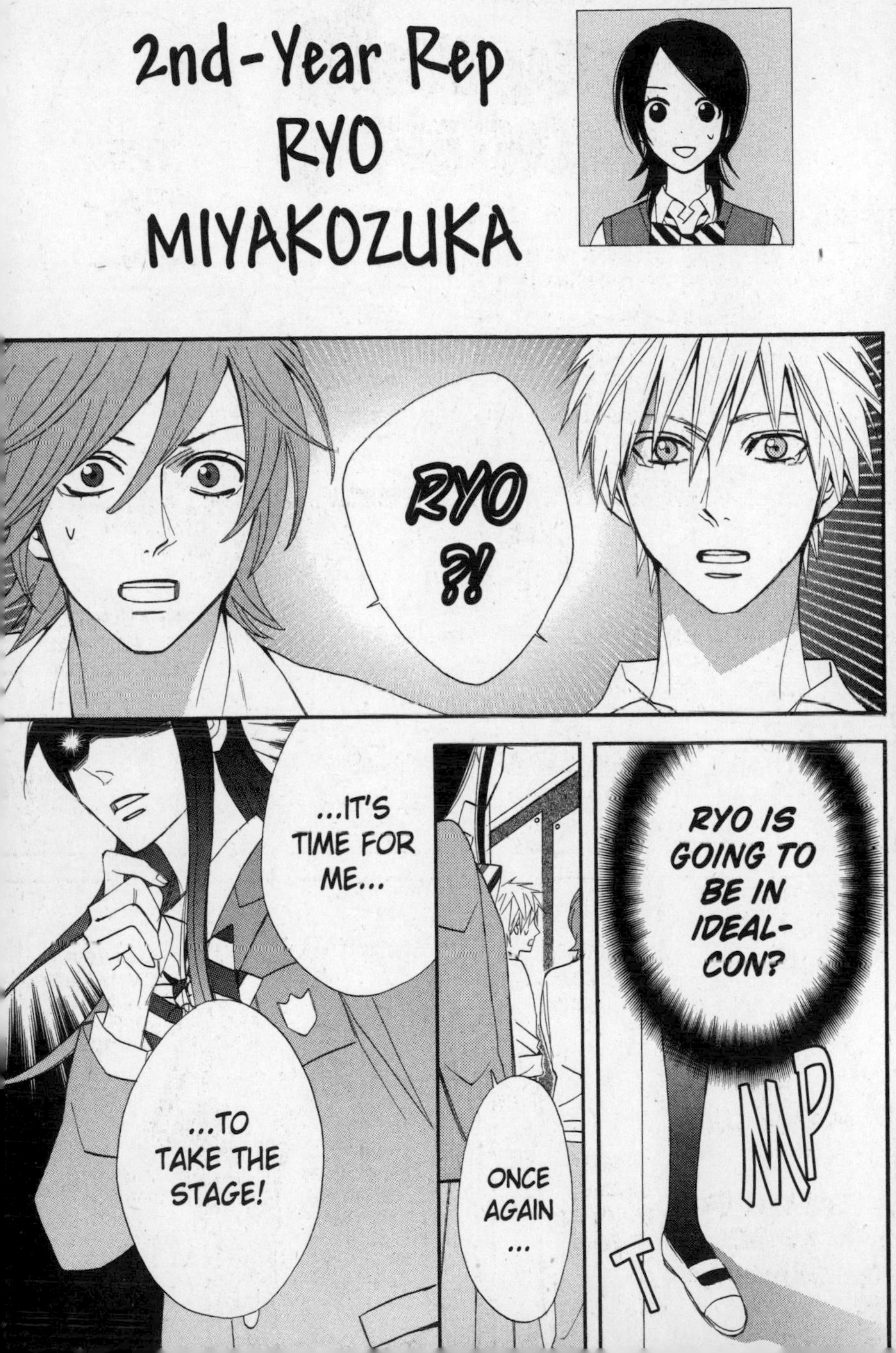
2nd-Year Rep
RYO MIYAKOZUKA
RYO ?!
RYO IS GOING TO BE IN IDEAL-CON?
TMP
ONCE AGAIN ...
...IT'S TIME FOR ME...
...TO TAKE THE STAGE!

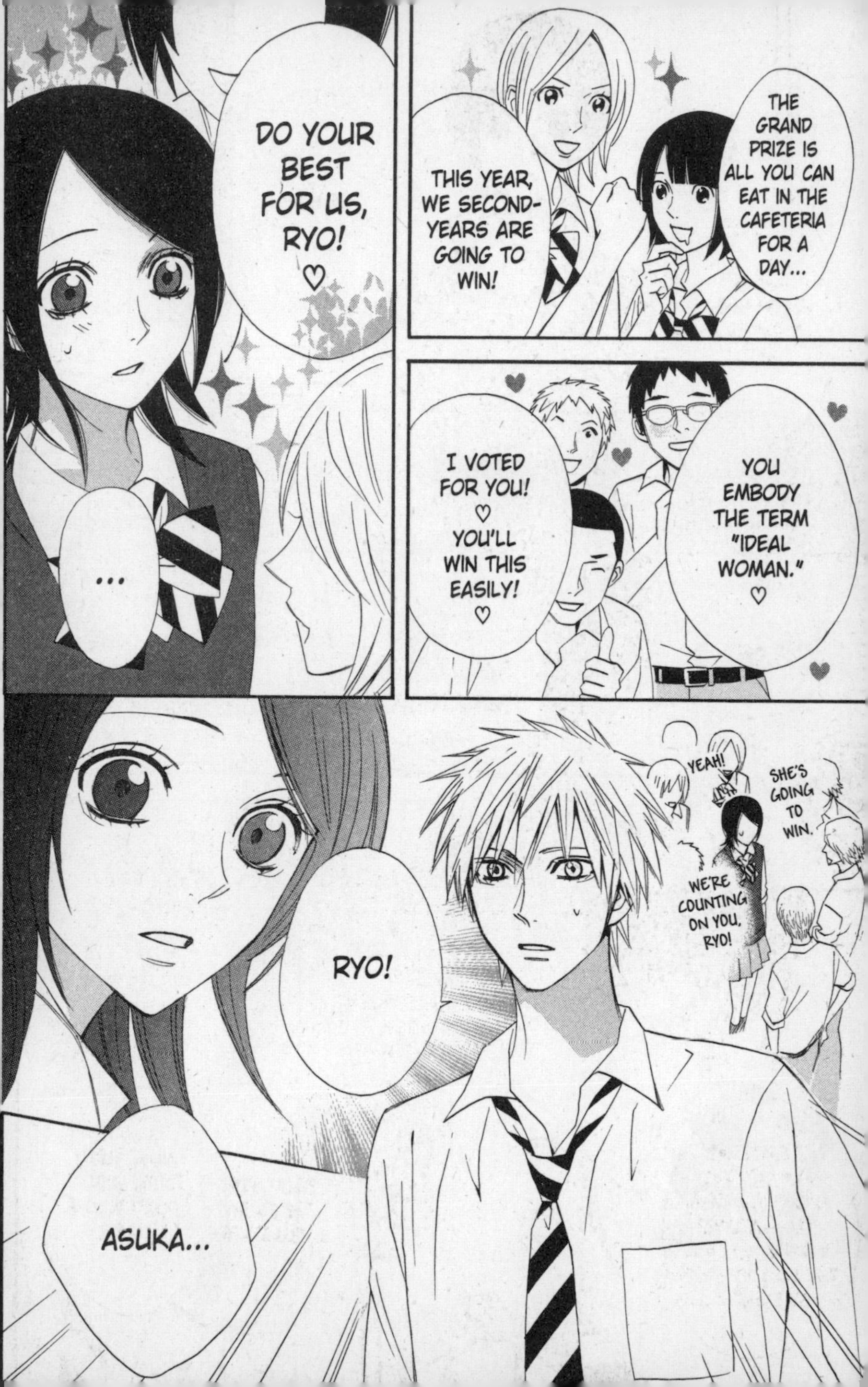
THE GRAND PRIZE IS ALL YOU CAN EAT IN THE CAFETERIA FOR A DAY...
THIS YEAR, WE SECOND-YEARS ARE GOING TO WIN!
YOU EMBODY THE TERM "IDEAL WOMAN." ♡
I VOTED FOR YOU! ♡ YOU'LL WIN THIS EASILY! ♡
DO YOUR BEST FOR US, RYO! ♡
...
SHE'S GOING TO WIN.
YEAH!
WE'RE COUNTING ON YOU, RYO!
RYO!
ASUKA...

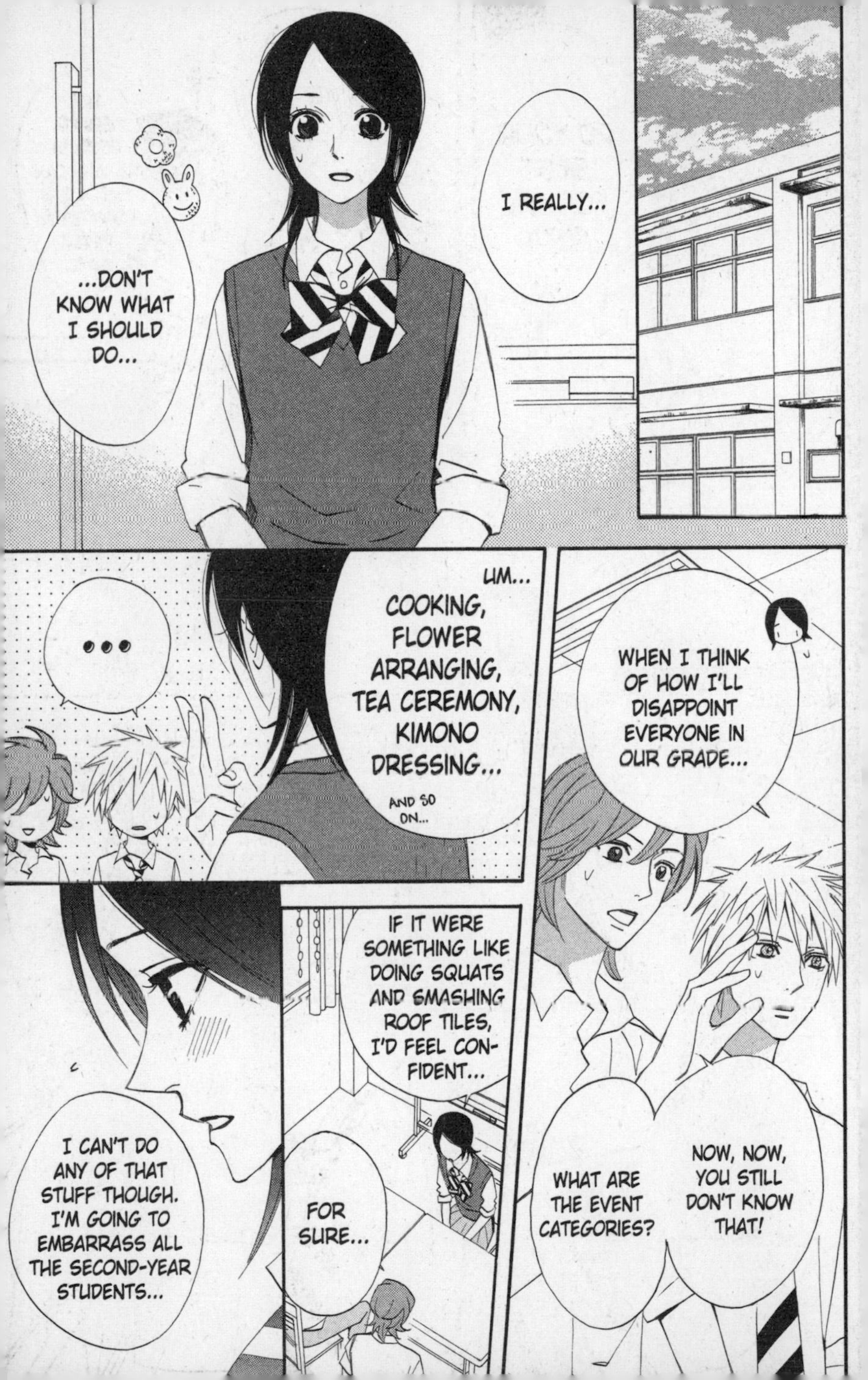
I REALLY...
...DON'T KNOW WHAT I SHOULD DO...
WHEN I THINK OF HOW I'LL DISAPPOINT EVERYONE IN OUR GRADE...
NOW, NOW, YOU STILL DON'T KNOW THAT!
WHAT ARE THE EVENT CATEGORIES?
UM...
COOKING, FLOWER ARRANGING, TEA CEREMONY, KIMONO DRESSING...
AND SO ON...
...
IF IT WERE SOMETHING LIKE DOING SQUATS AND SMASHING ROOF TILES, I'D FEEL CON-FIDENT...
FOR SURE...
I CAN'T DO ANY OF THAT STUFF THOUGH. I'M GOING TO EMBARRASS ALL THE SECOND-YEAR STUDENTS...

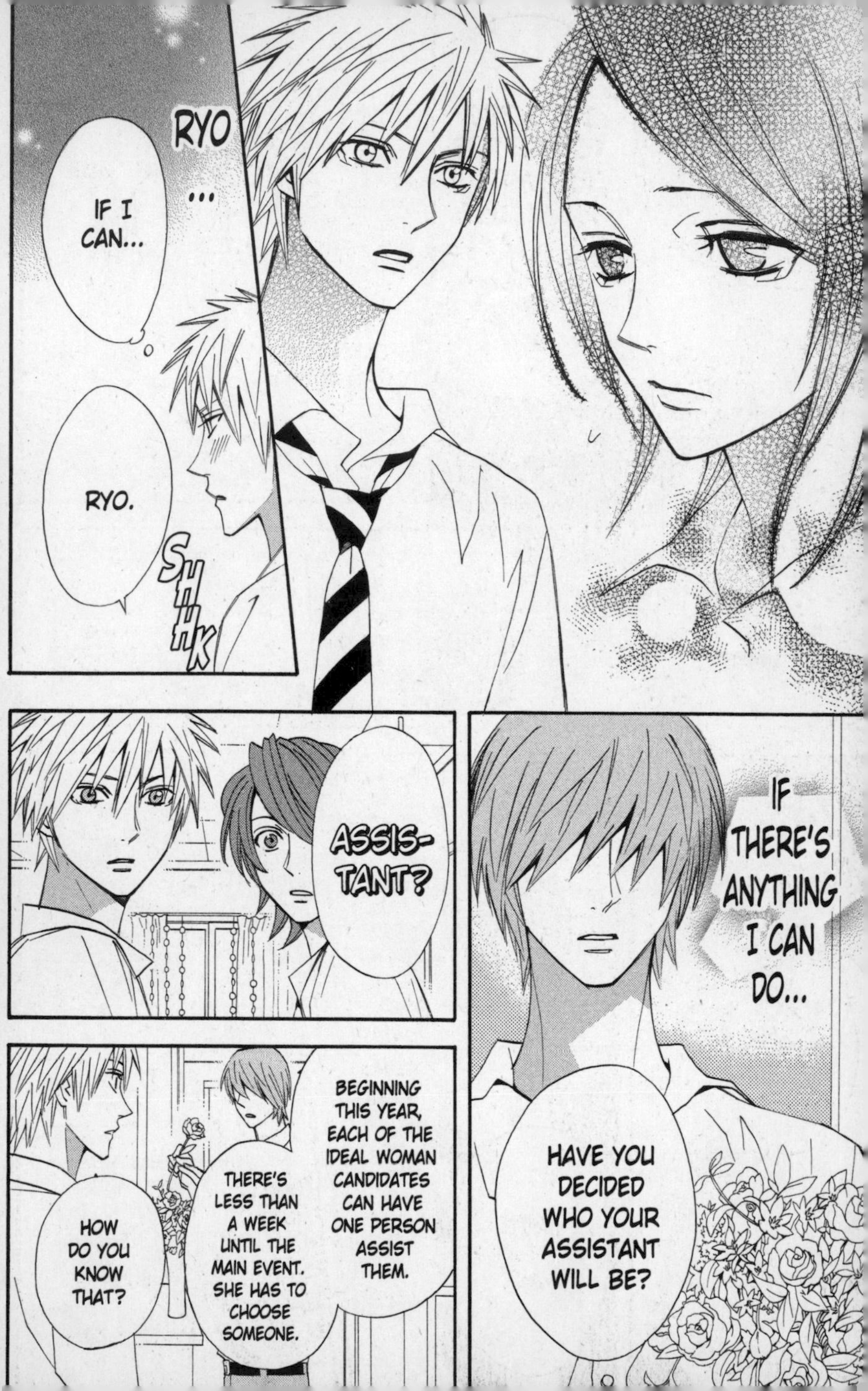
RYO
...
IF I CAN...
RYO.
SHHK
IF THERE'S ANYTHING I CAN DO...
HAVE YOU DECIDED WHO YOUR ASSISTANT WILL BE?
ASSIS-TANT?
BEGINNING THIS YEAR, EACH OF THE IDEAL WOMAN CANDIDATES CAN HAVE ONE PERSON ASSIST THEM.
THERE'S LESS THAN A WEEK UNTIL THE MAIN EVENT. SHE HAS TO CHOOSE SOMEONE.
HOW DO YOU KNOW THAT?

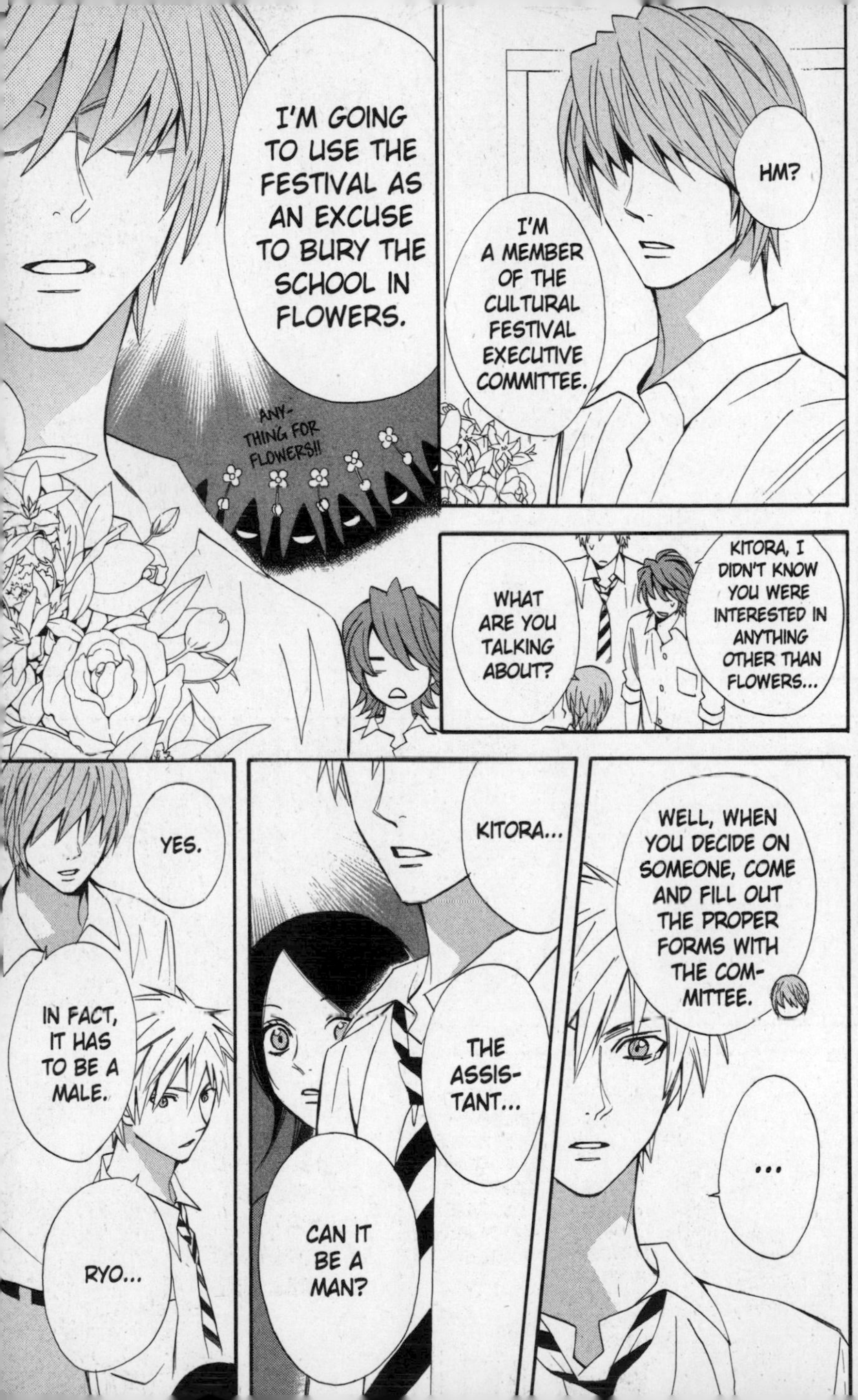
HM?
I'M A MEMBER OF THE CULTURAL FESTIVAL EXECUTIVE COMMITTEE.
KITORA, I DIDN'T KNOW YOU WERE INTERESTED IN ANYTHING OTHER THAN FLOWERS...
WHAT ARE YOU TALKING ABOUT?
I'M GOING TO USE THE FESTIVAL AS AN EXCUSE TO BURY THE SCHOOL IN FLOWERS.
ANY-THING FOR FLOWERS!!
WELL, WHEN YOU DECIDE ON SOMEONE, COME AND FILL OUT THE PROPER FORMS WITH THE COM-MITTEE.
...
KITORA...
THE ASSIS-TANT...
CAN IT BE A MAN?
YES.
IN FACT, IT HAS TO BE A MALE.
RYO...

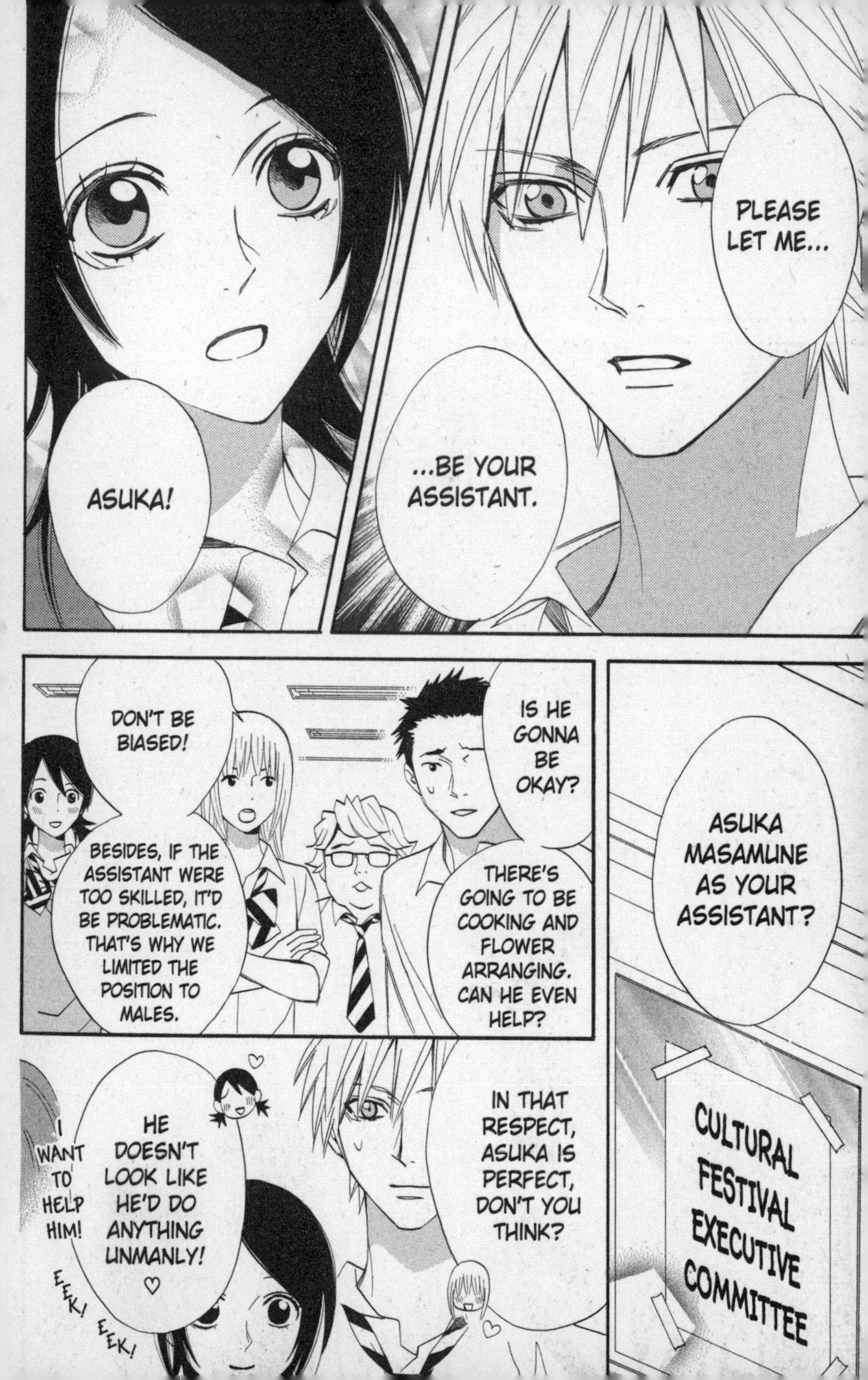
PLEASE LET ME...
...BE YOUR ASSISTANT.
ASUKA!
ASUKA MASAMUNE AS YOUR ASSISTANT?
CULTURAL FESTIVAL EXECUTIVE COMMITTEE
IS HE GONNA BE OKAY?
THERE'S GOING TO BE COOKING AND FLOWER ARRANGING. CAN HE EVEN HELP?
DON'T BE BIASED!
BESIDES, IF THE ASSISTANT WERE TOO SKILLED, IT'D BE PROBLEMATIC. THAT'S WHY WE LIMITED THE POSITION TO MALES.
IN THAT RESPECT, ASUKA IS PERFECT, DON'T YOU THINK?
HE DOESN'T LOOK LIKE HE'D DO ANYTHING UNMANLY! ♡
I WANT TO HELP HIM!
EEK! EEK!

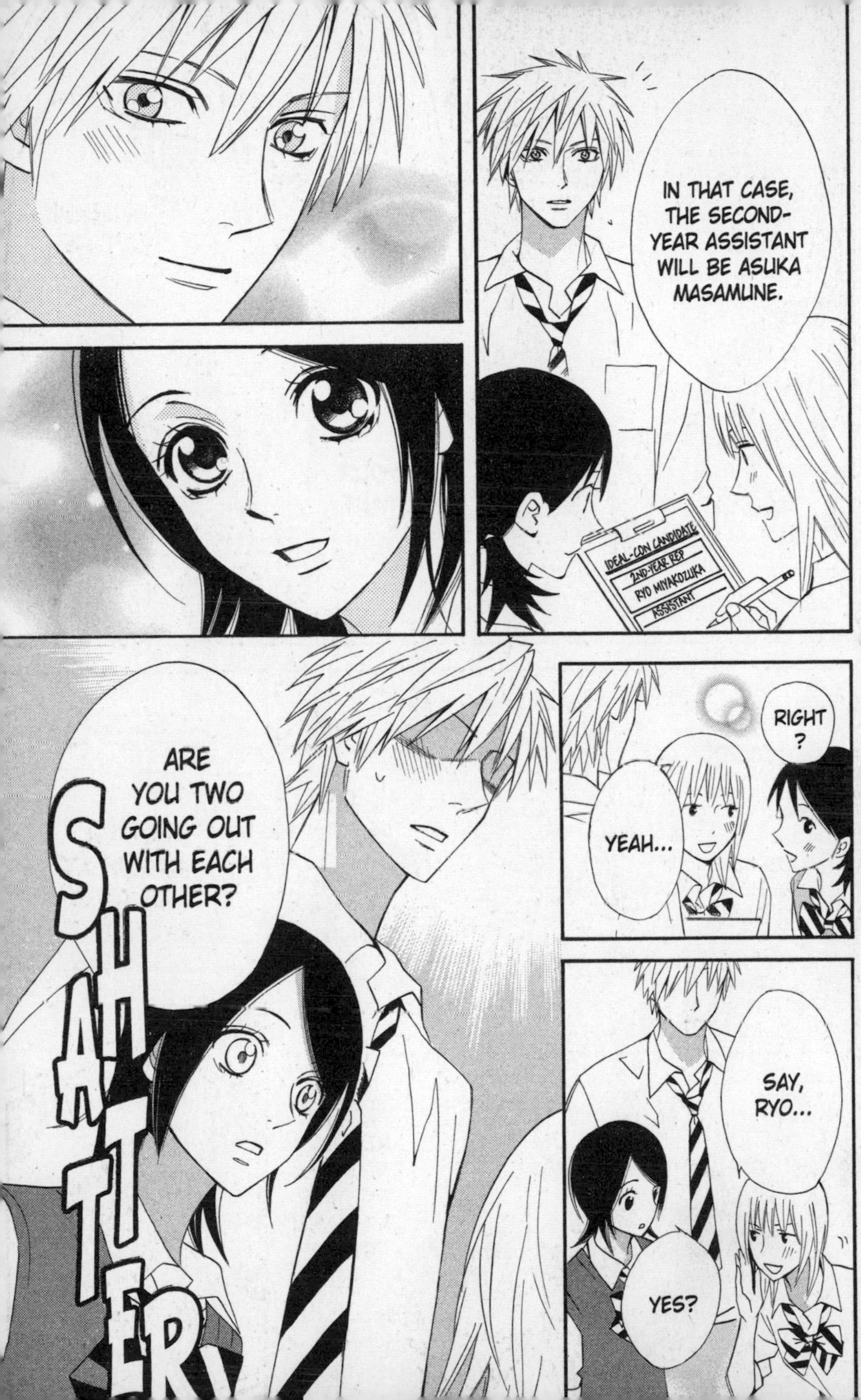
IN THAT CASE, THE SECOND-YEAR ASSISTANT WILL BE ASUKA MASAMUNE.
IDEAL-CON CANDIDATE
2ND-YEAR REP
RYO MIYAKOZUKA
ASSISTANT
RIGHT?
YEAH...
SAY, RYO...
YES?
ARE YOU TWO GOING OUT WITH EACH OTHER?
SHATTER!

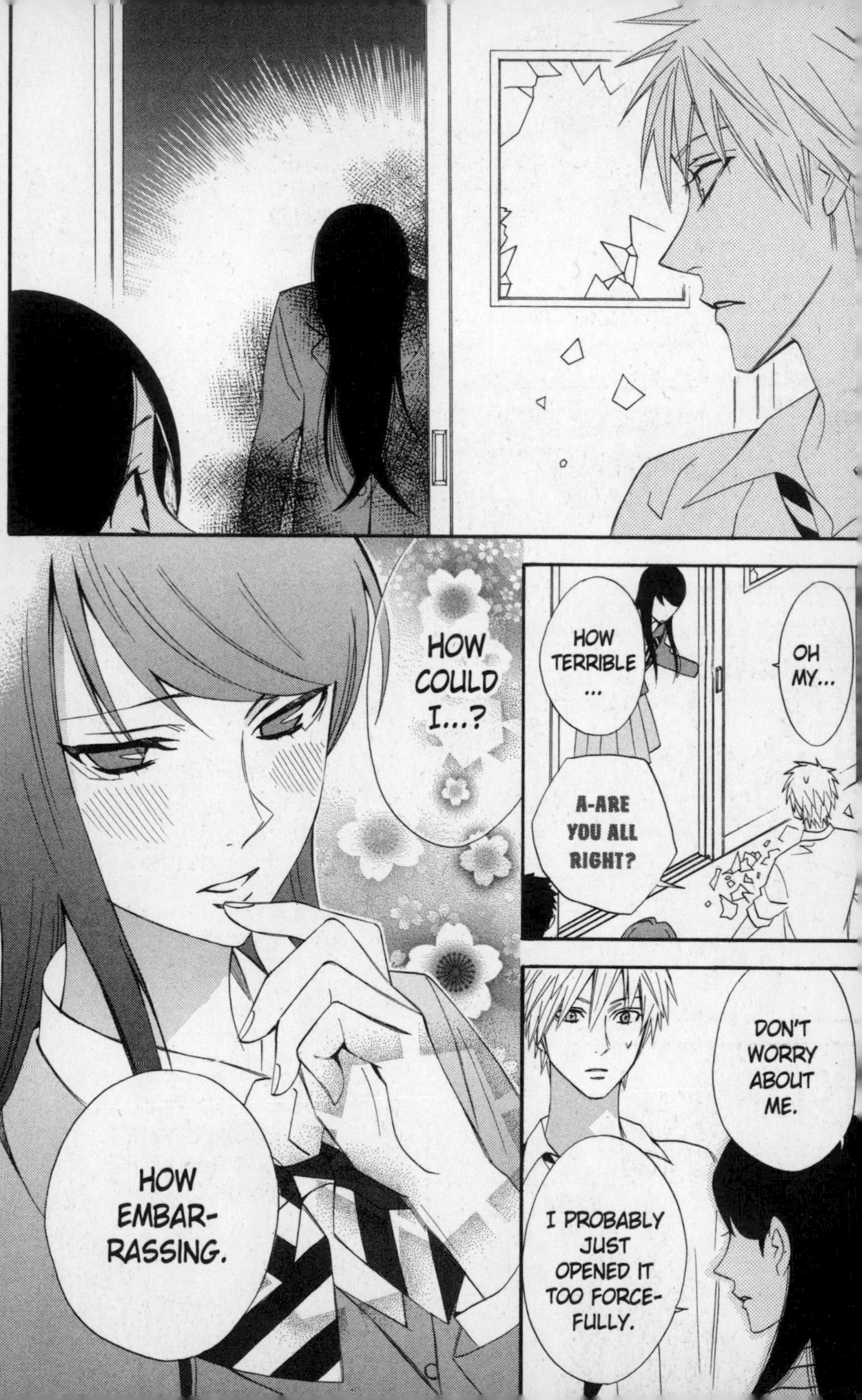
OH MY...
HOW TERRIBLE ...
A-ARE YOU ALL RIGHT?
DON'T WORRY ABOUT ME.
I PROBABLY JUST OPENED IT TOO FORCE-FULLY.
HOW COULD I...?
HOW EMBAR-RASSING.

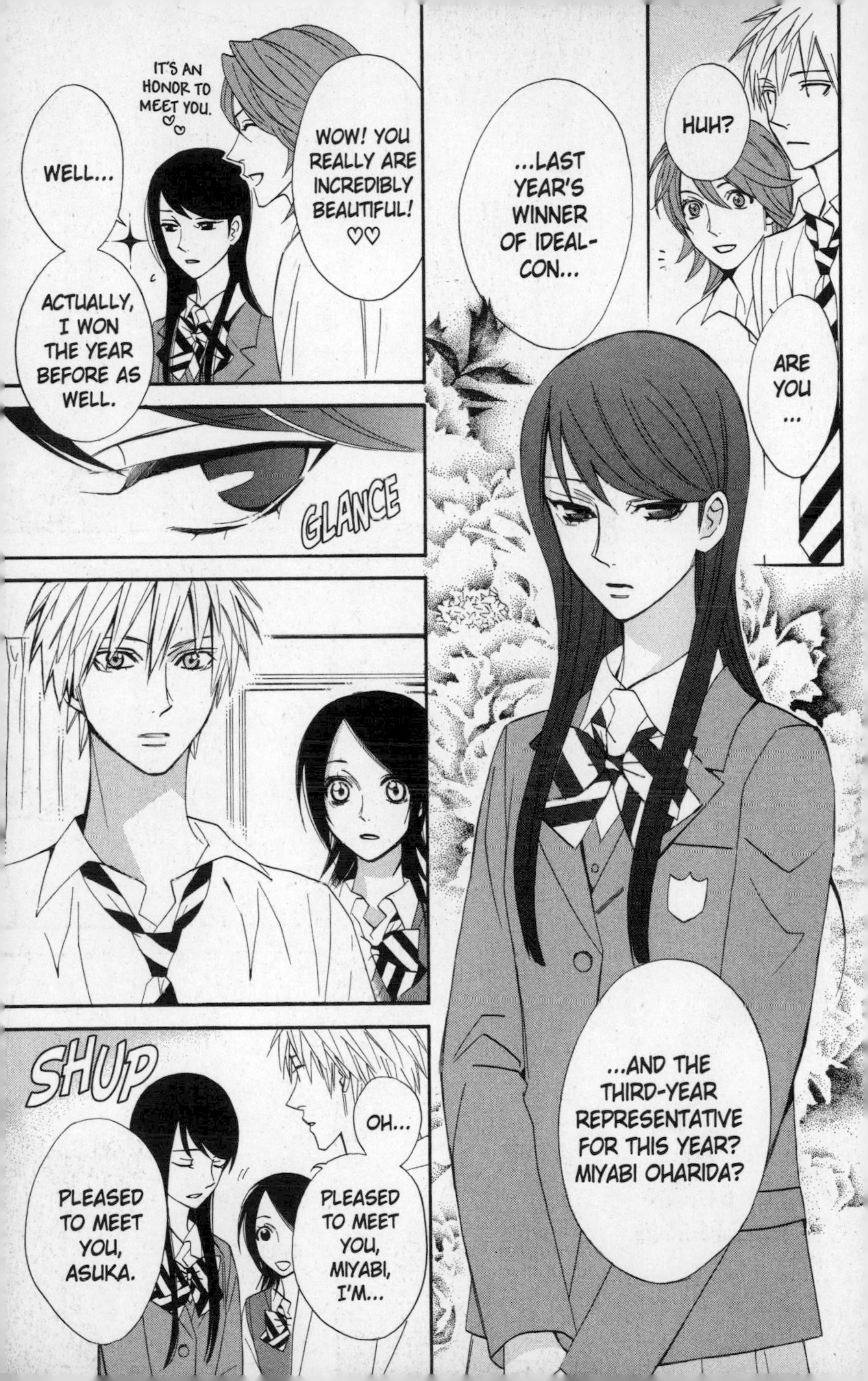
HUH?
ARE YOU ...
...LAST YEAR'S WINNER OF IDEAL-CON...
...AND THE THIRD-YEAR REPRESENTATIVE FOR THIS YEAR? MIYABI OHARIDA?
WOW! YOU REALLY ARE INCREDIBLY BEAUTIFUL! ♡♡
IT'S AN HONOR TO MEET YOU. ♡♡
WELL...
ACTUALLY, I WON THE YEAR BEFORE AS WELL.
GLANCE
SHUP
OH...
PLEASED TO MEET YOU, MIYABI, I'M...
PLEASED TO MEET YOU, ASUKA.

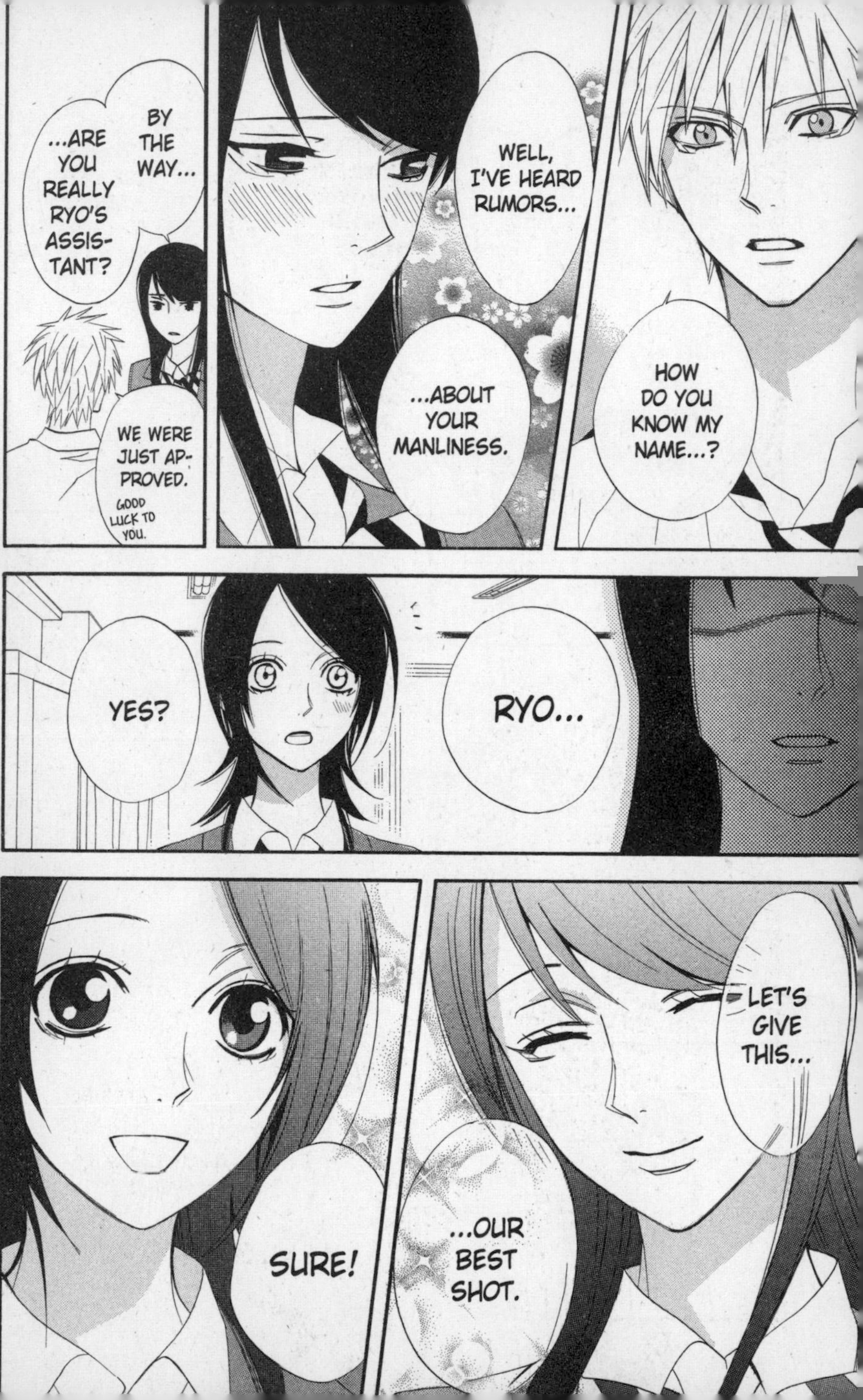
HOW DO YOU KNOW MY NAME...?
WELL, I'VE HEARD RUMORS...
...ABOUT YOUR MANLINESS.
BY THE WAY...
...ARE YOU REALLY RYO'S ASSISTANT?
WE WERE JUST APPROVED.
GOOD LUCK TO YOU.
RYO...
YES?
LET'S GIVE THIS...
...OUR BEST SHOT.
SURE!

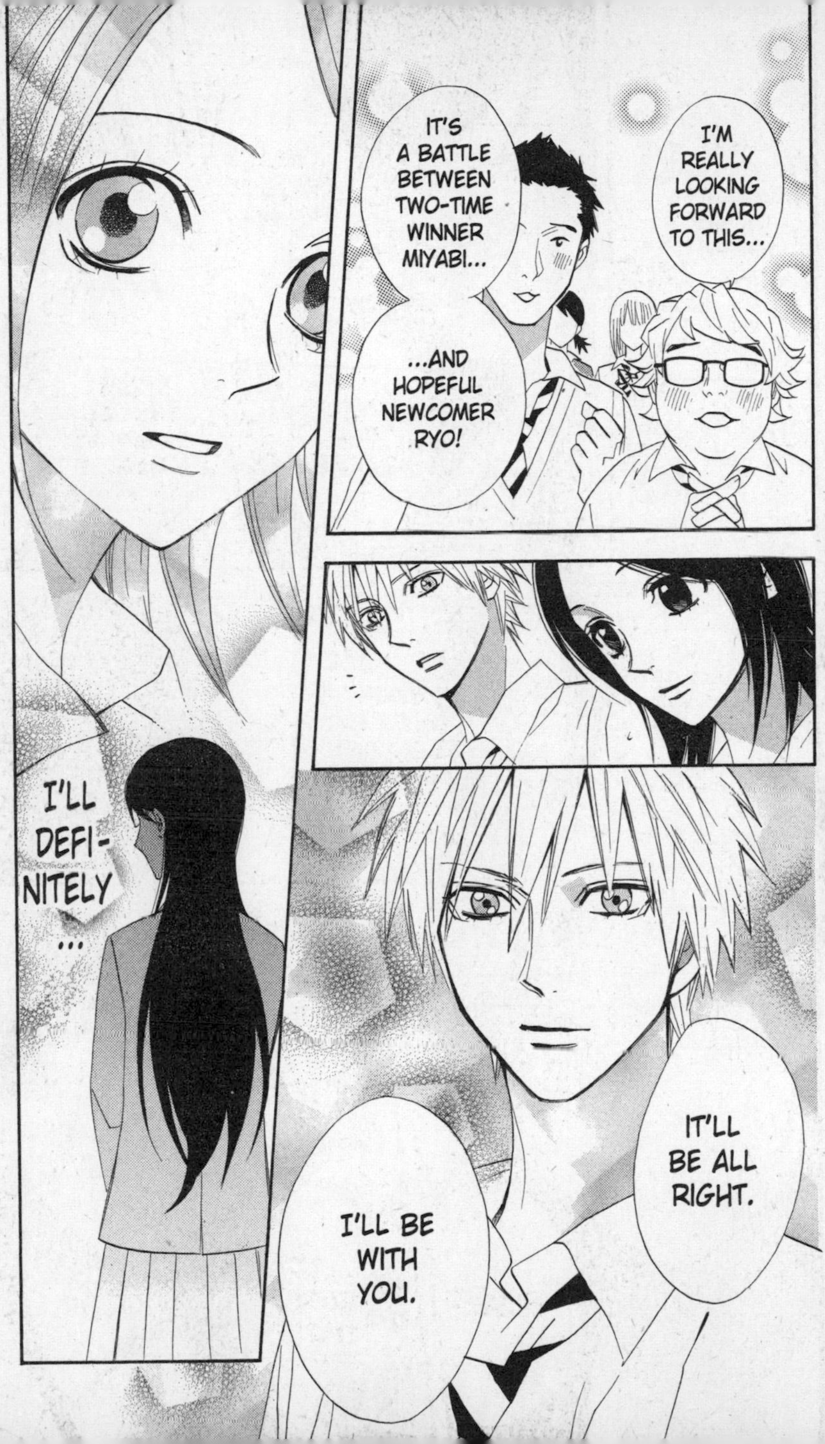
I'M REALLY LOOKING FORWARD TO THIS...
IT'S A BATTLE BETWEEN TWO-TIME WINNER MIYABI...
...AND HOPEFUL NEWCOMER RYO!
IT'LL BE ALL RIGHT.
I'LL BE WITH YOU.
I'LL DEFI-NITELY ...

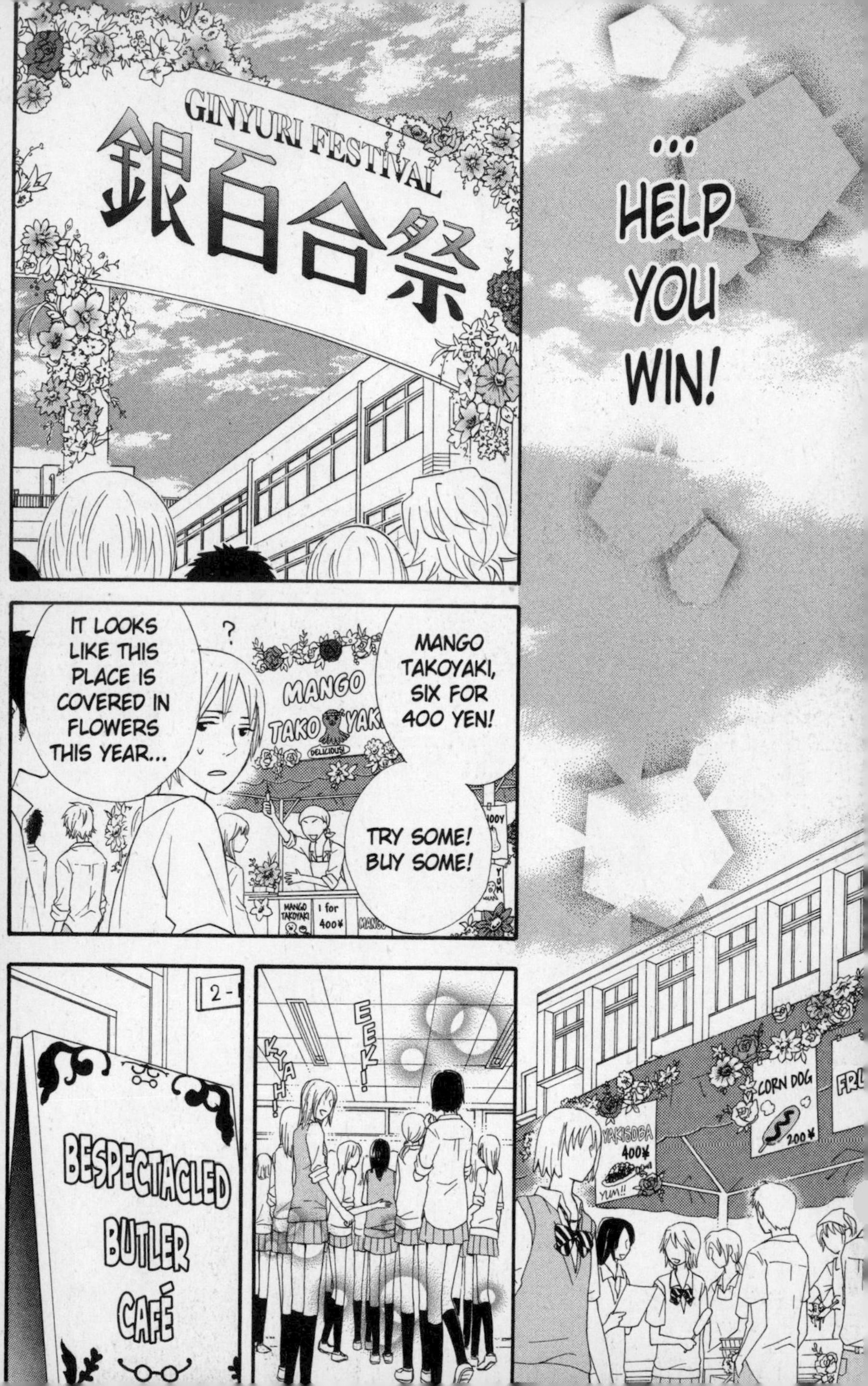
...HELP YOU WIN!
CORN DOG
200¥
YAKISOBA
400¥
YUM!!
GINYURI FESTIVAL
銀百合祭
MANGO TAKOYAKI, SIX FOR 400 YEN!
TRY SOME! BUY SOME!
MANGO TAKOYAKI
DELICIOUS!
MANGO TAKOYAKI
1 for 400¥
?
IT LOOKS LIKE THIS PLACE IS COVERED IN FLOWERS THIS YEAR...
EEK!
KYAH!
BESPECTACLED BUTLER CAFÉ

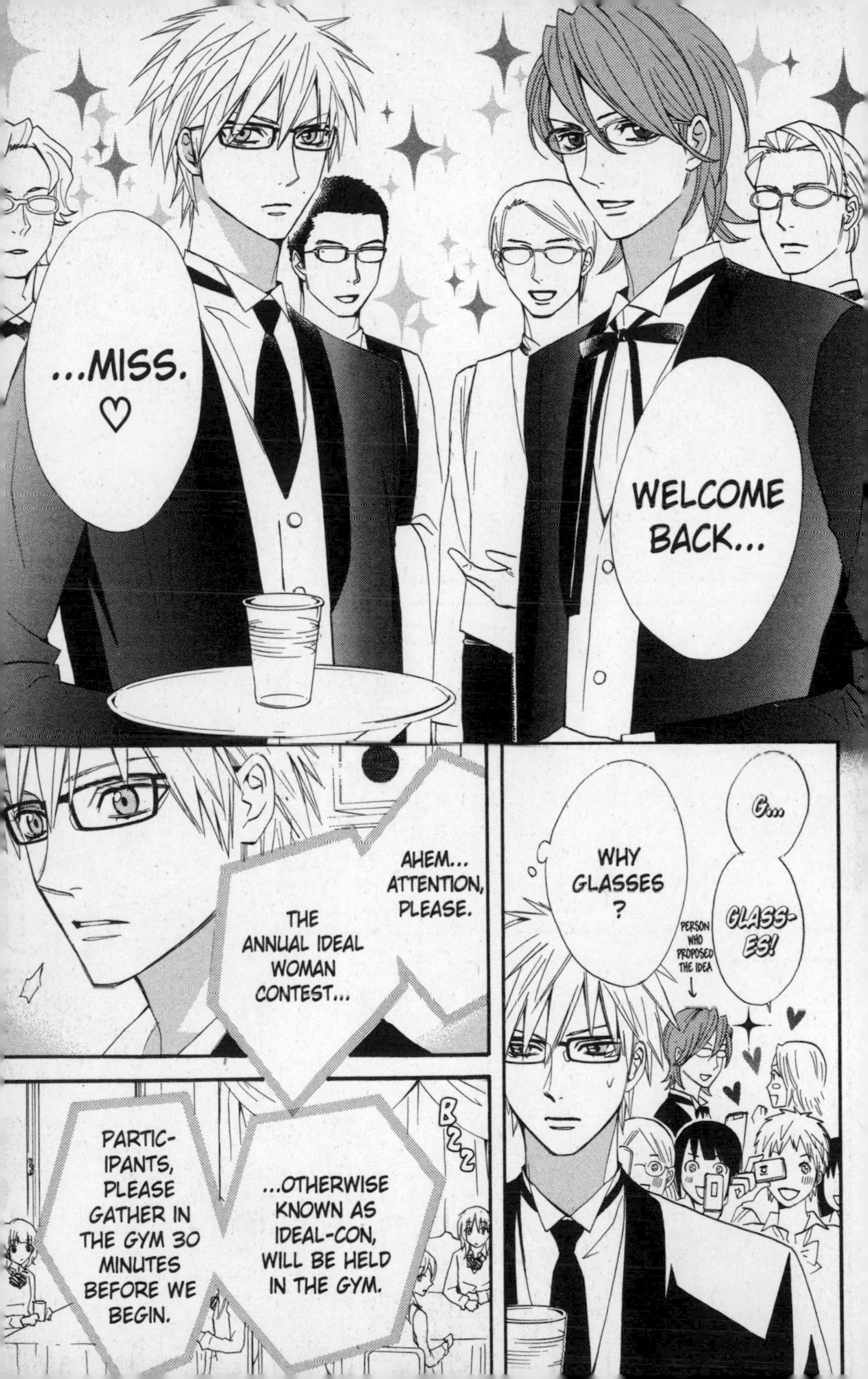
WELCOME BACK...
...MISS. ♡
G...
GLASS-ES!
WHY GLASSES ?
PERSON WHO PROPOSED THE IDEA
AHEM... ATTENTION, PLEASE.
THE ANNUAL IDEAL WOMAN CONTEST...
BZZ
...OTHERWISE KNOWN AS IDEAL-CON, WILL BE HELD IN THE GYM.
PARTIC-IPANTS, PLEASE GATHER IN THE GYM 30 MINUTES BEFORE WE BEGIN.

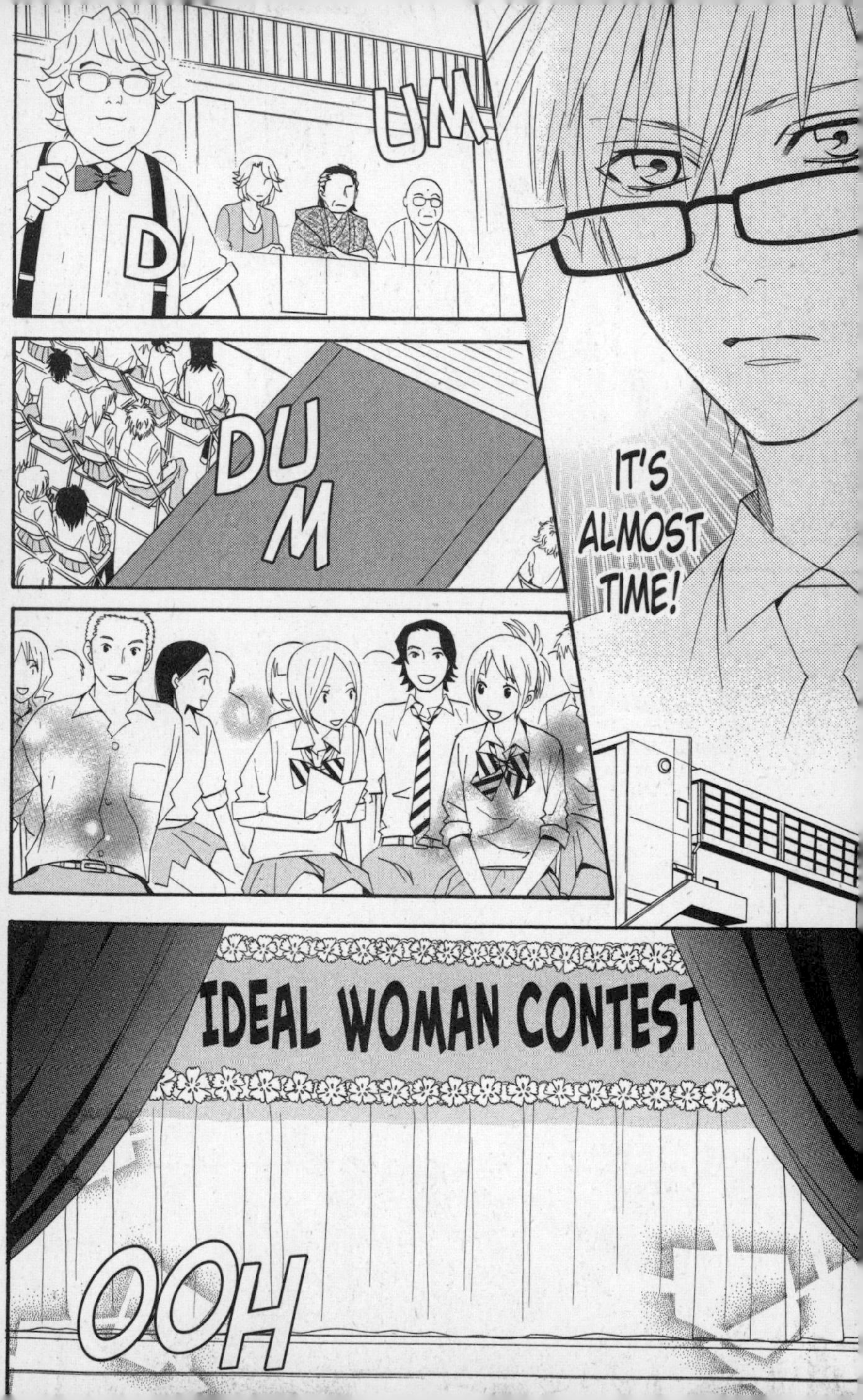
IT'S ALMOST TIME!
UM
D
DUM
IDEAL WOMAN CONTEST
OOH

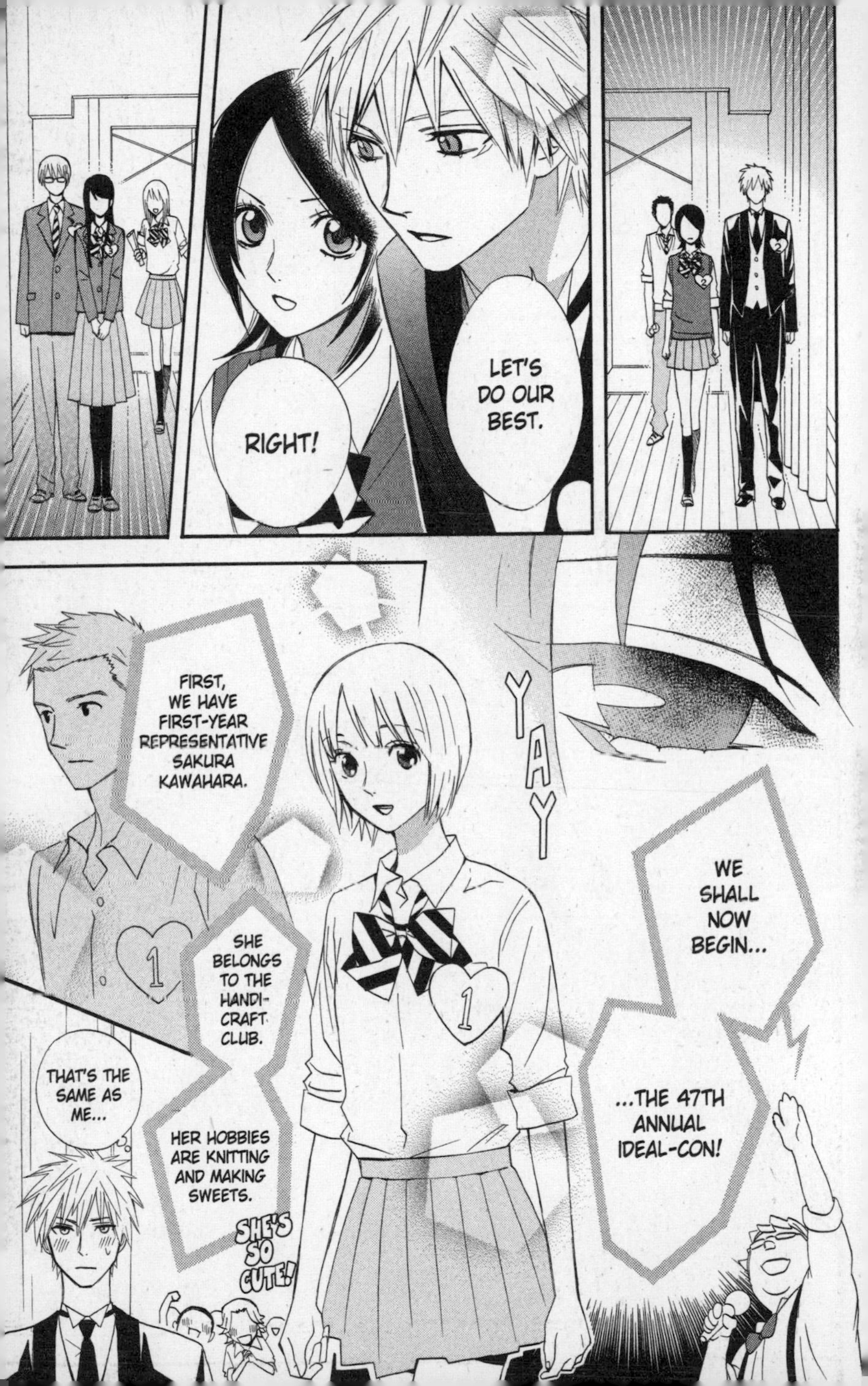
LET'S DO OUR BEST.
RIGHT!
YAY
WE SHALL NOW BEGIN...
...THE 47TH ANNUAL IDEAL-CON!
FIRST, WE HAVE FIRST-YEAR REPRESENTATIVE SAKURA KAWAHARA.
SHE BELONGS TO THE HANDI-CRAFT CLUB.
HER HOBBIES ARE KNITTING AND MAKING SWEETS.
SHE'S SO CUTE!
THAT'S THE SAME AS ME...

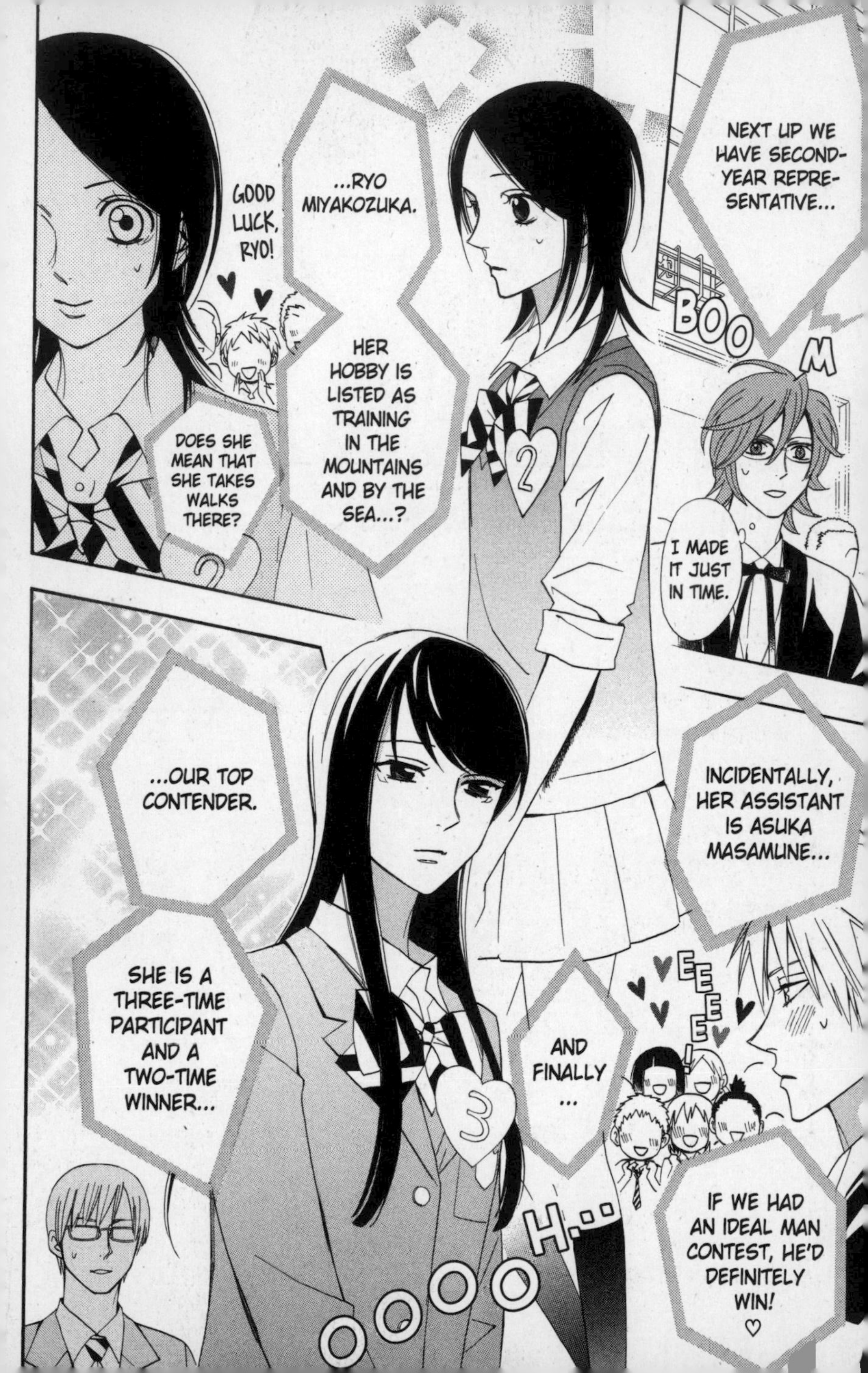
NEXT UP WE HAVE SECOND-YEAR REPRESENTATIVE...
BOOOM
...RYO MIYAKOZUKA.
I MADE IT JUST IN TIME.
HER HOBBY IS LISTED AS TRAINING IN THE MOUNTAINS AND BY THE SEA...?
GOOD LUCK, RYO!
DOES SHE MEAN THAT SHE TAKES WALKS THERE?
INCIDENTALLY, HER ASSISTANT IS ASUKA MASAMUNE...
EEEE!
IF WE HAD AN IDEAL MAN CONTEST, HE'D DEFINITELY WIN! ♡
AND FINALLY ...
...OUR TOP CONTENDER.
SHE IS A THREE-TIME PARTICIPANT AND A TWO-TIME WINNER...
OOOOH...

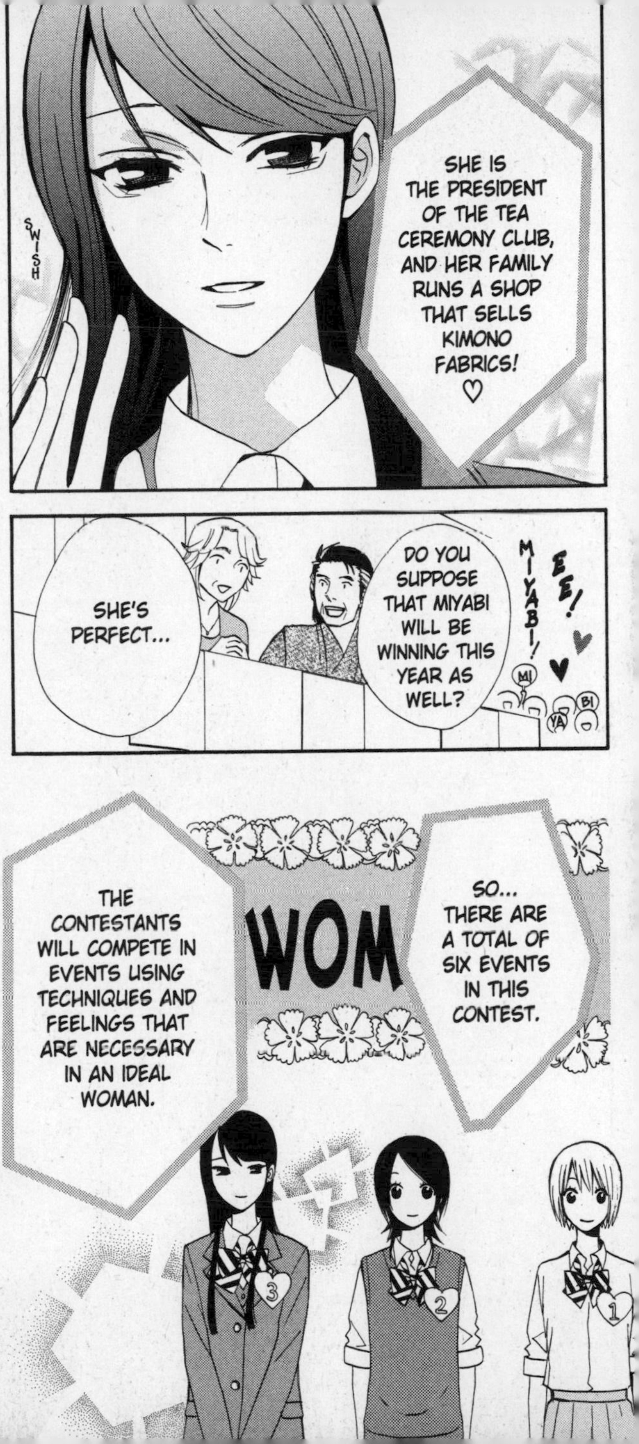
SWISH
SHE IS THE PRESIDENT OF THE TEA CEREMONY CLUB, AND HER FAMILY RUNS A SHOP THAT SELLS KIMONO FABRICS! ♡
EE!
MIYABI!
MI
YA
BI
DO YOU SUPPOSE THAT MIYABI WILL BE WINNING THIS YEAR AS WELL?
SHE'S PERFECT...
SO... THERE ARE A TOTAL OF SIX EVENTS IN THIS CONTEST.
WOM
THE CONTESTANTS WILL COMPETE IN EVENTS USING TECHNIQUES AND FEELINGS THAT ARE NECESSARY IN AN IDEAL WOMAN.
3
2
1

Hello. This is volume 5.

This is *Otomen* but a girl is at the center of this chapter.

I received requests for it before, so I made Ryo the focus of this story. I had wanted to do this story before, but when I get a request, I want to make it live up to expectations.

What do you think of it?

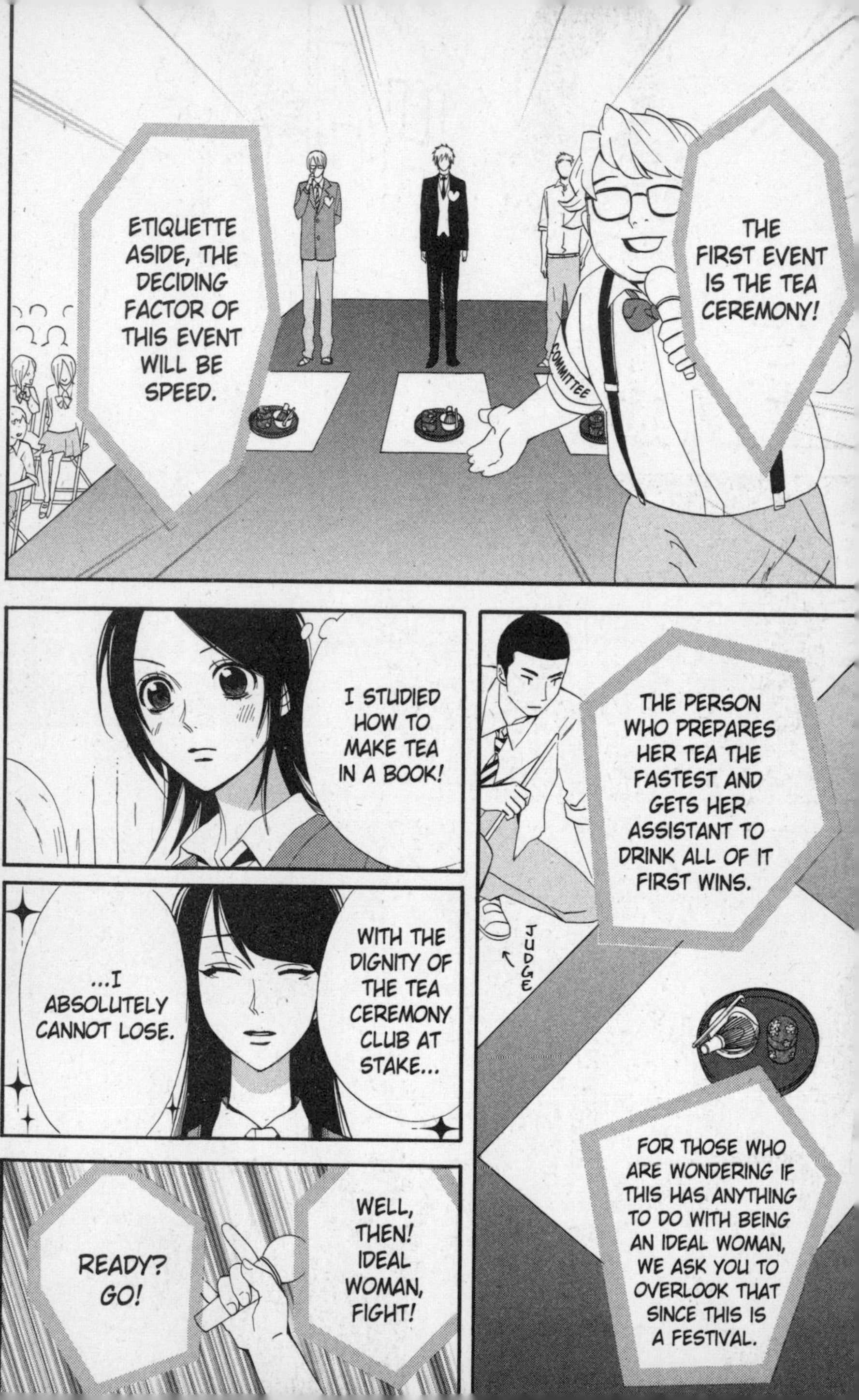
THE FIRST EVENT IS THE TEA CEREMONY!
COMMITTEE
ETIQUETTE ASIDE, THE DECIDING FACTOR OF THIS EVENT WILL BE SPEED.
THE PERSON WHO PREPARES HER TEA THE FASTEST AND GETS HER ASSISTANT TO DRINK ALL OF IT FIRST WINS.
JUDGE
FOR THOSE WHO ARE WONDERING IF THIS HAS ANYTHING TO DO WITH BEING AN IDEAL WOMAN, WE ASK YOU TO OVERLOOK THAT SINCE THIS IS A FESTIVAL.
I STUDIED HOW TO MAKE TEA IN A BOOK!
WITH THE DIGNITY OF THE TEA CEREMONY CLUB AT STAKE...
...I ABSOLUTELY CANNOT LOSE.
WELL, THEN! IDEAL WOMAN, FIGHT!
READY? GO!

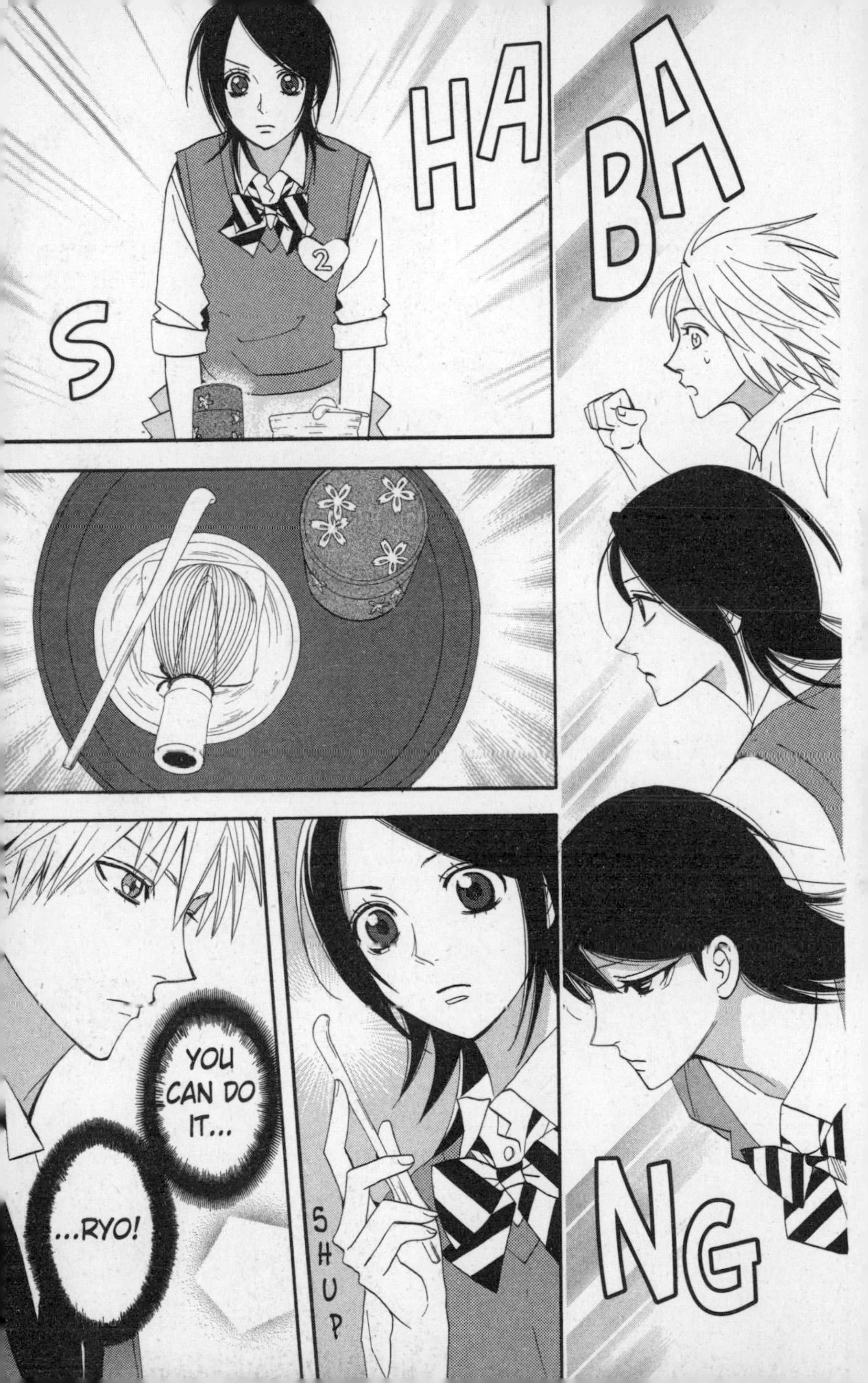
S HA BA NG
SHUP
YOU CAN DO IT...
...RYO!

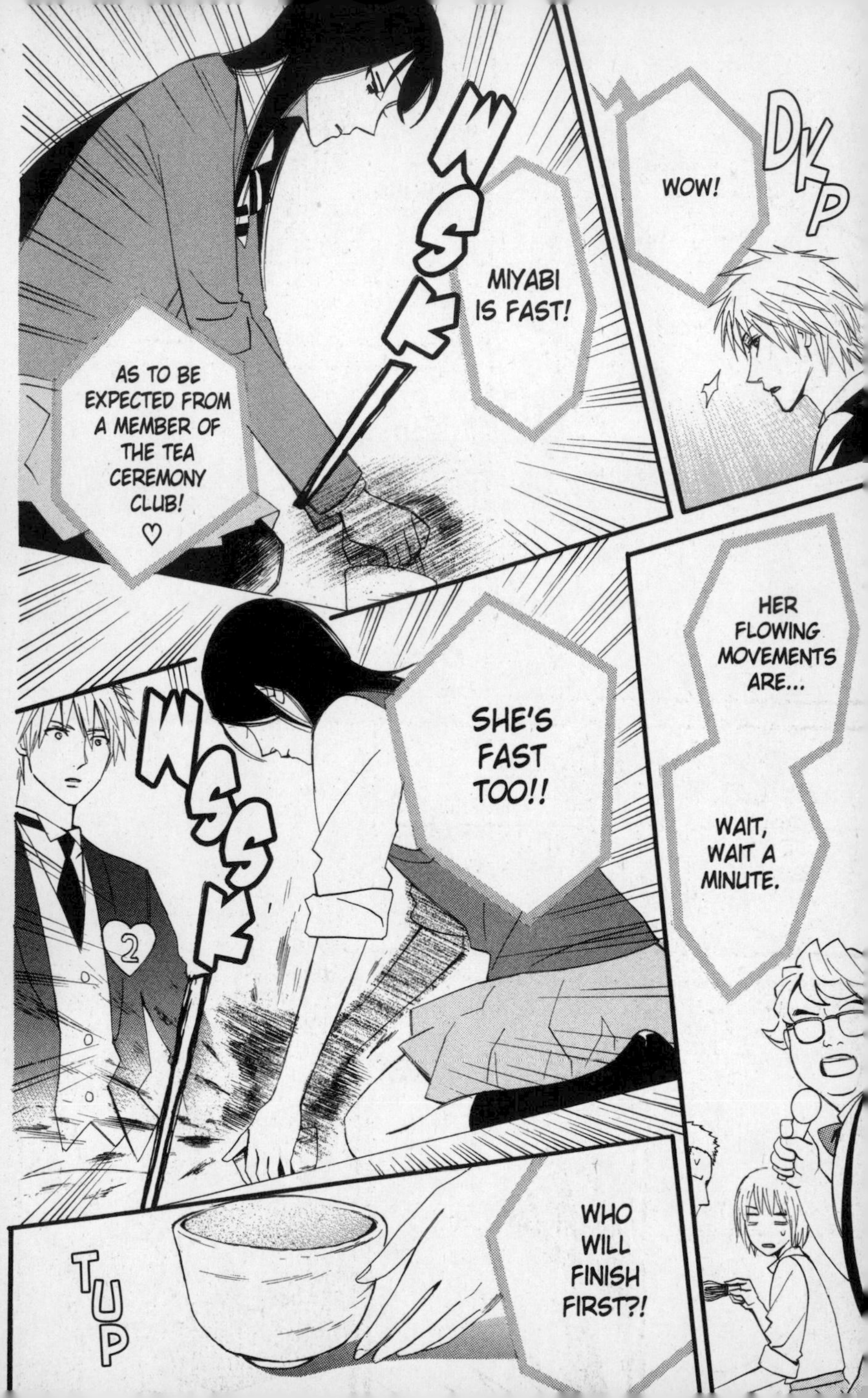
WOW!
DKP
MIYABI IS FAST!
WSSK
AS TO BE EXPECTED FROM A MEMBER OF THE TEA CEREMONY CLUB! ♡
HER FLOWING MOVEMENTS ARE...
WAIT, WAIT A MINUTE.
SHE'S FAST TOO!!
WSSK
2
WHO WILL FINISH FIRST?!
TUP

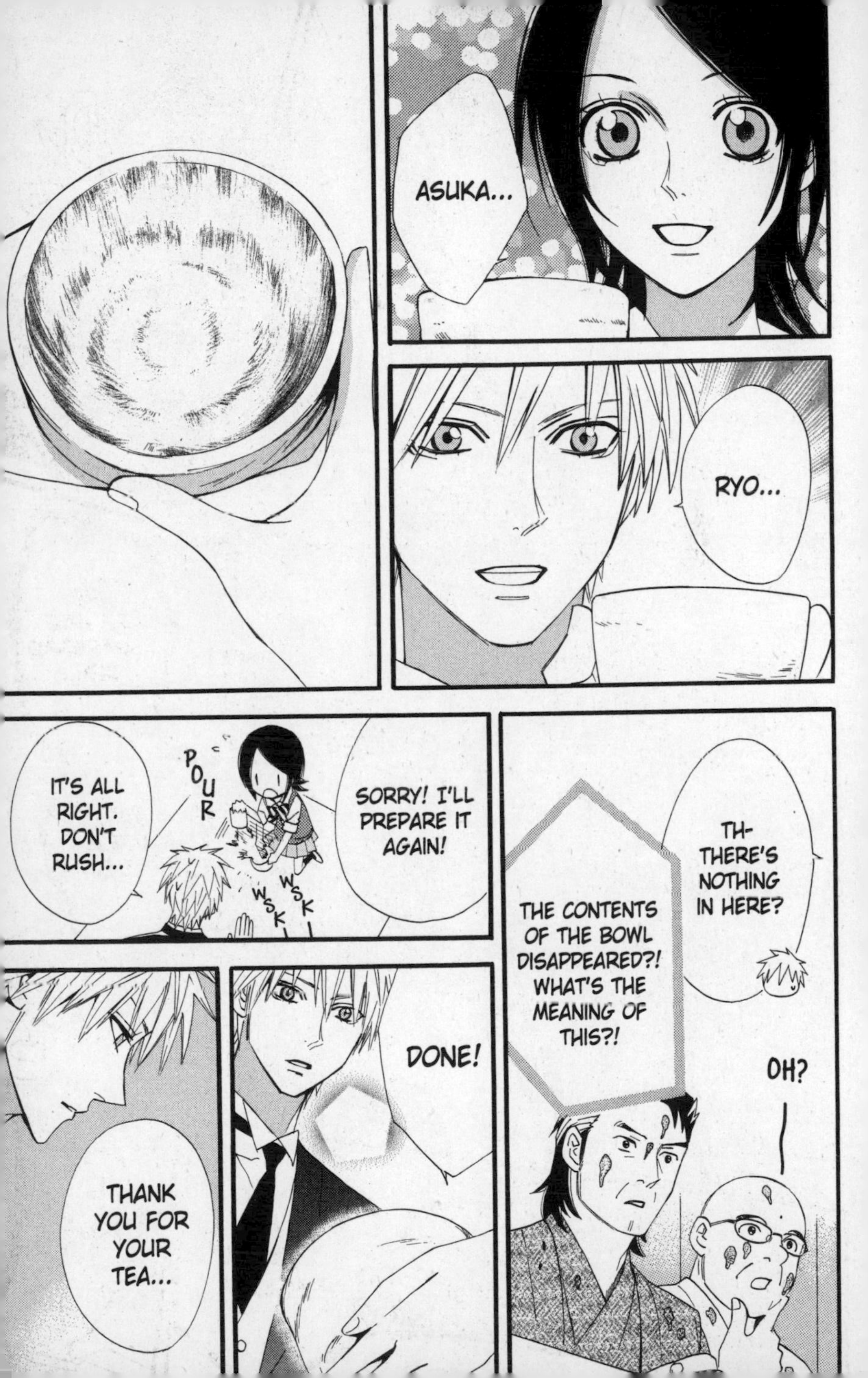

ASUKA...
RYO...
TH- THERE'S NOTHING IN HERE?
THE CONTENTS OF THE BOWL DISAPPEARED?! WHAT'S THE MEANING OF THIS?!
OH?
SORRY! I'LL PREPARE IT AGAIN!
POUR
WSK WSK
IT'S ALL RIGHT. DON'T RUSH...
DONE!
THANK YOU FOR YOUR TEA...

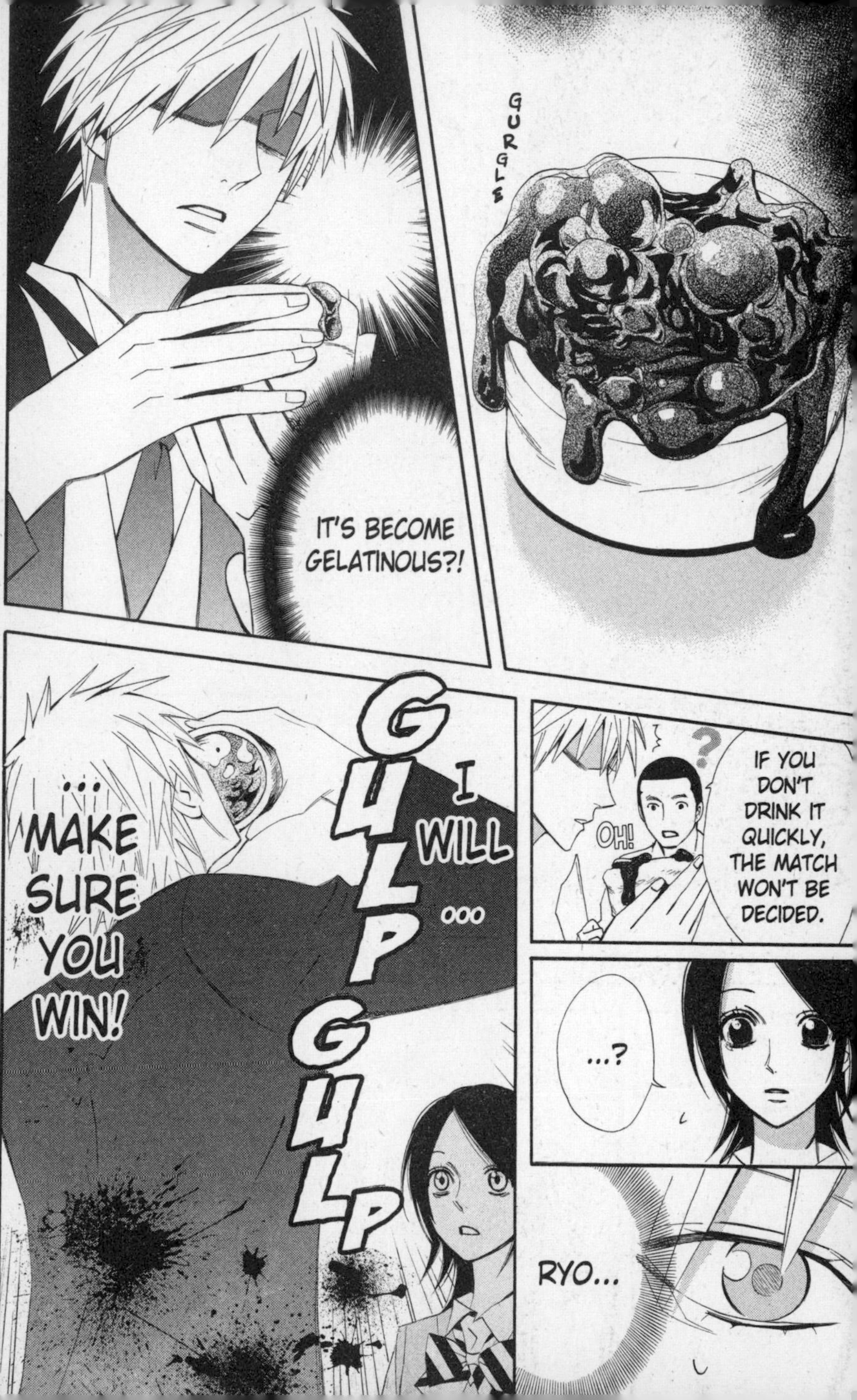
GURGLE
IT'S BECOME GELATINOUS?!
?
OH!
IF YOU DON'T DRINK IT QUICKLY, THE MATCH WON'T BE DECIDED.
...?
RYO...
I WILL...
...MAKE SURE YOU WIN!
GULP
GULP

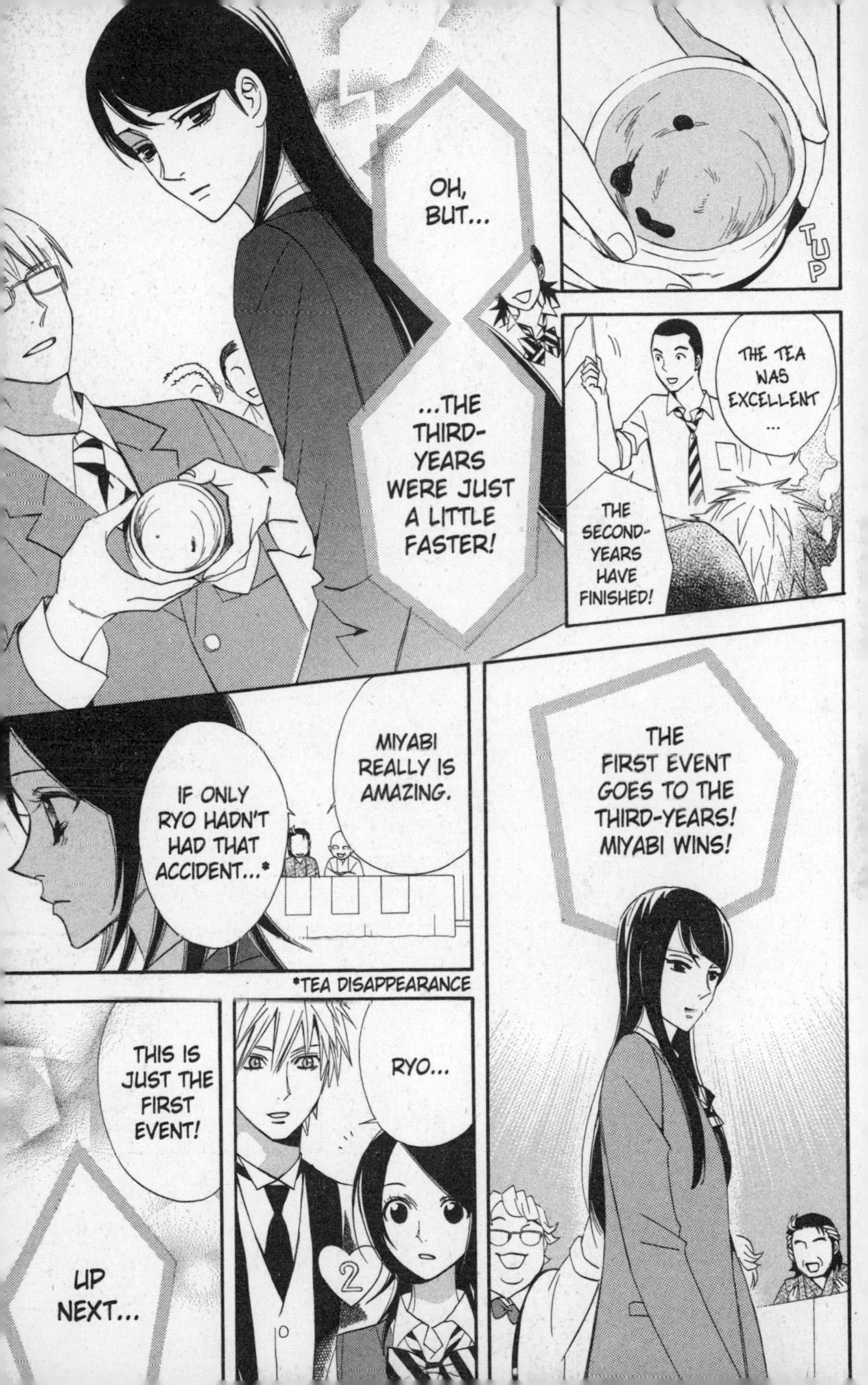
TUP
THE TEA WAS EXCELLENT...
THE SECOND-YEARS HAVE FINISHED!
OH, BUT...
...THE THIRD-YEARS WERE JUST A LITTLE FASTER!
THE FIRST EVENT GOES TO THE THIRD-YEARS! MIYABI WINS!
MIYABI REALLY IS AMAZING.
IF ONLY RYO HADN'T HAD THAT ACCIDENT...*
*TEA DISAPPEARANCE
RYO...
THIS IS JUST THE FIRST EVENT!
UP NEXT...

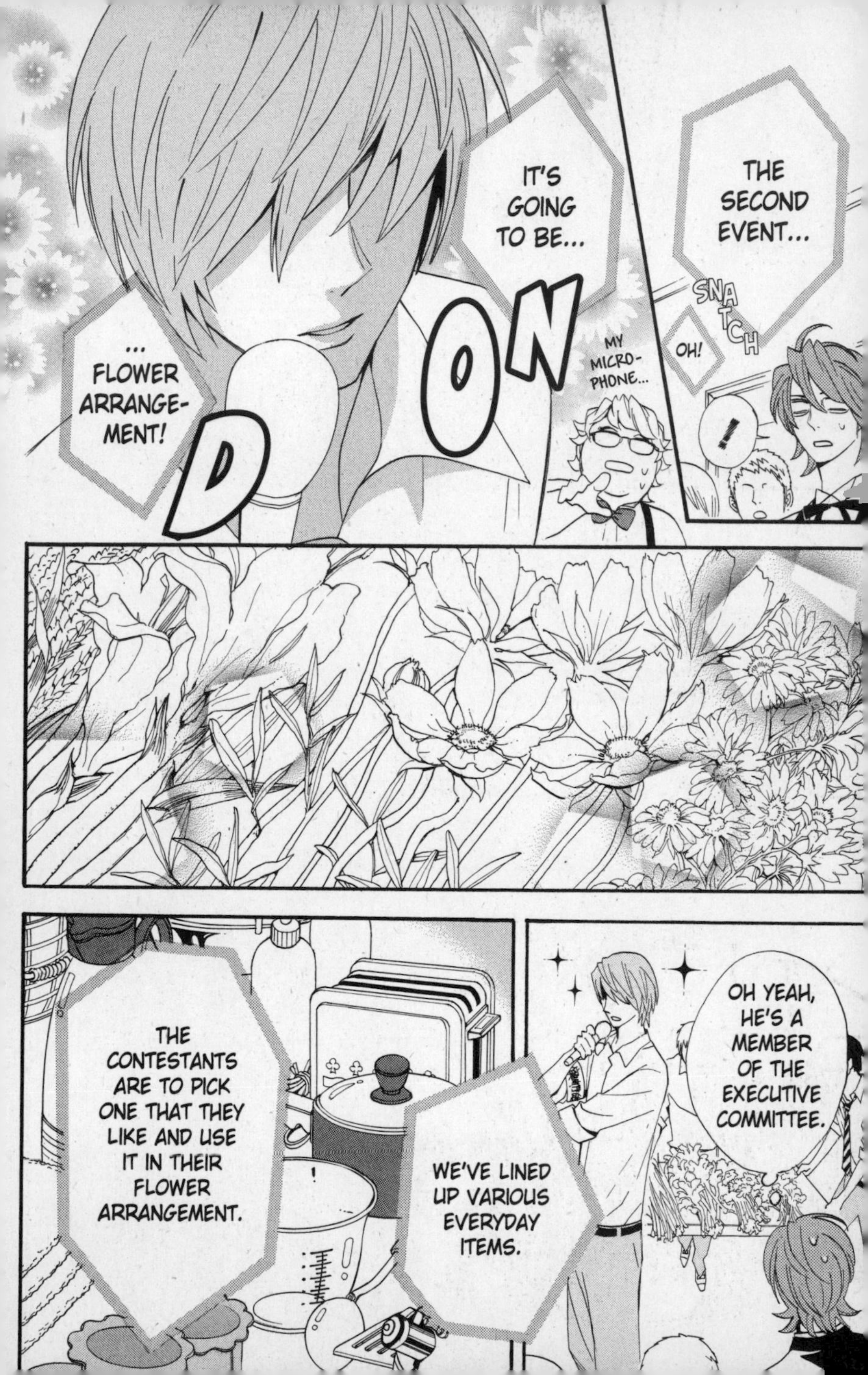
THE SECOND EVENT...
SNATCH
OH!
MY MICRO-PHONE...
!
IT'S GOING TO BE...
DON
... FLOWER ARRANGE-MENT!
OH YEAH, HE'S A MEMBER OF THE EXECUTIVE COMMITTEE.
WE'VE LINED UP VARIOUS EVERYDAY ITEMS.
THE CONTESTANTS ARE TO PICK ONE THAT THEY LIKE AND USE IT IN THEIR FLOWER ARRANGEMENT.

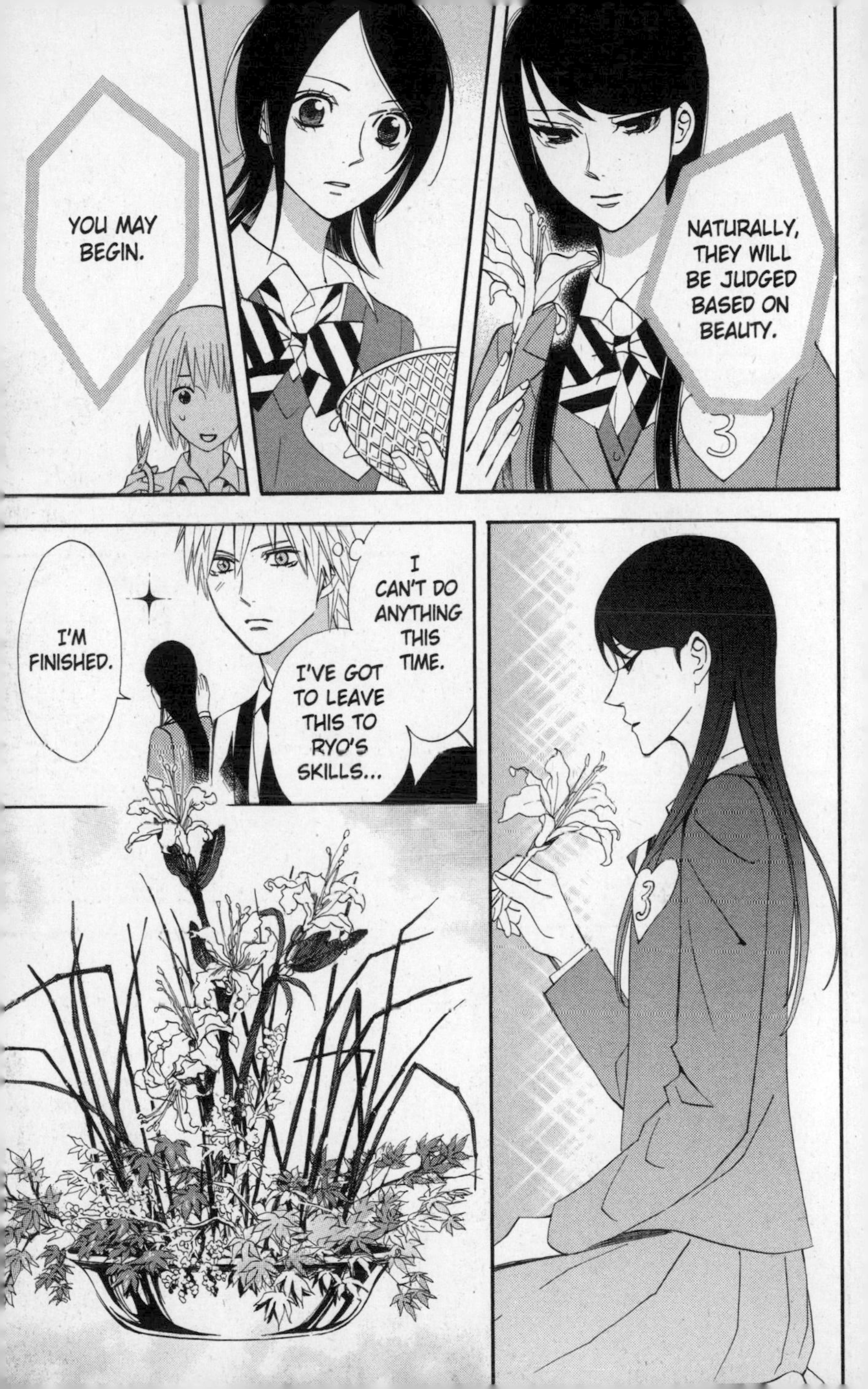
NATURALLY, THEY WILL BE JUDGED BASED ON BEAUTY.
YOU MAY BEGIN.
3
3
I CAN'T DO ANYTHING THIS TIME.
I'VE GOT TO LEAVE THIS TO RYO'S SKILLS...
I'M FINISHED.

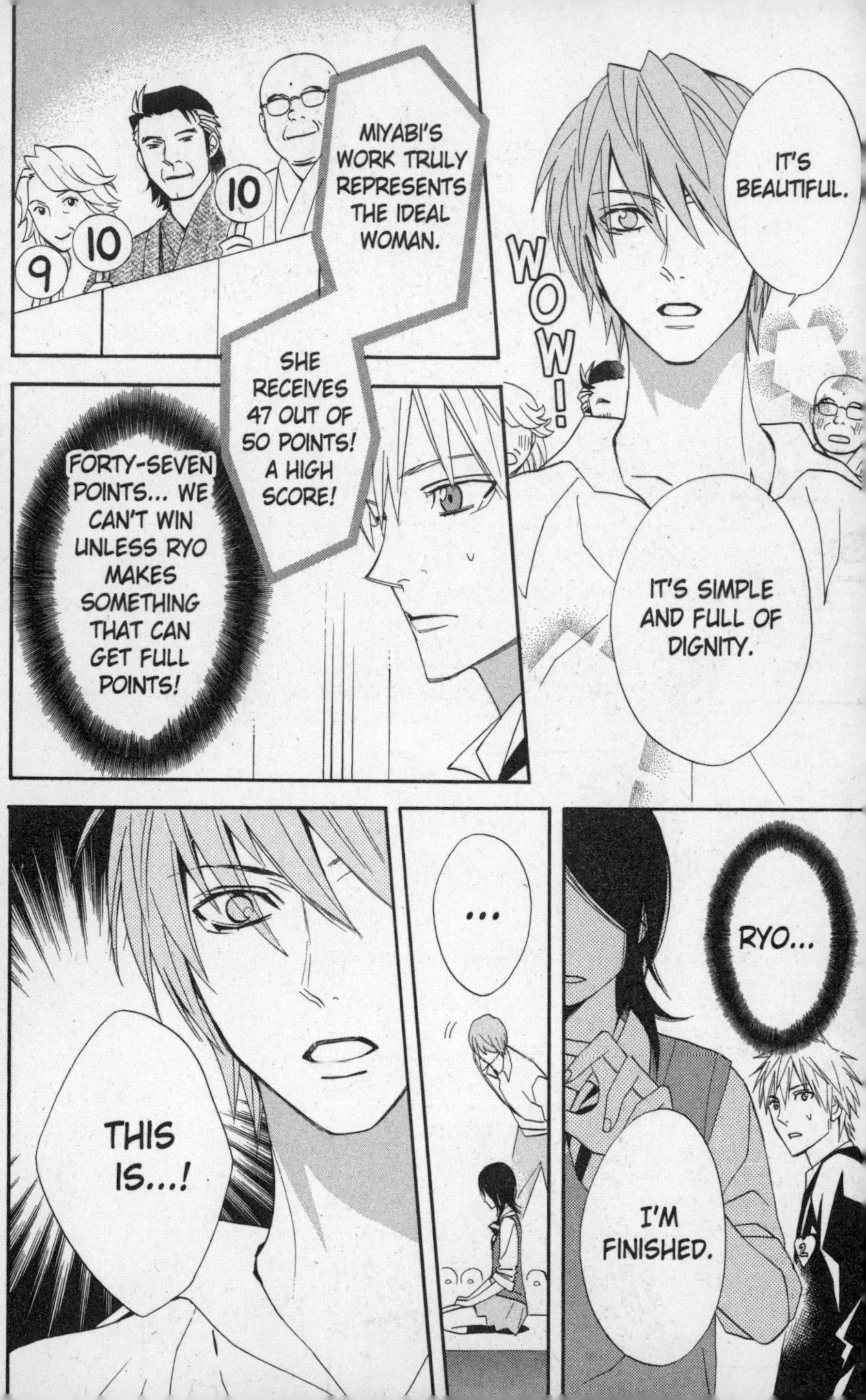
IT'S BEAUTIFUL.
WOW!
IT'S SIMPLE AND FULL OF DIGNITY.
10
10
9
MIYABI'S WORK TRULY REPRESENTS THE IDEAL WOMAN.
SHE RECEIVES 47 OUT OF 50 POINTS! A HIGH SCORE!
FORTY-SEVEN POINTS... WE CAN'T WIN UNLESS RYO MAKES SOMETHING THAT CAN GET FULL POINTS!
RYO...
I'M FINISHED.
...
THIS IS...!

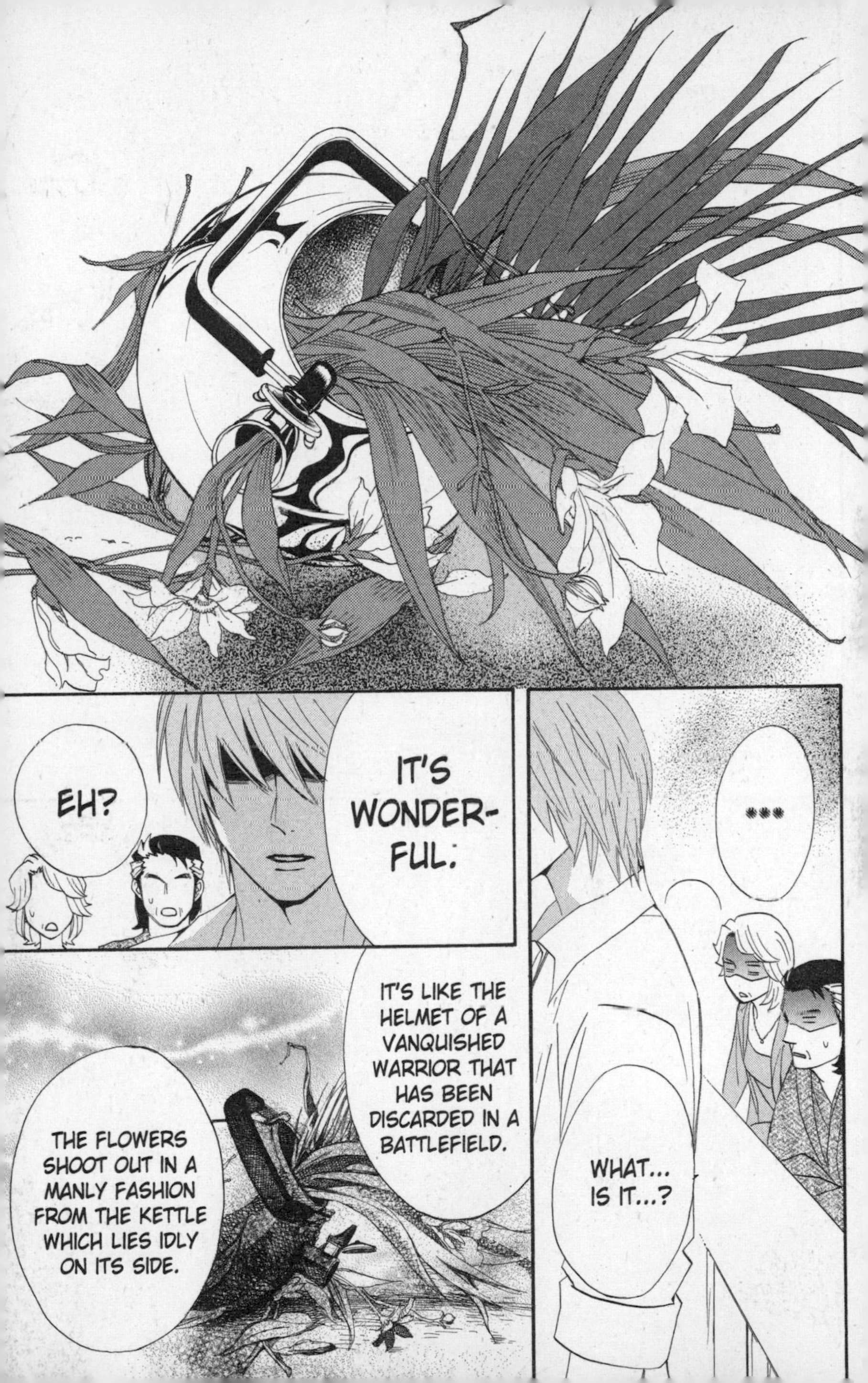
...
WHAT... IS IT...?
IT'S WONDERFUL.
EH?
IT'S LIKE THE HELMET OF A VANQUISHED WARRIOR THAT HAS BEEN DISCARDED IN A BATTLEFIELD.
THE FLOWERS SHOOT OUT IN A MANLY FASHION FROM THE KETTLE WHICH LIES IDLY ON ITS SIDE.

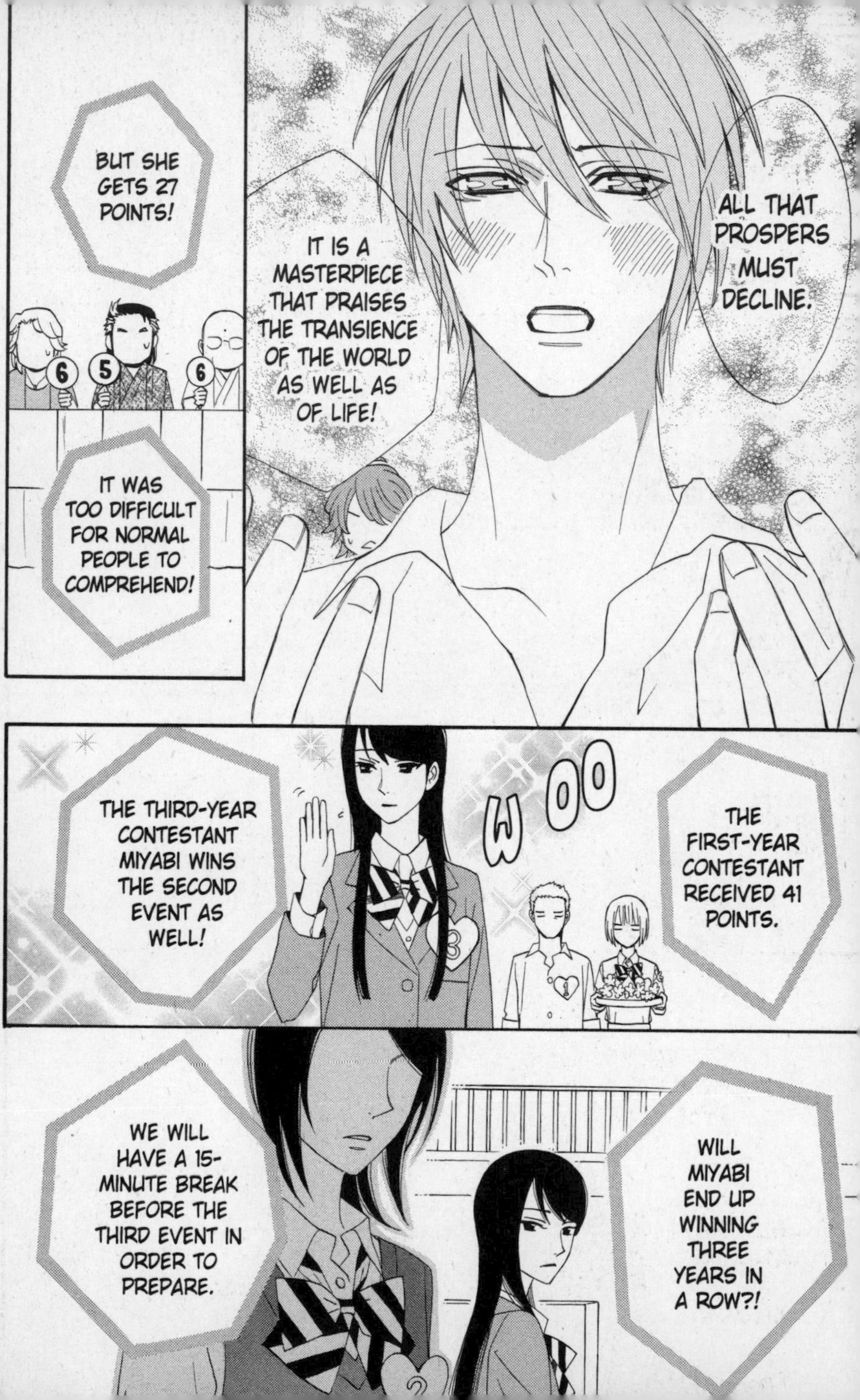
ALL THAT PROSPERS MUST DECLINE.
IT IS A MASTERPIECE THAT PRAISES THE TRANSIENCE OF THE WORLD AS WELL AS OF LIFE!
BUT SHE GETS 27 POINTS!
6
5
6
IT WAS TOO DIFFICULT FOR NORMAL PEOPLE TO COMPREHEND!
THE FIRST-YEAR CONTESTANT RECEIVED 41 POINTS.
WOO
THE THIRD-YEAR CONTESTANT MIYABI WINS THE SECOND EVENT AS WELL!
WILL MIYABI END UP WINNING THREE YEARS IN A ROW?!
WE WILL HAVE A 15-MINUTE BREAK BEFORE THE THIRD EVENT IN ORDER TO PREPARE.

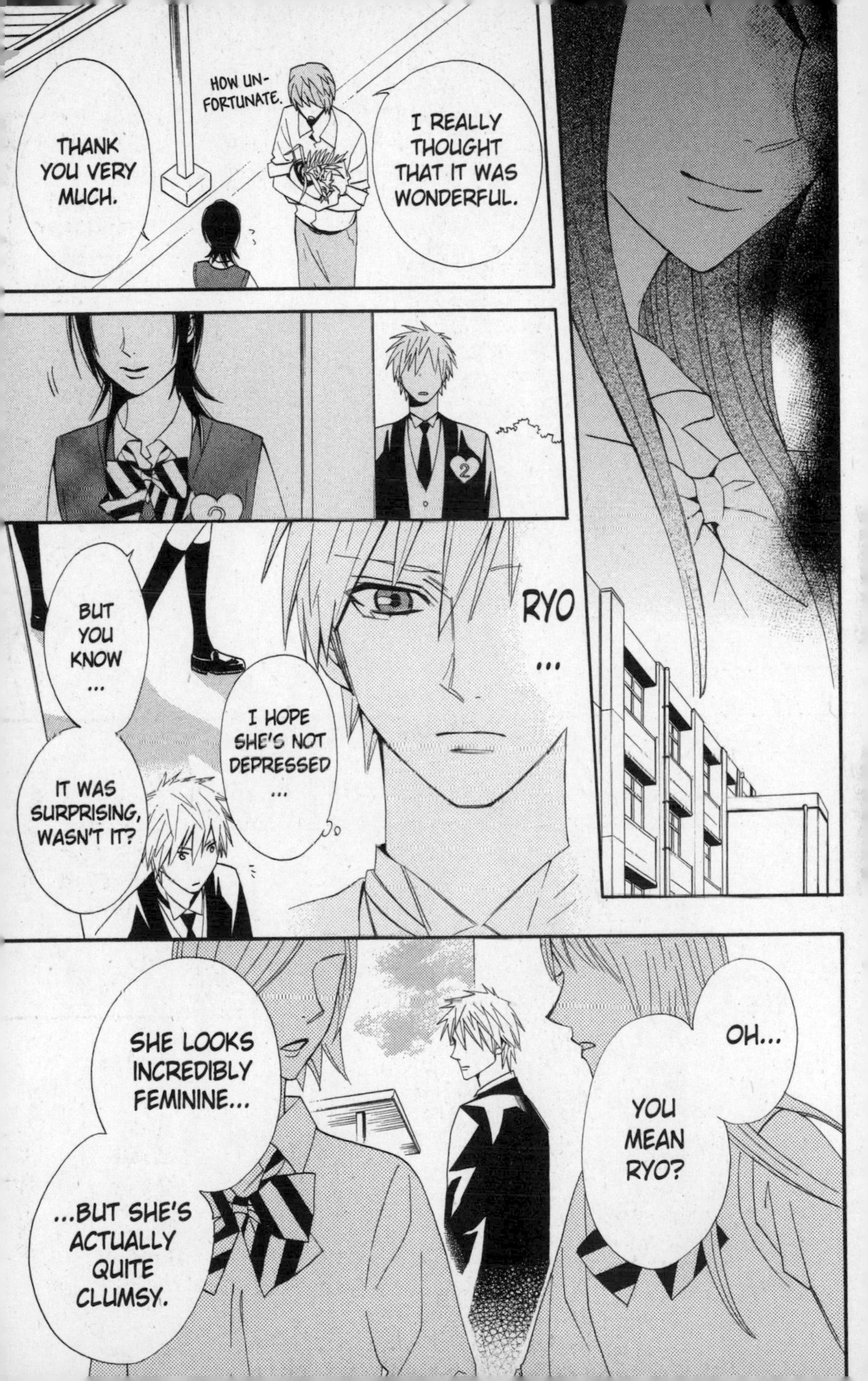
I REALLY THOUGHT THAT IT WAS WONDERFUL.
HOW UN-FORTUNATE.
THANK YOU VERY MUCH.
RYO ...
I HOPE SHE'S NOT DEPRESSED ...
BUT YOU KNOW ...
IT WAS SURPRISING, WASN'T IT?
OH...
YOU MEAN RYO?
SHE LOOKS INCREDIBLY FEMININE...
...BUT SHE'S ACTUALLY QUITE CLUMSY.

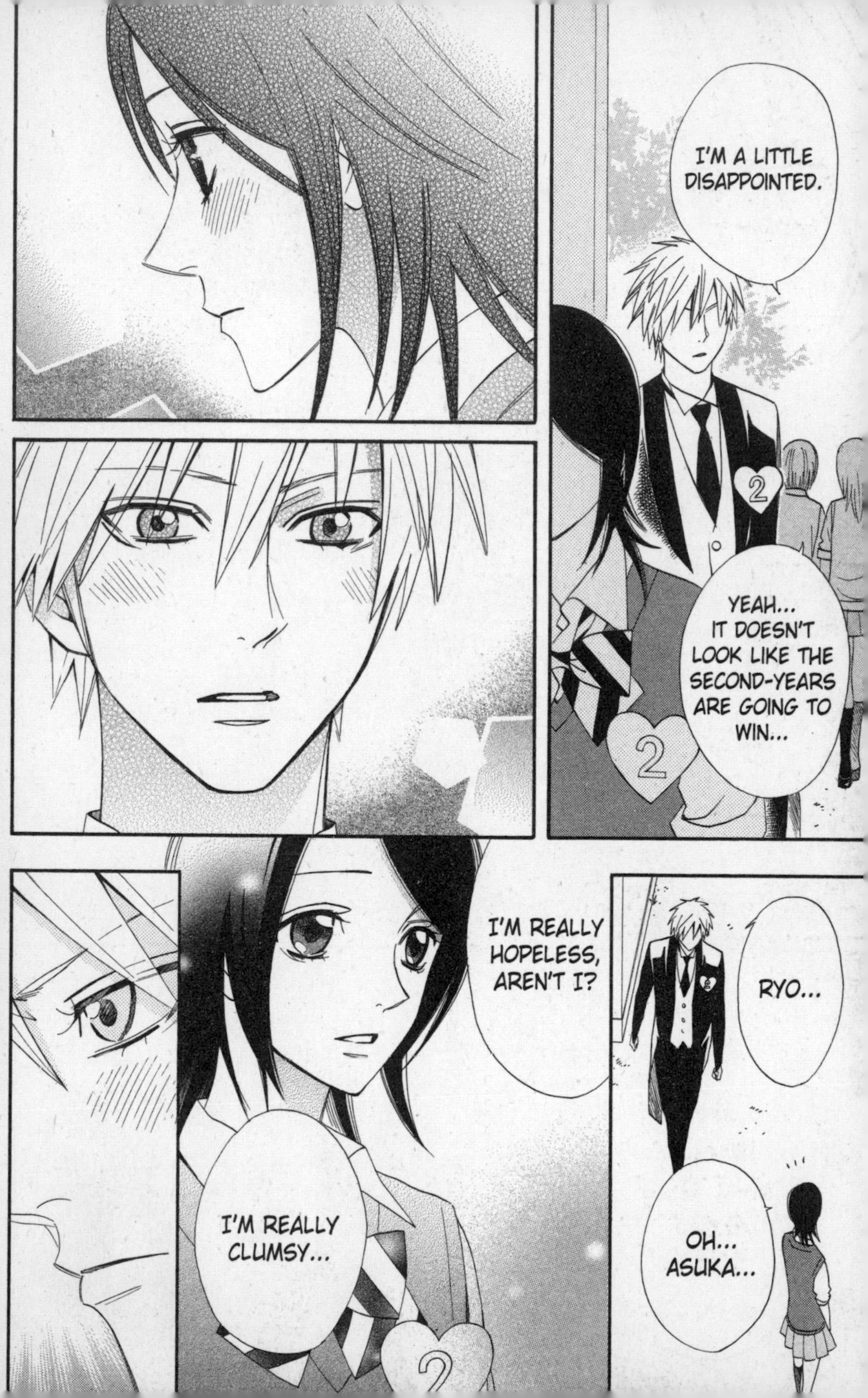
I'M A LITTLE DISAPPOINTED.
YEAH... IT DOESN'T LOOK LIKE THE SECOND-YEARS ARE GOING TO WIN...
RYO...
OH... ASUKA...
I'M REALLY HOPELESS, AREN'T I?
I'M REALLY CLUMSY...

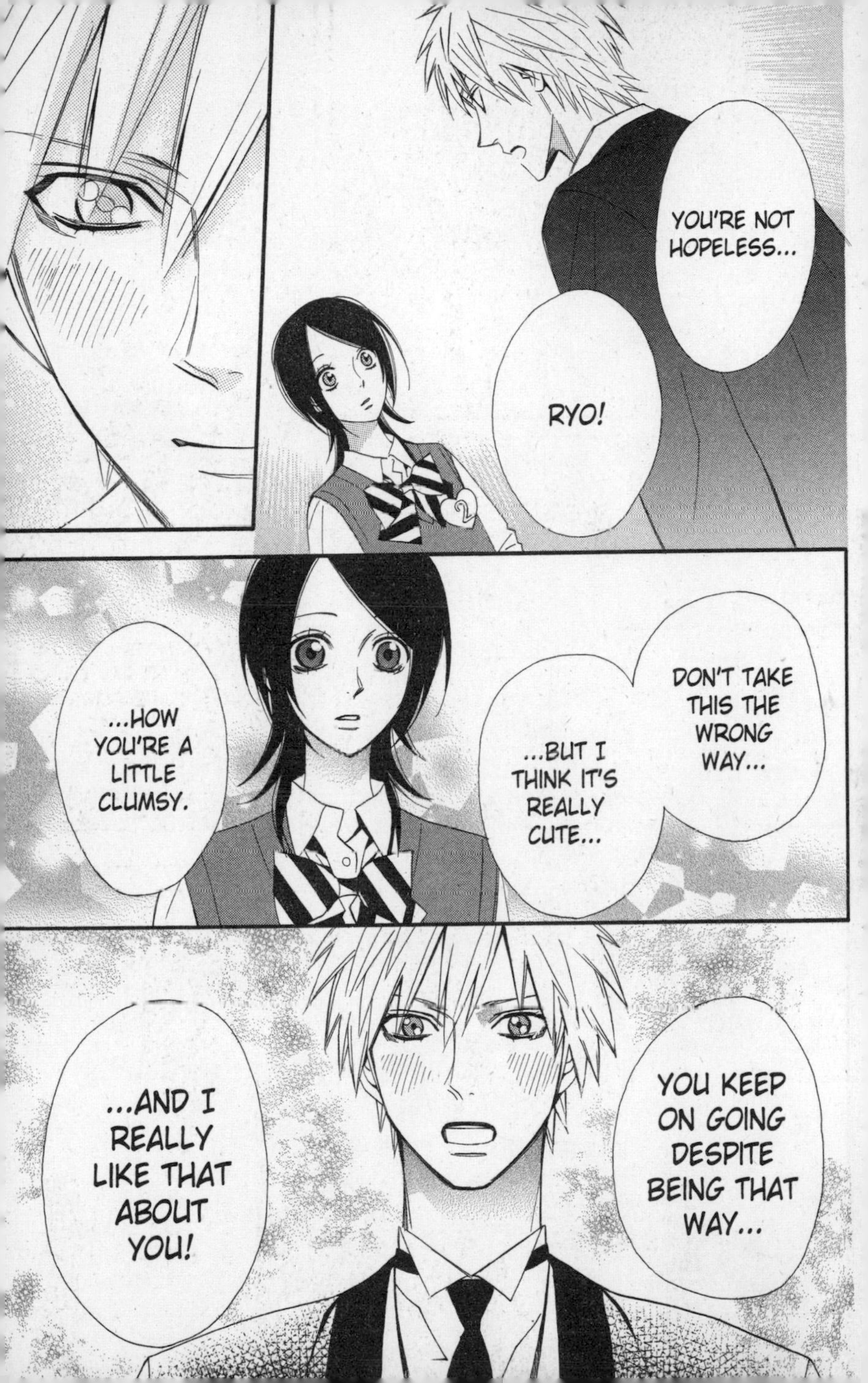
YOU'RE NOT HOPELESS...
RYO!
DON'T TAKE THIS THE WRONG WAY...
...BUT I THINK IT'S REALLY CUTE...
...HOW YOU'RE A LITTLE CLUMSY.
YOU KEEP ON GOING DESPITE BEING THAT WAY...
...AND I REALLY LIKE THAT ABOUT YOU!

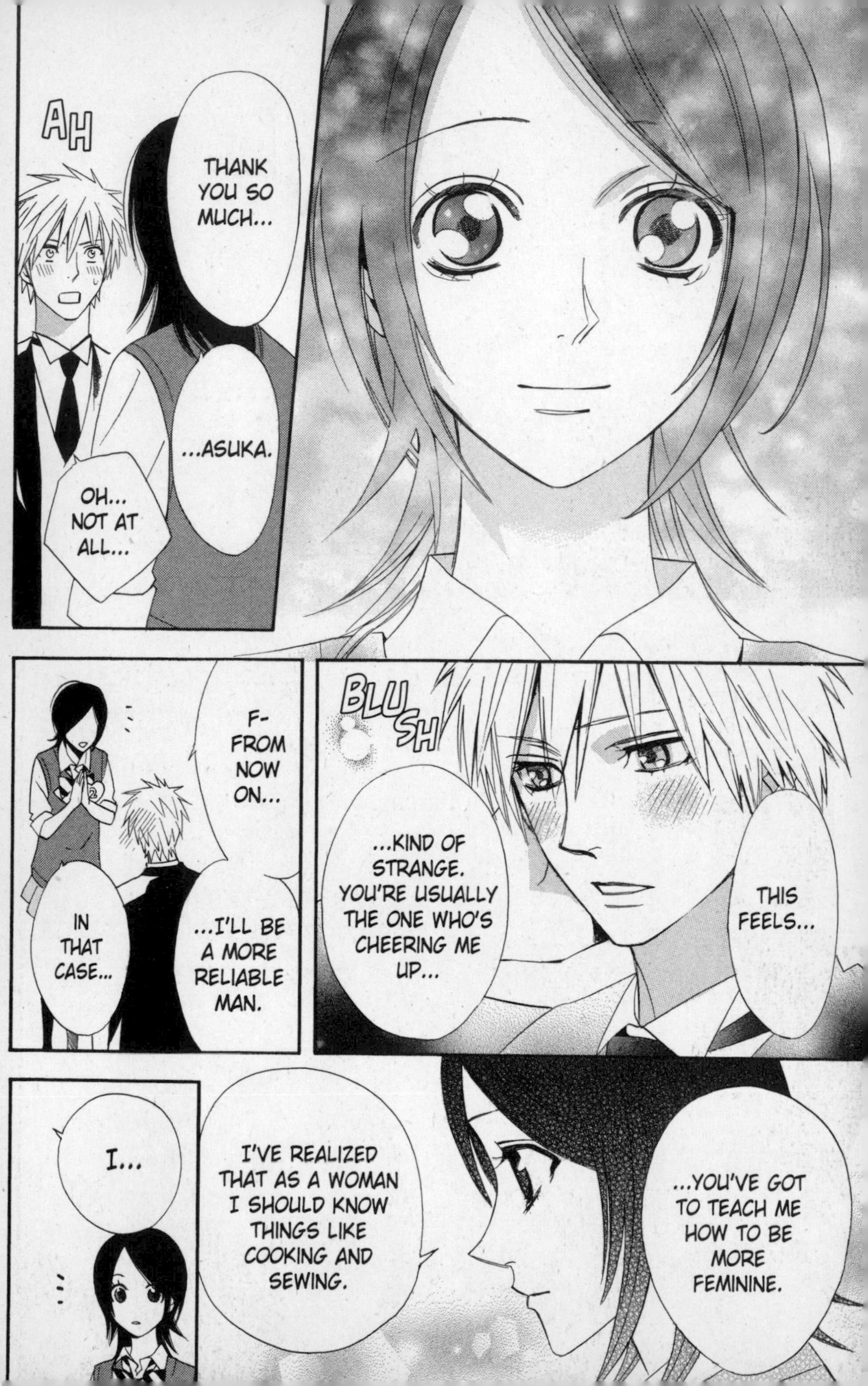
THANK YOU SO MUCH...
AH
...ASUKA.
OH... NOT AT ALL...
BLUSH
THIS FEELS...
...KIND OF STRANGE. YOU'RE USUALLY THE ONE WHO'S CHEERING ME UP...
F-FROM NOW ON...
...I'LL BE A MORE RELIABLE MAN.
IN THAT CASE...
...YOU'VE GOT TO TEACH ME HOW TO BE MORE FEMININE.
I'VE REALIZED THAT AS A WOMAN I SHOULD KNOW THINGS LIKE COOKING AND SEWING.
I...

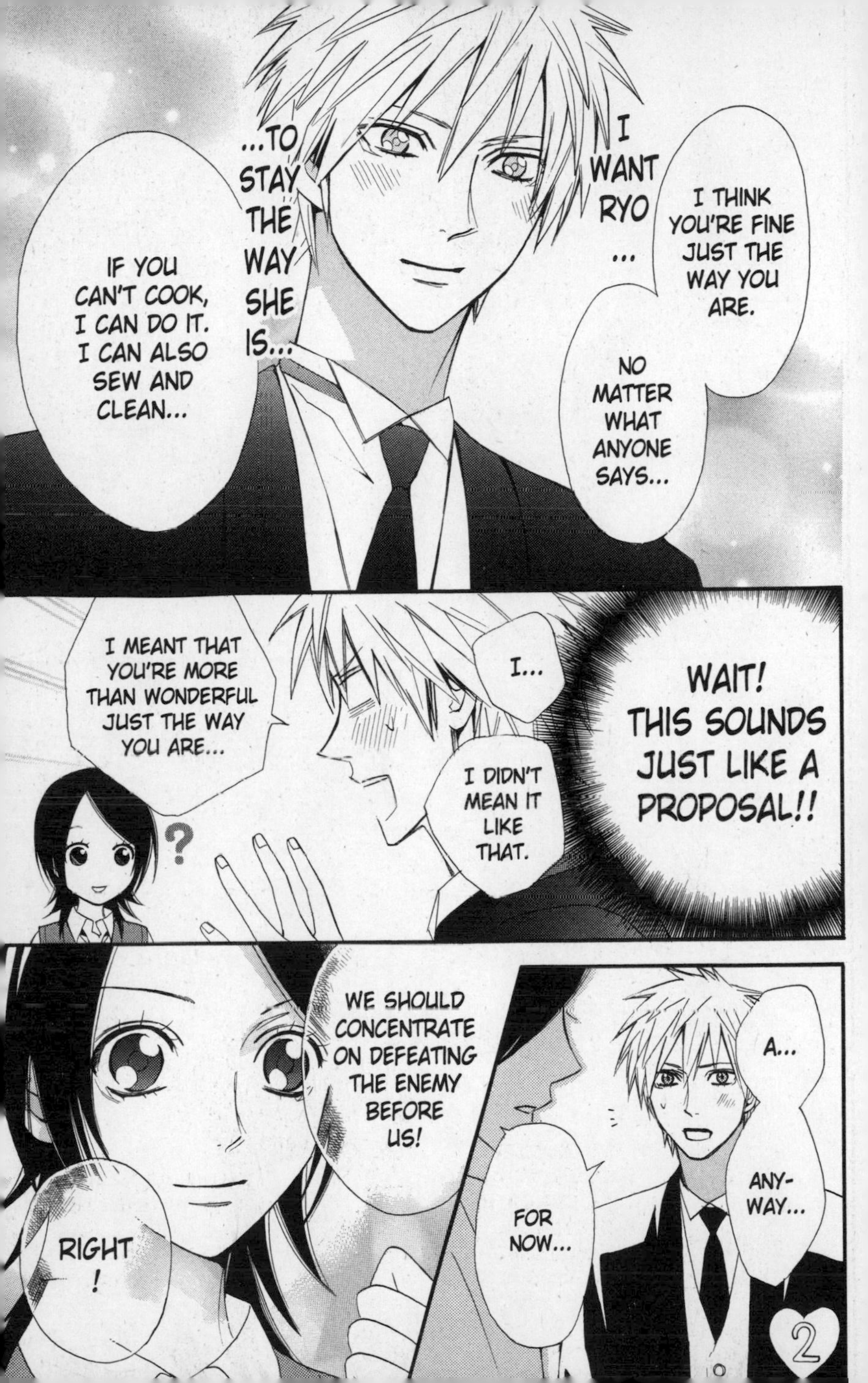
I THINK YOU'RE FINE JUST THE WAY YOU ARE.
NO MATTER WHAT ANYONE SAYS...
I WANT RYO ...
...TO STAY THE WAY SHE IS...
IF YOU CAN'T COOK, I CAN DO IT. I CAN ALSO SEW AND CLEAN...
WAIT! THIS SOUNDS JUST LIKE A PROPOSAL!!
I...
I DIDN'T MEAN IT LIKE THAT.
I MEANT THAT YOU'RE MORE THAN WONDERFUL JUST THE WAY YOU ARE...
?
A...
ANY-WAY...
FOR NOW...
WE SHOULD CONCENTRATE ON DEFEATING THE ENEMY BEFORE US!
RIGHT!
2

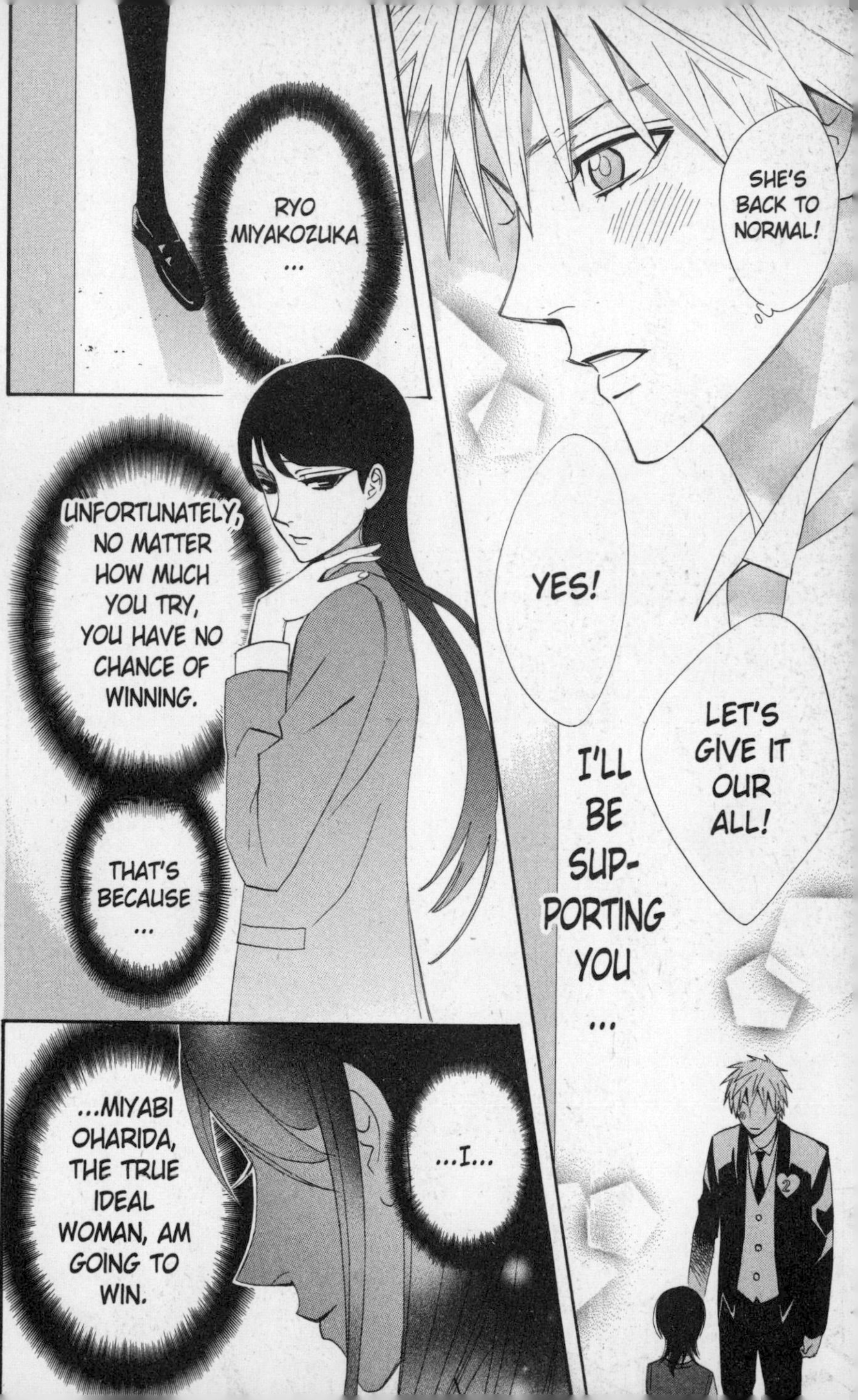
SHE'S BACK TO NORMAL!
YES!
LET'S GIVE IT OUR ALL!
I'LL BE SUP-PORTING YOU ...
RYO MIYAKOZUKA ...
UNFORTUNATELY, NO MATTER HOW MUCH YOU TRY, YOU HAVE NO CHANCE OF WINNING.
THAT'S BECAUSE ...
...I...
...MIYABI OHARIDA, THE TRUE IDEAL WOMAN, AM GOING TO WIN.

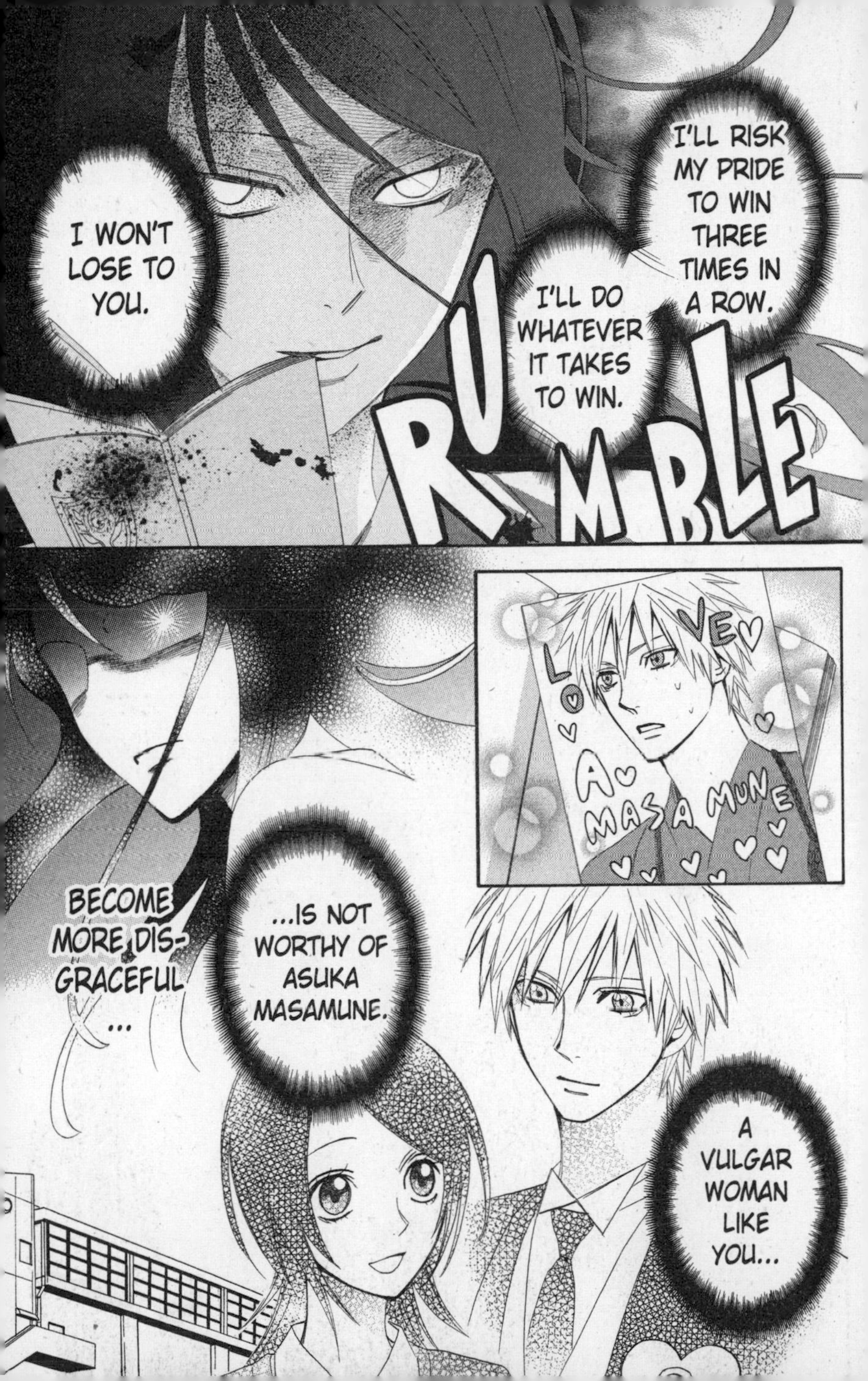
I'LL RISK MY PRIDE TO WIN THREE TIMES IN A ROW.
I'LL DO WHATEVER IT TAKES TO WIN.
RUMBLE
I WON'T LOSE TO YOU.
LOVE
A
MASAMUNE
A VULGAR WOMAN LIKE YOU...
...IS NOT WORTHY OF ASUKA MASAMUNE.
BECOME MORE DIS-GRACEFUL...

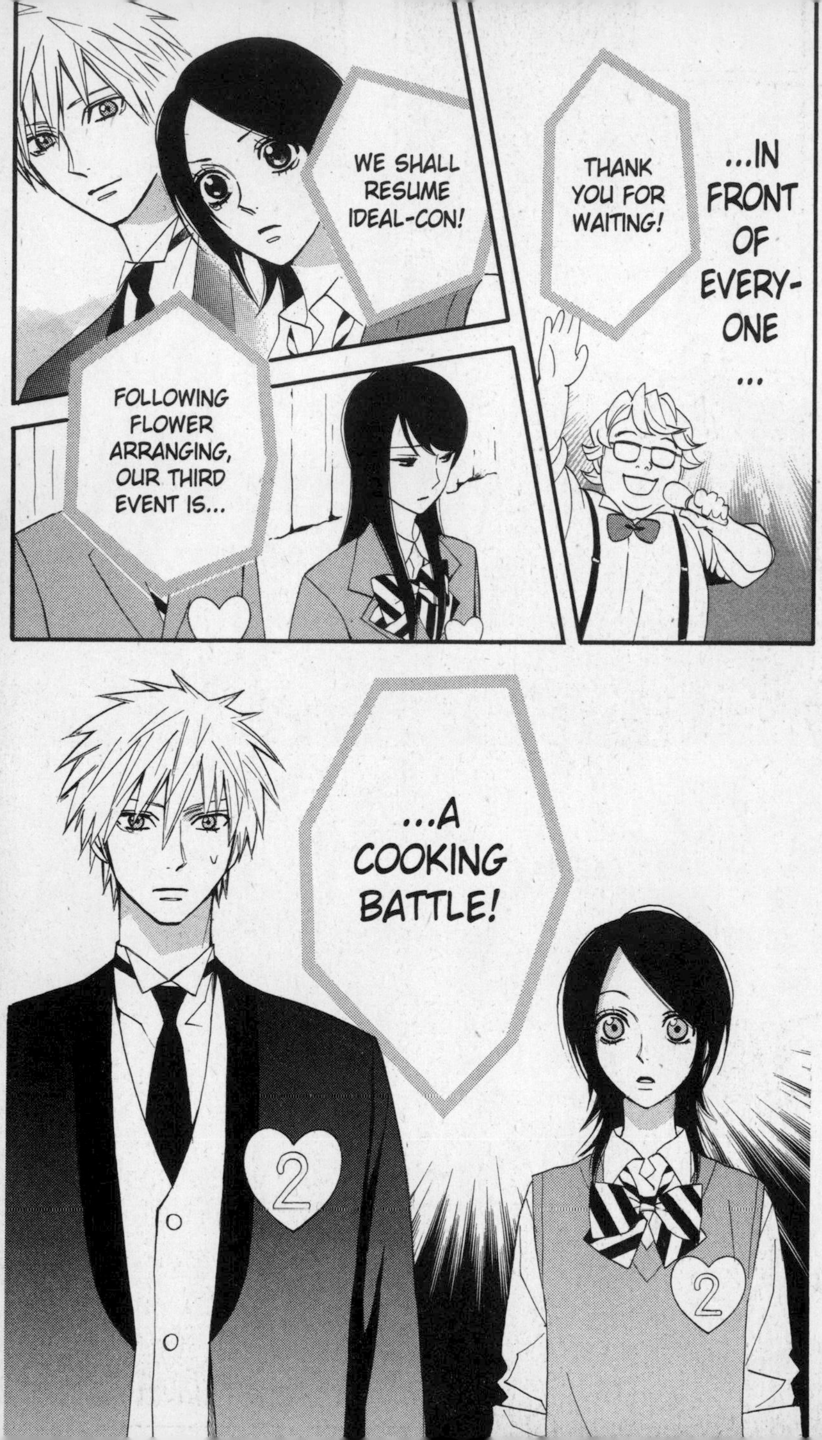
...IN FRONT OF EVERY-ONE...
THANK YOU FOR WAITING!
WE SHALL RESUME IDEAL-CON!
FOLLOWING FLOWER ARRANGING, OUR THIRD EVENT IS...
...A COOKING BATTLE!

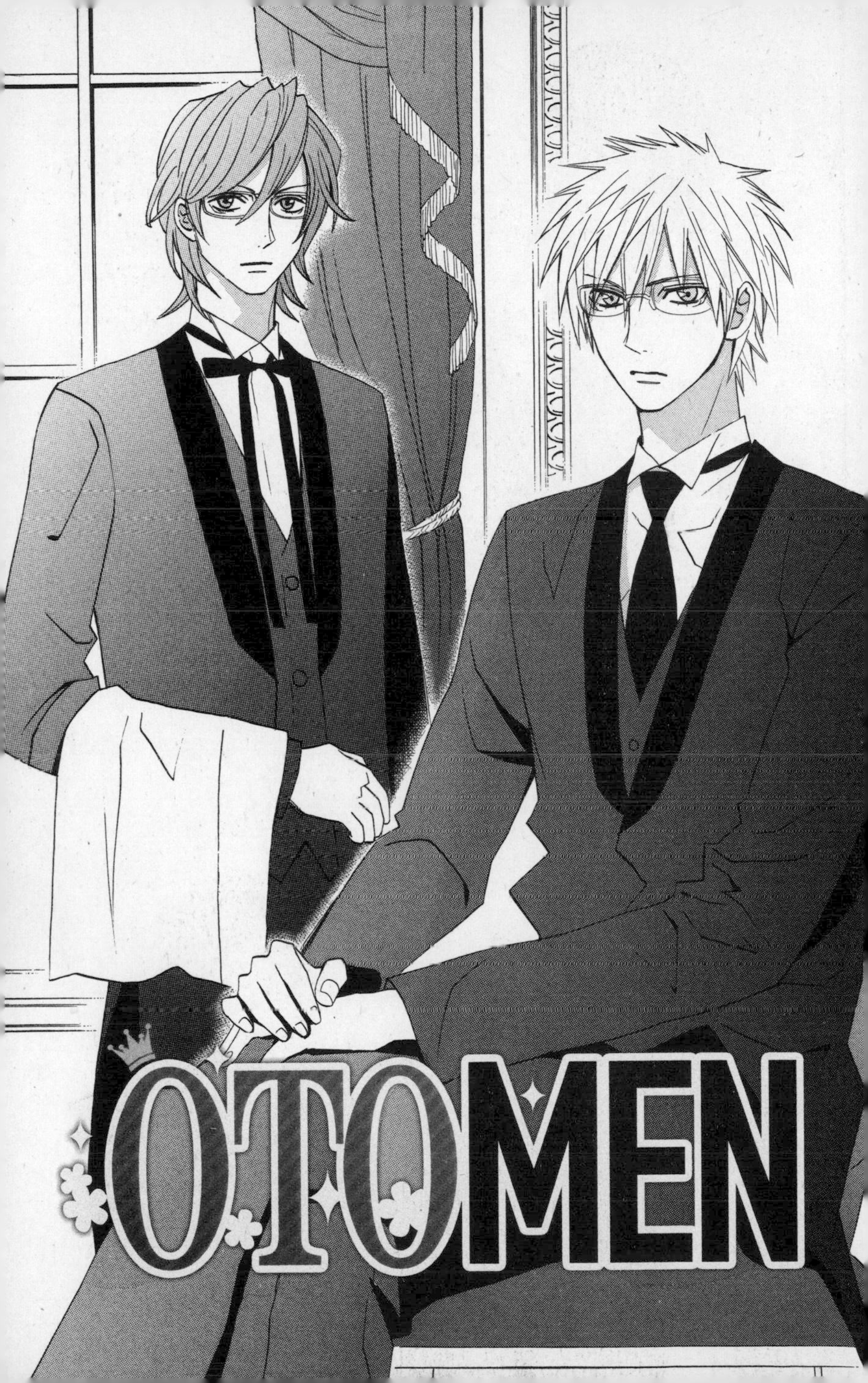
OTOMEN

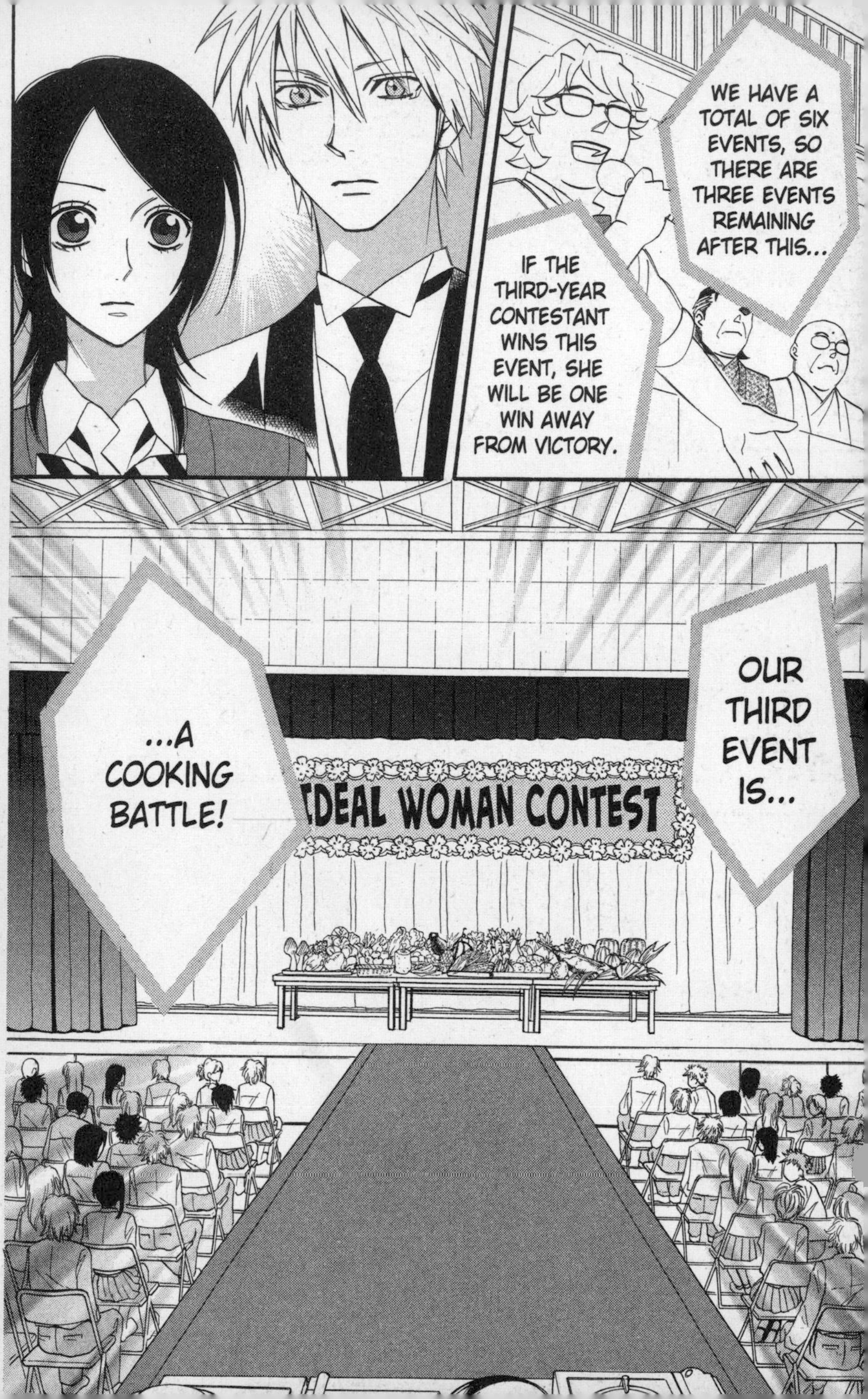
WE HAVE A TOTAL OF SIX EVENTS, SO THERE ARE THREE EVENTS REMAINING AFTER THIS...
IF THE THIRD-YEAR CONTESTANT WINS THIS EVENT, SHE WILL BE ONE WIN AWAY FROM VICTORY.
OUR THIRD EVENT IS...
...A COOKING BATTLE!
IDEAL WOMAN CONTEST

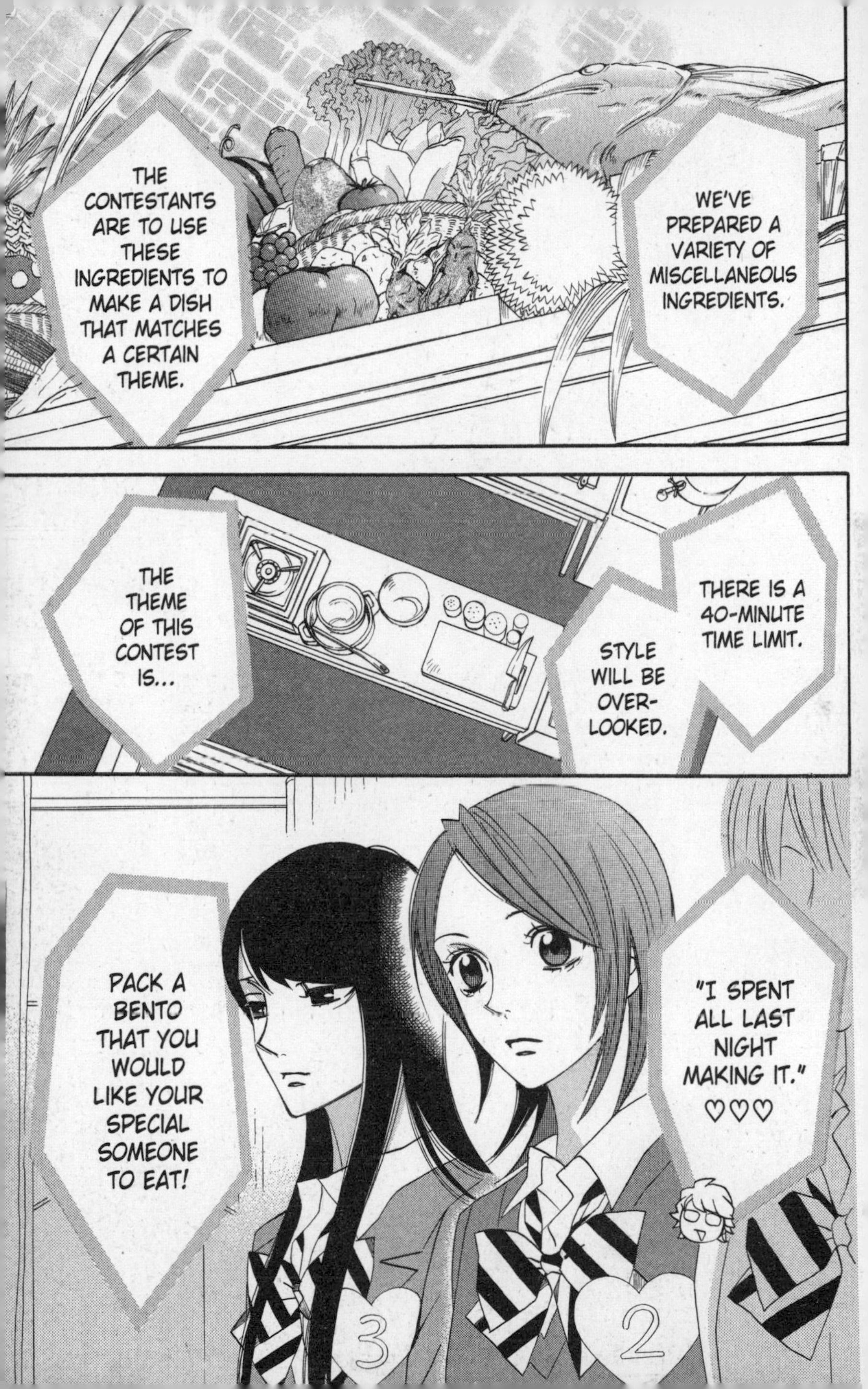
WE'VE PREPARED A VARIETY OF MISCELLANEOUS INGREDIENTS.
THE CONTESTANTS ARE TO USE THESE INGREDIENTS TO MAKE A DISH THAT MATCHES A CERTAIN THEME.
THERE IS A 40-MINUTE TIME LIMIT.
STYLE WILL BE OVER-LOOKED.
THE THEME OF THIS CONTEST IS...
"I SPENT ALL LAST NIGHT MAKING IT." ♡♡♡
PACK A BENTO THAT YOU WOULD LIKE YOUR SPECIAL SOMEONE TO EAT!
2
3

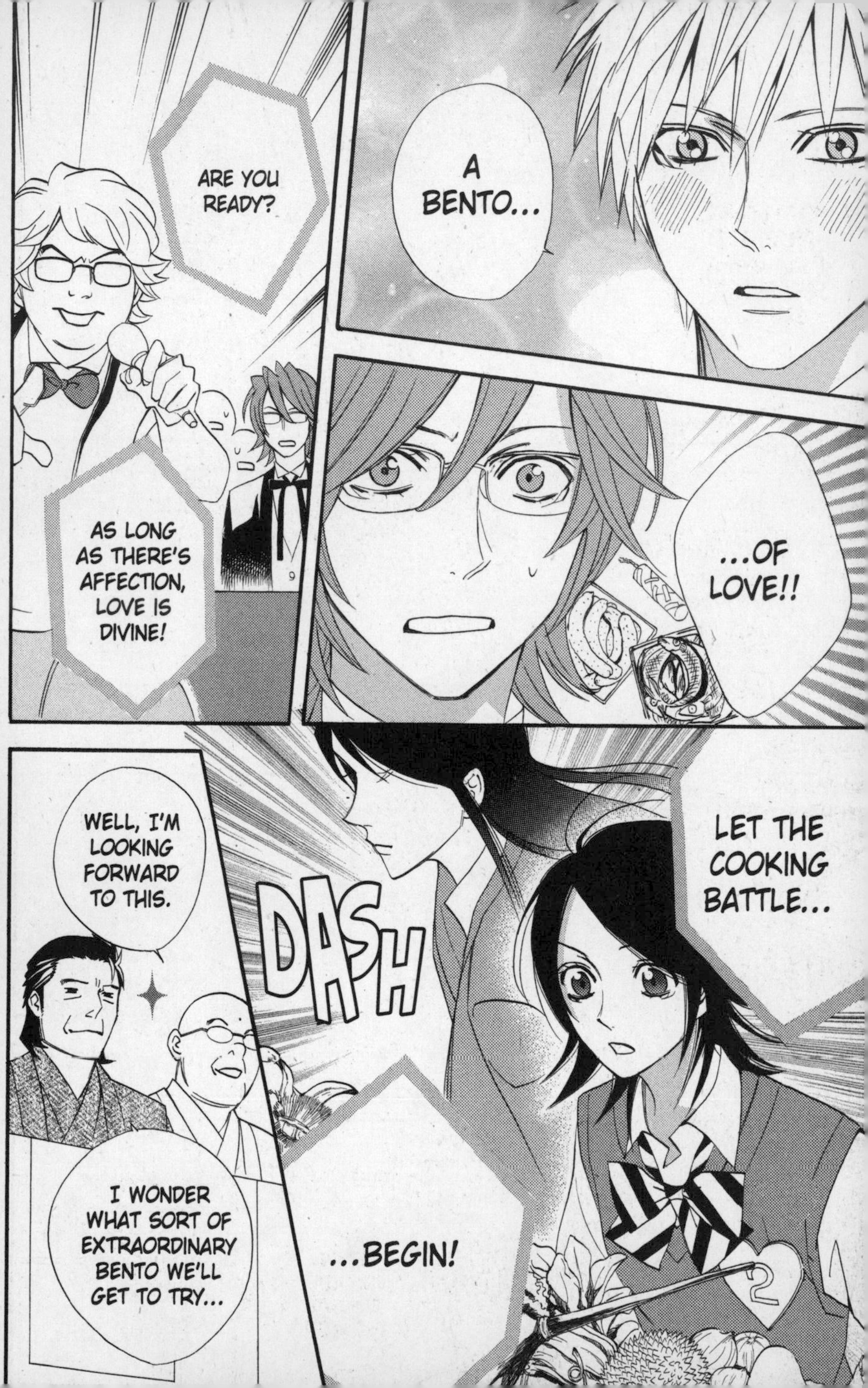
A BENTO...
...OF LOVE!!
ARE YOU READY?
AS LONG AS THERE'S AFFECTION, LOVE IS DIVINE!
LET THE COOKING BATTLE...
DASH
...BEGIN!
WELL, I'M LOOKING FORWARD TO THIS.
I WONDER WHAT SORT OF EXTRAORDINARY BENTO WE'LL GET TO TRY...

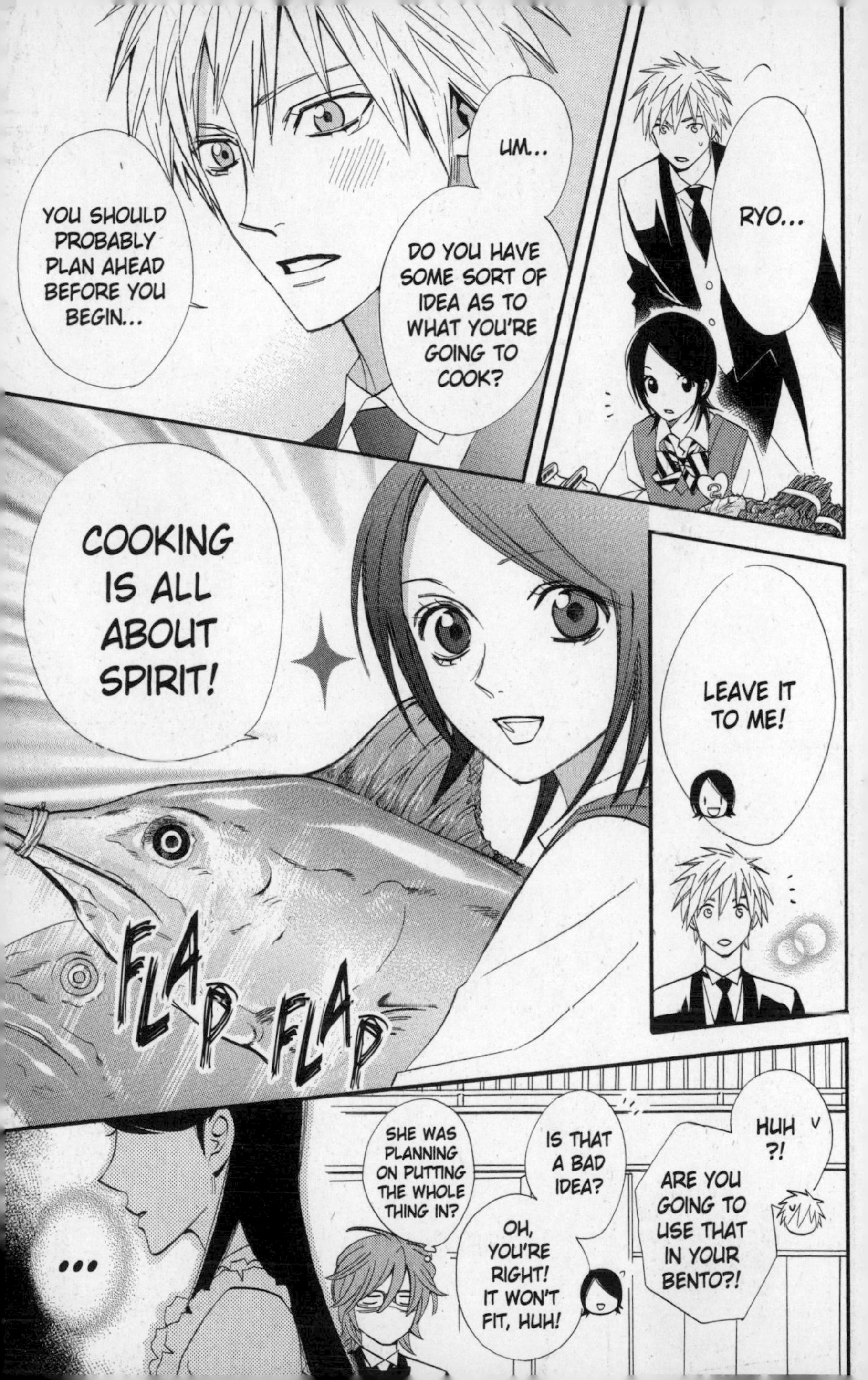
RYO...
UM...
DO YOU HAVE SOME SORT OF IDEA AS TO WHAT YOU'RE GOING TO COOK?
YOU SHOULD PROBABLY PLAN AHEAD BEFORE YOU BEGIN...
LEAVE IT TO ME!
COOKING IS ALL ABOUT SPIRIT!
FLAP FLAP
HUH?!
ARE YOU GOING TO USE THAT IN YOUR BENTO?!
IS THAT A BAD IDEA?
OH, YOU'RE RIGHT! IT WON'T FIT, HUH!
SHE WAS PLANNING ON PUTTING THE WHOLE THING IN?
...

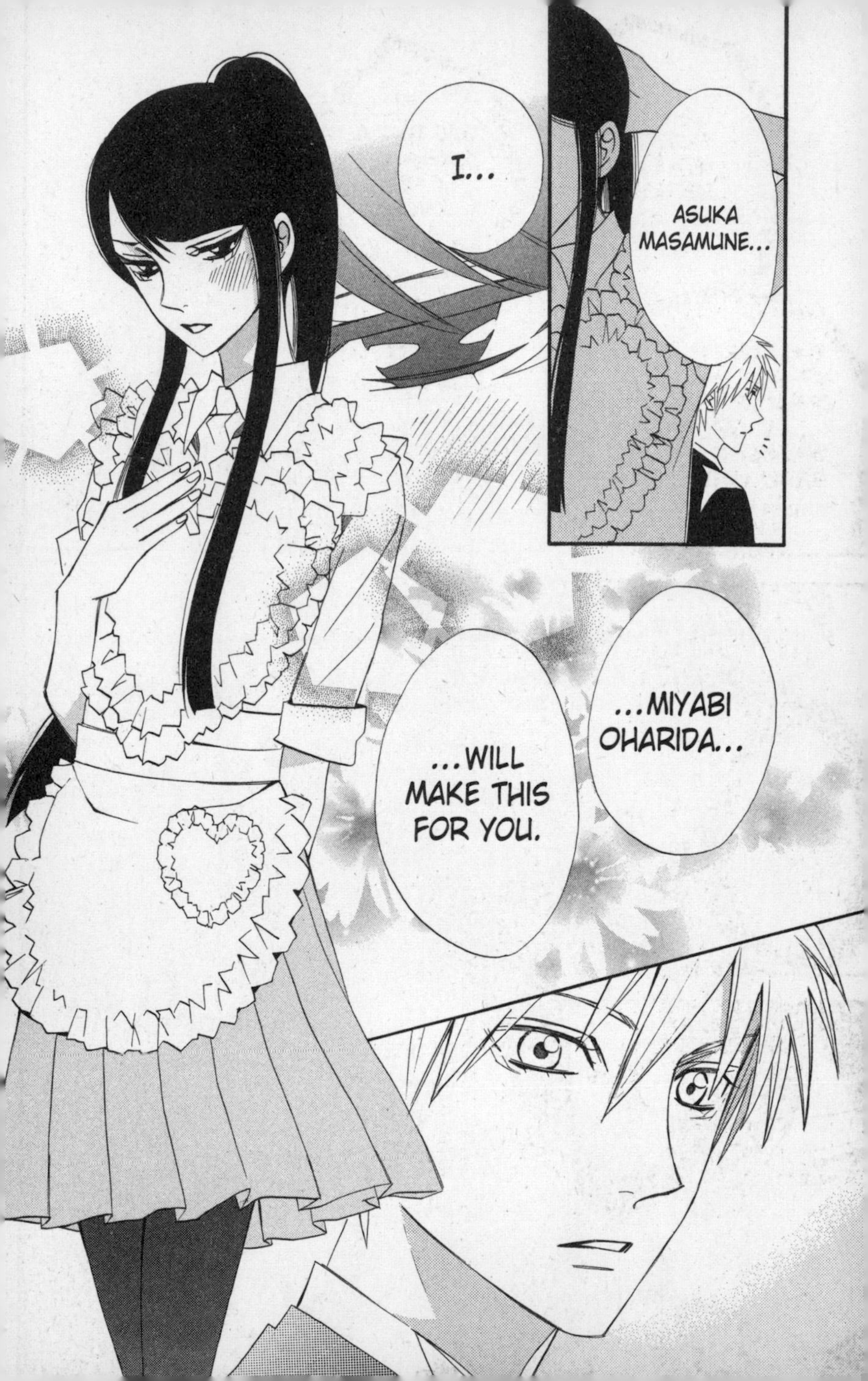
I...
ASUKA MASAMUNE...
...MIYABI OHARIDA...
...WILL MAKE THIS FOR YOU.

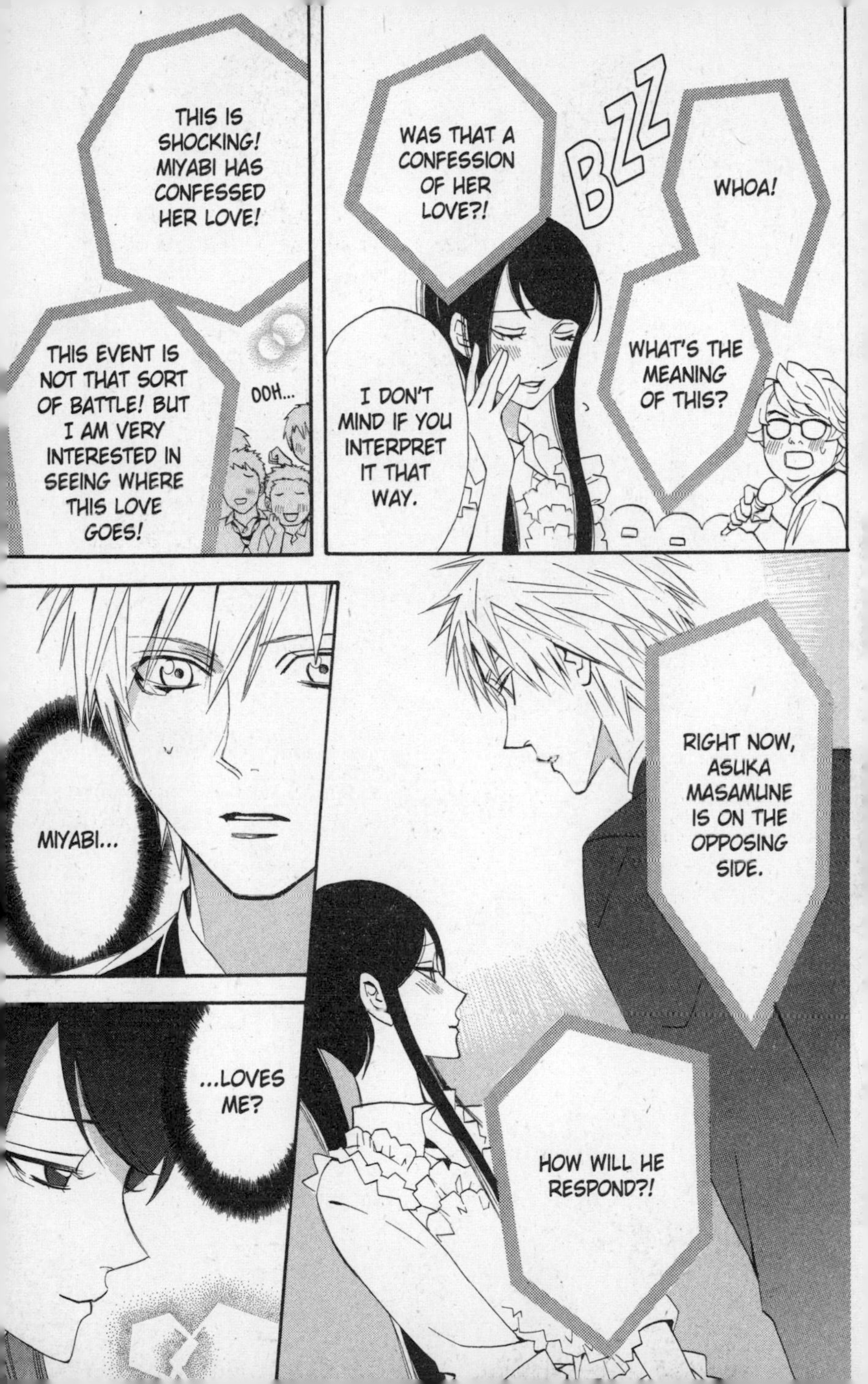
WHOA!
BZZ
WAS THAT A CONFESSION OF HER LOVE?!
WHAT'S THE MEANING OF THIS?
I DON'T MIND IF YOU INTERPRET IT THAT WAY.
THIS IS SHOCKING! MIYABI HAS CONFESSED HER LOVE!
OOH...
THIS EVENT IS NOT THAT SORT OF BATTLE! BUT I AM VERY INTERESTED IN SEEING WHERE THIS LOVE GOES!
RIGHT NOW, ASUKA MASAMUNE IS ON THE OPPOSING SIDE.
HOW WILL HE RESPOND?!
MIYABI...
...LOVES ME?

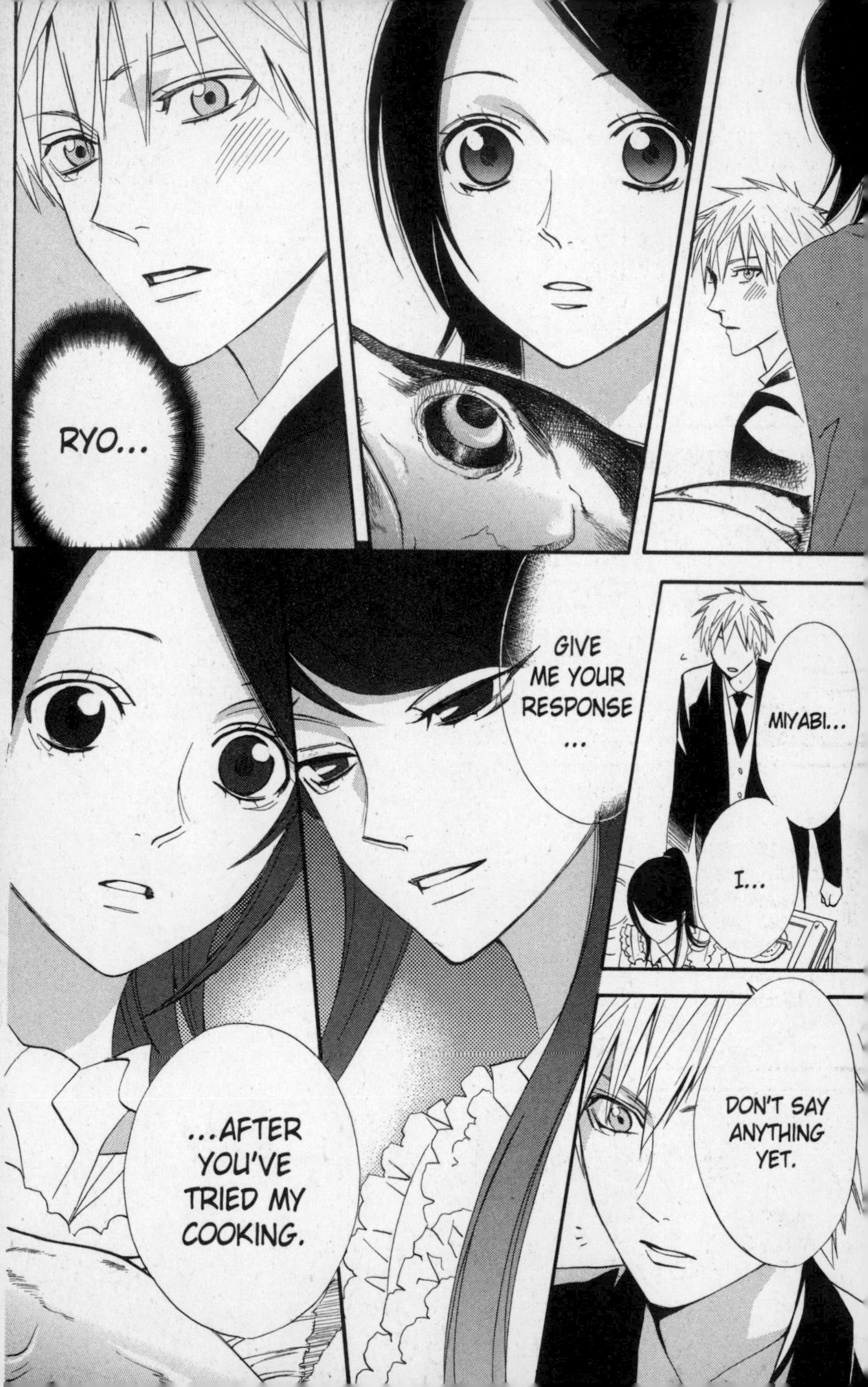
RYO...
MIYABI...
I...
DON'T SAY ANYTHING YET.
GIVE ME YOUR RESPONSE ...
...AFTER YOU'VE TRIED MY COOKING.

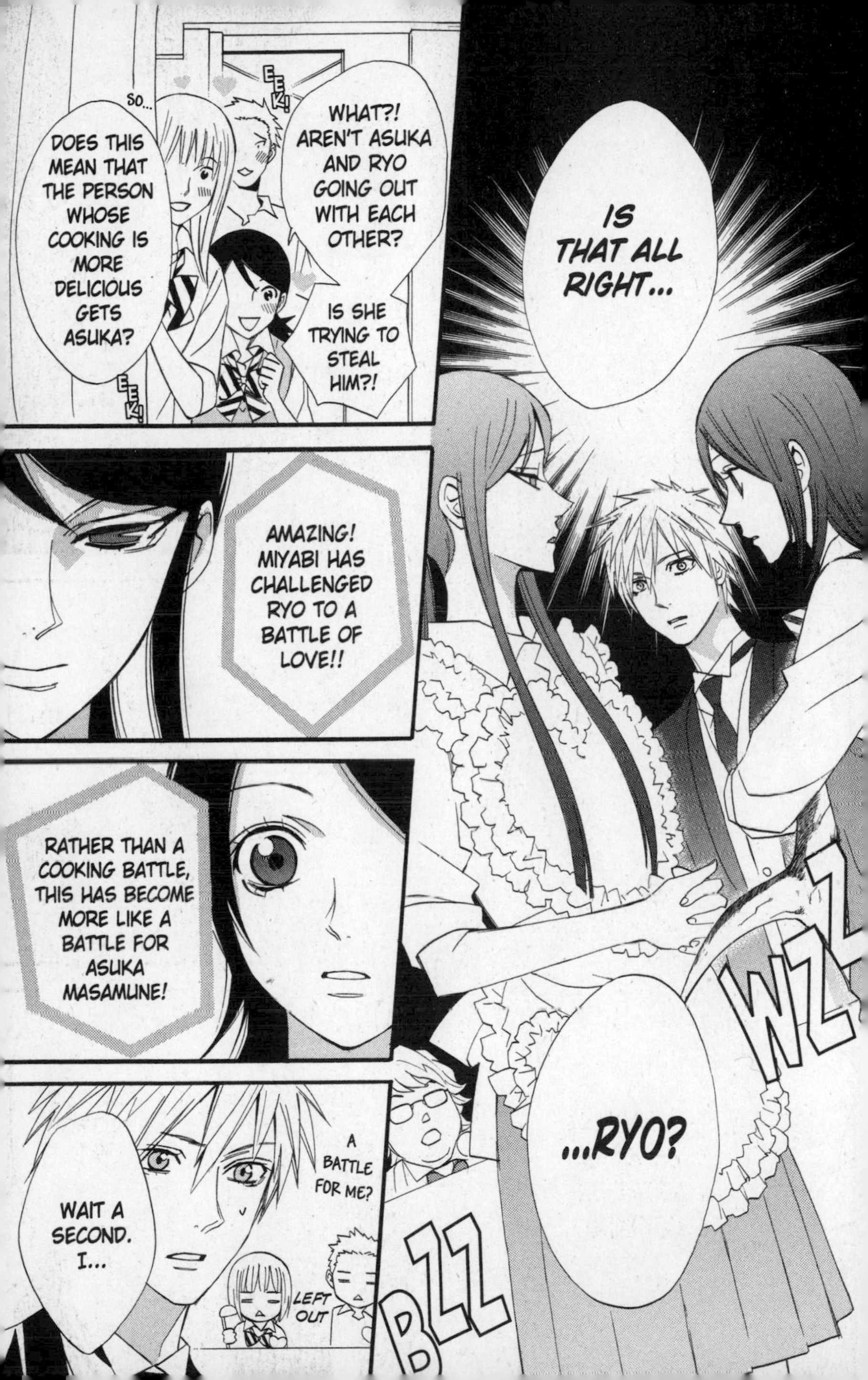
IS THAT ALL RIGHT...
WZZ
...RYO?
BZZ
WHAT?! AREN'T ASUKA AND RYO GOING OUT WITH EACH OTHER?
EEK!
IS SHE TRYING TO STEAL HIM?!
SO...
DOES THIS MEAN THAT THE PERSON WHOSE COOKING IS MORE DELICIOUS GETS ASUKA?
EEK!
AMAZING! MIYABI HAS CHALLENGED RYO TO A BATTLE OF LOVE!!
RATHER THAN A COOKING BATTLE, THIS HAS BECOME MORE LIKE A BATTLE FOR ASUKA MASAMUNE!
A BATTLE FOR ME?
WAIT A SECOND. I...
LEFT OUT

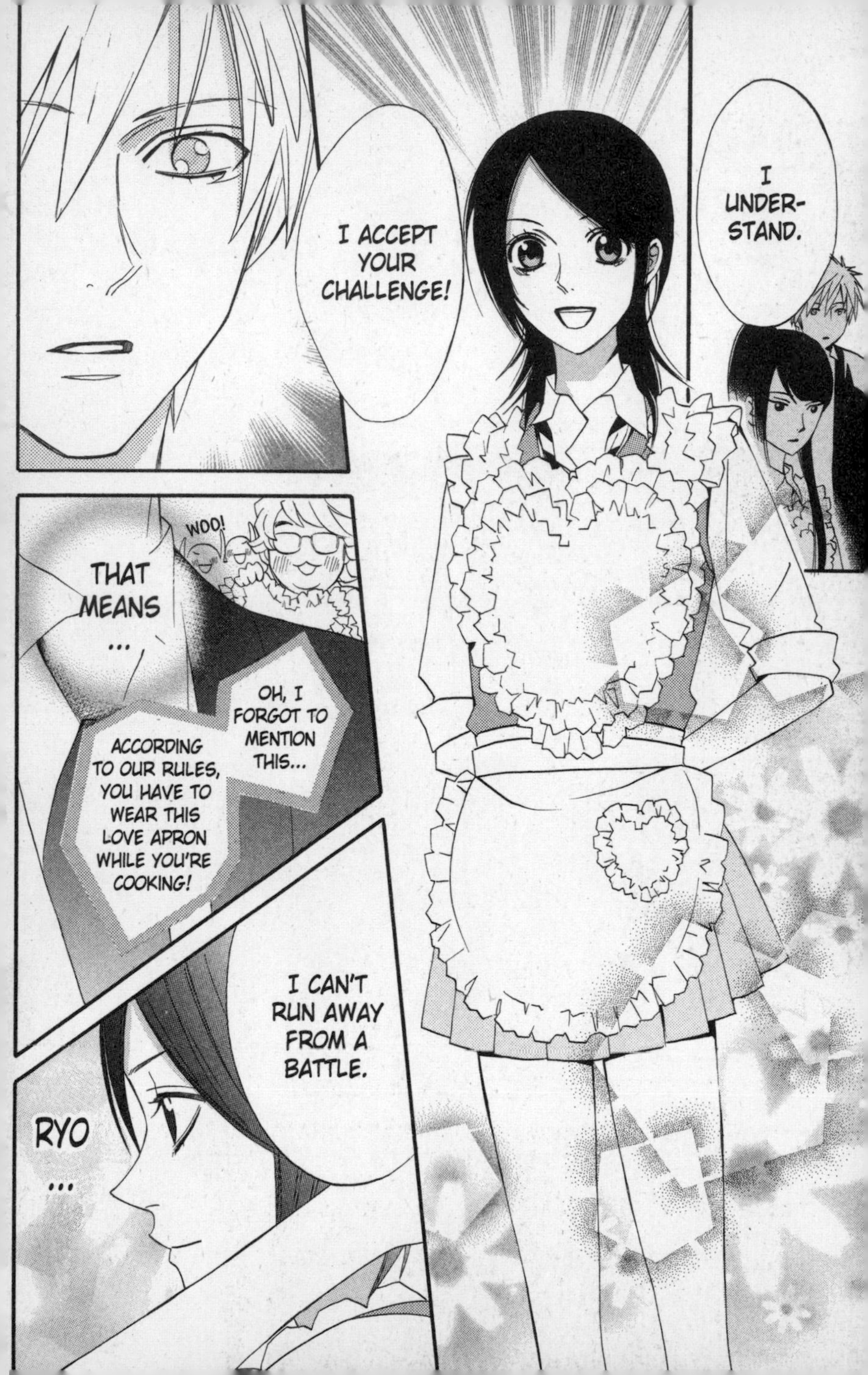
I UNDER-STAND.
I ACCEPT YOUR CHALLENGE!
WOO!
THAT MEANS ...
OH, I FORGOT TO MENTION THIS...
ACCORDING TO OUR RULES, YOU HAVE TO WEAR THIS LOVE APRON WHILE YOU'RE COOKING!
I CAN'T RUN AWAY FROM A BATTLE.
RYO ...

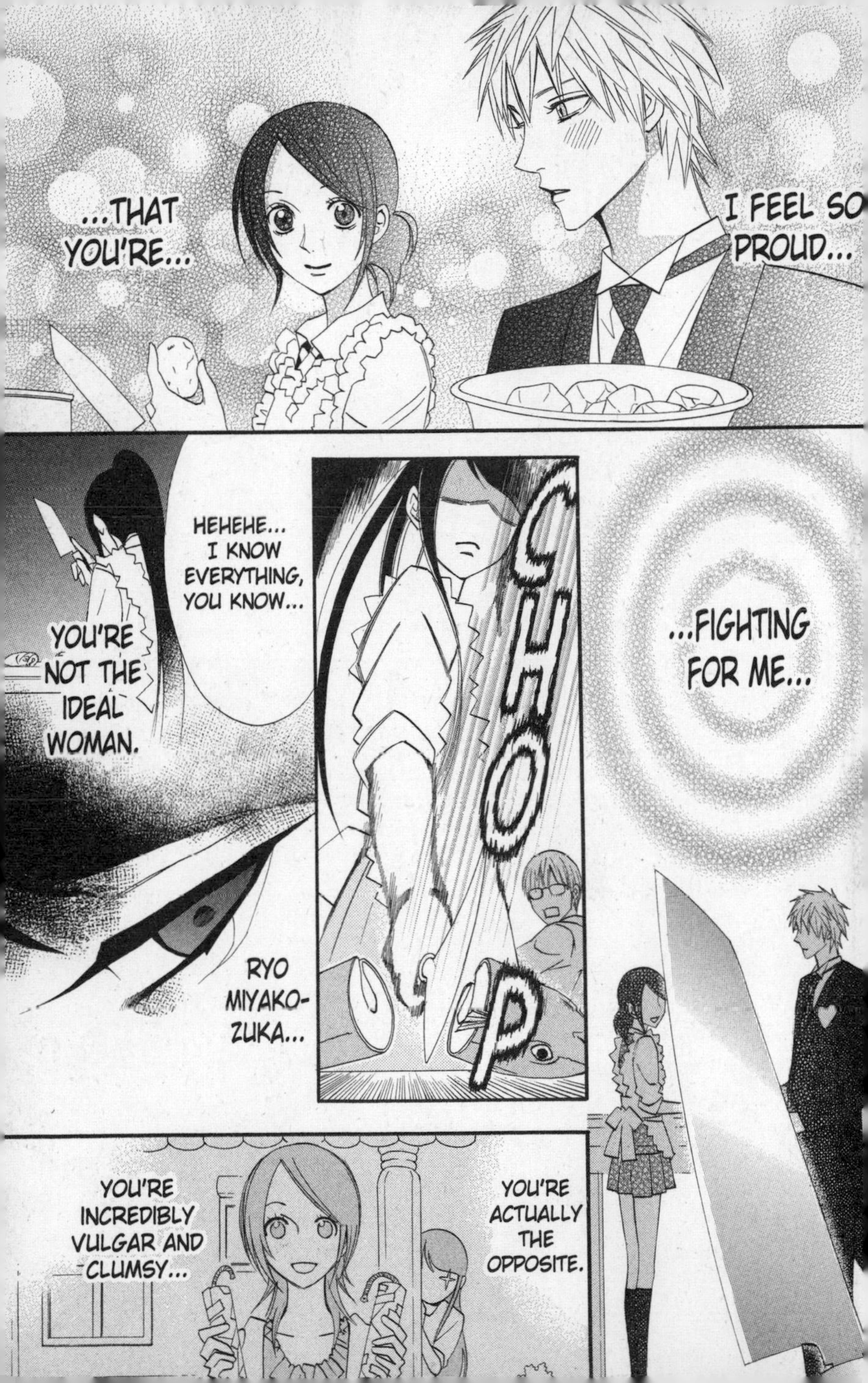
I FEEL SO PROUD...
...THAT YOU'RE...
...FIGHTING FOR ME...
CHOP
HEHEHE... I KNOW EVERYTHING, YOU KNOW...
YOU'RE NOT THE IDEAL WOMAN.
RYO MIYAKO-ZUKA...
YOU'RE ACTUALLY THE OPPOSITE.
YOU'RE INCREDIBLY VULGAR AND CLUMSY...

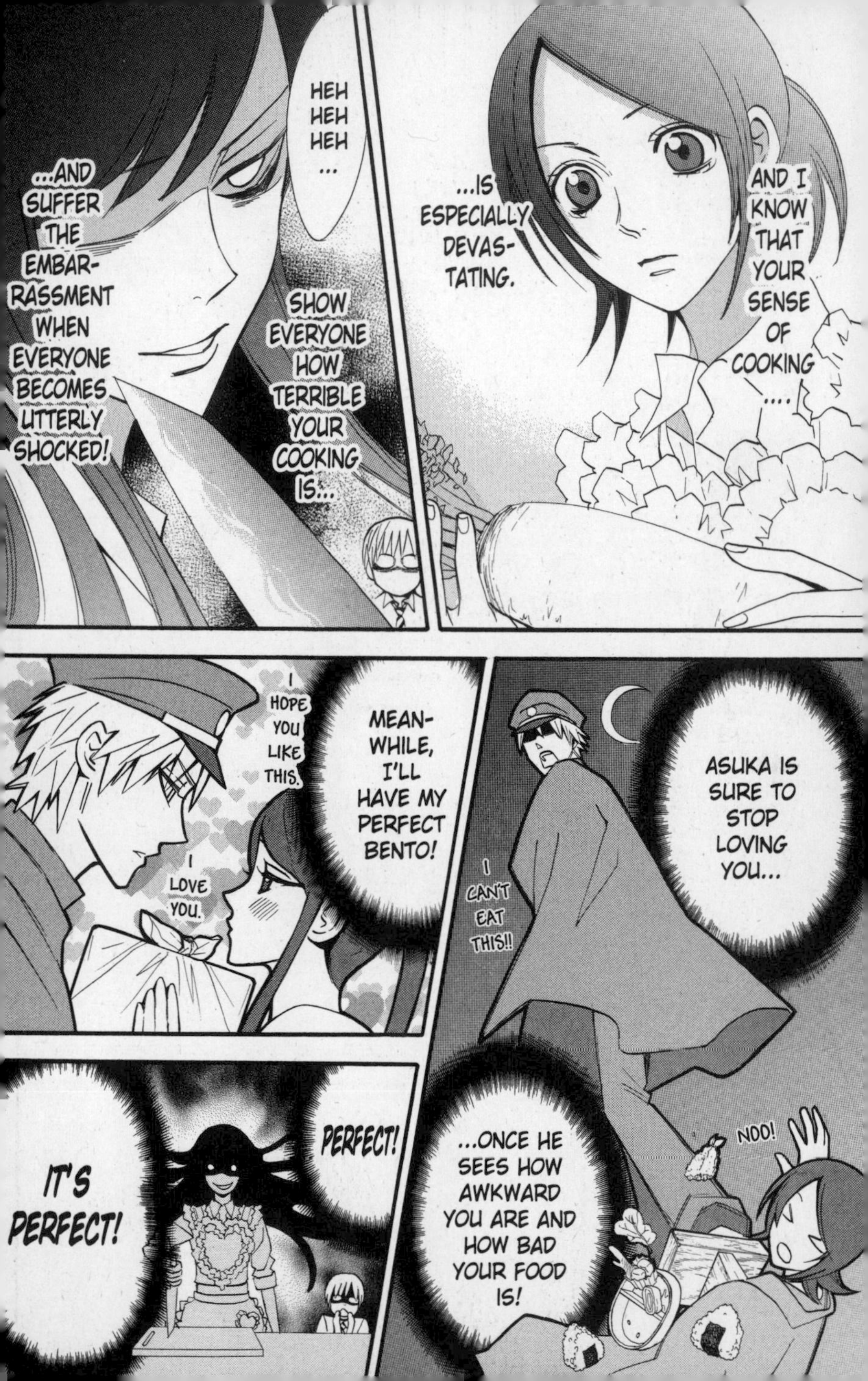
AND I KNOW THAT YOUR SENSE OF COOKING ....
...IS ESPECIALLY DEVAS-TATING.
HEH HEH HEH ...
SHOW EVERYONE HOW TERRIBLE YOUR COOKING IS...
...AND SUFFER THE EMBAR-RASSMENT WHEN EVERYONE BECOMES UTTERLY SHOCKED!
ASUKA IS SURE TO STOP LOVING YOU...
I CAN'T EAT THIS!!
NOO!
...ONCE HE SEES HOW AWKWARD YOU ARE AND HOW BAD YOUR FOOD IS!
MEAN-WHILE, I'LL HAVE MY PERFECT BENTO!
I HOPE YOU LIKE THIS.
I LOVE YOU.
PERFECT!
IT'S PERFECT!

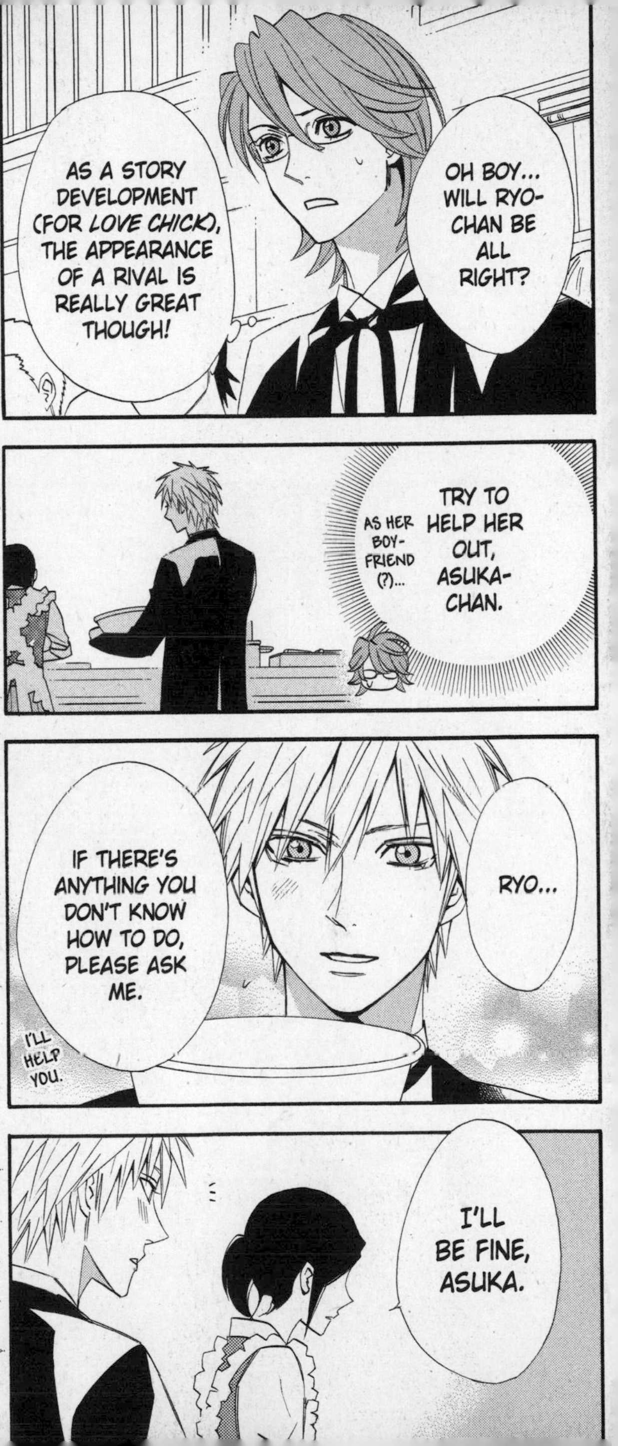
OH BOY... WILL RYO-CHAN BE ALL RIGHT?
AS A STORY DEVELOPMENT (FOR *LOVE CHICK*), THE APPEARANCE OF A RIVAL IS REALLY GREAT THOUGH!
TRY TO HELP HER OUT, ASUKA-CHAN.
AS HER BOY-FRIEND (?)...
RYO...
IF THERE'S ANYTHING YOU DON'T KNOW HOW TO DO, PLEASE ASK ME.
I'LL HELP YOU.
I'LL BE FINE, ASUKA.

HERE'S HOW MIYABI MET ASUKA, WHICH I COULDN'T PUT IN THE STORY BECAUSE OF LACK OF SPACE.

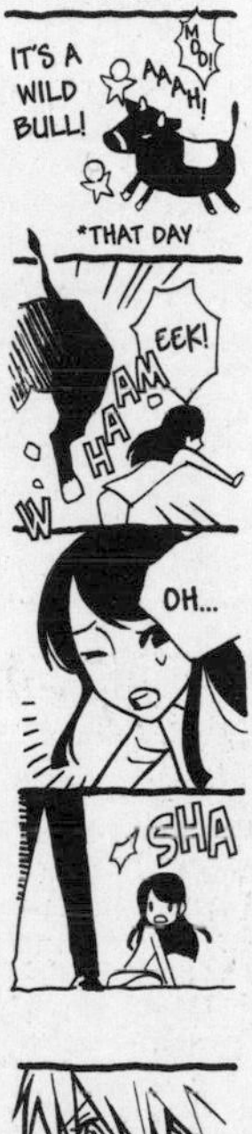
IT'S A WILD BULL!
MOO!
AAAH!
*THAT DAY
EEK!
WHAM
OH...
SHA
HURRY, GET AWAY!

IT CONTINUES AFTER HE SAYS, "COME ON!!"

THERE IS NO PUNCH LINE.

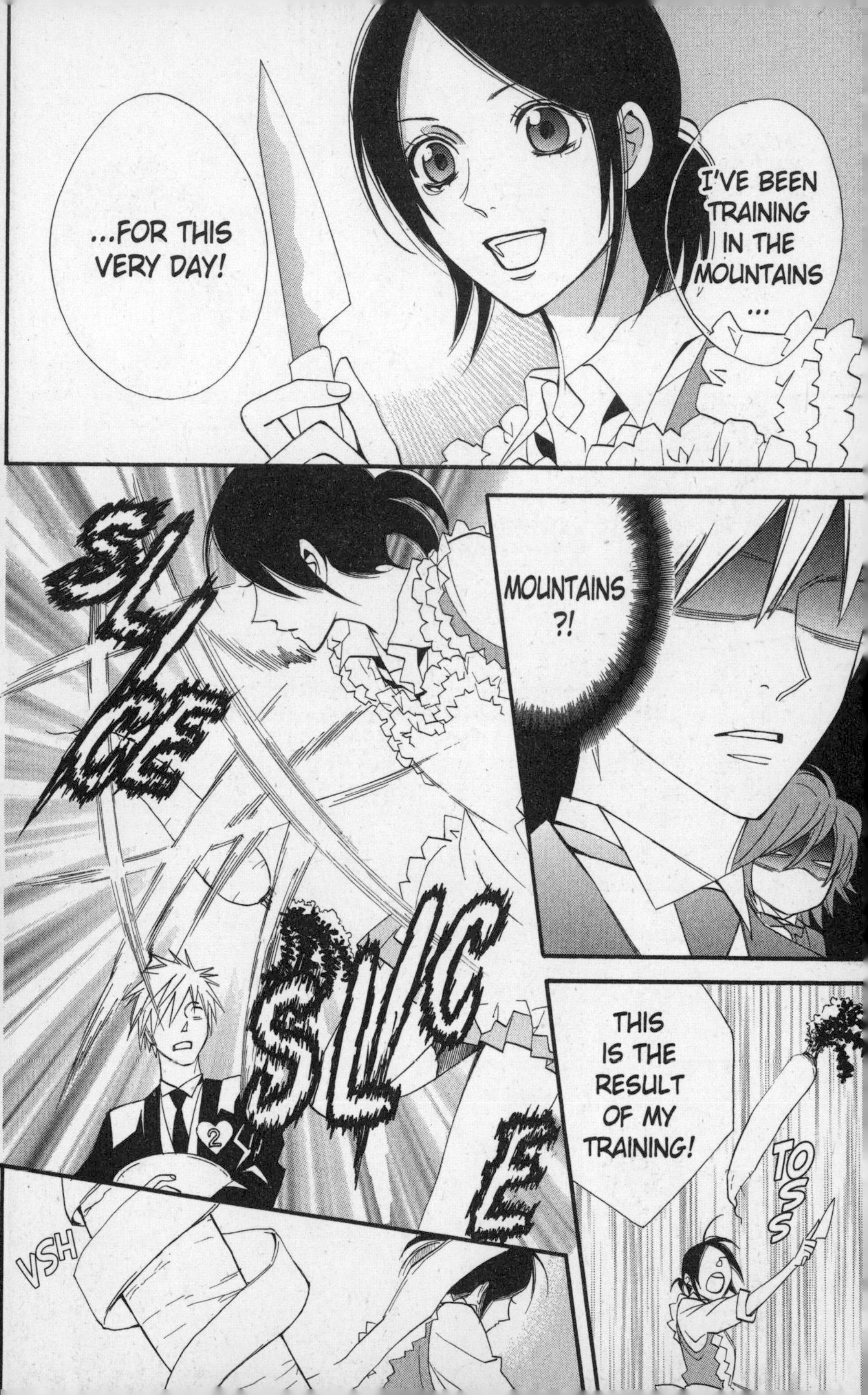

I'VE BEEN TRAINING IN THE MOUNTAINS ...
...FOR THIS VERY DAY!
MOUNTAINS ?!
SLICE
SLICE
THIS IS THE RESULT OF MY TRAINING!
TOSS
VSH

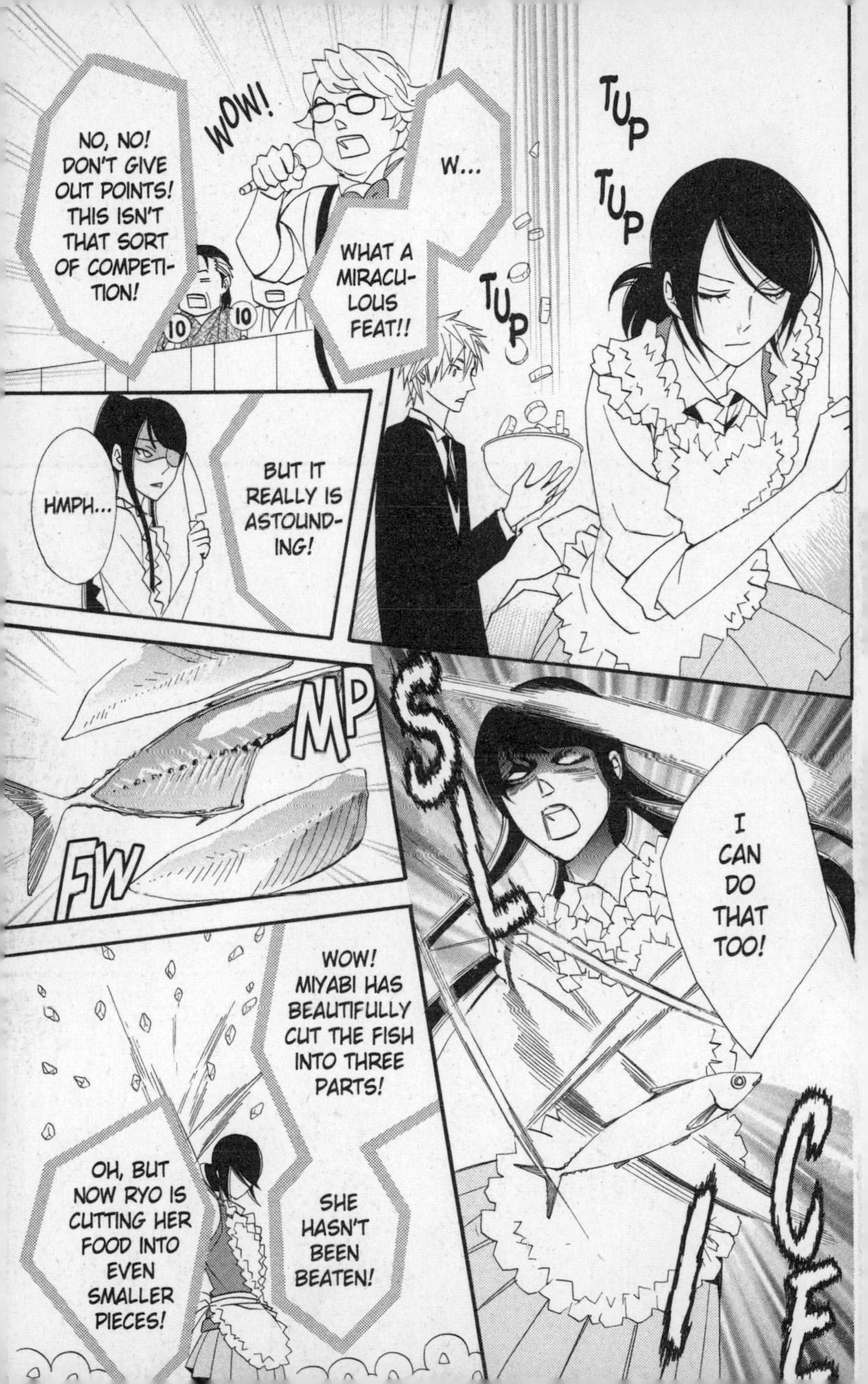
TUP
TUP
TUP
W...
WOW!
WHAT A MIRACULOUS FEAT!!
NO, NO! DON'T GIVE OUT POINTS! THIS ISN'T THAT SORT OF COMPETITION!
10
10
BUT IT REALLY IS ASTOUNDING!
HMPH...
SLICE
I CAN DO THAT TOO!
MP
FW
WOW! MIYABI HAS BEAUTIFULLY CUT THE FISH INTO THREE PARTS!
SHE HASN'T BEEN BEATEN!
OH, BUT NOW RYO IS CUTTING HER FOOD INTO EVEN SMALLER PIECES!

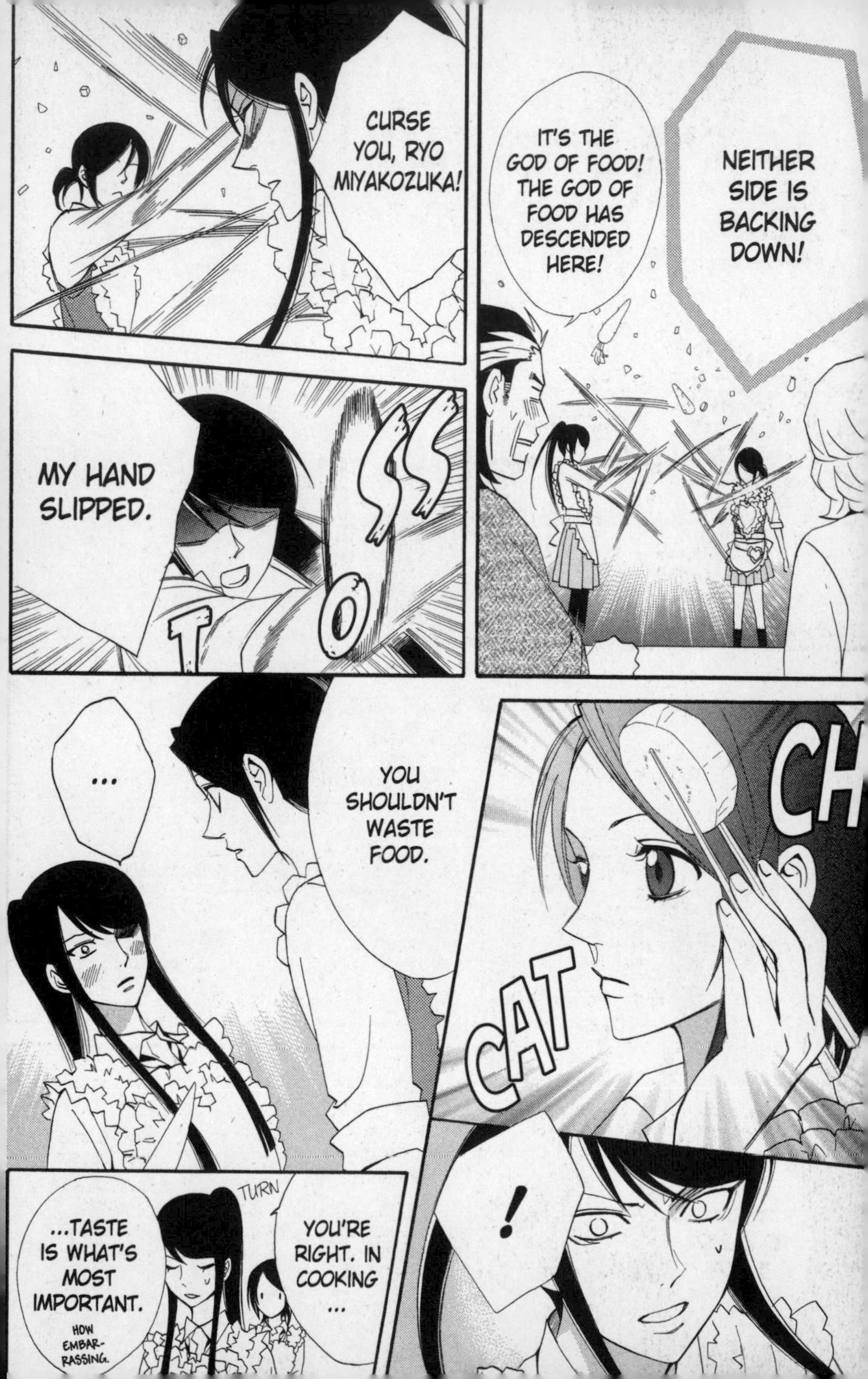
NEITHER SIDE IS BACKING DOWN!
IT'S THE GOD OF FOOD! THE GOD OF FOOD HAS DESCENDED HERE!
CURSE YOU, RYO MIYAKOZUKA!
TOSS
MY HAND SLIPPED.
CH
CAT
YOU SHOULDN'T WASTE FOOD.
...
!
TURN
YOU'RE RIGHT. IN COOKING ...
...TASTE IS WHAT'S MOST IMPORTANT.
HOW EMBARRASSING.

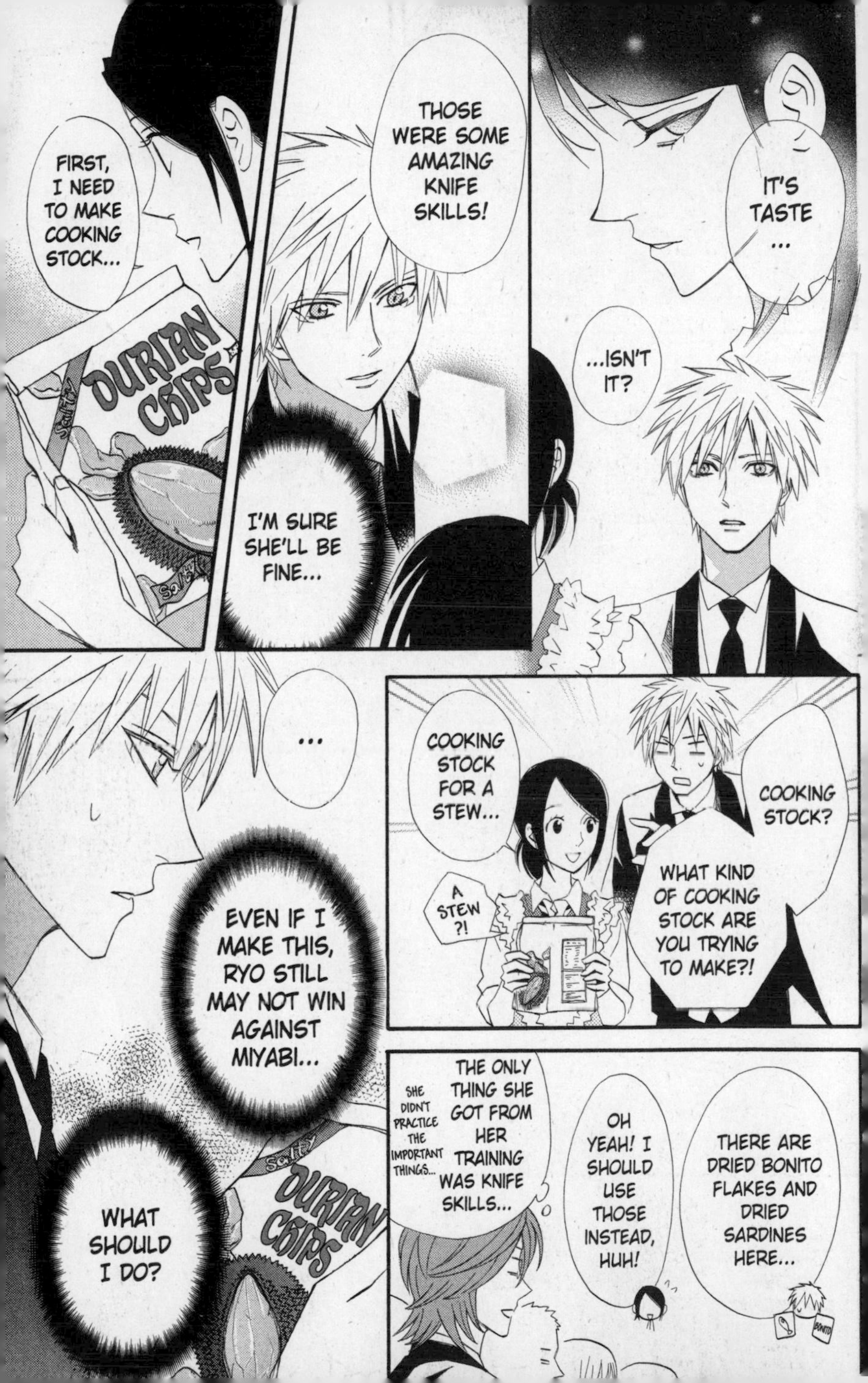
IT'S TASTE ...
...ISN'T IT?
THOSE WERE SOME AMAZING KNIFE SKILLS!
I'M SURE SHE'LL BE FINE...
FIRST, I NEED TO MAKE COOKING STOCK...
DURIAN CHIPS
COOKING STOCK?
WHAT KIND OF COOKING STOCK ARE YOU TRYING TO MAKE?!
COOKING STOCK FOR A STEW...
A STEW ?!
THERE ARE DRIED BONITO FLAKES AND DRIED SARDINES HERE...
BONITO
OH YEAH! I SHOULD USE THOSE INSTEAD, HUH!
THE ONLY THING SHE GOT FROM HER TRAINING WAS KNIFE SKILLS...
SHE DIDN'T PRACTICE THE IMPORTANT THINGS...
...
EVEN IF I MAKE THIS, RYO STILL MAY NOT WIN AGAINST MIYABI...
WHAT SHOULD I DO?
DURIAN CHIPS

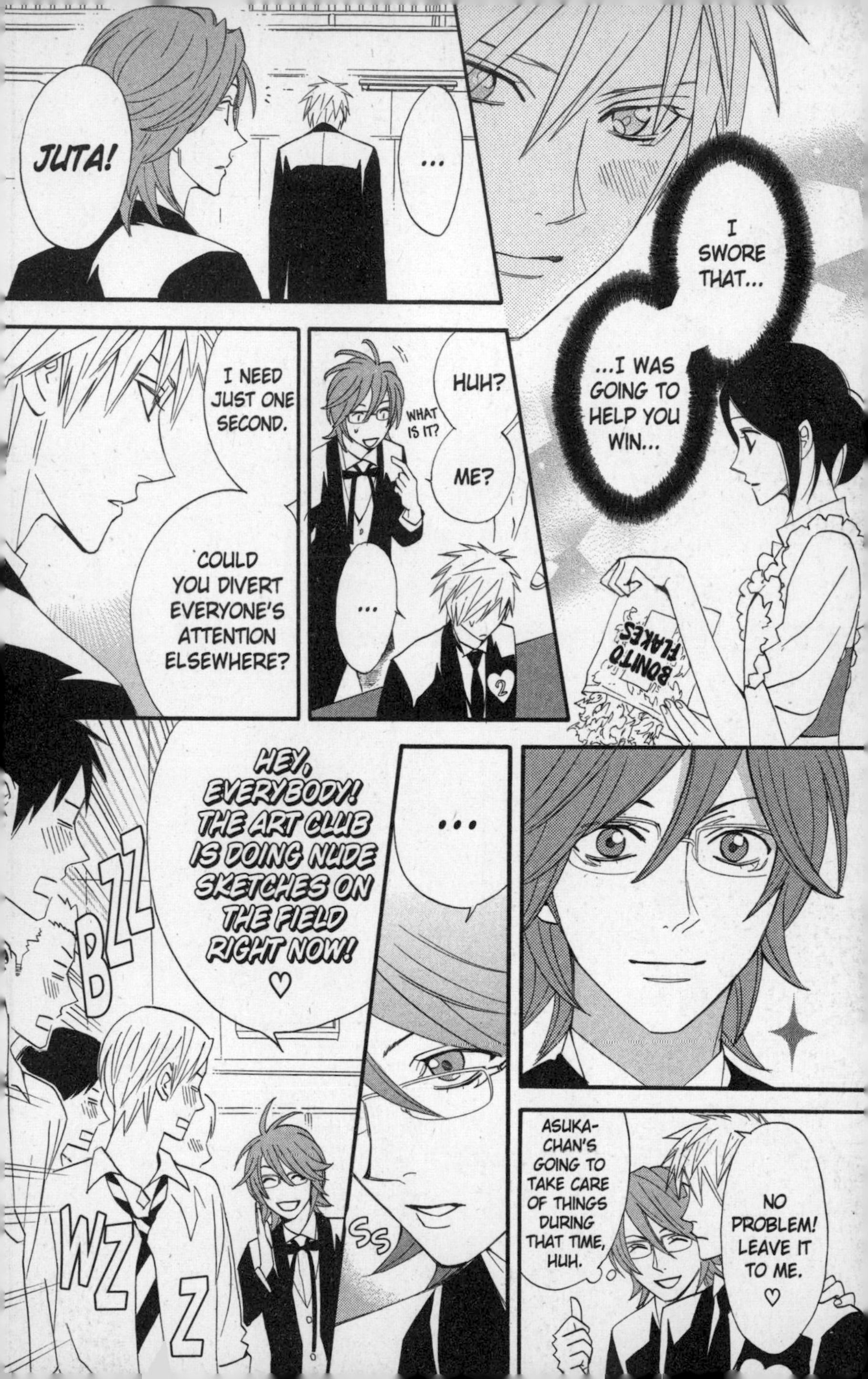
I SWORE THAT...
...I WAS GOING TO HELP YOU WIN...
BONITO FLAKES
...
JUTA!
HUH?
WHAT IS IT?
ME?
...
I NEED JUST ONE SECOND.
COULD YOU DIVERT EVERYONE'S ATTENTION ELSEWHERE?
...
SS
HEY, EVERYBODY! THE ART CLUB IS DOING NUDE SKETCHES ON THE FIELD RIGHT NOW! ♡
BZZ
WZZ
Z
NO PROBLEM! LEAVE IT TO ME. ♡
ASUKA-CHAN'S GOING TO TAKE CARE OF THINGS DURING THAT TIME, HUH.

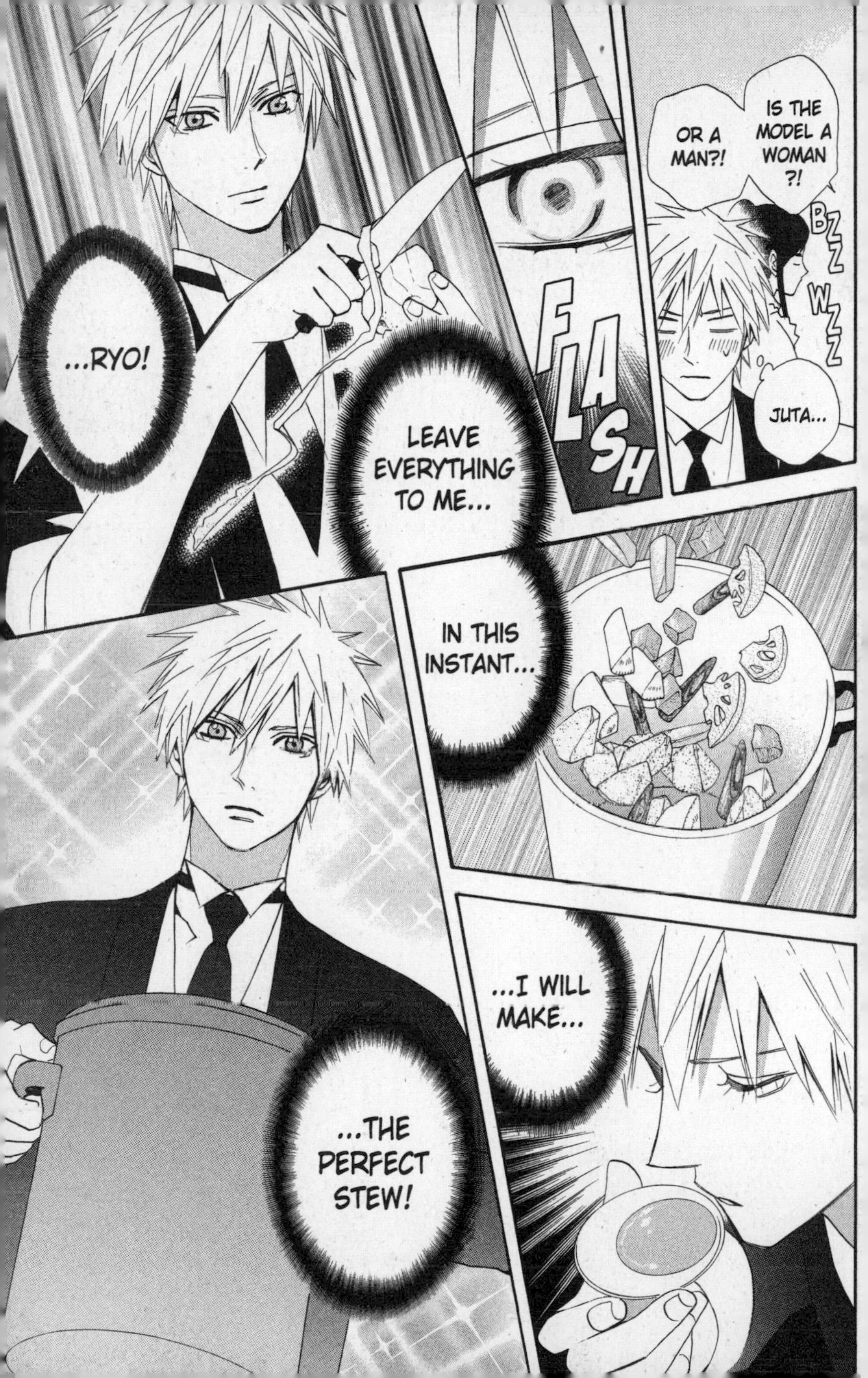
IS THE MODEL A WOMAN ?!
OR A MAN?!
BZZ
WZZ
JUTA...
FLASH
...RYO!
LEAVE EVERYTHING TO ME...
IN THIS INSTANT...
...I WILL MAKE...
...THE PERFECT STEW!

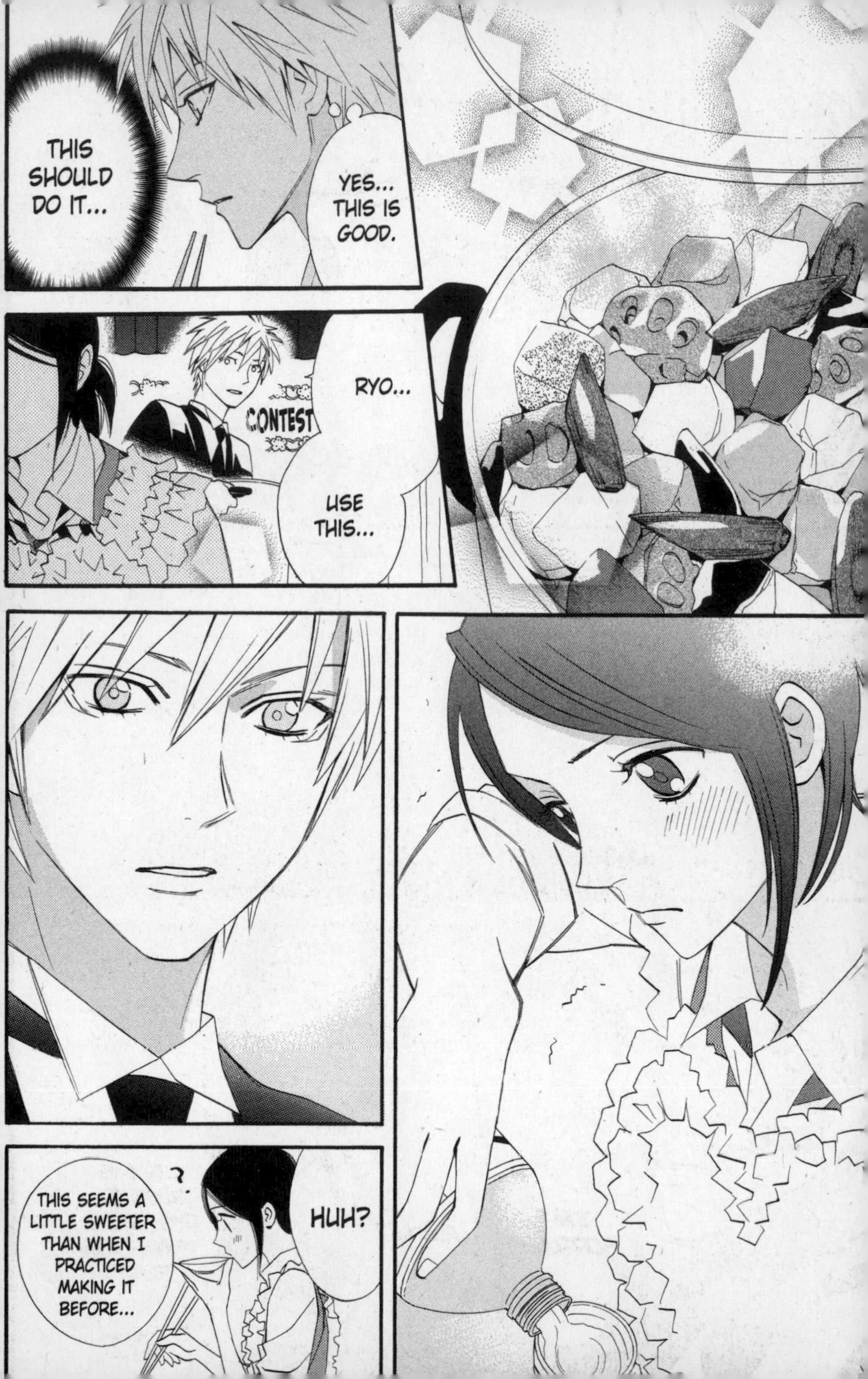
YES... THIS IS GOOD.
THIS SHOULD DO IT...
RYO...
CONTEST
USE THIS...
HUH?
THIS SEEMS A LITTLE SWEETER THAN WHEN I PRACTICED MAKING IT BEFORE...

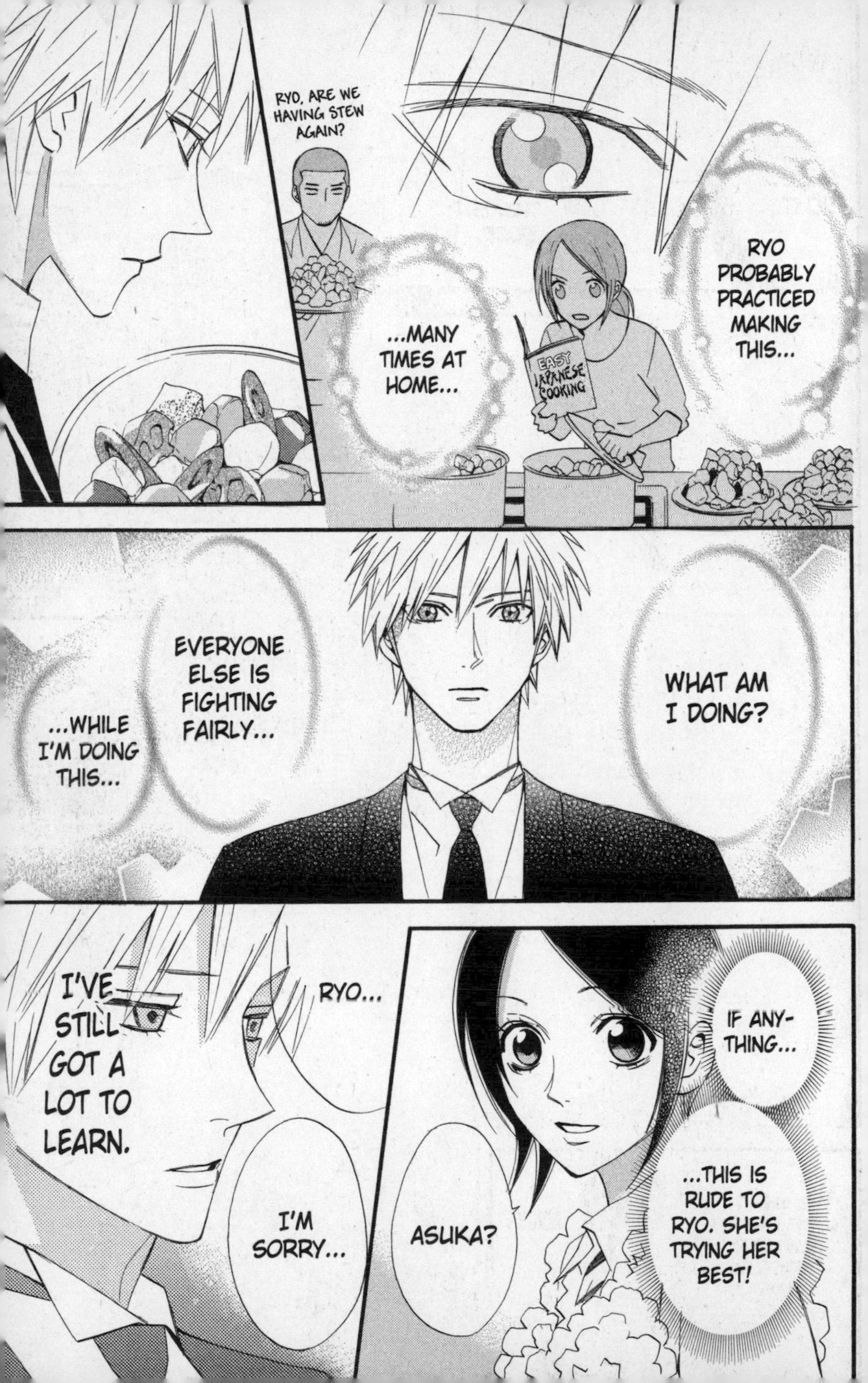
RYO PROBABLY PRACTICED MAKING THIS...
...MANY TIMES AT HOME...
EASY JAPANESE COOKING
RYO, ARE WE HAVING STEW AGAIN?
WHAT AM I DOING?
EVERYONE ELSE IS FIGHTING FAIRLY...
...WHILE I'M DOING THIS...
IF ANY-THING...
...THIS IS RUDE TO RYO. SHE'S TRYING HER BEST!
ASUKA?
RYO...
I'M SORRY...
I'VE STILL GOT A LOT TO LEARN.

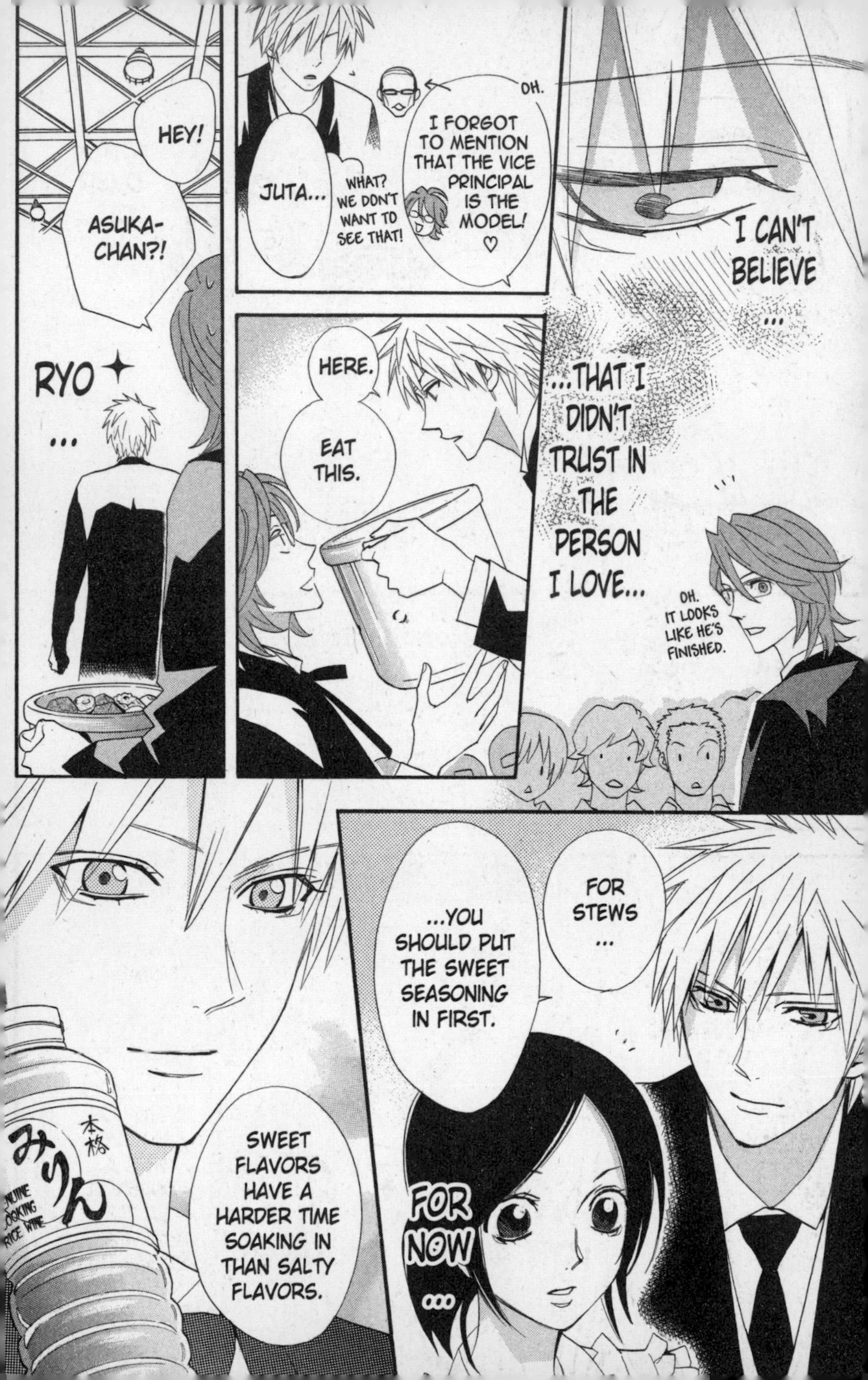
I CAN'T BELIEVE ...
...THAT I DIDN'T TRUST IN THE PERSON I LOVE...
OH. IT LOOKS LIKE HE'S FINISHED.
OH.
I FORGOT TO MENTION THAT THE VICE PRINCIPAL IS THE MODEL! ♡
WHAT? WE DON'T WANT TO SEE THAT!
JUTA...
HERE.
EAT THIS.
HEY!
ASUKA-CHAN?!
RYO ✦ ...
FOR STEWS ...
...YOU SHOULD PUT THE SWEET SEASONING IN FIRST.
FOR NOW ...
SWEET FLAVORS HAVE A HARDER TIME SOAKING IN THAN SALTY FLAVORS.
本格
みりん

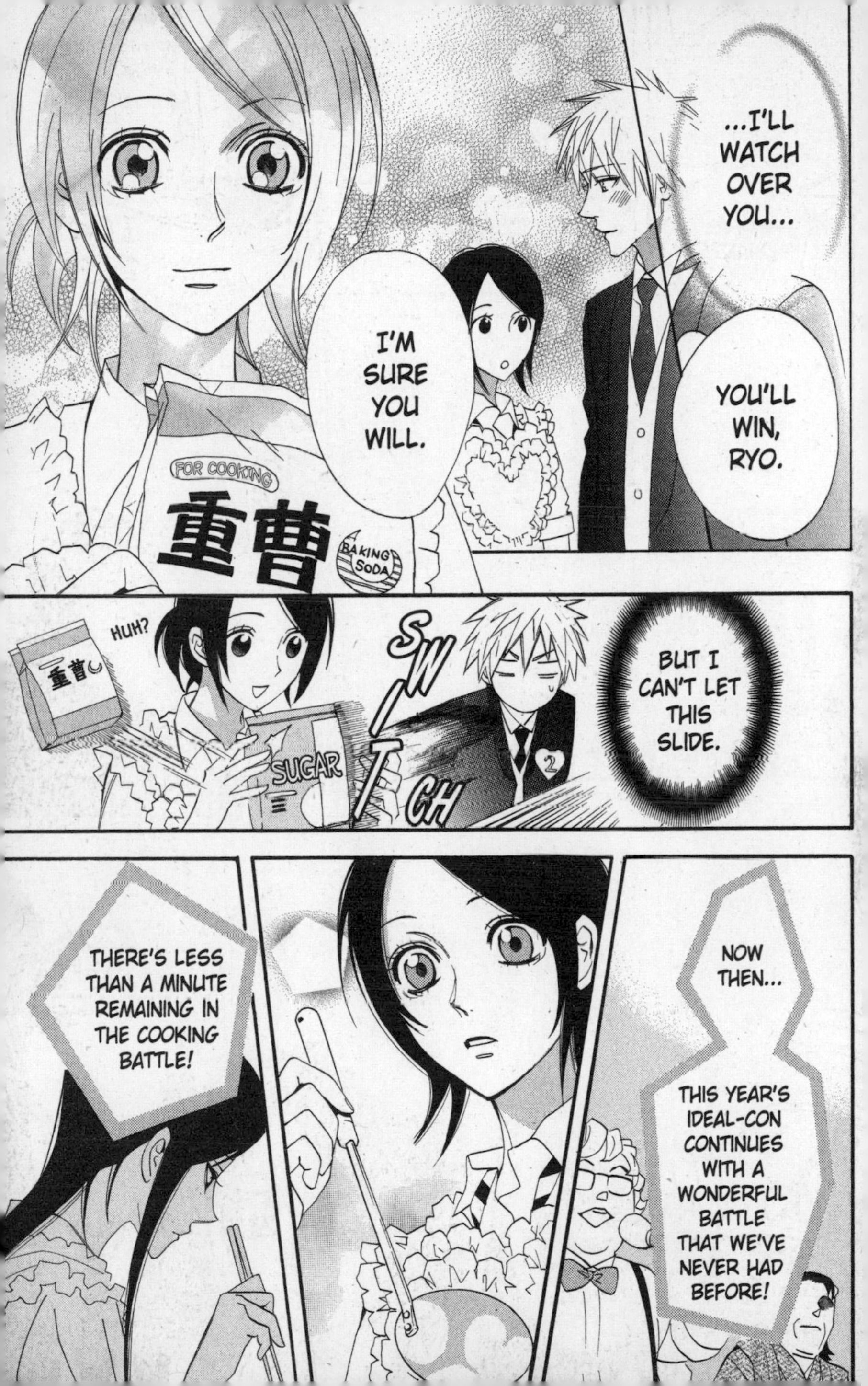
...I'LL WATCH OVER YOU...
YOU'LL WIN, RYO.
I'M SURE YOU WILL.
FOR COOKING
重曹
BAKING SODA
BUT I CAN'T LET THIS SLIDE.
SWITCH
SUGAR
HUH?
重曹
NOW THEN...
THIS YEAR'S IDEAL-CON CONTINUES WITH A WONDERFUL BATTLE THAT WE'VE NEVER HAD BEFORE!
THERE'S LESS THAN A MINUTE REMAINING IN THE COOKING BATTLE!

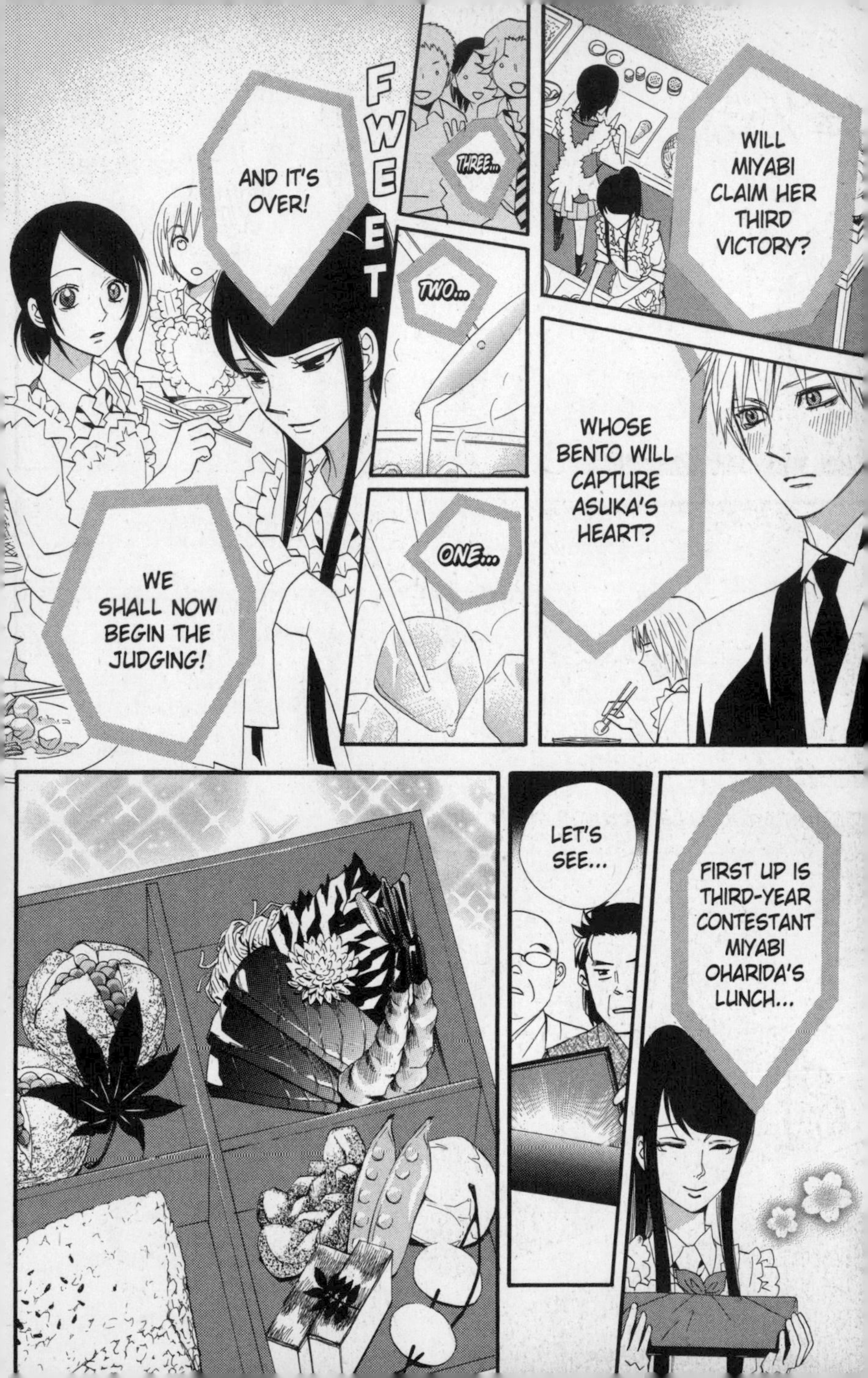
WILL MIYABI CLAIM HER THIRD VICTORY?
WHOSE BENTO WILL CAPTURE ASUKA'S HEART?
THREE...
TWO...
ONE...
FWEET
AND IT'S OVER!
WE SHALL NOW BEGIN THE JUDGING!
FIRST UP IS THIRD-YEAR CONTESTANT MIYABI OHARIDA'S LUNCH...
LET'S SEE...

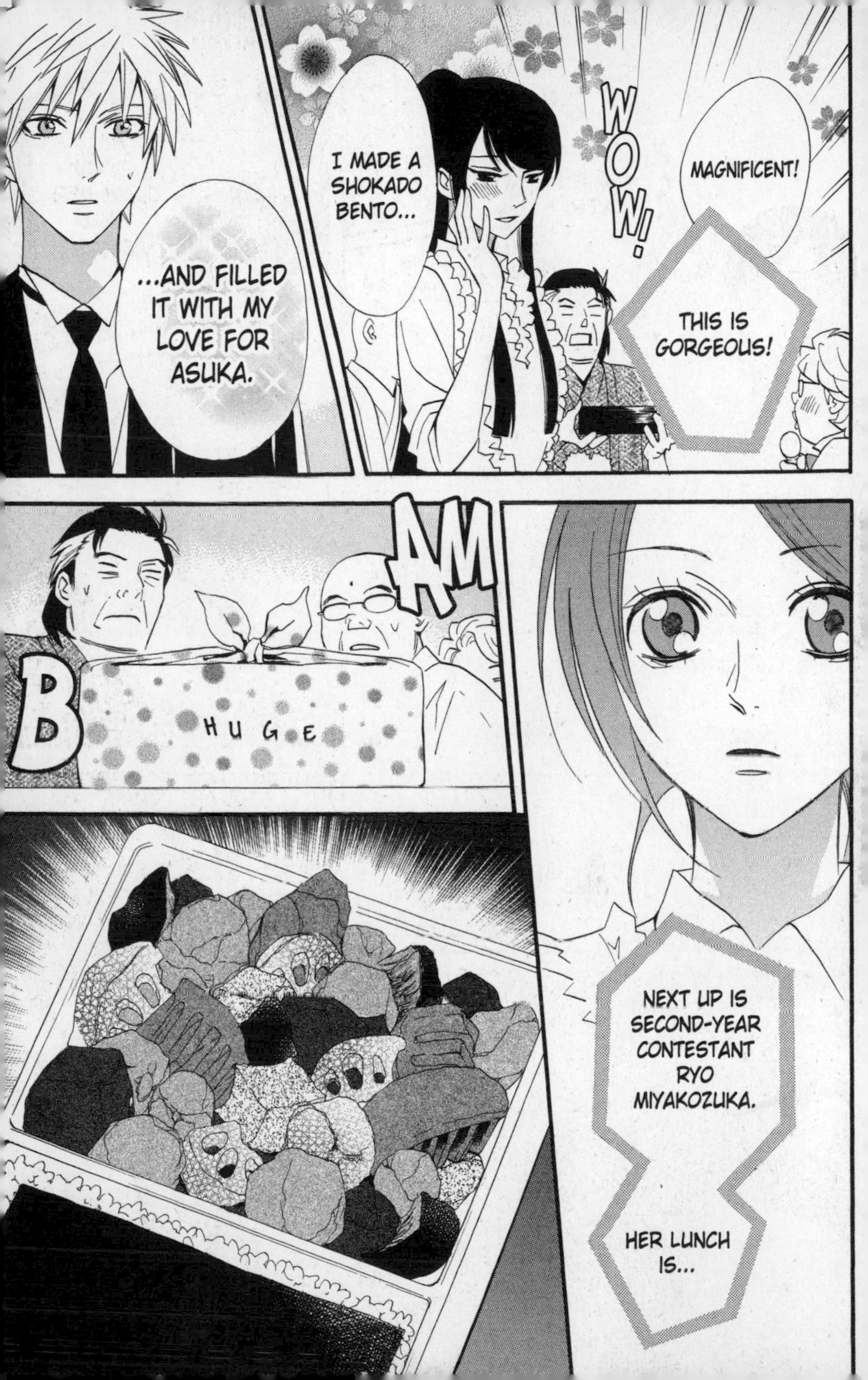
MAGNIFICENT!
WOW!
THIS IS GORGEOUS!
I MADE A SHOKADO BENTO...
...AND FILLED IT WITH MY LOVE FOR ASUKA.
NEXT UP IS SECOND-YEAR CONTESTANT RYO MIYAKOZUKA.
HER LUNCH IS...
BAM
HUGE

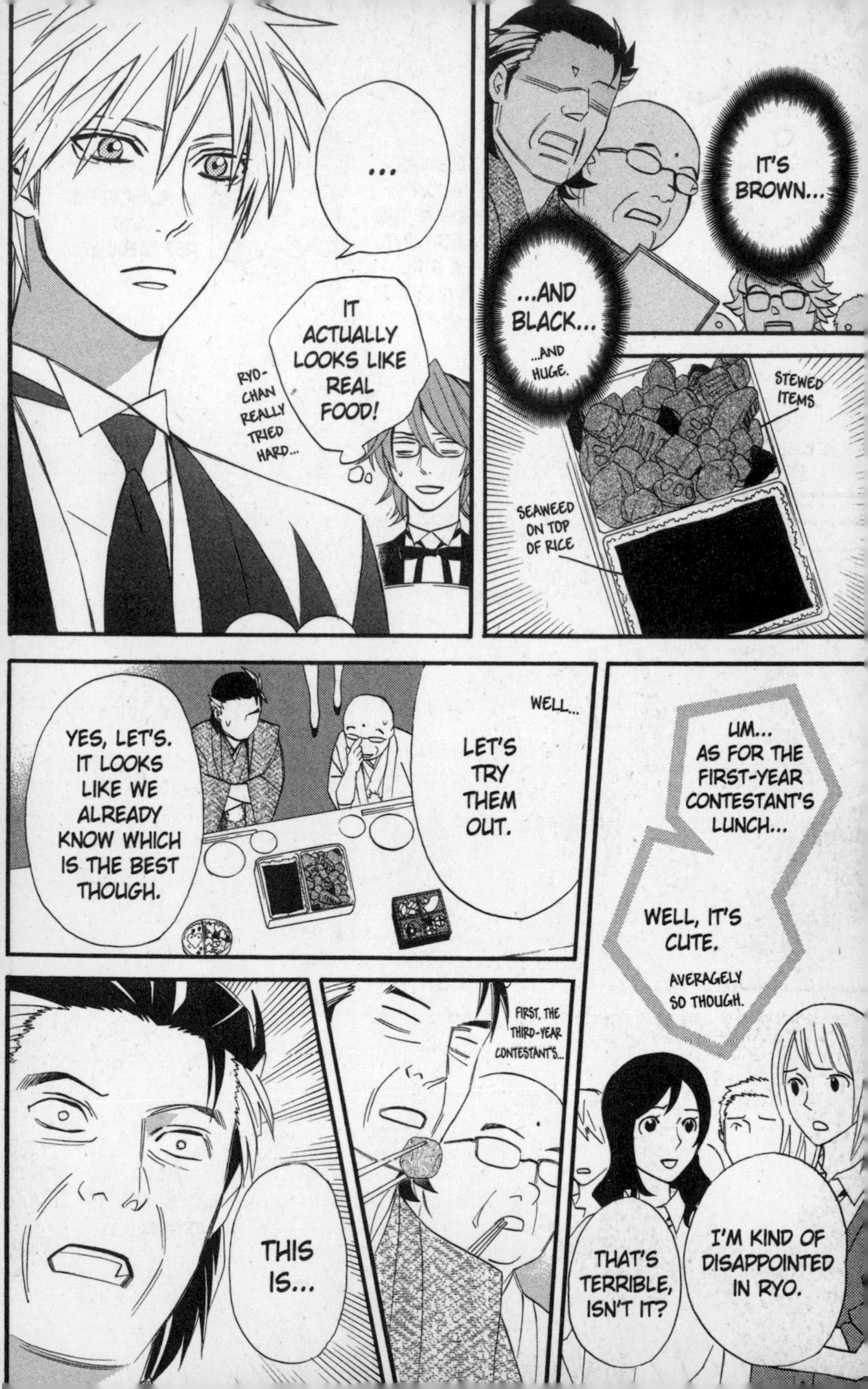
IT'S BROWN...
...AND BLACK...
...AND HUGE.
STEWED ITEMS
SEAWEED ON TOP OF RICE
...
IT ACTUALLY LOOKS LIKE REAL FOOD!
RYO-CHAN REALLY TRIED HARD...
UM... AS FOR THE FIRST-YEAR CONTESTANT'S LUNCH...
WELL, IT'S CUTE.
AVERAGELY SO THOUGH.
I'M KIND OF DISAPPOINTED IN RYO.
THAT'S TERRIBLE, ISN'T IT?
WELL...
LET'S TRY THEM OUT.
YES, LET'S. IT LOOKS LIKE WE ALREADY KNOW WHICH IS THE BEST THOUGH.
FIRST, THE THIRD-YEAR CONTESTANT'S...
THIS IS...

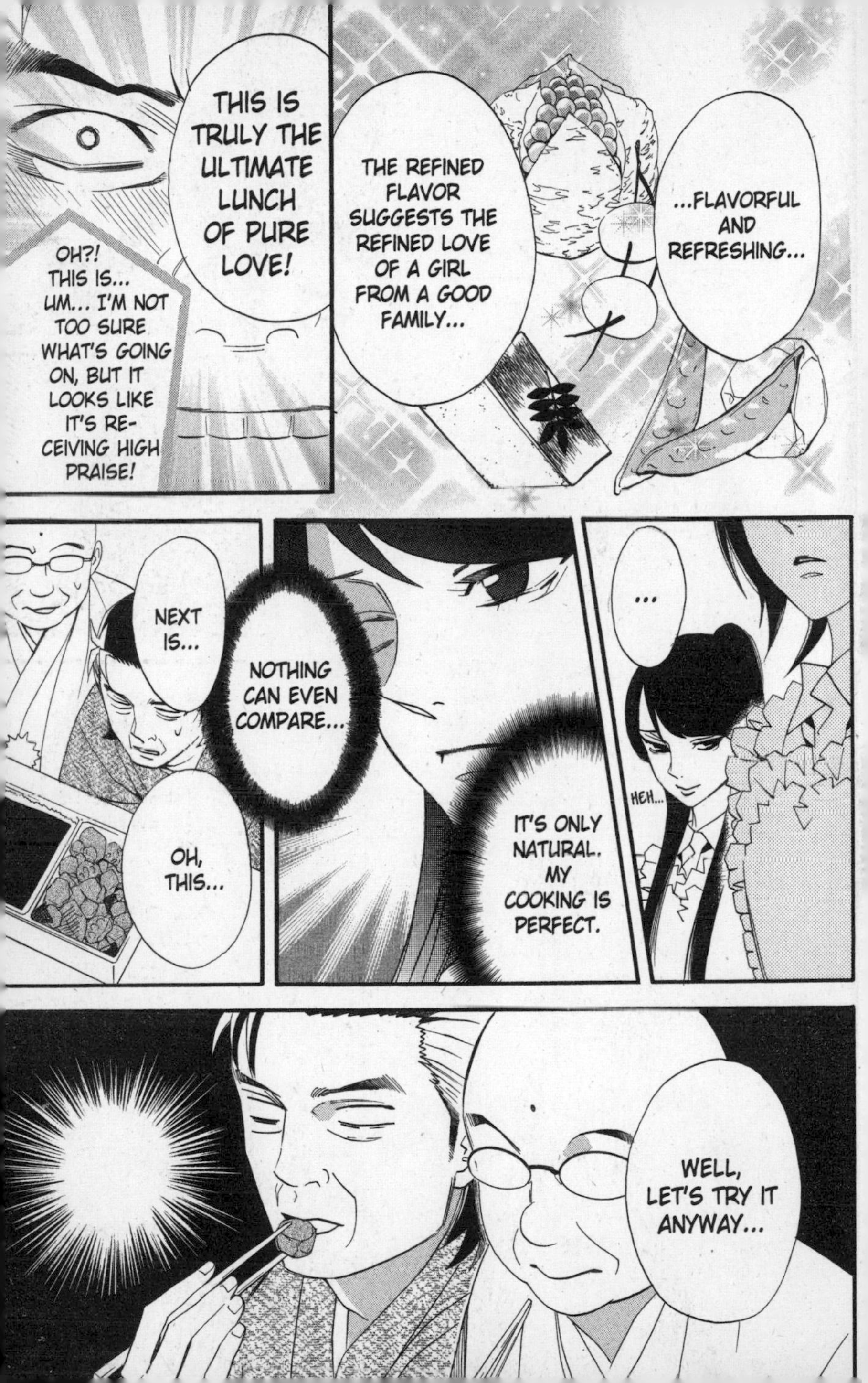
...FLAVORFUL AND REFRESHING...
THE REFINED FLAVOR SUGGESTS THE REFINED LOVE OF A GIRL FROM A GOOD FAMILY...
THIS IS TRULY THE ULTIMATE LUNCH OF PURE LOVE!
OH?! THIS IS... UM... I'M NOT TOO SURE WHAT'S GOING ON, BUT IT LOOKS LIKE IT'S RE-CEIVING HIGH PRAISE!
...
HEH...
NOTHING CAN EVEN COMPARE...
IT'S ONLY NATURAL. MY COOKING IS PERFECT.
NEXT IS...
OH, THIS...
WELL, LET'S TRY IT ANYWAY...

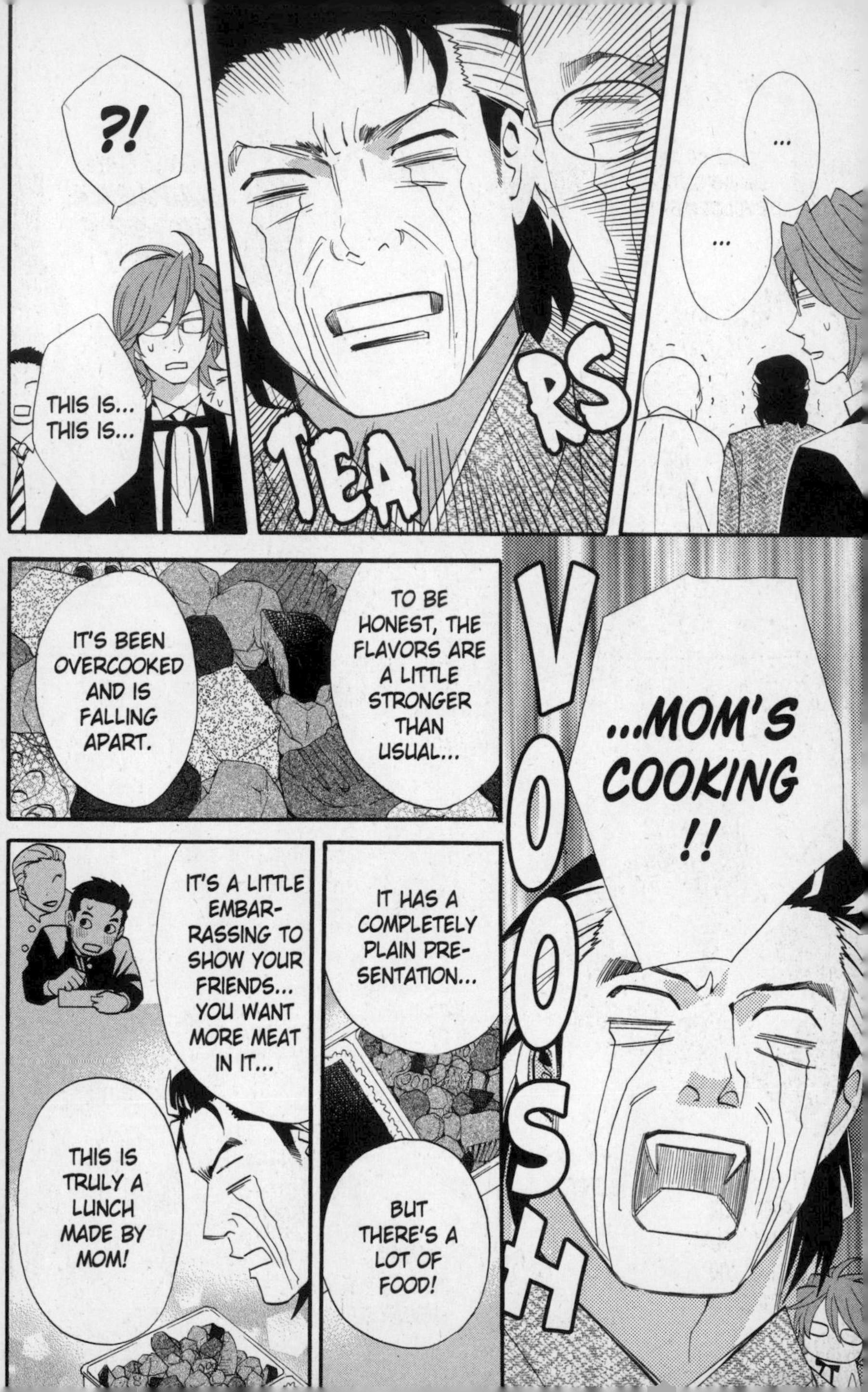
...
...
TEARS
?!
THIS IS... THIS IS...
VOOSH
...MOM'S COOKING !!
TO BE HONEST, THE FLAVORS ARE A LITTLE STRONGER THAN USUAL...
IT'S BEEN OVERCOOKED AND IS FALLING APART.
IT HAS A COMPLETELY PLAIN PRE-SENTATION...
BUT THERE'S A LOT OF FOOD!
IT'S A LITTLE EMBAR-RASSING TO SHOW YOUR FRIENDS... YOU WANT MORE MEAT IN IT...
THIS IS TRULY A LUNCH MADE BY MOM!

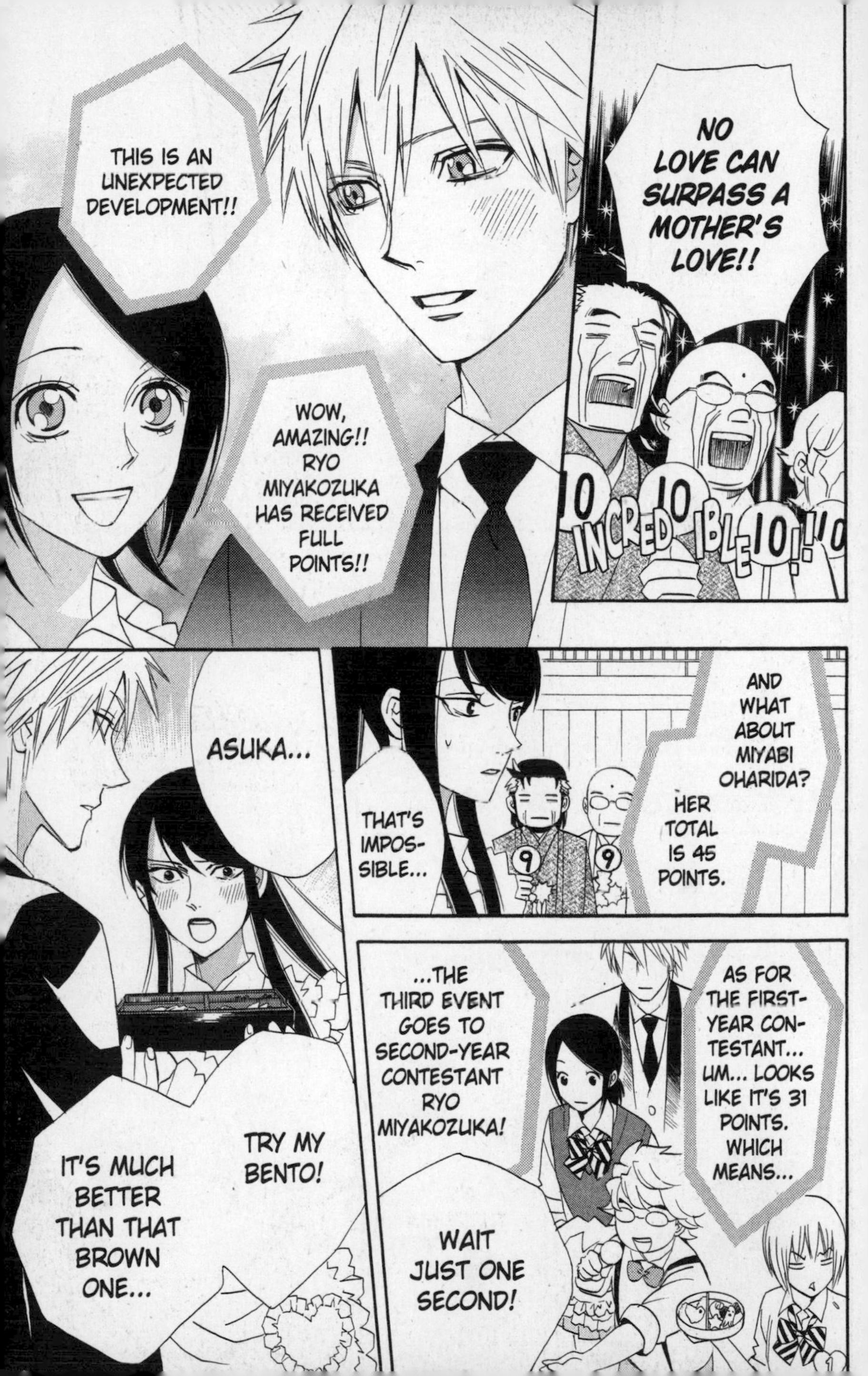
NO LOVE CAN SURPASS A MOTHER'S LOVE!!
10 10 INCREDIBLE 10!! 10
THIS IS AN UNEXPECTED DEVELOPMENT!!
WOW, AMAZING!! RYO MIYAKOZUKA HAS RECEIVED FULL POINTS!!
AND WHAT ABOUT MIYABI OHARIDA?
HER TOTAL IS 45 POINTS.
THAT'S IMPOSSIBLE...
9 9
AS FOR THE FIRST-YEAR CONTESTANT... UM... LOOKS LIKE IT'S 31 POINTS. WHICH MEANS...
...THE THIRD EVENT GOES TO SECOND-YEAR CONTESTANT RYO MIYAKOZUKA!
WAIT JUST ONE SECOND!
ASUKA...
TRY MY BENTO!
IT'S MUCH BETTER THAN THAT BROWN ONE...

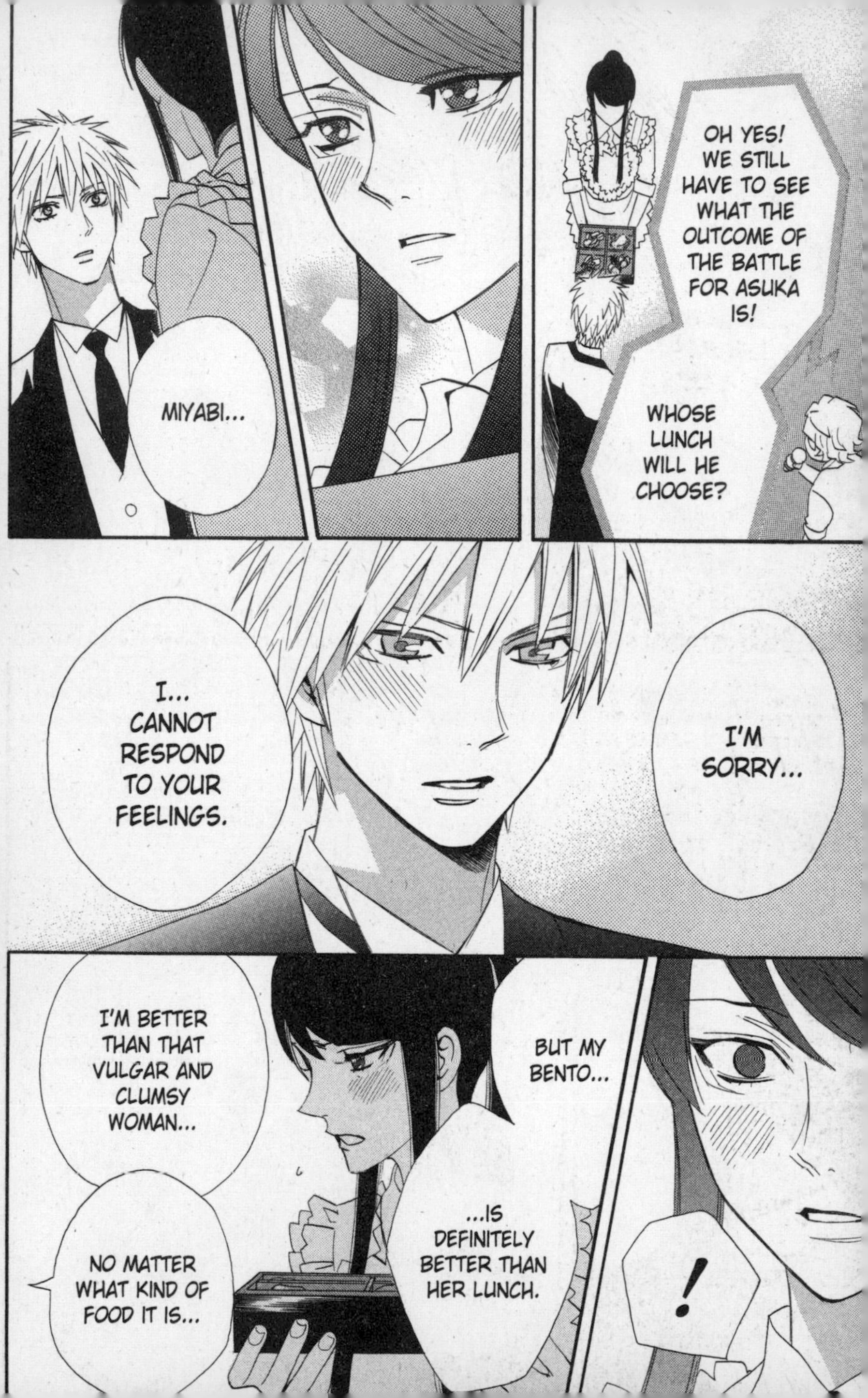
OH YES! WE STILL HAVE TO SEE WHAT THE OUTCOME OF THE BATTLE FOR ASUKA IS!
WHOSE LUNCH WILL HE CHOOSE?
MIYABI...
I'M SORRY...
I... CANNOT RESPOND TO YOUR FEELINGS.
!
BUT MY BENTO...
I'M BETTER THAN THAT VULGAR AND CLUMSY WOMAN...
...IS DEFINITELY BETTER THAN HER LUNCH.
NO MATTER WHAT KIND OF FOOD IT IS...

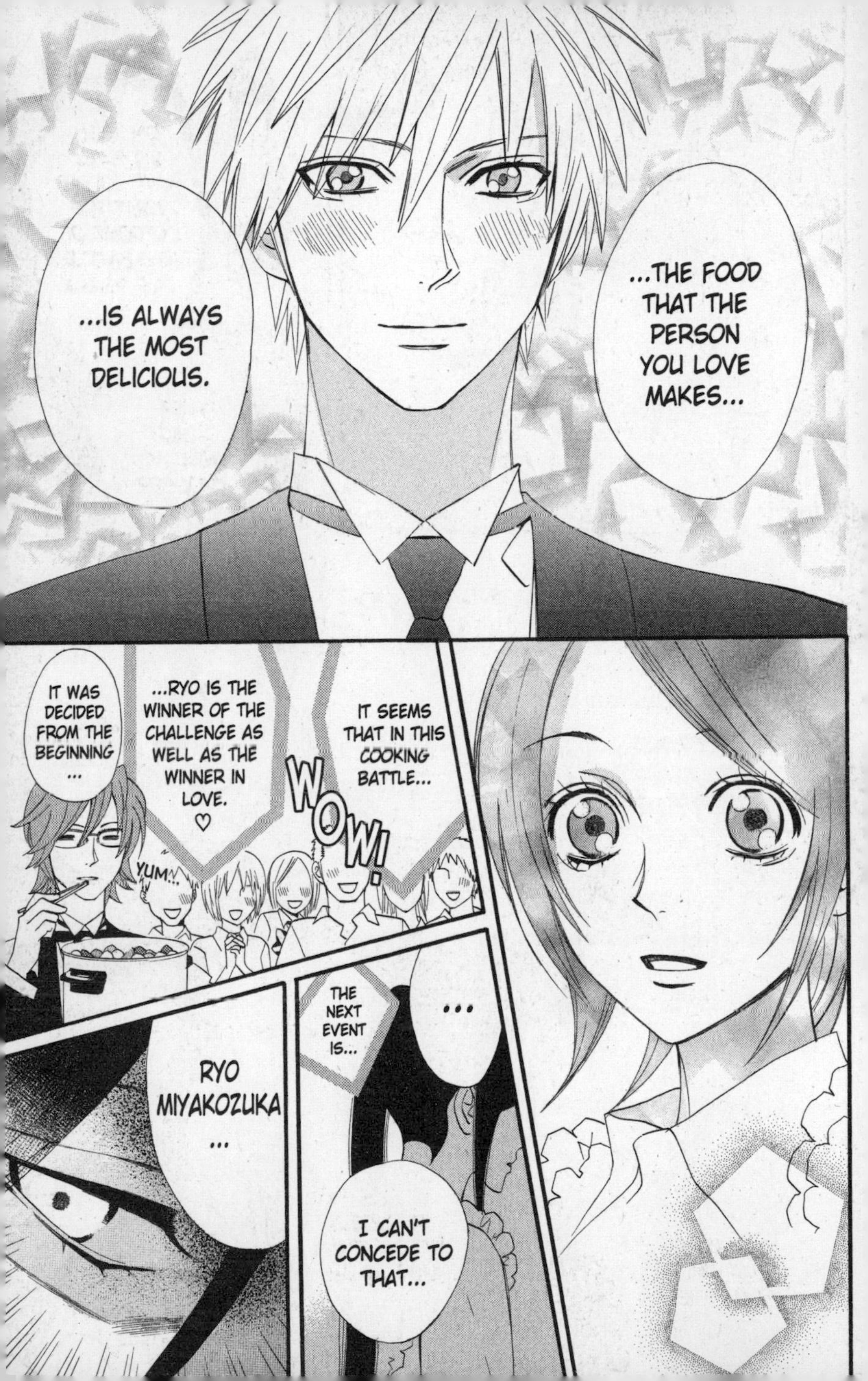
...THE FOOD THAT THE PERSON YOU LOVE MAKES...
...IS ALWAYS THE MOST DELICIOUS.
IT SEEMS THAT IN THIS COOKING BATTLE...
WOW!
...RYO IS THE WINNER OF THE CHALLENGE AS WELL AS THE WINNER IN LOVE. ♡
IT WAS DECIDED FROM THE BEGINNING...
YUM...
...
THE NEXT EVENT IS...
I CAN'T CONCEDE TO THAT...
RYO MIYAKOZUKA...

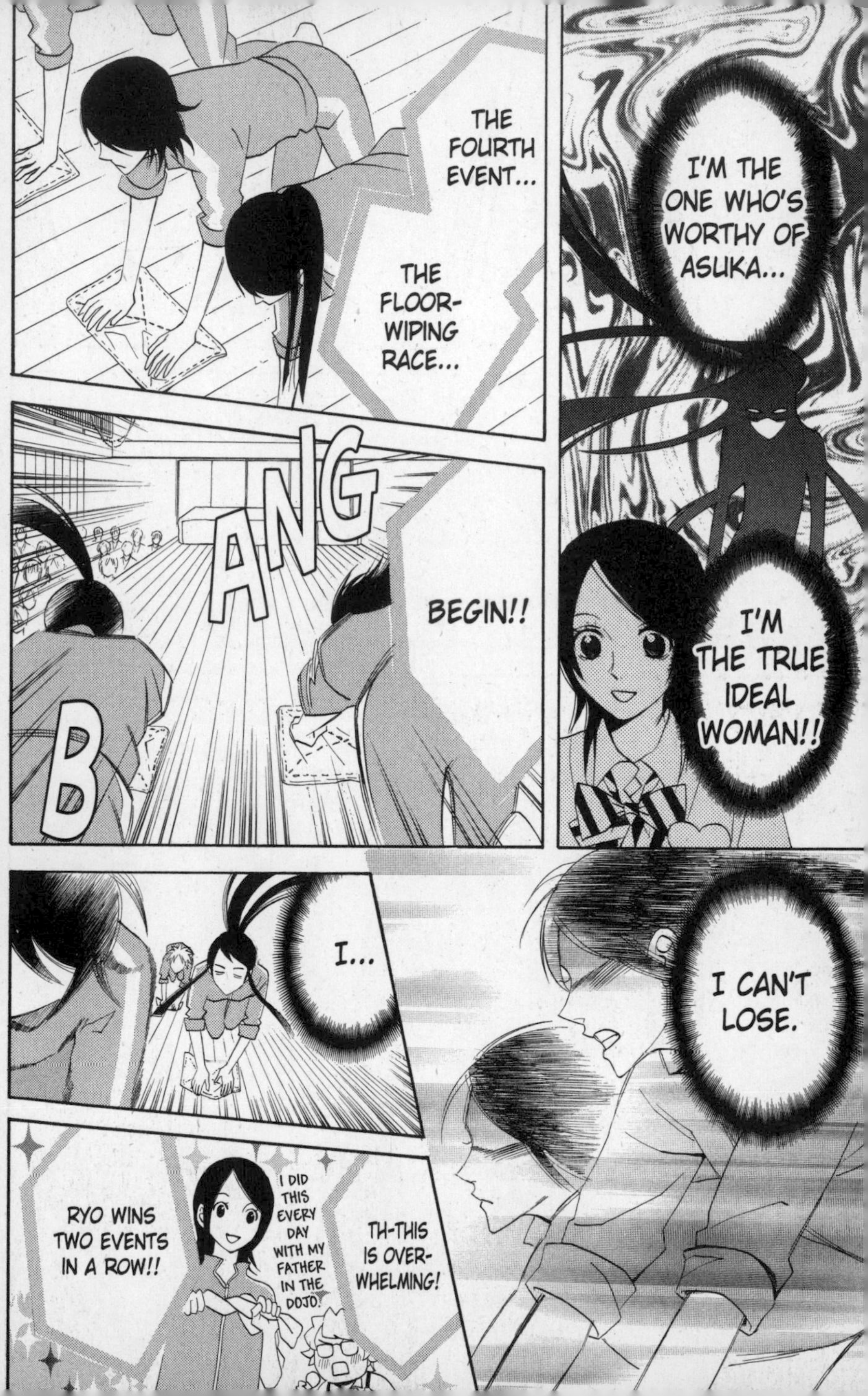

I'M THE ONE WHO'S WORTHY OF ASUKA...
I'M THE TRUE IDEAL WOMAN!!
THE FOURTH EVENT...
THE FLOOR-WIPING RACE...
BEGIN!!
BANG
I CAN'T LOSE.
I...
TH-THIS IS OVER-WHELMING!
I DID THIS EVERY DAY WITH MY FATHER IN THE DOJO.
RYO WINS TWO EVENTS IN A ROW!!

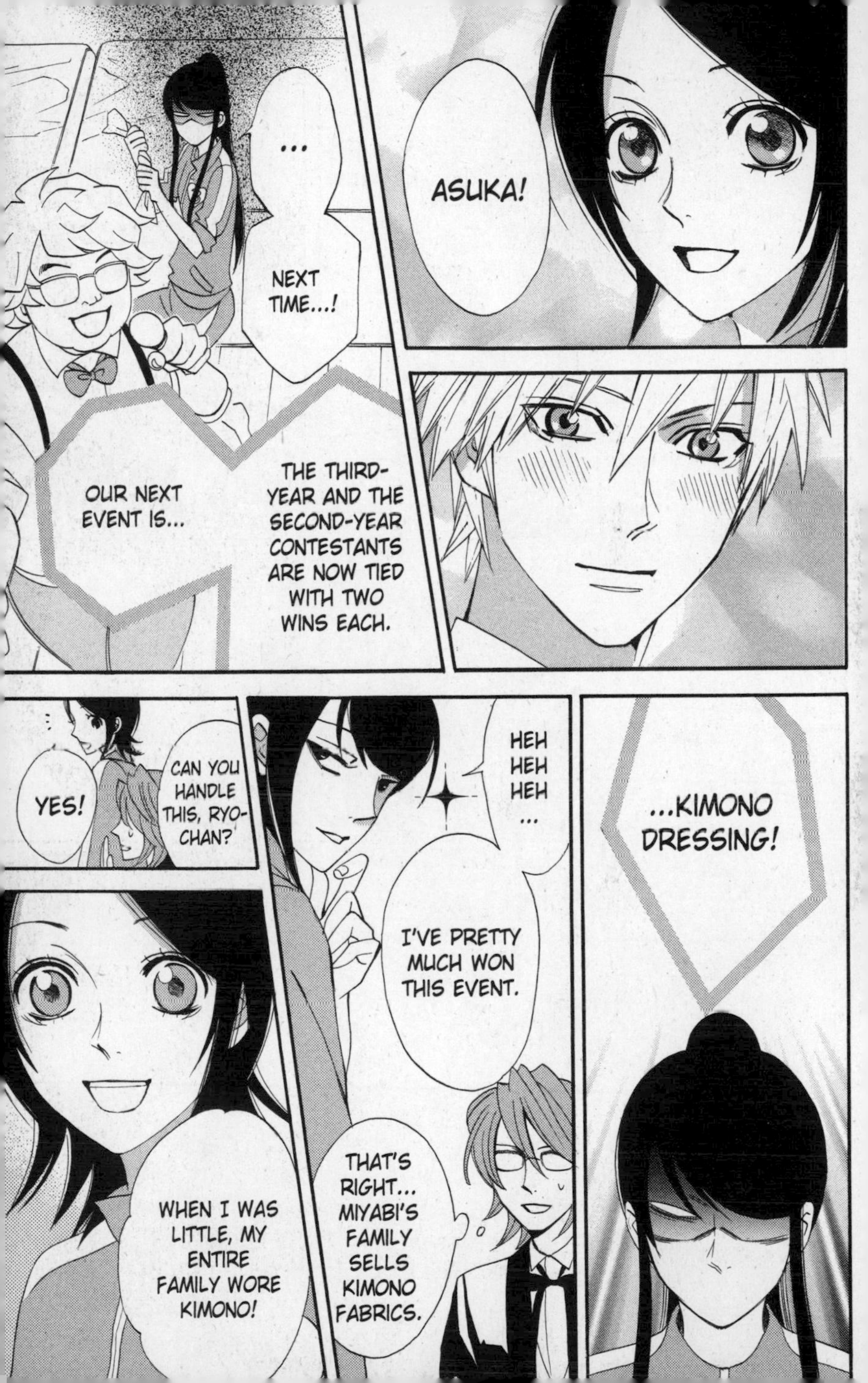
ASUKA!
...
NEXT TIME...!
THE THIRD-YEAR AND THE SECOND-YEAR CONTESTANTS ARE NOW TIED WITH TWO WINS EACH.
OUR NEXT EVENT IS...
...KIMONO DRESSING!
HEH HEH HEH ...
I'VE PRETTY MUCH WON THIS EVENT.
THAT'S RIGHT... MIYABI'S FAMILY SELLS KIMONO FABRICS.
CAN YOU HANDLE THIS, RYO-CHAN?
YES!
WHEN I WAS LITTLE, MY ENTIRE FAMILY WORE KIMONO!

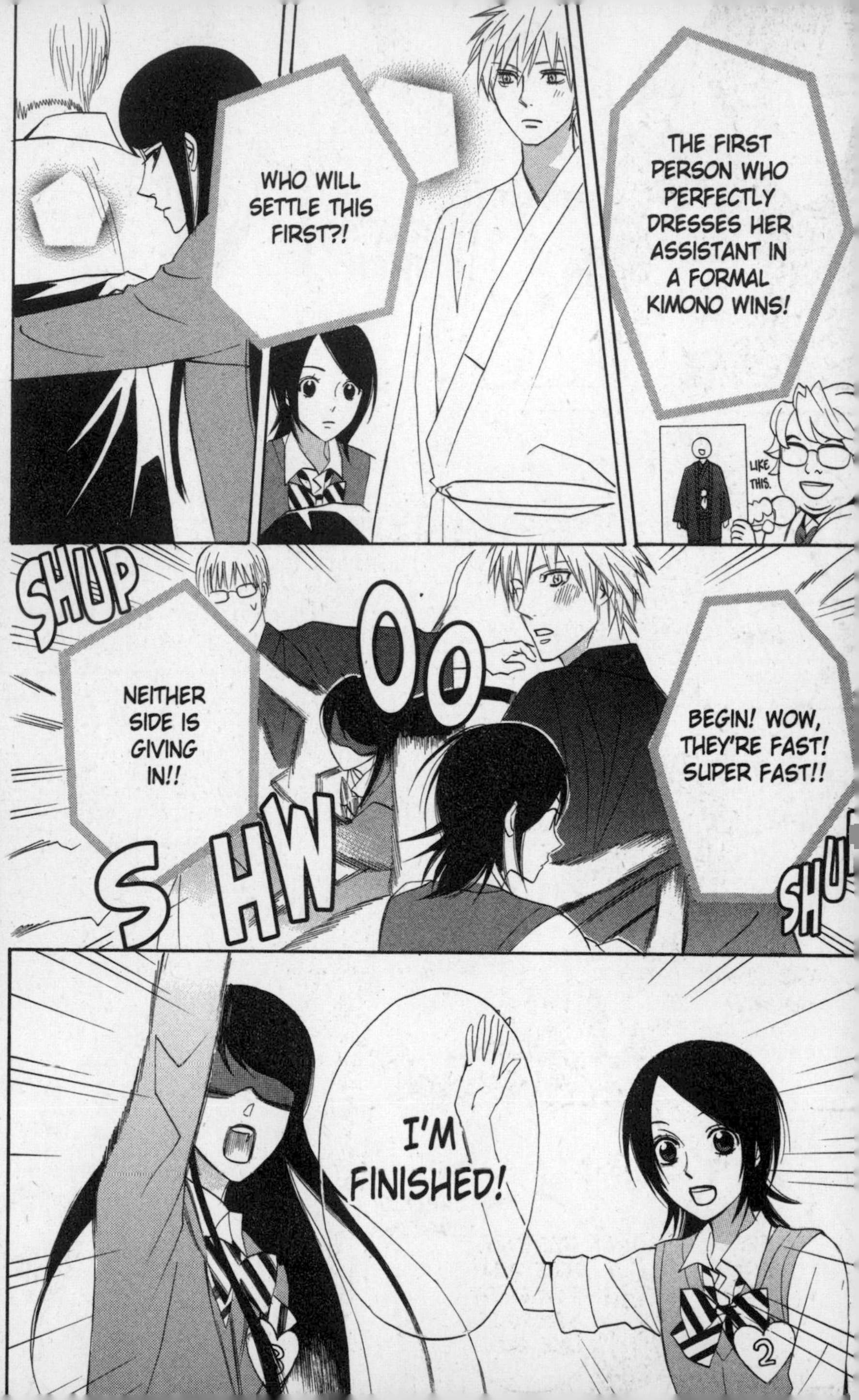
THE FIRST PERSON WHO PERFECTLY DRESSES HER ASSISTANT IN A FORMAL KIMONO WINS!
LIKE THIS.
WHO WILL SETTLE THIS FIRST?!
BEGIN! WOW, THEY'RE FAST! SUPER FAST!!
SHU
SHUP
NEITHER SIDE IS GIVING IN!!
SHWOO
I'M FINISHED!

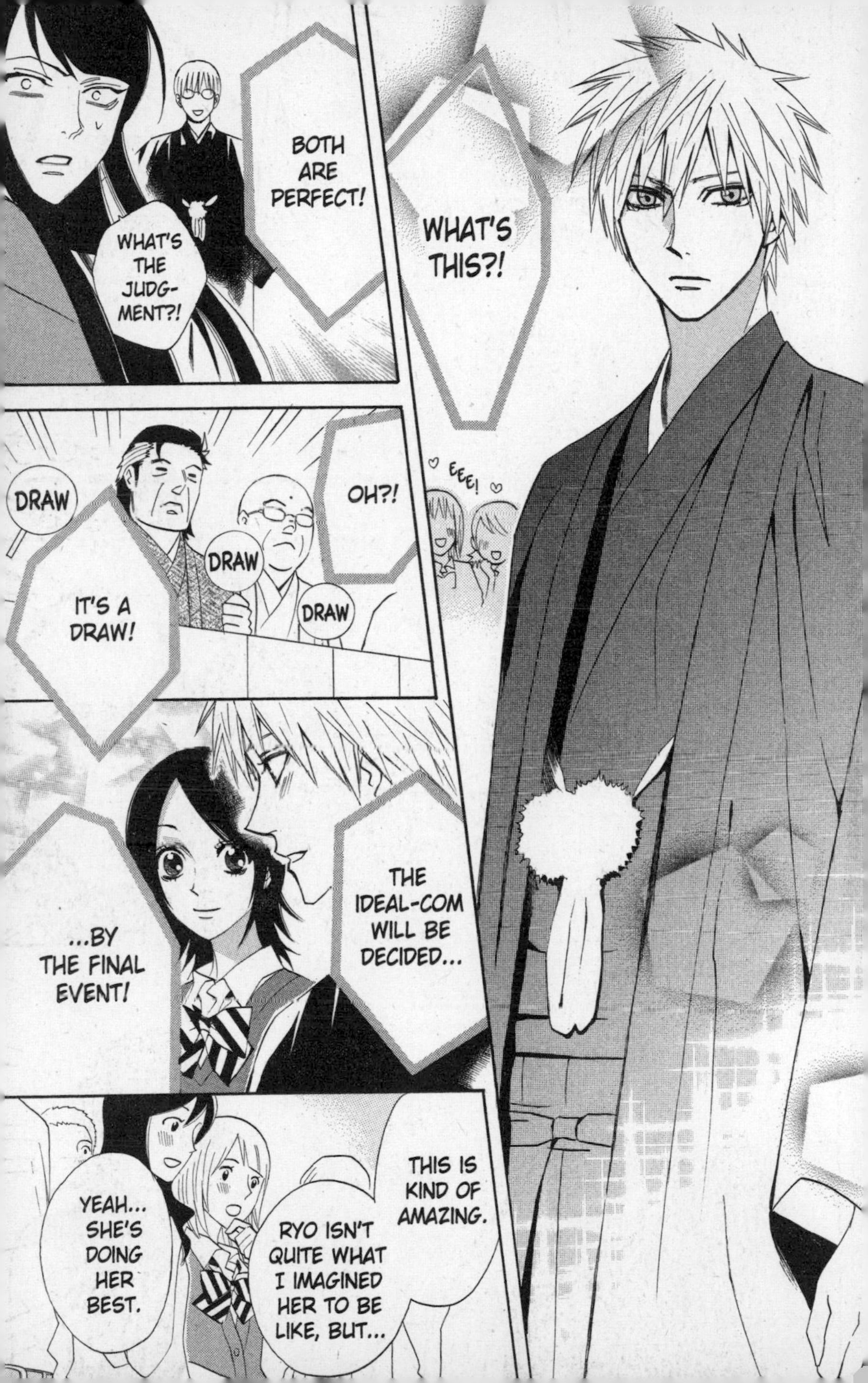
WHAT'S THIS?!
EEE!
BOTH ARE PERFECT!
WHAT'S THE JUDG-MENT?!
OH?!
DRAW
DRAW
DRAW
IT'S A DRAW!
THE IDEAL-COM WILL BE DECIDED...
...BY THE FINAL EVENT!
THIS IS KIND OF AMAZING.
RYO ISN'T QUITE WHAT I IMAGINED HER TO BE LIKE, BUT...
YEAH... SHE'S DOING HER BEST.

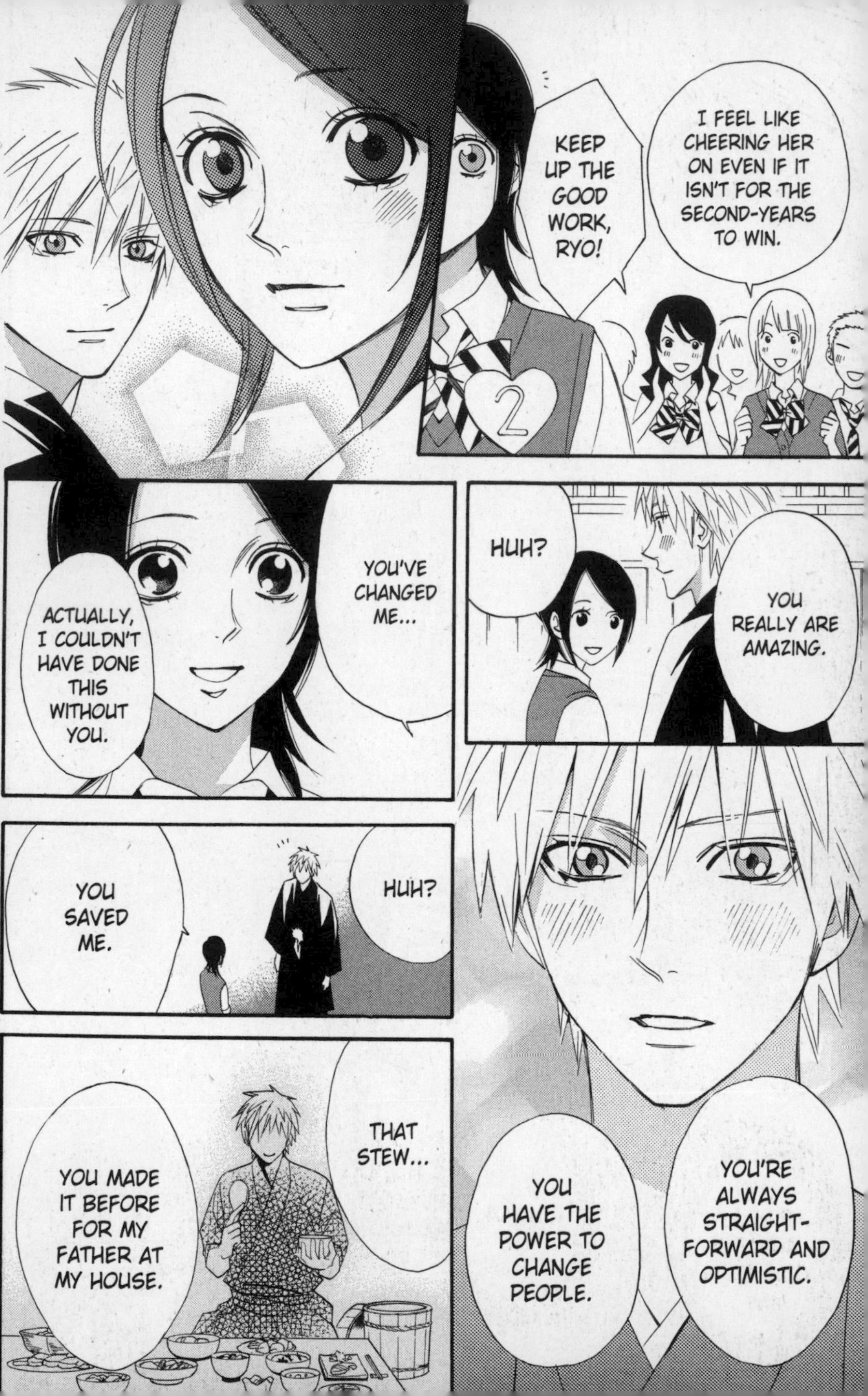
I FEEL LIKE CHEERING HER ON EVEN IF IT ISN'T FOR THE SECOND-YEARS TO WIN.
KEEP UP THE GOOD WORK, RYO!
YOU REALLY ARE AMAZING.
HUH?
YOU'VE CHANGED ME...
ACTUALLY, I COULDN'T HAVE DONE THIS WITHOUT YOU.
YOU'RE ALWAYS STRAIGHT-FORWARD AND OPTIMISTIC.
YOU HAVE THE POWER TO CHANGE PEOPLE.
HUH?
YOU SAVED ME.
THAT STEW...
YOU MADE IT BEFORE FOR MY FATHER AT MY HOUSE.

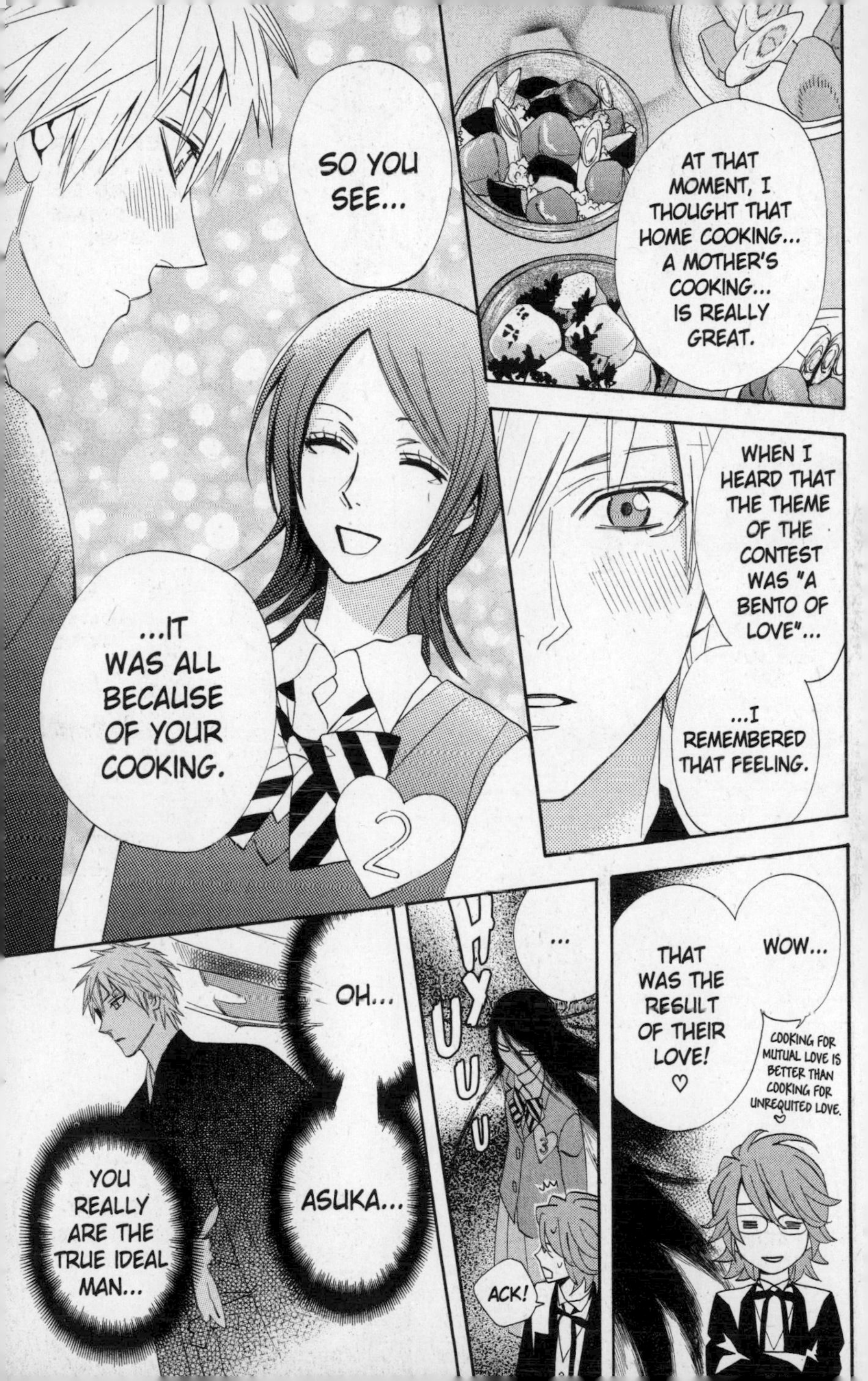
AT THAT MOMENT, I THOUGHT THAT HOME COOKING... A MOTHER'S COOKING... IS REALLY GREAT.
WHEN I HEARD THAT THE THEME OF THE CONTEST WAS "A BENTO OF LOVE"...
...I REMEMBERED THAT FEELING.
SO YOU SEE...
...IT WAS ALL BECAUSE OF YOUR COOKING.
WOW...
THAT WAS THE RESULT OF THEIR LOVE! ♡
COOKING FOR MUTUAL LOVE IS BETTER THAN COOKING FOR UNREQUITED LOVE. ♡
...
HYUUUU
ACK!
OH...
ASUKA...
YOU REALLY ARE THE TRUE IDEAL MAN...

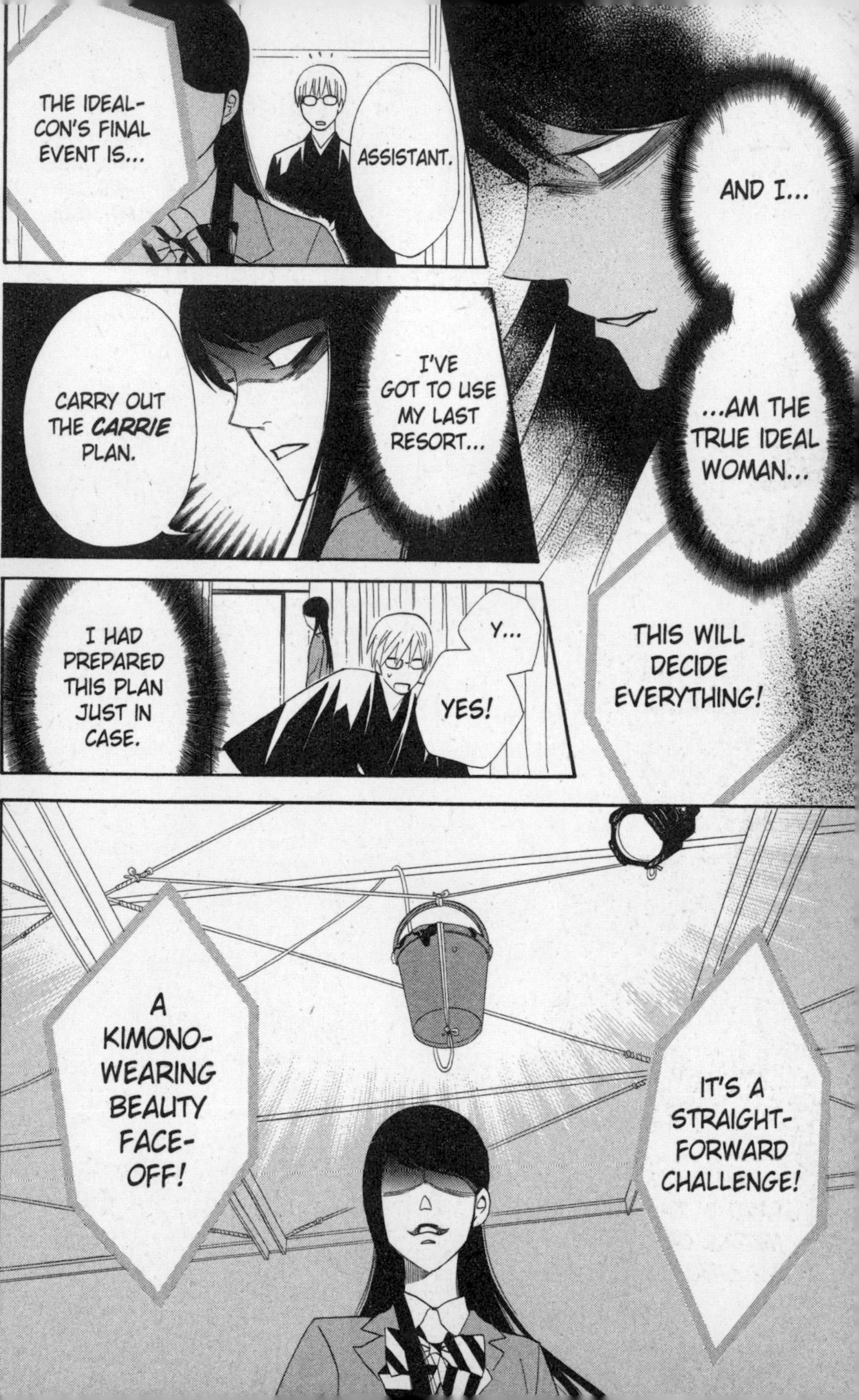
AND I...
...AM THE TRUE IDEAL WOMAN...
THIS WILL DECIDE EVERYTHING!
ASSISTANT.
THE IDEAL-CON'S FINAL EVENT IS...
I'VE GOT TO USE MY LAST RESORT...
CARRY OUT THE *CARRIE* PLAN.
Y... YES!
I HAD PREPARED THIS PLAN JUST IN CASE.
IT'S A STRAIGHT-FORWARD CHALLENGE!
A KIMONO-WEARING BEAUTY FACE-OFF!

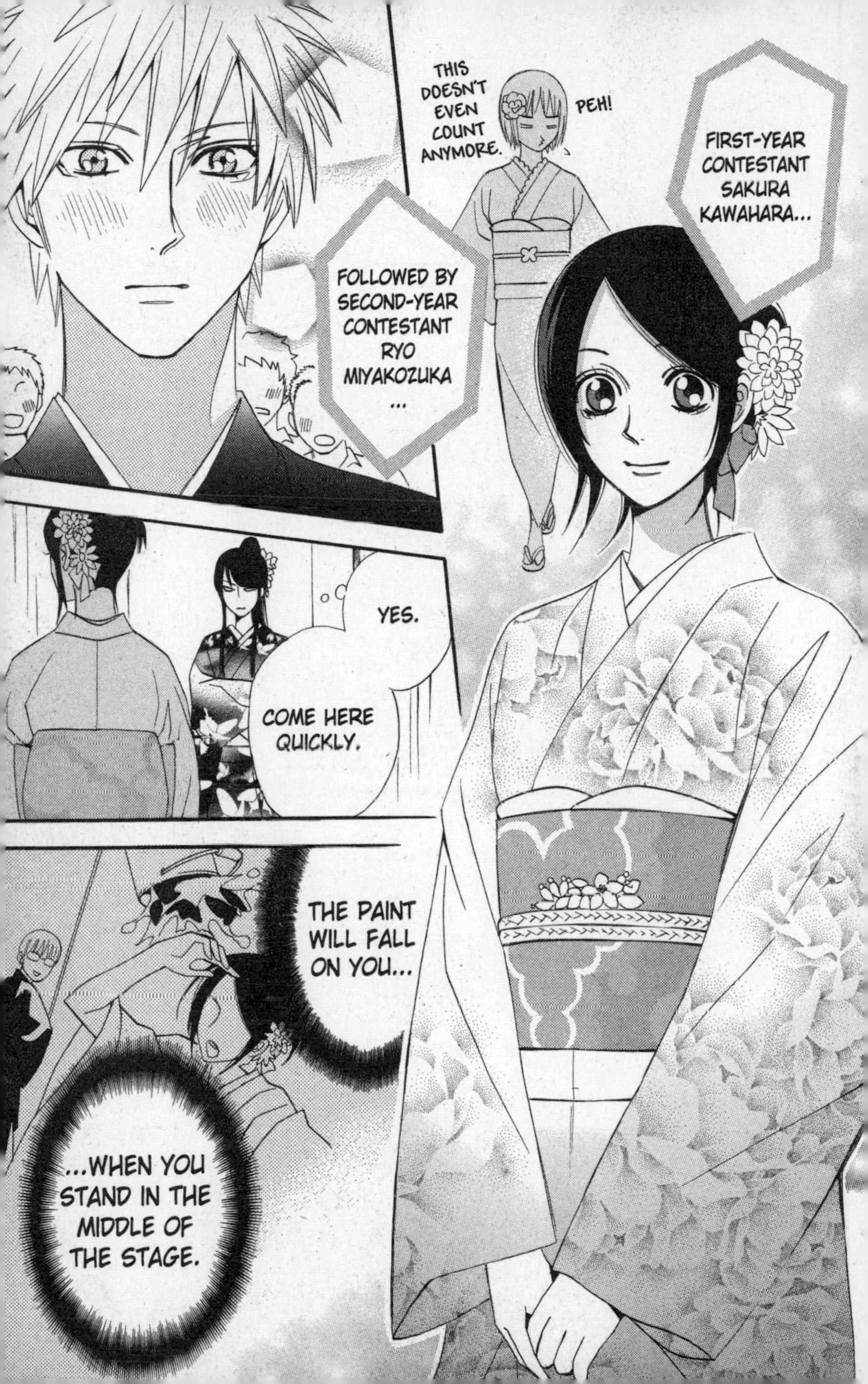
FIRST-YEAR CONTESTANT SAKURA KAWAHARA...
PEH!
THIS DOESN'T EVEN COUNT ANYMORE.
FOLLOWED BY SECOND-YEAR CONTESTANT RYO MIYAKOZUKA ...
YES.
COME HERE QUICKLY.
THE PAINT WILL FALL ON YOU...
...WHEN YOU STAND IN THE MIDDLE OF THE STAGE.

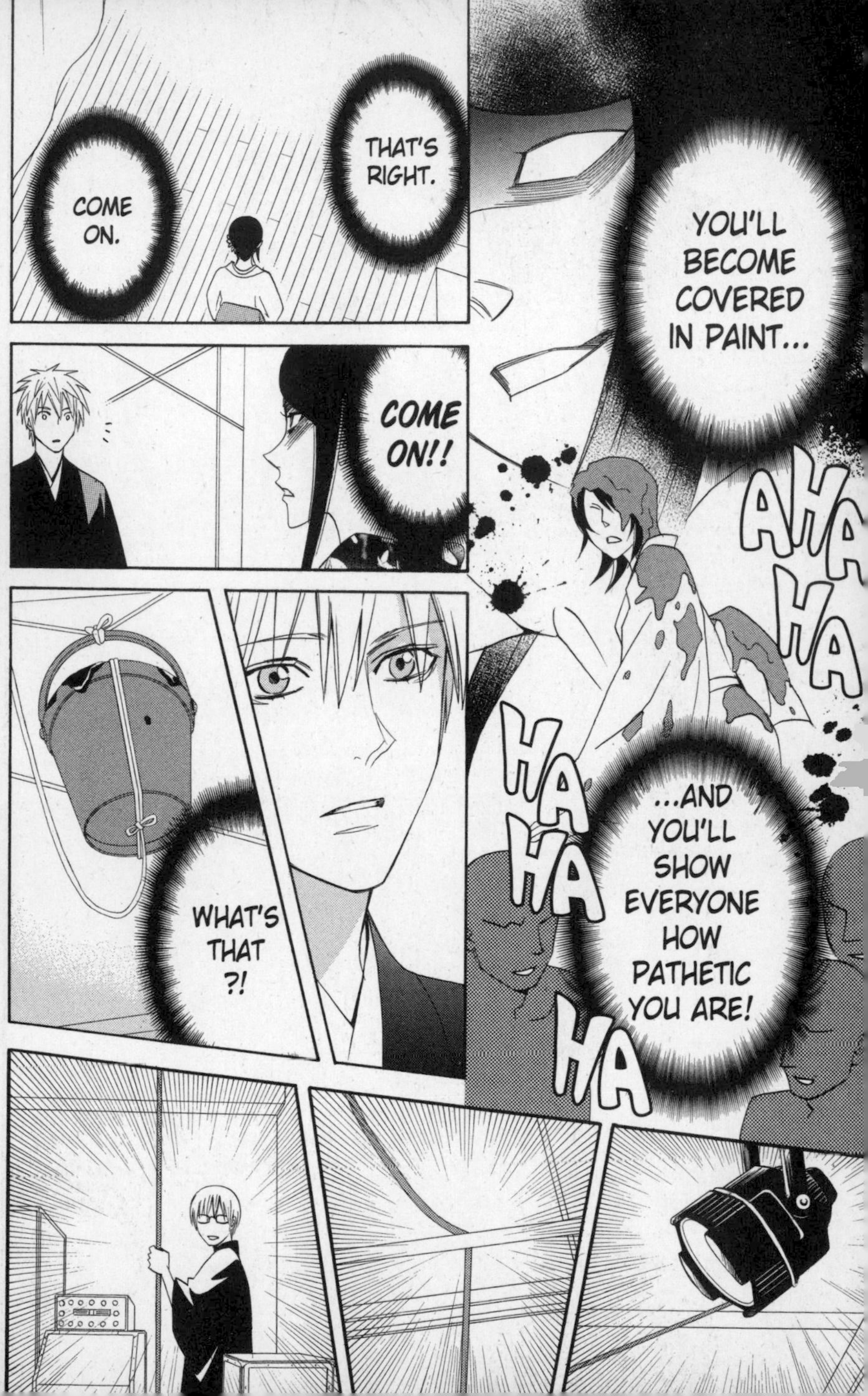
YOU'LL BECOME COVERED IN PAINT...
AHAHAHA
HAHAHAHA
...AND YOU'LL SHOW EVERYONE HOW PATHETIC YOU ARE!
THAT'S RIGHT.
COME ON.
COME ON!!
WHAT'S THAT?!

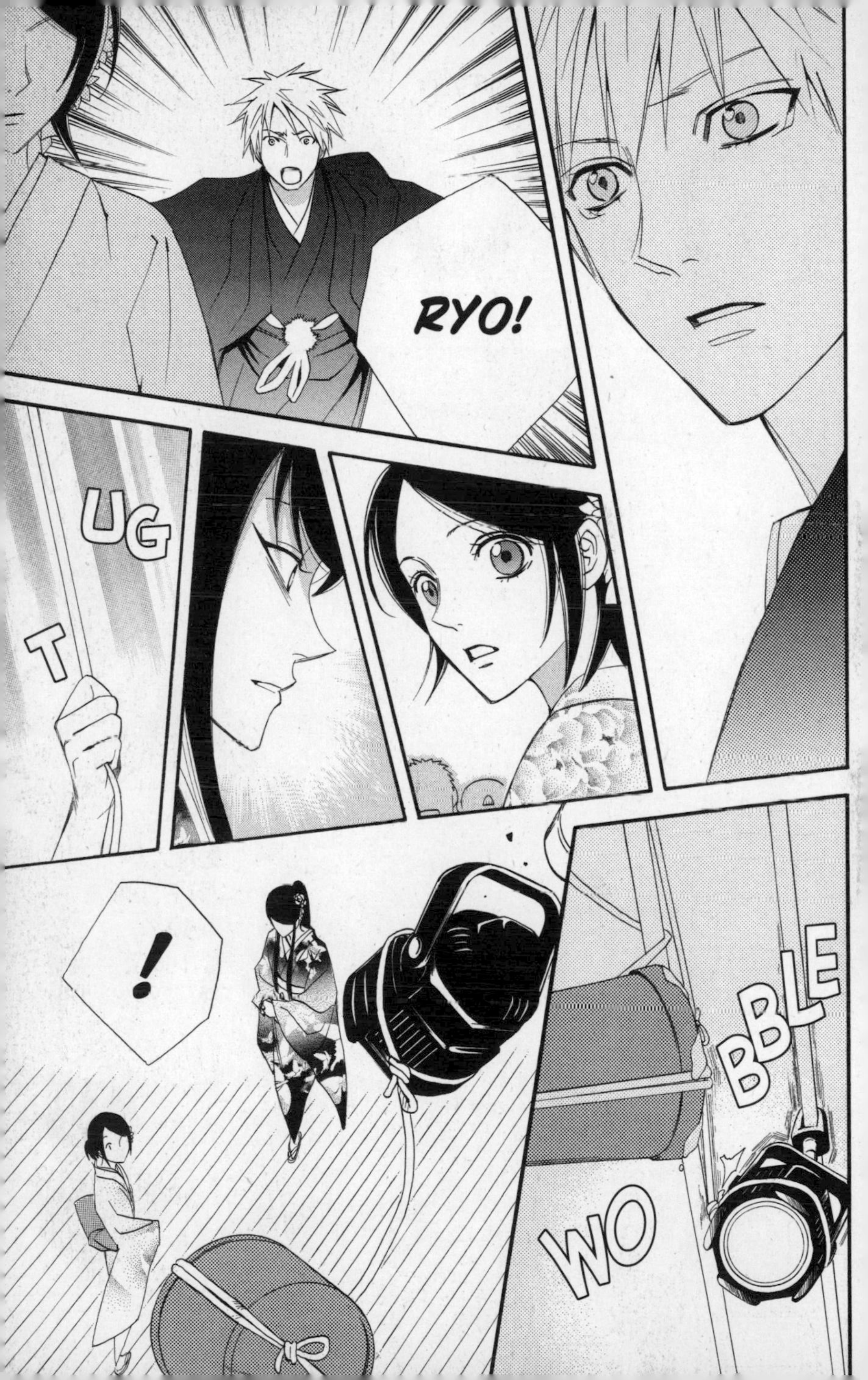
RYO!
TUG
WOBBLE
!

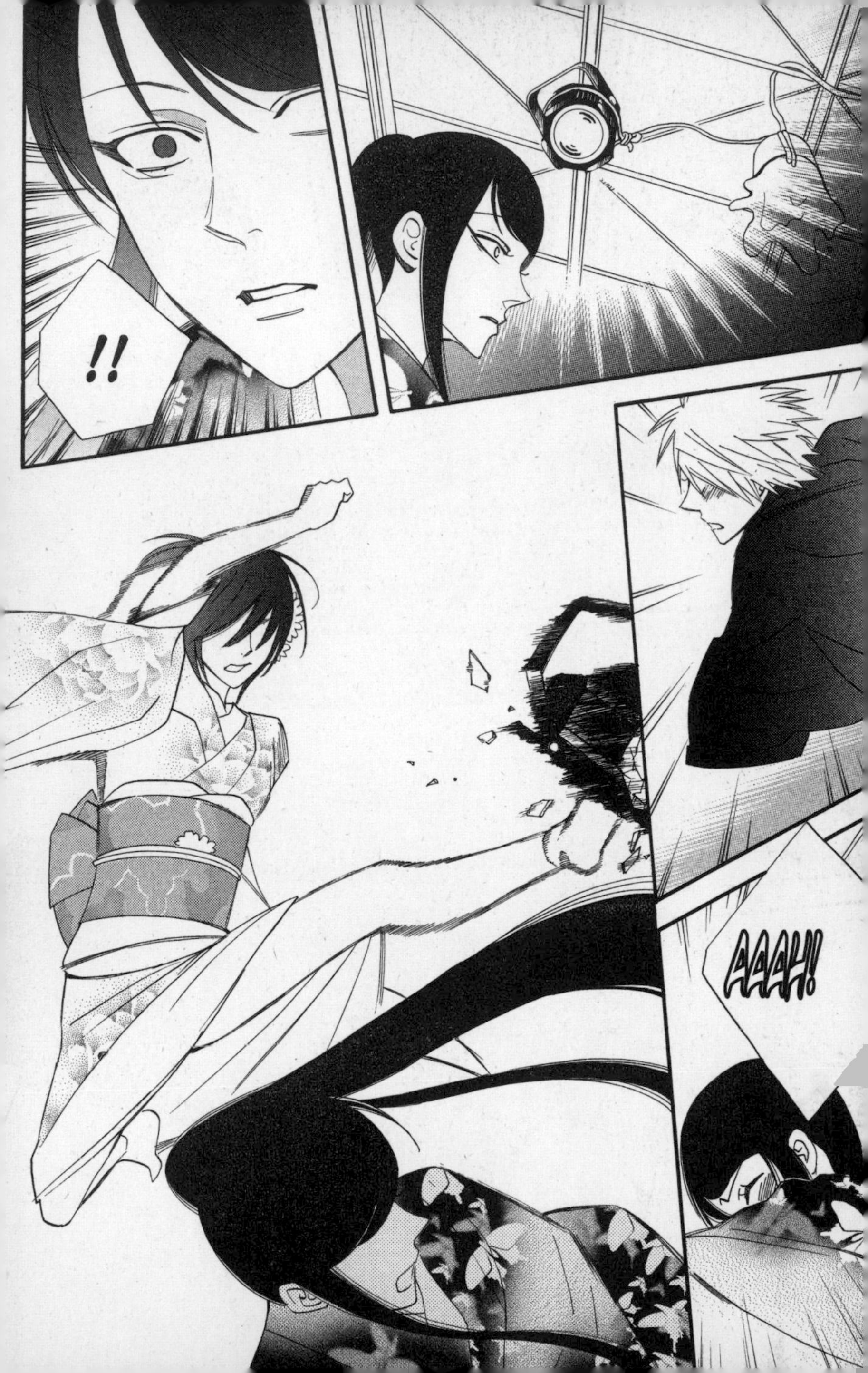
!!
AAAH!

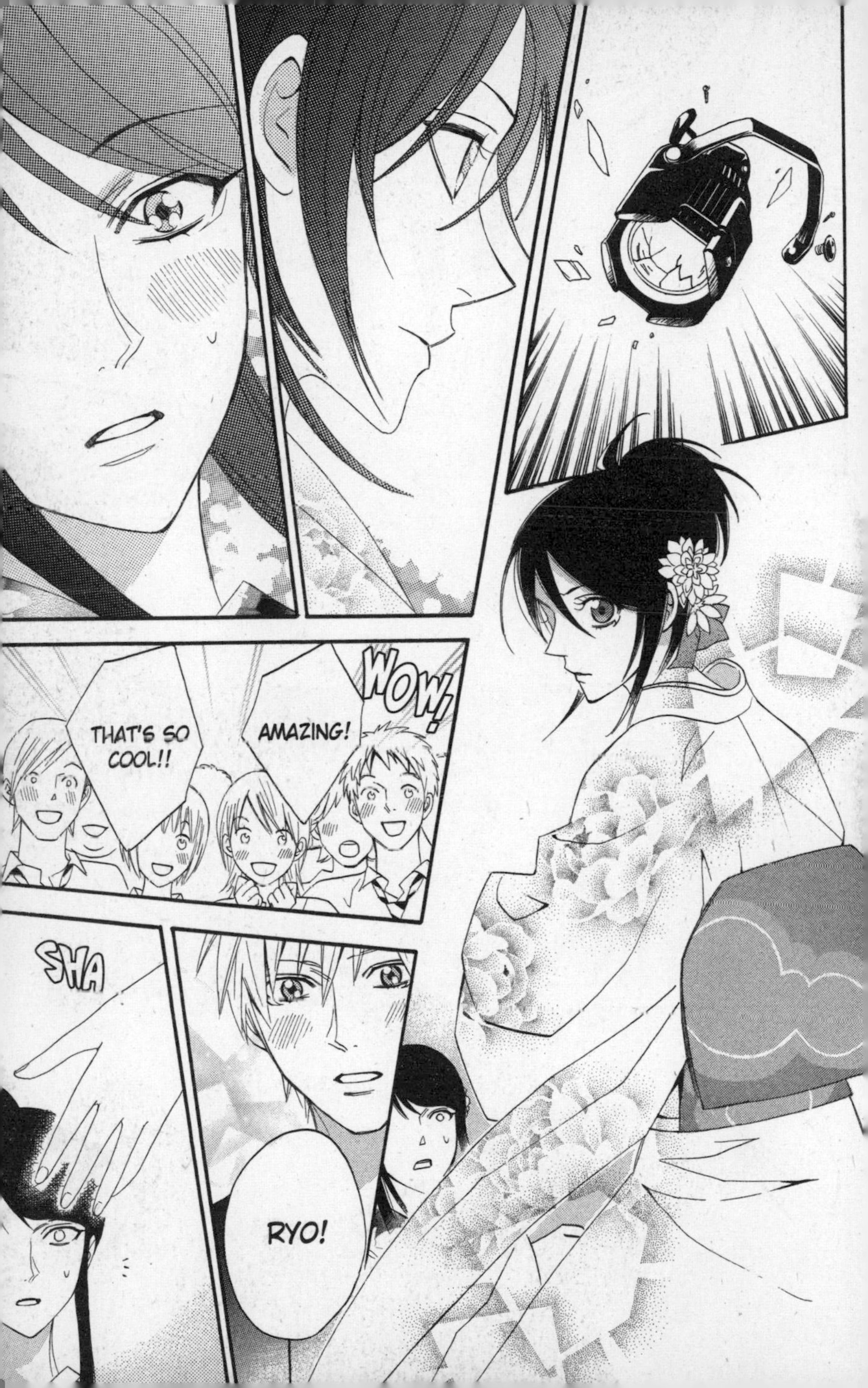
WOW!
AMAZING!
THAT'S SO COOL!!
RYO!
SHA

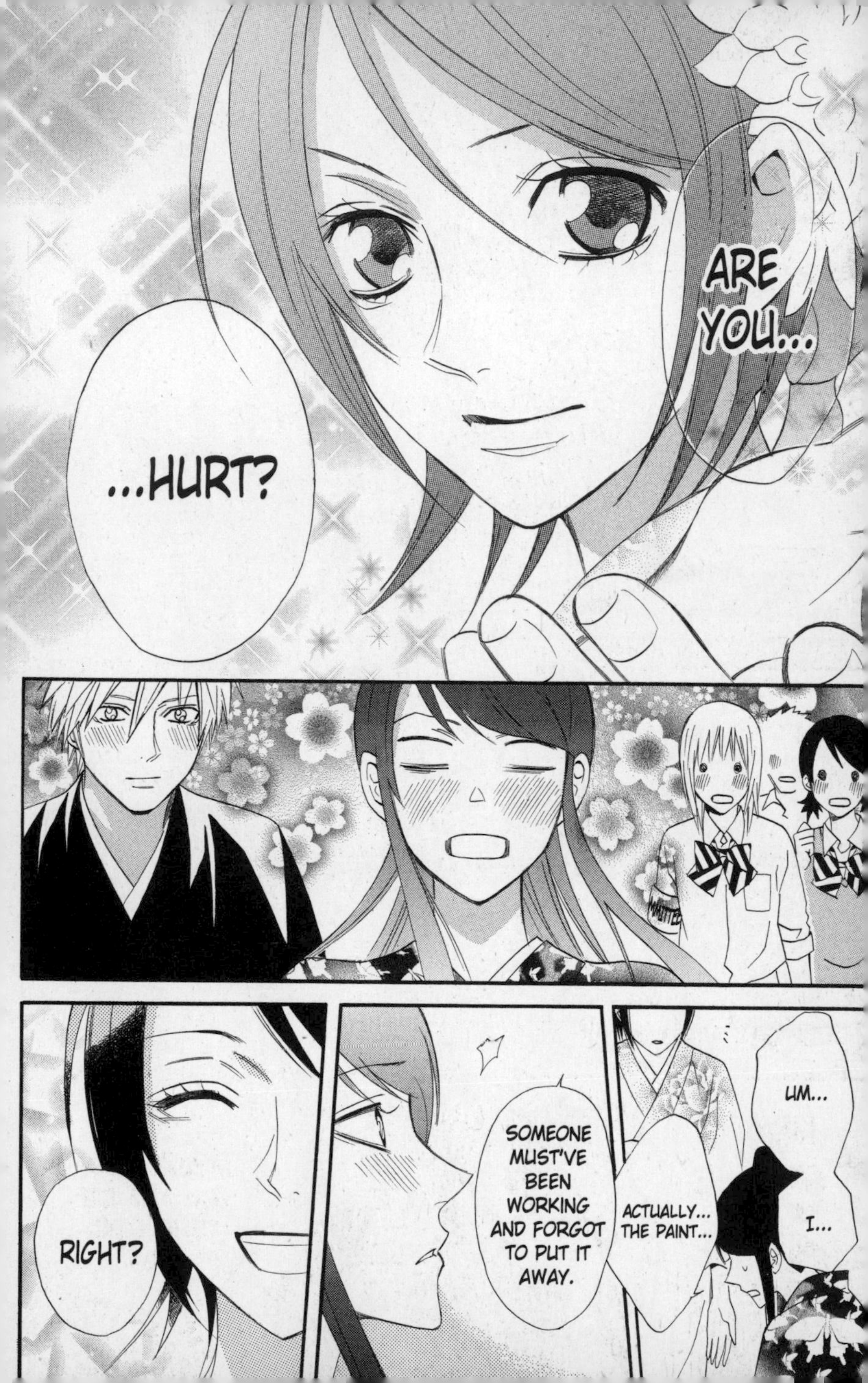
ARE YOU...
...HURT?
UM...
I...
ACTUALLY... THE PAINT...
SOMEONE MUST'VE BEEN WORKING AND FORGOT TO PUT IT AWAY.
RIGHT?

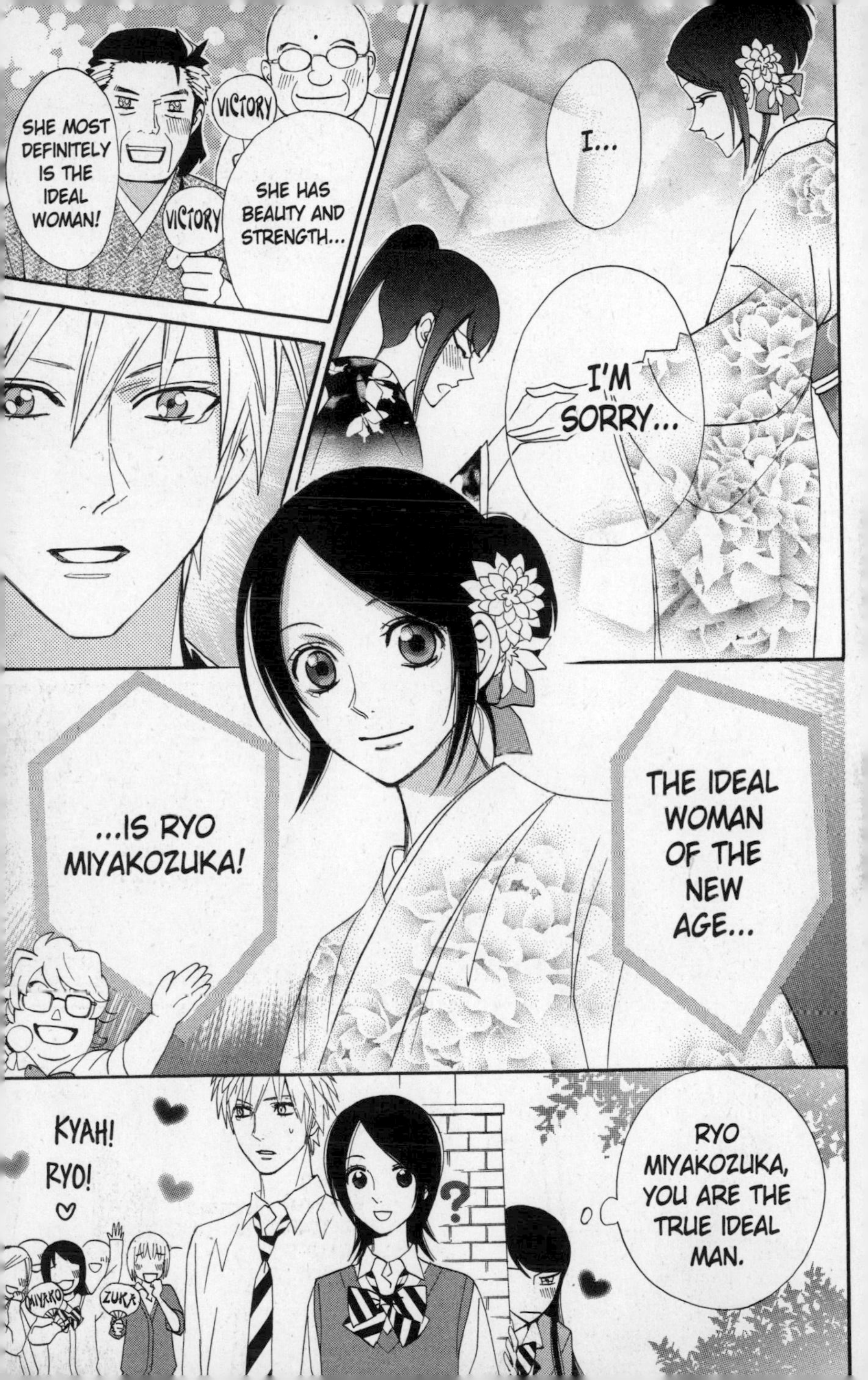
I...
I'M SORRY...
VICTORY
SHE HAS BEAUTY AND STRENGTH...
SHE MOST DEFINITELY IS THE IDEAL WOMAN!
VICTORY
THE IDEAL WOMAN OF THE NEW AGE...
...IS RYO MIYAKOZUKA!
RYO MIYAKOZUKA, YOU ARE THE TRUE IDEAL MAN.
?
KYAH! RYO! ♡
ZUKA
MIYAKO

OTOMEN

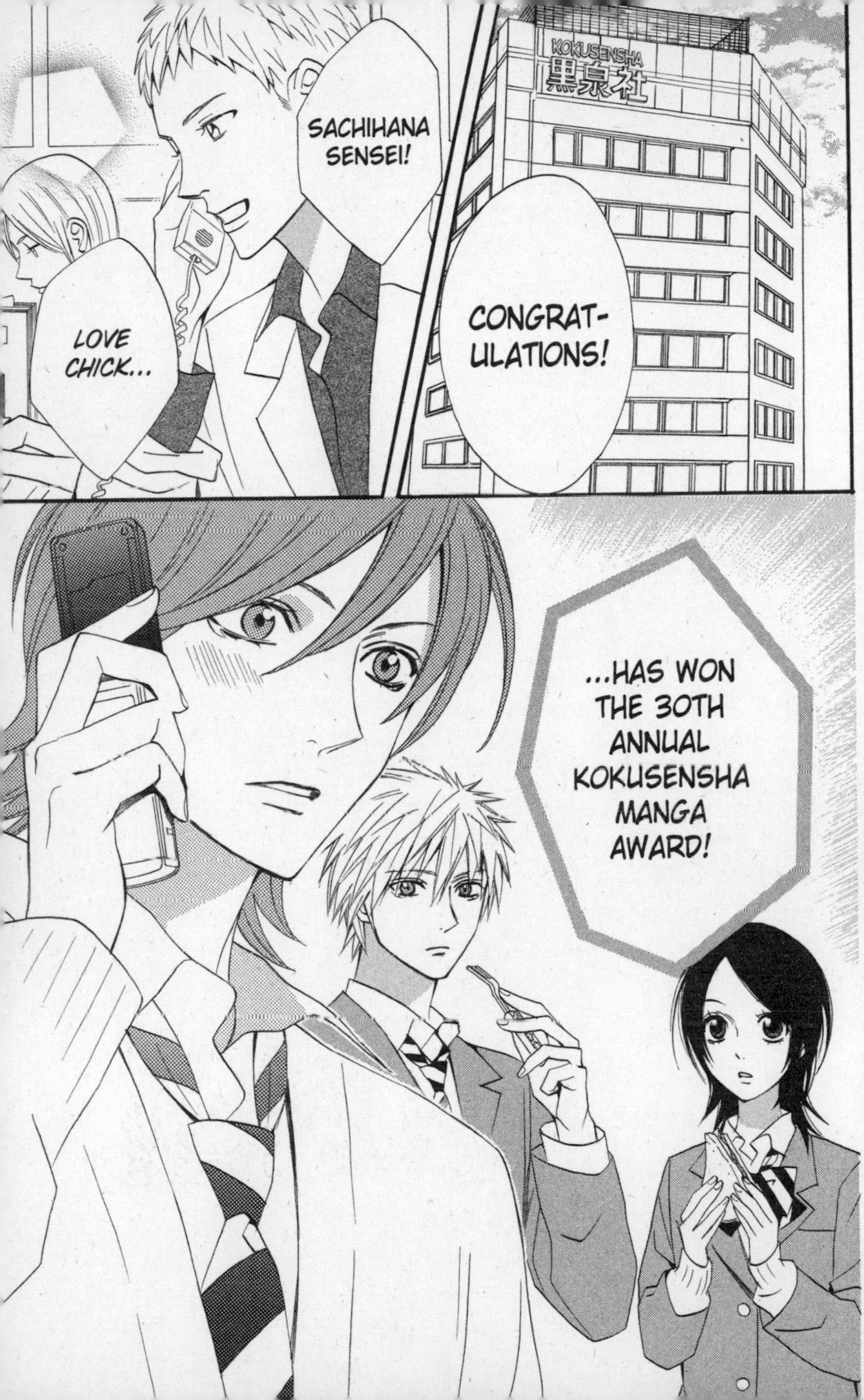
KOKUSENSHA
黒泉社
CONGRAT-ULATIONS!
SACHIHANA SENSEI!
LOVE CHICK...
...HAS WON THE 30TH ANNUAL KOKUSENSHA MANGA AWARD!

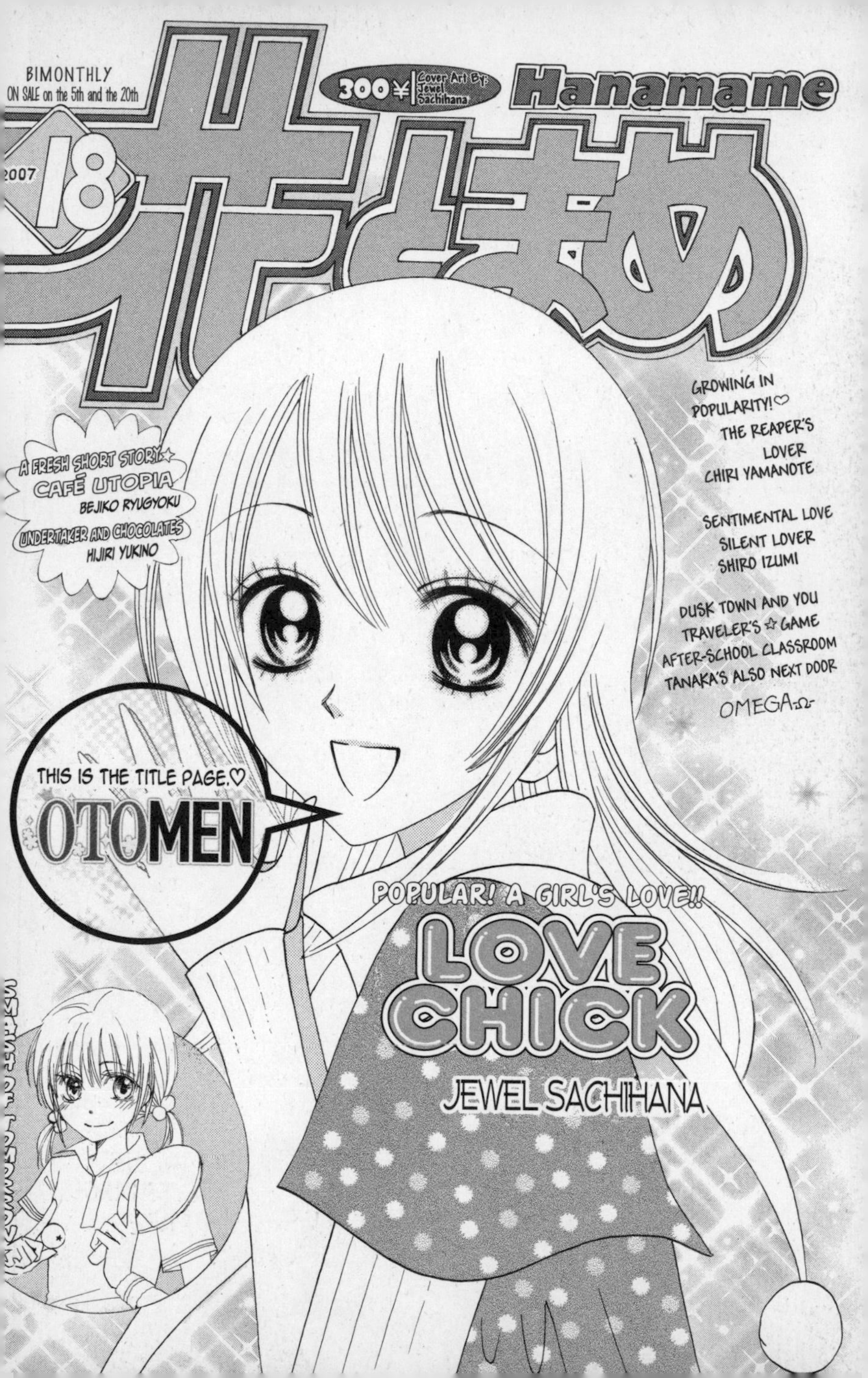
BIMONTHLY
ON SALE on the 5th and the 20th
2007
18
300¥
Cover Art By: Jewel Sachihana
Hanamame
GROWING IN POPULARITY!♡
THE REAPER'S LOVER
CHIRI YAMANOTE
A FRESH SHORT STORY☆
CAFÉ UTOPIA
BEJIKO RYUGYOKU
UNDERTAKER AND CHOCOLATES
HIJIRI YUKINO
SENTIMENTAL LOVE
SILENT LOVER
SHIRO IZUMI
DUSK TOWN AND YOU
TRAVELER'S ☆ GAME
AFTER-SCHOOL CLASSROOM
TANAKA'S ALSO NEXT DOOR
OMEGA-Ω-
THIS IS THE TITLE PAGE.♡
OTOMEN
POPULAR! A GIRL'S LOVE!!
LOVE CHICK
JEWEL SACHIHANA

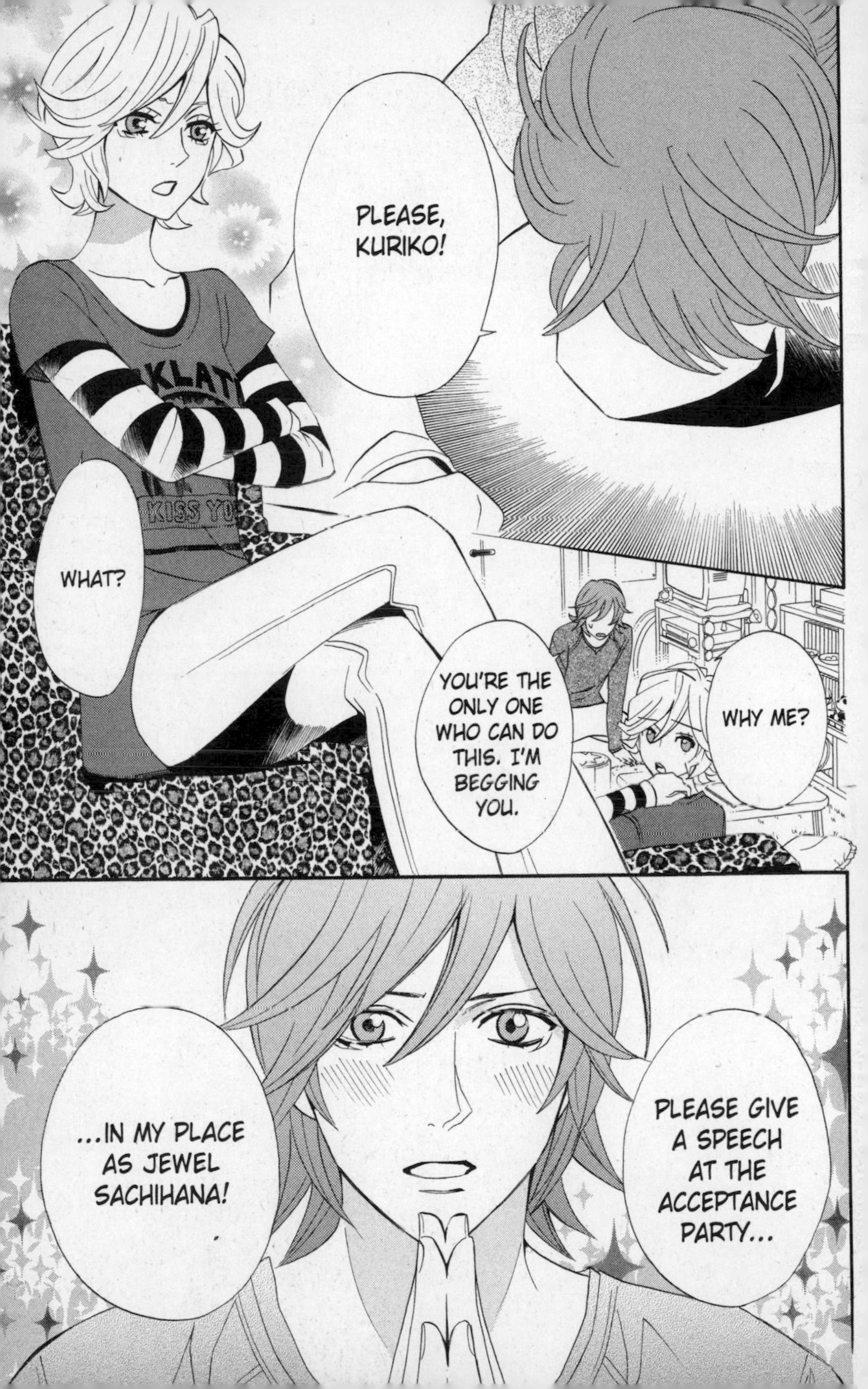
PLEASE, KURIKO!
WHAT?
WHY ME?
YOU'RE THE ONLY ONE WHO CAN DO THIS. I'M BEGGING YOU.
PLEASE GIVE A SPEECH AT THE ACCEPTANCE PARTY...
...IN MY PLACE AS JEWEL SACHIHANA!

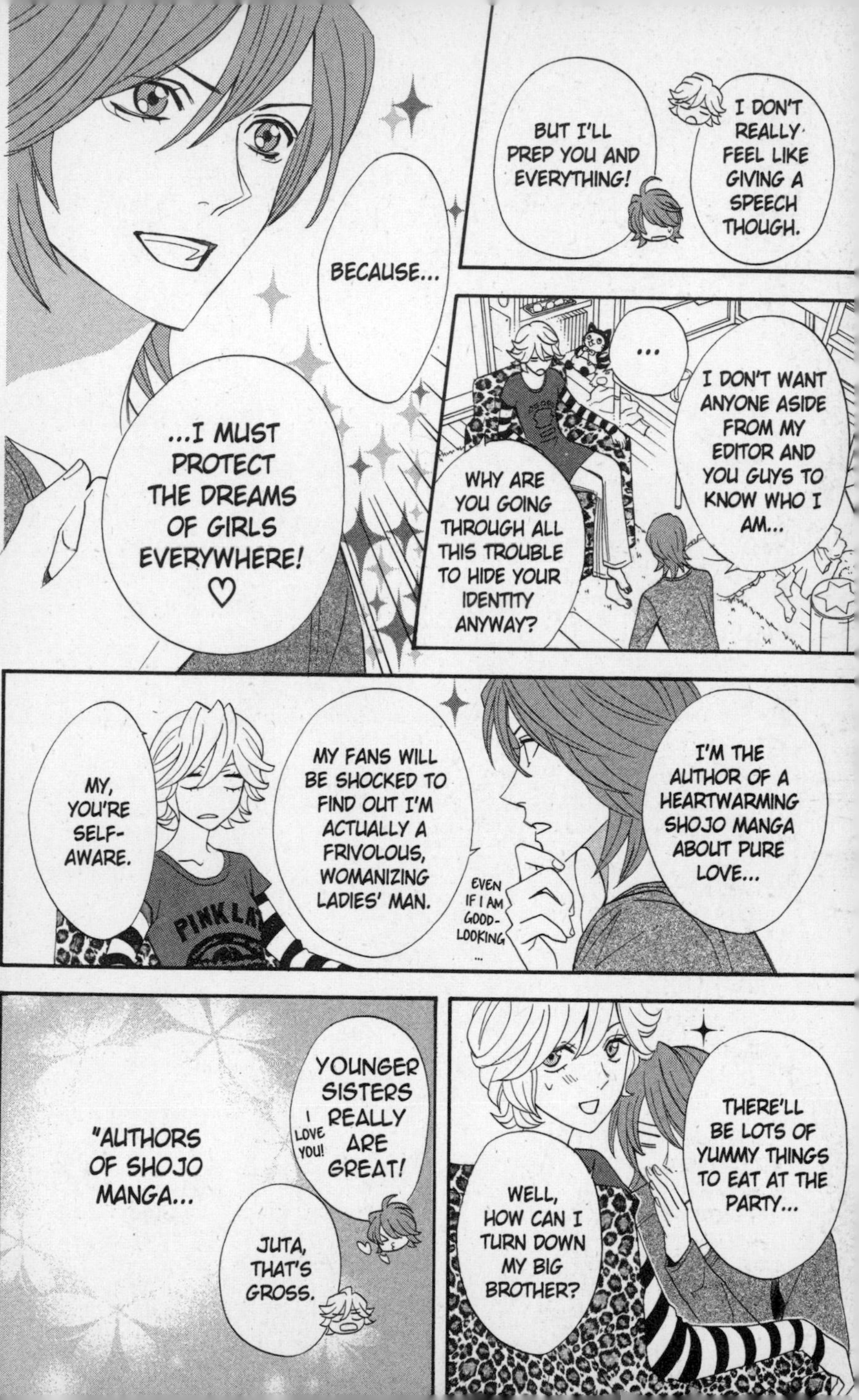
I DON'T REALLY FEEL LIKE GIVING A SPEECH THOUGH.
BUT I'LL PREP YOU AND EVERYTHING!
...
I DON'T WANT ANYONE ASIDE FROM MY EDITOR AND YOU GUYS TO KNOW WHO I AM...
WHY ARE YOU GOING THROUGH ALL THIS TROUBLE TO HIDE YOUR IDENTITY ANYWAY?
BECAUSE...
...I MUST PROTECT THE DREAMS OF GIRLS EVERYWHERE! ♡
I'M THE AUTHOR OF A HEARTWARMING SHOJO MANGA ABOUT PURE LOVE...
EVEN IF I AM GOOD-LOOKING...
MY FANS WILL BE SHOCKED TO FIND OUT I'M ACTUALLY A FRIVOLOUS, WOMANIZING LADIES' MAN.
MY, YOU'RE SELF-AWARE.
PINK LA
THERE'LL BE LOTS OF YUMMY THINGS TO EAT AT THE PARTY...
WELL, HOW CAN I TURN DOWN MY BIG BROTHER?
YOUNGER SISTERS REALLY ARE GREAT!
I LOVE YOU!
"AUTHORS OF SHOJO MANGA...
JUTA, THAT'S GROSS.

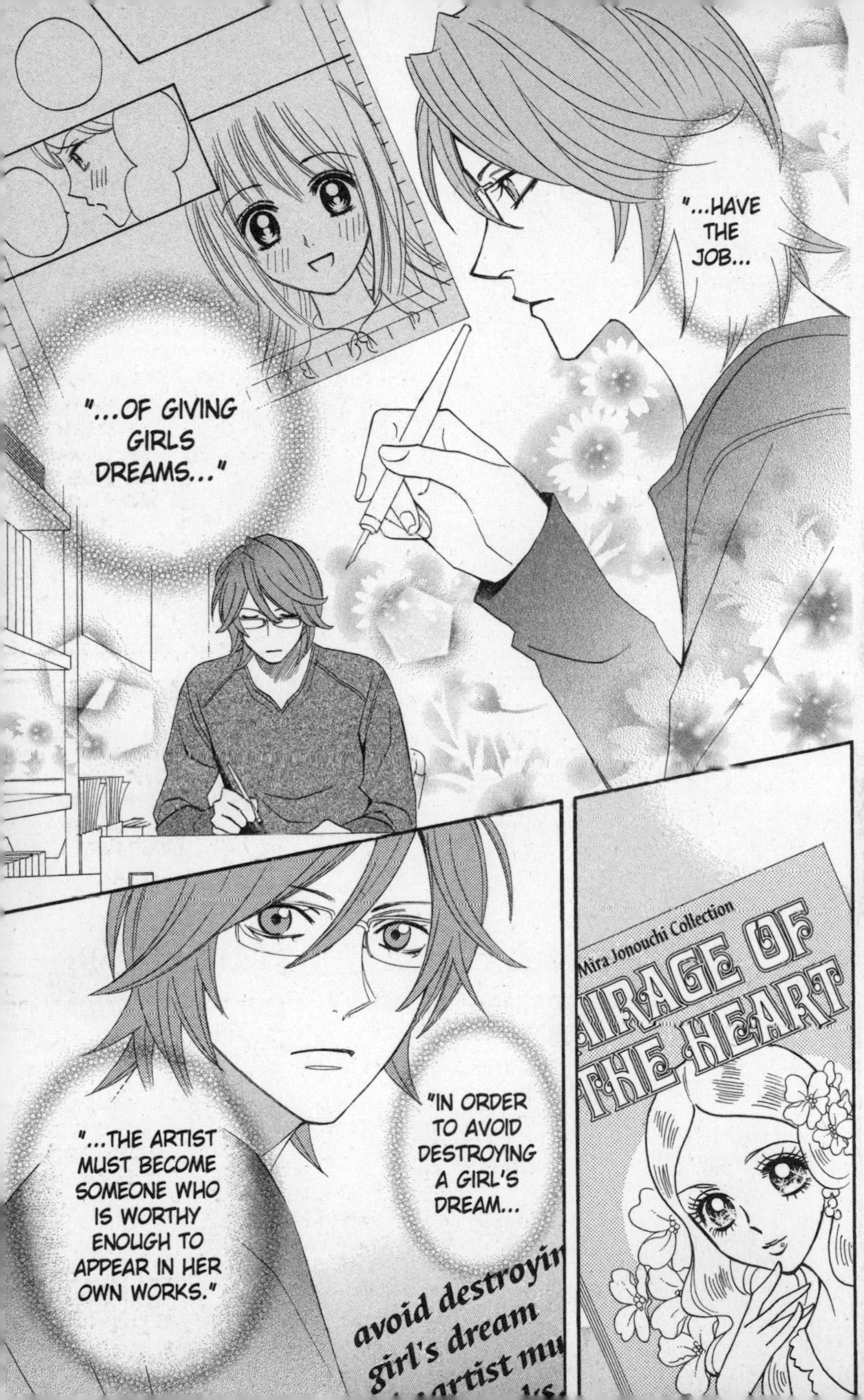
"...HAVE THE JOB...
"...OF GIVING GIRLS DREAMS..."
Mira Jonouchi Collection
IRAGE OF THE HEART
"IN ORDER TO AVOID DESTROYING A GIRL'S DREAM...
"...THE ARTIST MUST BECOME SOMEONE WHO IS WORTHY ENOUGH TO APPEAR IN HER OWN WORKS."
avoid destroyin
girl's dream
artist mu

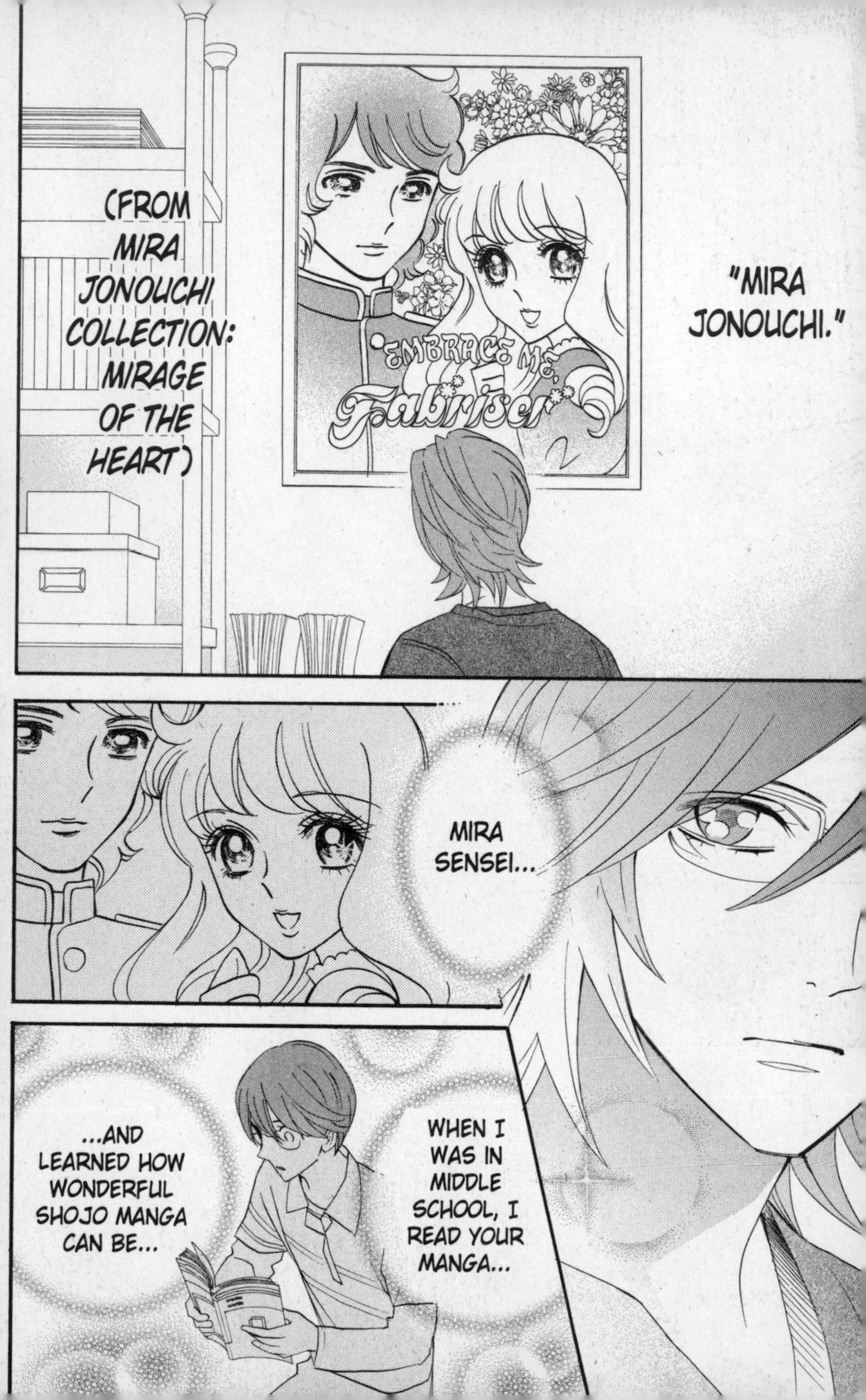
"MIRA JONOUCHI."
EMBRACE ME, Fabriser
(FROM MIRA JONOUCHI COLLECTION: MIRAGE OF THE HEART)
MIRA SENSEI...
WHEN I WAS IN MIDDLE SCHOOL, I READ YOUR MANGA...
...AND LEARNED HOW WONDERFUL SHOJO MANGA CAN BE...

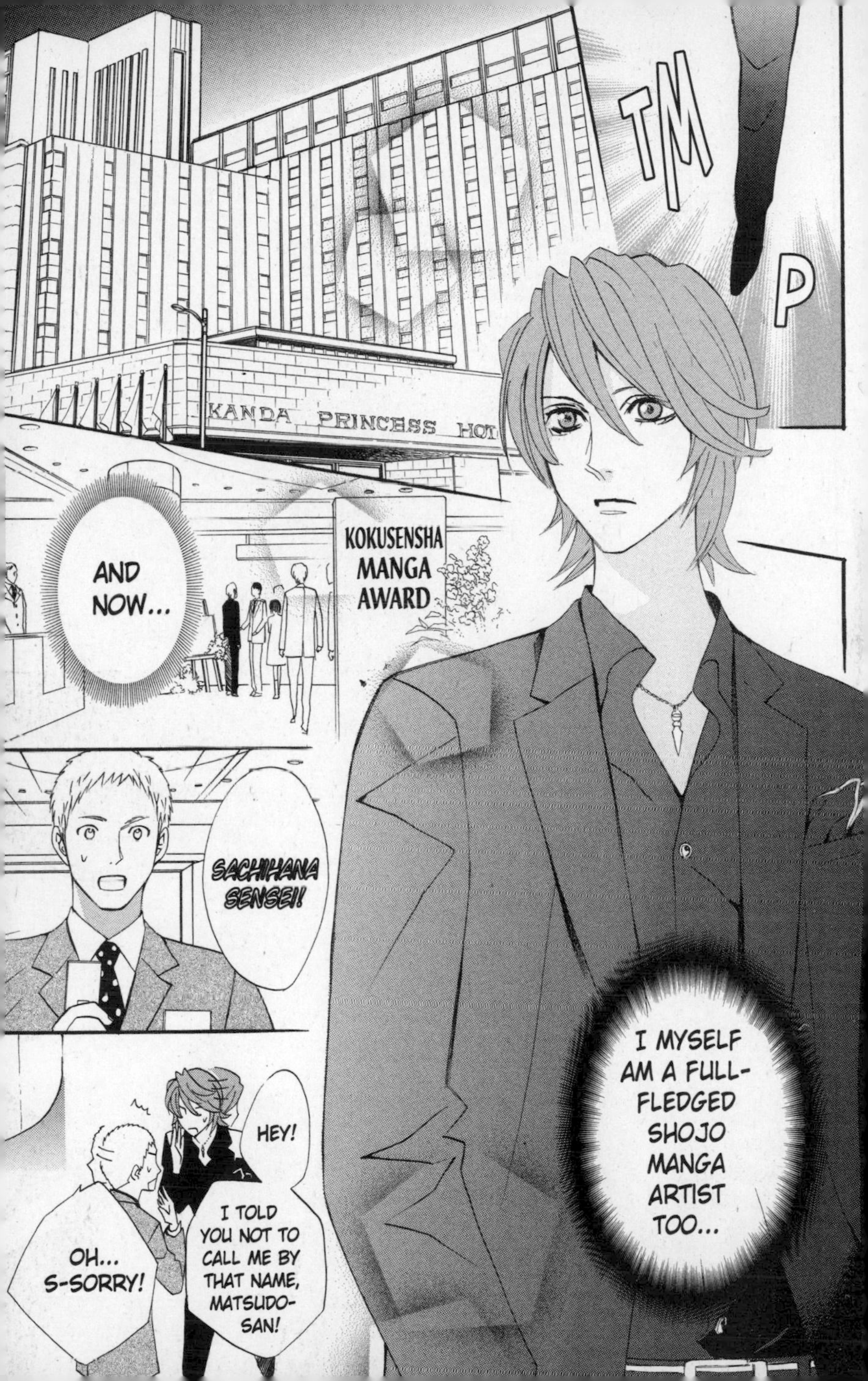
TMP
KANDA PRINCESS HOT
KOKUSENSHA MANGA AWARD
AND NOW...
I MYSELF AM A FULL-FLEDGED SHOJO MANGA ARTIST TOO...
SACHIHANA SENSEI!
HEY!
I TOLD YOU NOT TO CALL ME BY THAT NAME, MATSUDO-SAN!
OH... S-SORRY!

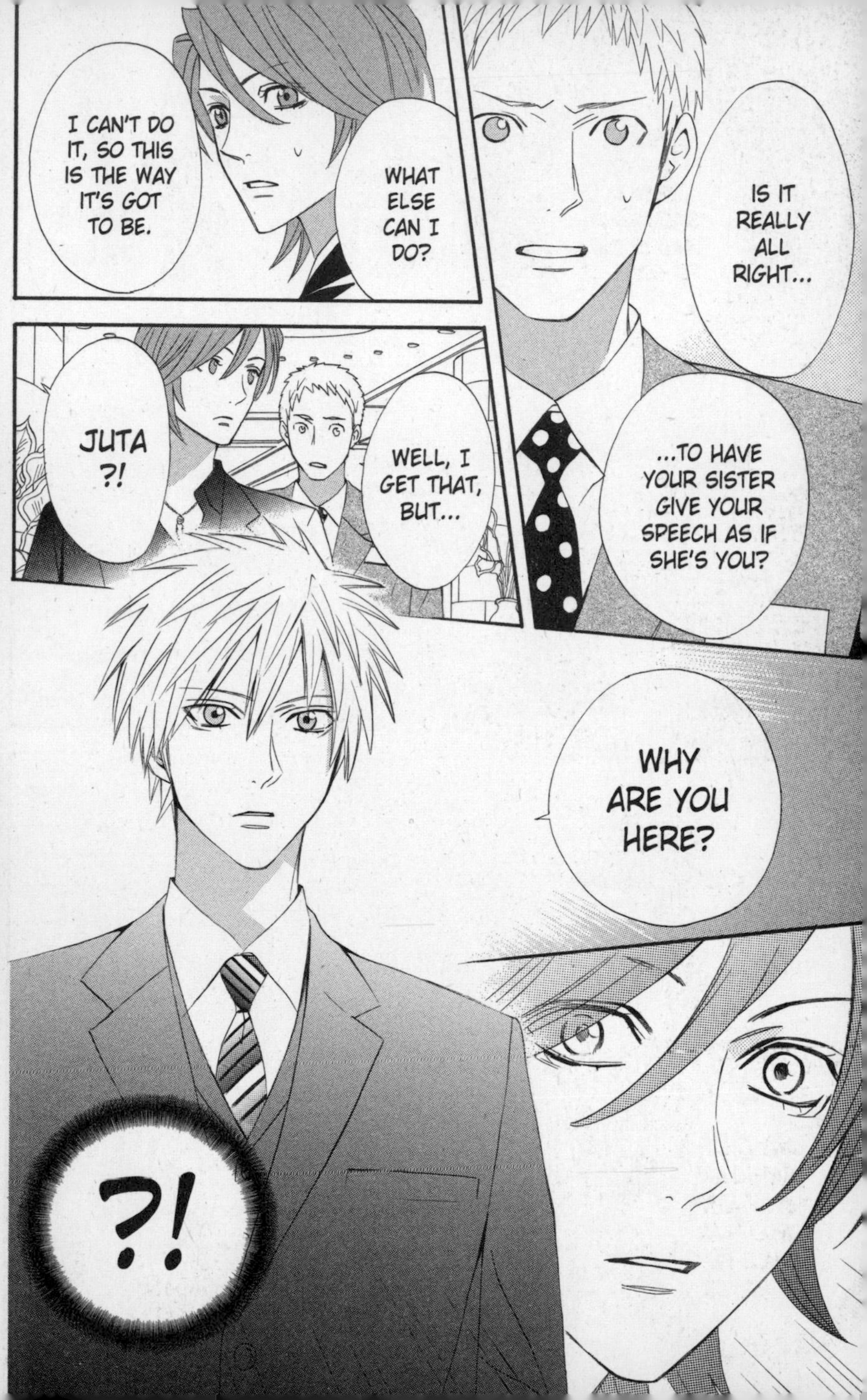
IS IT REALLY ALL RIGHT...
...TO HAVE YOUR SISTER GIVE YOUR SPEECH AS IF SHE'S YOU?
WHAT ELSE CAN I DO?
I CAN'T DO IT, SO THIS IS THE WAY IT'S GOT TO BE.
WELL, I GET THAT, BUT...
JUTA ?!
WHY ARE YOU HERE?
?!

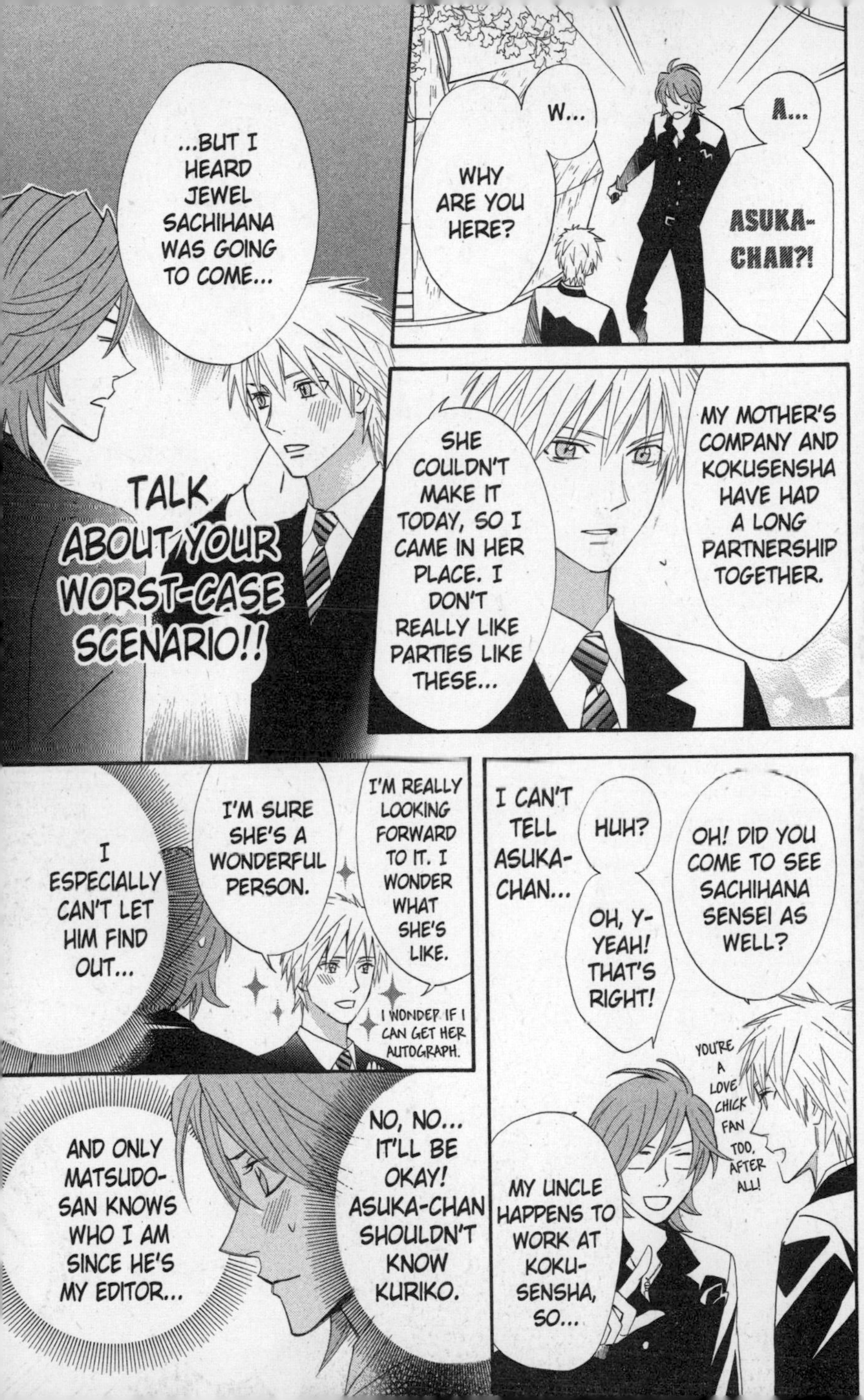
A...
ASUKA-CHAN?!
W...
WHY ARE YOU HERE?
MY MOTHER'S COMPANY AND KOKUSENSHA HAVE HAD A LONG PARTNERSHIP TOGETHER.
SHE COULDN'T MAKE IT TODAY, SO I CAME IN HER PLACE. I DON'T REALLY LIKE PARTIES LIKE THESE...
...BUT I HEARD JEWEL SACHIHANA WAS GOING TO COME...
TALK ABOUT YOUR WORST-CASE SCENARIO!!
OH! DID YOU COME TO SEE SACHIHANA SENSEI AS WELL?
HUH?
OH, Y-YEAH! THAT'S RIGHT!
I CAN'T TELL ASUKA-CHAN...
YOU'RE A LOVE CHICK FAN TOO, AFTER ALL!
MY UNCLE HAPPENS TO WORK AT KOKU-SENSHA, SO...
I'M REALLY LOOKING FORWARD TO IT. I WONDER WHAT SHE'S LIKE.
I'M SURE SHE'S A WONDERFUL PERSON.
I WONDEP IF I CAN GET HER AUTOGRAPH.
I ESPECIALLY CAN'T LET HIM FIND OUT...
NO, NO... IT'LL BE OKAY! ASUKA-CHAN SHOULDN'T KNOW KURIKO.
AND ONLY MATSUDO-SAN KNOWS WHO I AM SINCE HE'S MY EDITOR...

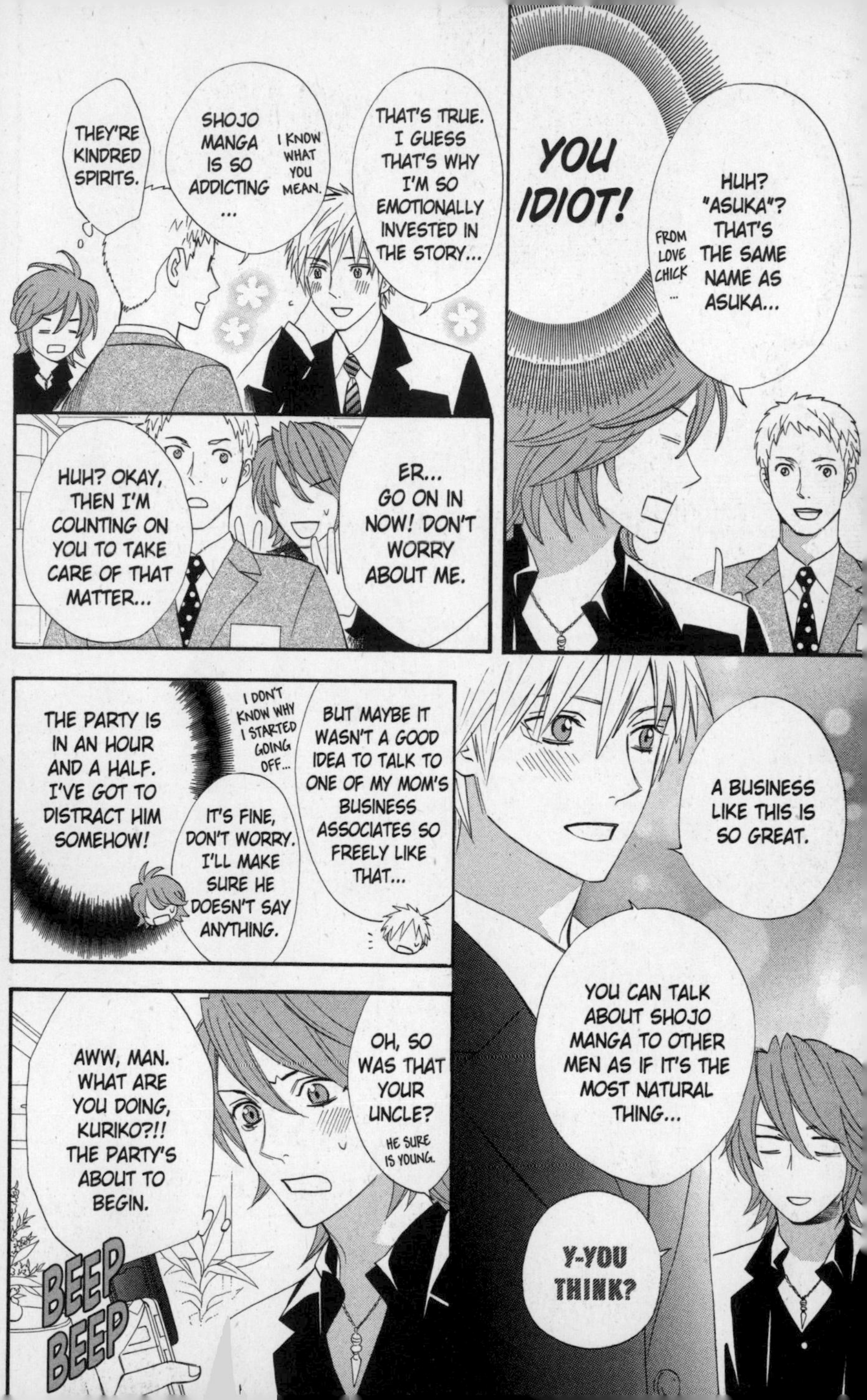
HUH? "ASUKA"? THAT'S THE SAME NAME AS ASUKA...
FROM LOVE CHICK ...
YOU IDIOT!
THAT'S TRUE. I GUESS THAT'S WHY I'M SO EMOTIONALLY INVESTED IN THE STORY...
I KNOW WHAT YOU MEAN.
SHOJO MANGA IS SO ADDICTING ...
THEY'RE KINDRED SPIRITS.
ER... GO ON IN NOW! DON'T WORRY ABOUT ME.
HUH? OKAY, THEN I'M COUNTING ON YOU TO TAKE CARE OF THAT MATTER...
A BUSINESS LIKE THIS IS SO GREAT.
YOU CAN TALK ABOUT SHOJO MANGA TO OTHER MEN AS IF IT'S THE MOST NATURAL THING...
Y-YOU THINK?
BUT MAYBE IT WASN'T A GOOD IDEA TO TALK TO ONE OF MY MOM'S BUSINESS ASSOCIATES SO FREELY LIKE THAT...
I DON'T KNOW WHY I STARTED GOING OFF...
THE PARTY IS IN AN HOUR AND A HALF. I'VE GOT TO DISTRACT HIM SOMEHOW!
IT'S FINE, DON'T WORRY. I'LL MAKE SURE HE DOESN'T SAY ANYTHING.
OH, SO WAS THAT YOUR UNCLE?
HE SURE IS YOUNG.
AWW, MAN. WHAT ARE YOU DOING, KURIKO?!! THE PARTY'S ABOUT TO BEGIN.
BEEP BEEP

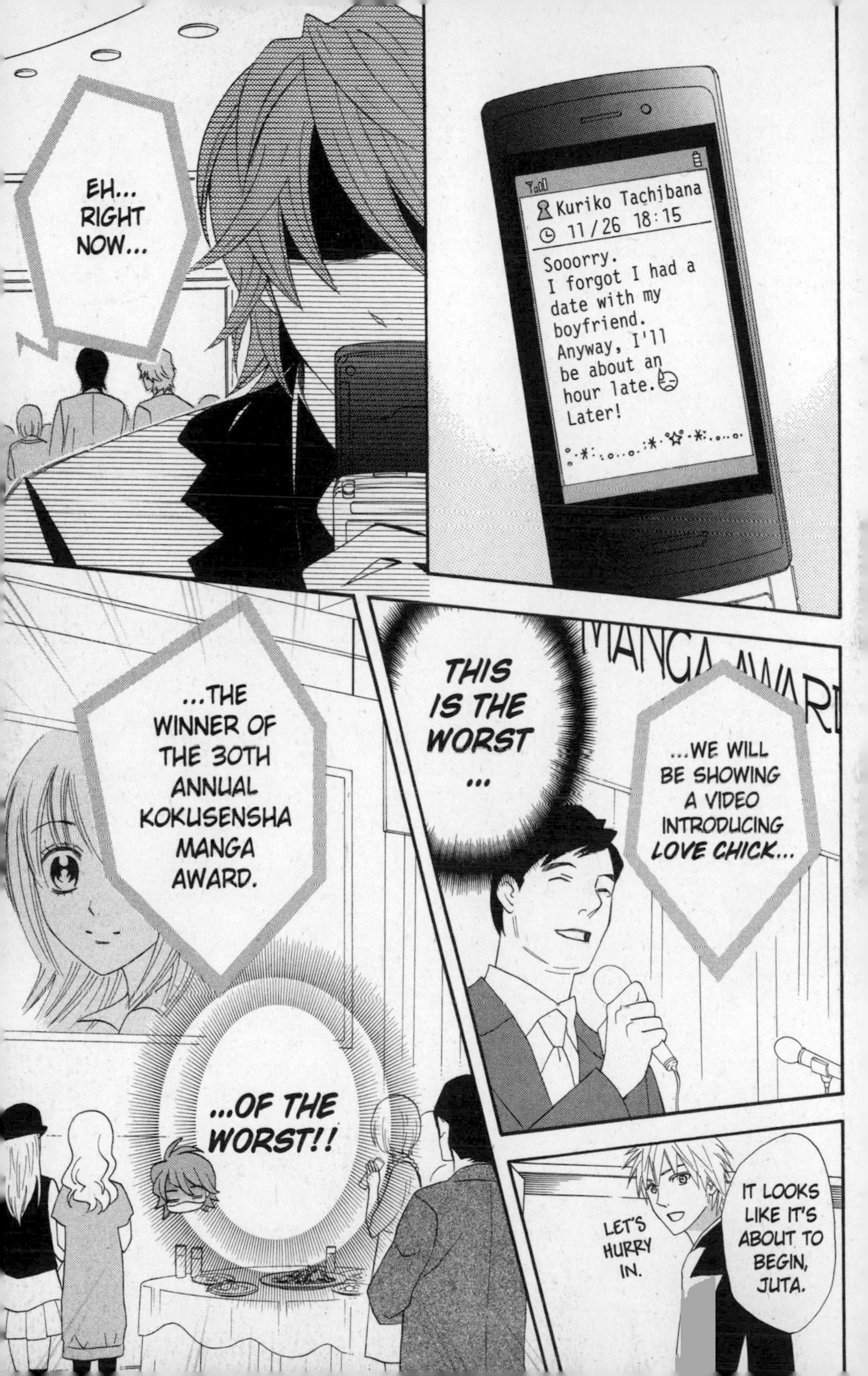
Kuriko Tachibana
11/26 18:15
Sooorry.
I forgot I had a date with my boyfriend. Anyway, I'll be about an hour late.
Later!
EH... RIGHT NOW...
MANGA AWARD
...WE WILL BE SHOWING A VIDEO INTRODUCING *LOVE CHICK*...
THIS IS THE WORST ...
IT LOOKS LIKE IT'S ABOUT TO BEGIN, JUTA.
LET'S HURRY IN.
...THE WINNER OF THE 30TH ANNUAL KOKUSENSHA MANGA AWARD.
...OF THE WORST!!

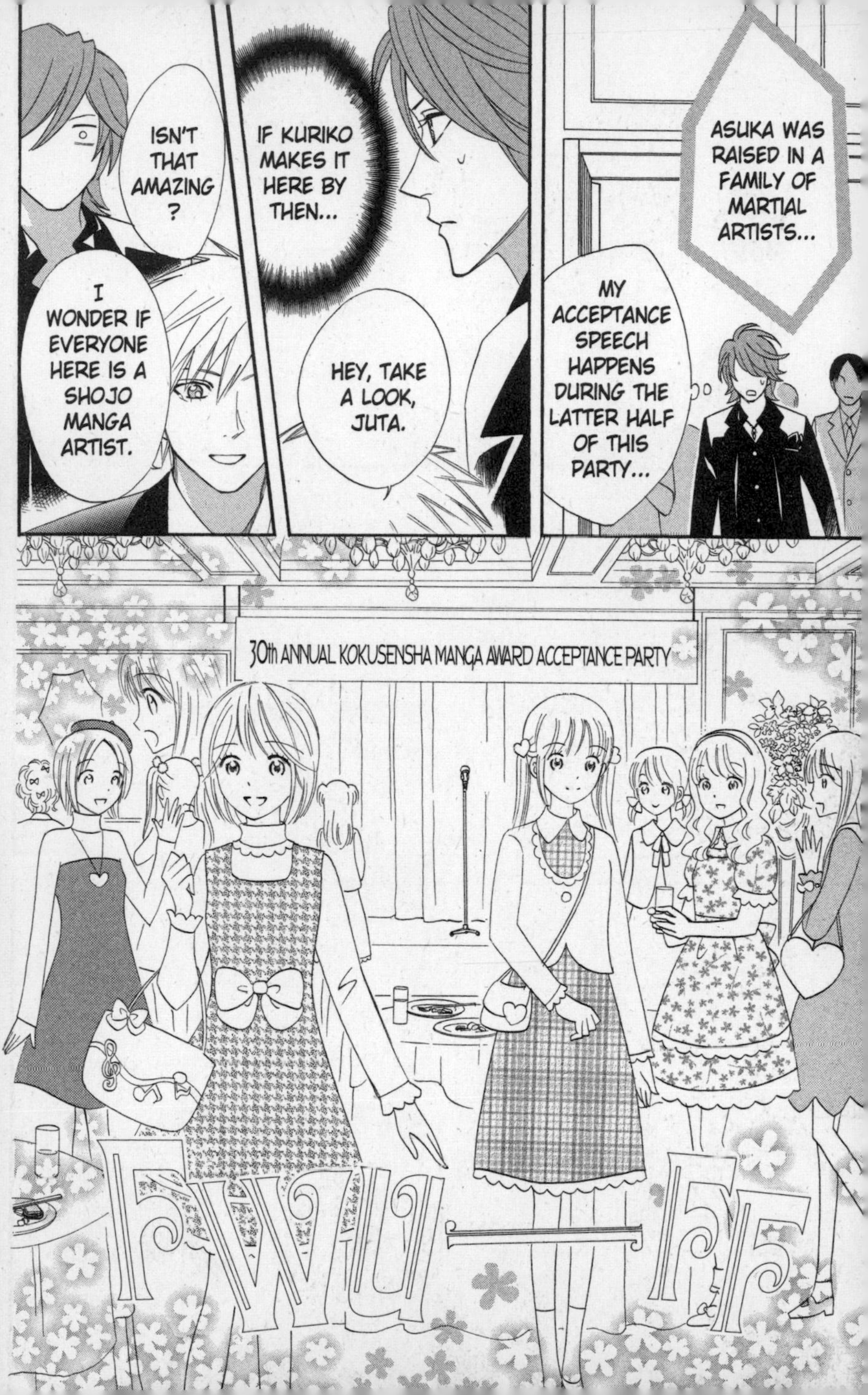
ASUKA WAS RAISED IN A FAMILY OF MARTIAL ARTISTS...
MY ACCEPTANCE SPEECH HAPPENS DURING THE LATTER HALF OF THIS PARTY...
IF KURIKO MAKES IT HERE BY THEN...
HEY, TAKE A LOOK, JUTA.
ISN'T THAT AMAZING?
I WONDER IF EVERYONE HERE IS A SHOJO MANGA ARTIST.
30th ANNUAL KOKUSENSHA MANGA AWARD ACCEPTANCE PARTY
FWU—FF

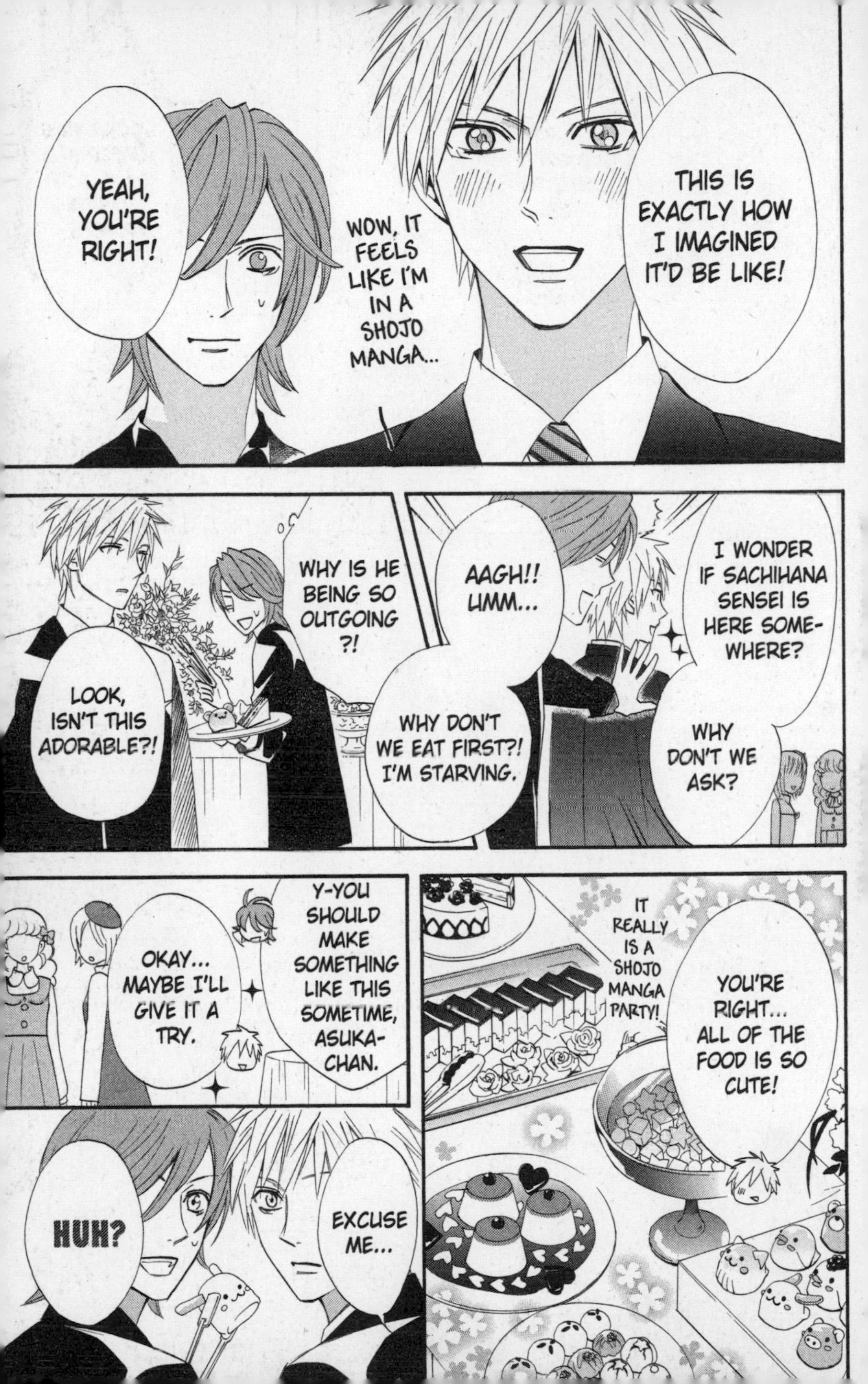
THIS IS EXACTLY HOW I IMAGINED IT'D BE LIKE!
WOW, IT FEELS LIKE I'M IN A SHOJO MANGA...
YEAH, YOU'RE RIGHT!
I WONDER IF SACHIHANA SENSEI IS HERE SOMEWHERE?
AAGH!! UMM...
WHY DON'T WE ASK?
WHY DON'T WE EAT FIRST?! I'M STARVING.
WHY IS HE BEING SO OUTGOING?!
LOOK, ISN'T THIS ADORABLE?!
IT REALLY IS A SHOJO MANGA PARTY!
YOU'RE RIGHT... ALL OF THE FOOD IS SO CUTE!
Y-YOU SHOULD MAKE SOMETHING LIKE THIS SOMETIME, ASUKA-CHAN.
OKAY... MAYBE I'LL GIVE IT A TRY.
EXCUSE ME...
HUH?

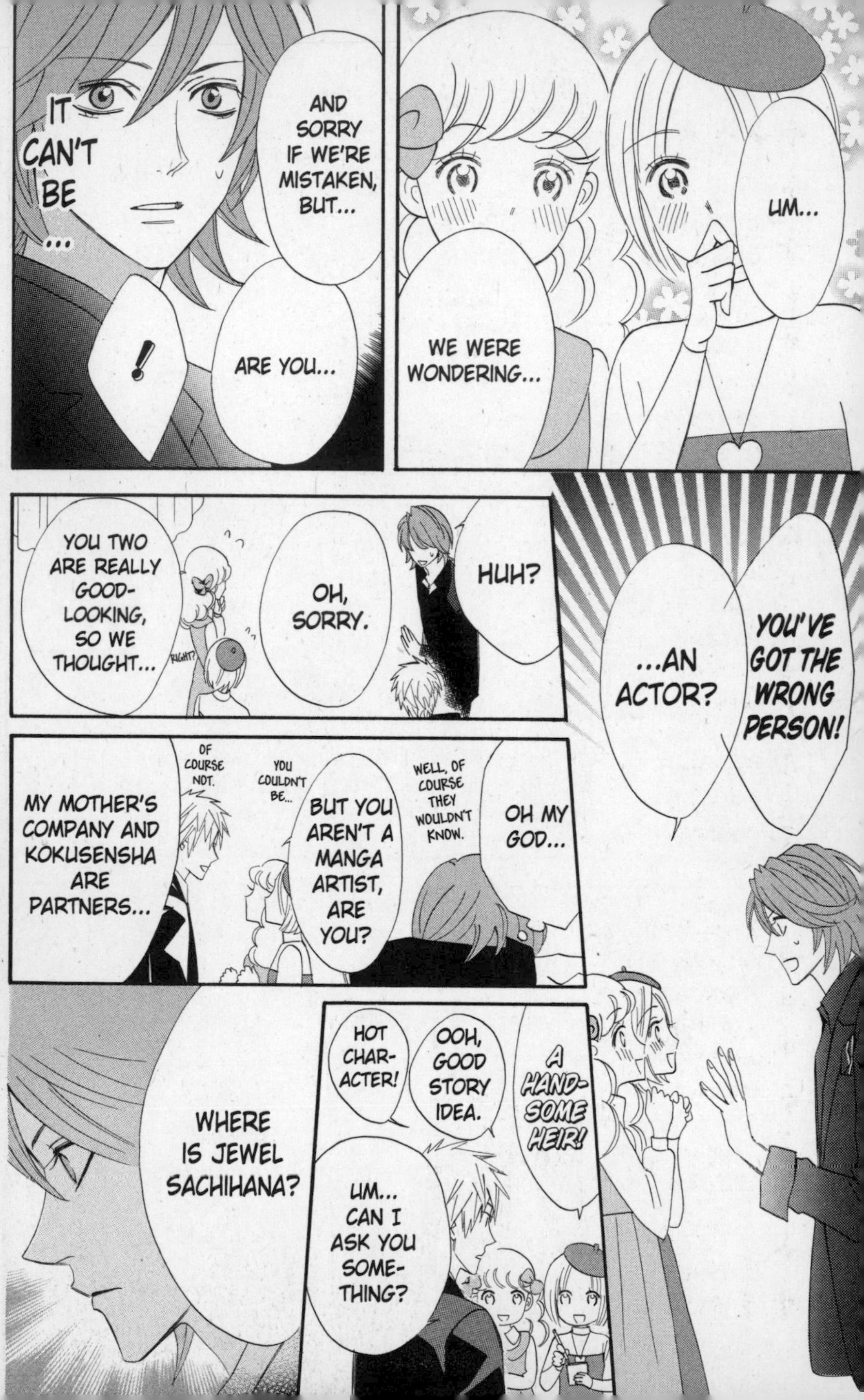
UM...
WE WERE WONDERING...
AND SORRY IF WE'RE MISTAKEN, BUT...
ARE YOU...
!
IT CAN'T BE ...
YOU'VE GOT THE WRONG PERSON!
...AN ACTOR?
HUH?
OH, SORRY.
YOU TWO ARE REALLY GOOD-LOOKING, SO WE THOUGHT...
RIGHT?
OH MY GOD...
WELL, OF COURSE THEY WOULDN'T KNOW.
BUT YOU AREN'T A MANGA ARTIST, ARE YOU?
YOU COULDN'T BE...
OF COURSE NOT.
MY MOTHER'S COMPANY AND KOKUSENSHA ARE PARTNERS...
A HANDSOME HEIR!
OOH, GOOD STORY IDEA.
HOT CHARACTER!
UM... CAN I ASK YOU SOMETHING?
WHERE IS JEWEL SACHIHANA?

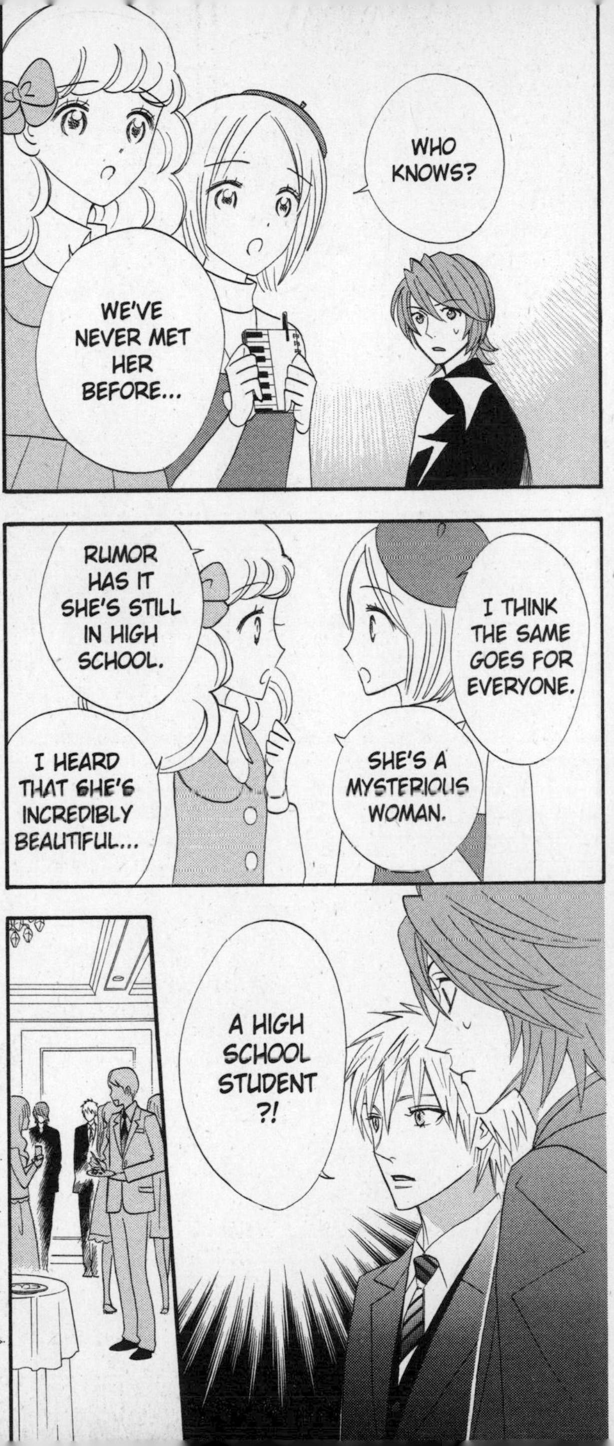
WHO KNOWS?
WE'VE NEVER MET HER BEFORE...
I THINK THE SAME GOES FOR EVERYONE.
RUMOR HAS IT SHE'S STILL IN HIGH SCHOOL.
SHE'S A MYSTERIOUS WOMAN.
I HEARD THAT SHE'S INCREDIBLY BEAUTIFUL...
A HIGH SCHOOL STUDENT ?!

This chapter is entirely fictional.

The story focuses on Juta, who hasn't been appearing much lately. I wrote it to broaden his character, but I can't deny I have a feeling I overdid things a bit. When I started this chapter, I didn't plan on having the ending be this way... but it happened just the same.

I realize that it was unreasonable to get so carried away with my drawings. But it was so **fun**.

I really like Mira Sensei.

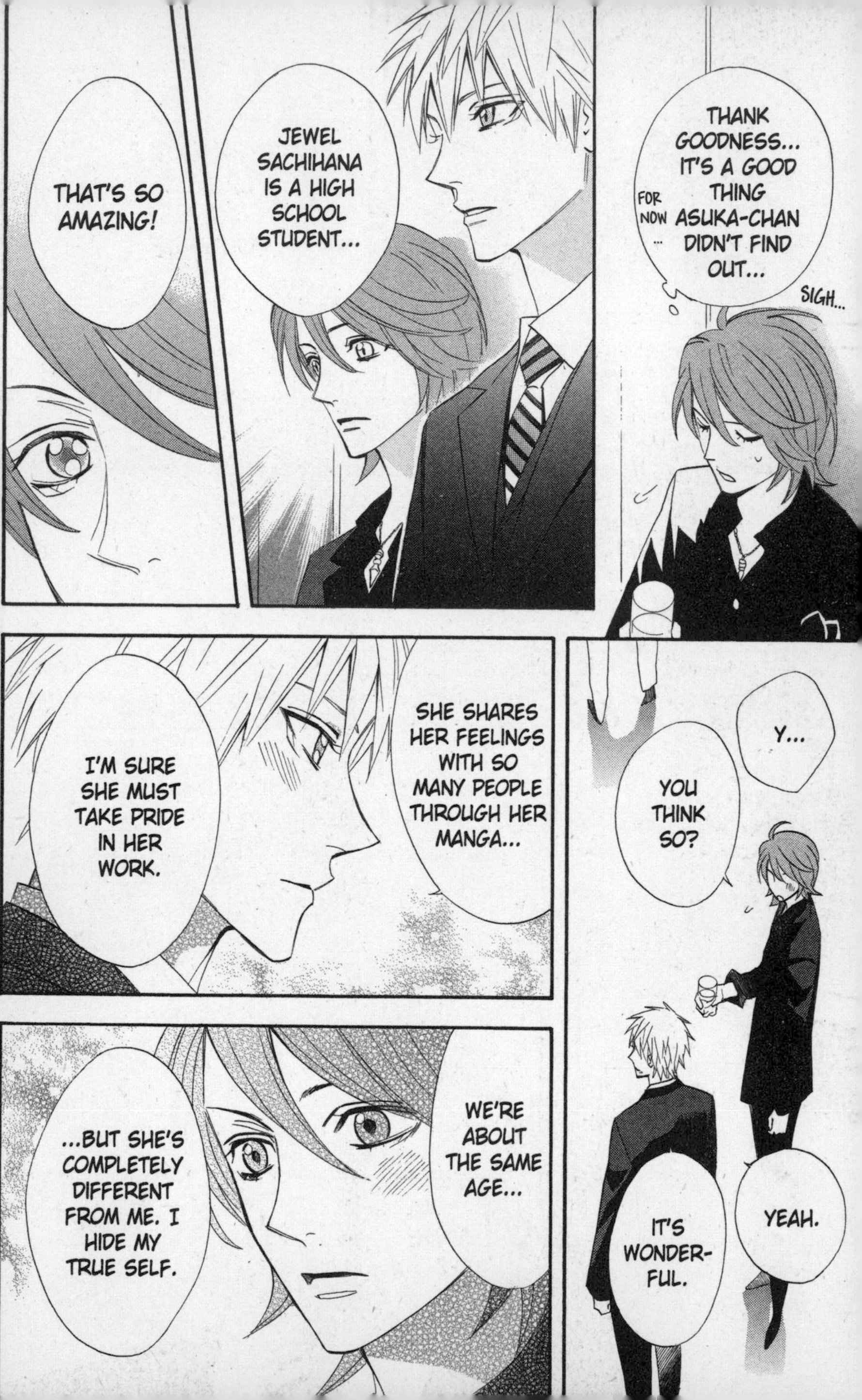
THANK GOODNESS... IT'S A GOOD THING ASUKA-CHAN DIDN'T FIND OUT...
FOR NOW ...
SIGH...
JEWEL SACHIHANA IS A HIGH SCHOOL STUDENT...
THAT'S SO AMAZING!
Y...
YOU THINK SO?
YEAH.
IT'S WONDER-FUL.
SHE SHARES HER FEELINGS WITH SO MANY PEOPLE THROUGH HER MANGA...
I'M SURE SHE MUST TAKE PRIDE IN HER WORK.
WE'RE ABOUT THE SAME AGE...
...BUT SHE'S COMPLETELY DIFFERENT FROM ME. I HIDE MY TRUE SELF.

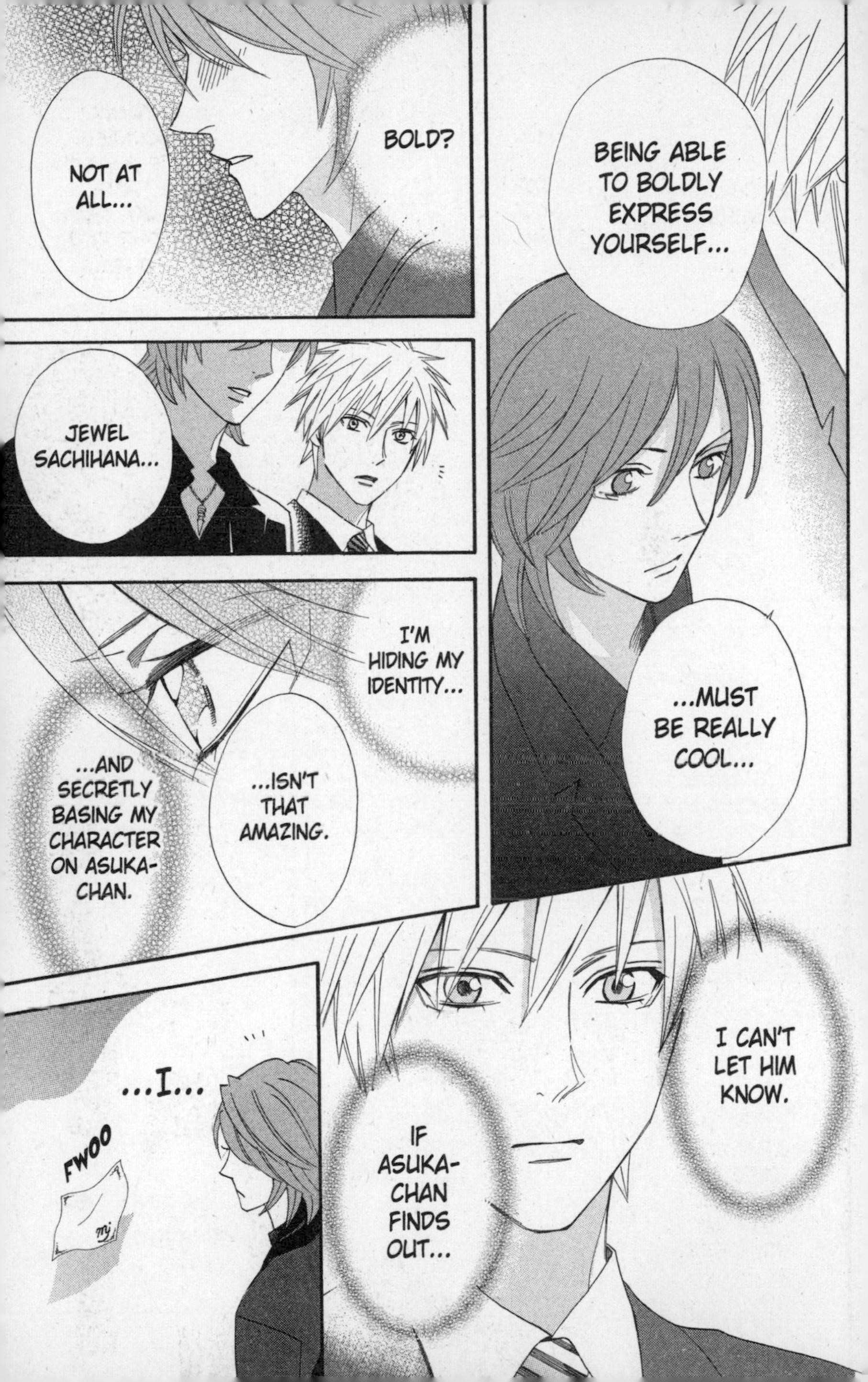
BEING ABLE TO BOLDLY EXPRESS YOURSELF...
...MUST BE REALLY COOL...
BOLD?
NOT AT ALL...
JEWEL SACHIHANA...
I'M HIDING MY IDENTITY...
...AND SECRETLY BASING MY CHARACTER ON ASUKA-CHAN.
...ISN'T THAT AMAZING.
I CAN'T LET HIM KNOW.
IF ASUKA-CHAN FINDS OUT...
...I...
FWOO

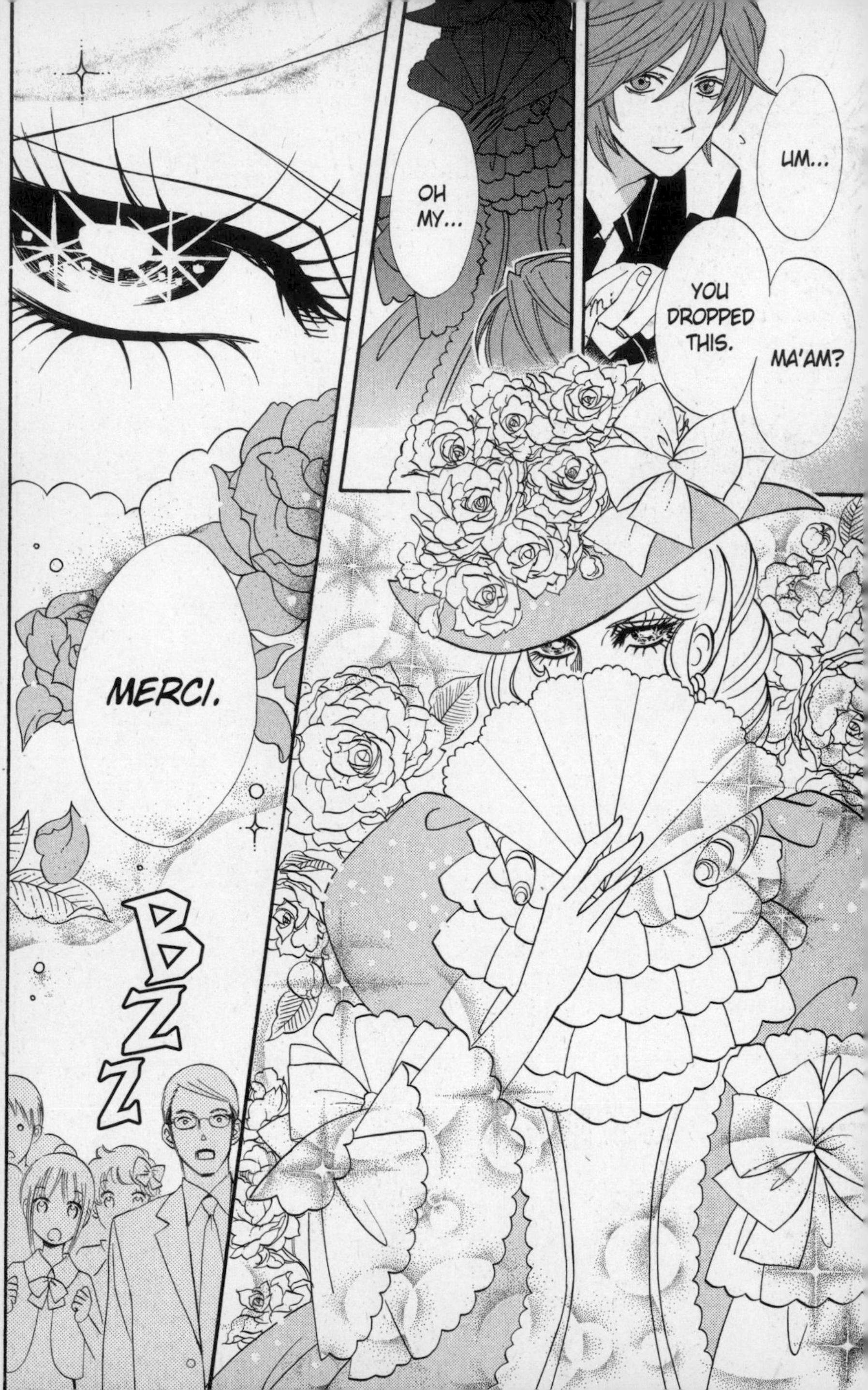
UM...
YOU DROPPED THIS.
MA'AM?
OH MY...
MERCI.
BZZ

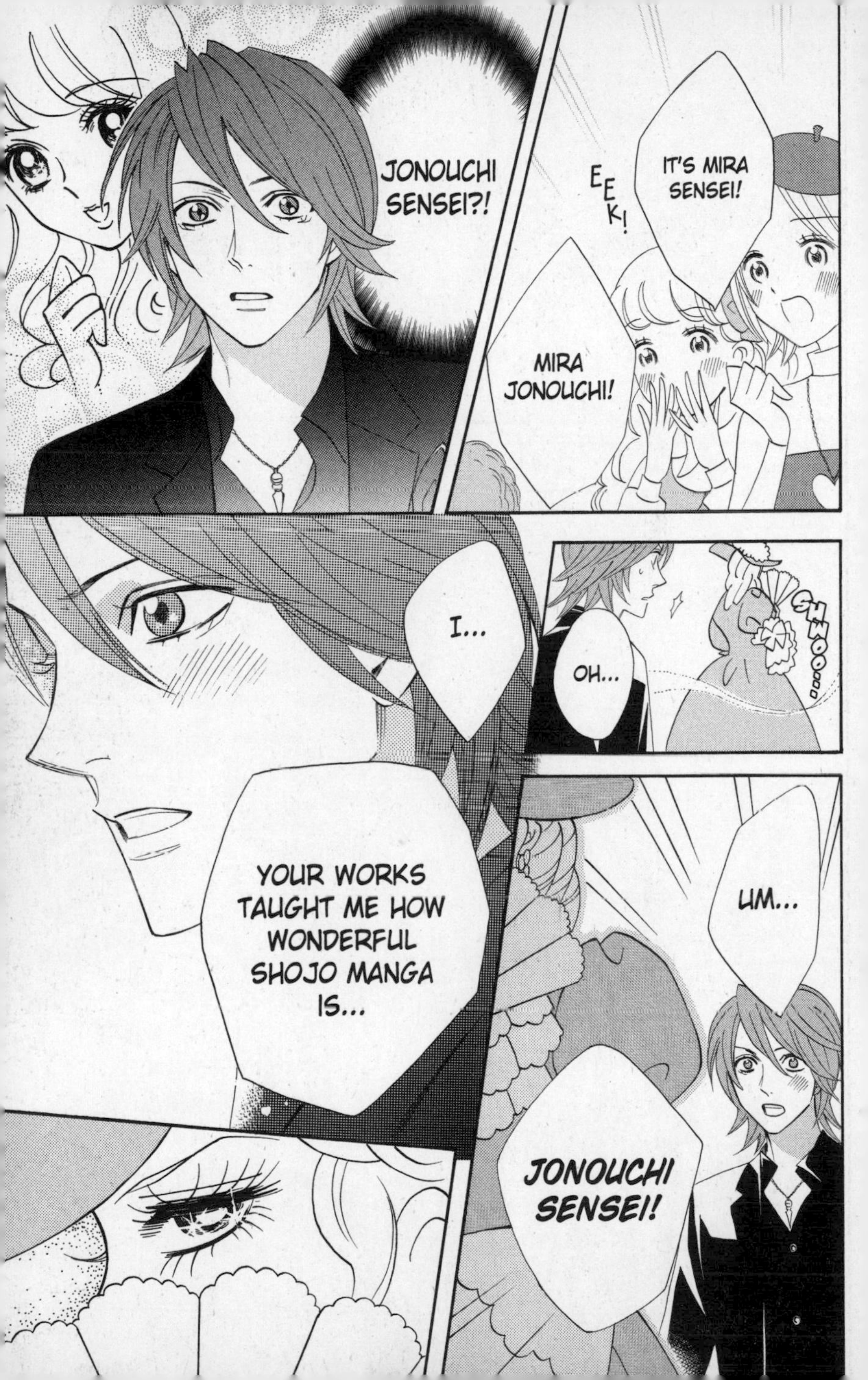
IT'S MIRA SENSEI!
EEK!
MIRA JONOUCHI!
JONOUCHI SENSEI?!
SHWOO...
OH...
UM...
JONOUCHI SENSEI!
I...
YOUR WORKS TAUGHT ME HOW WONDERFUL SHOJO MANGA IS...

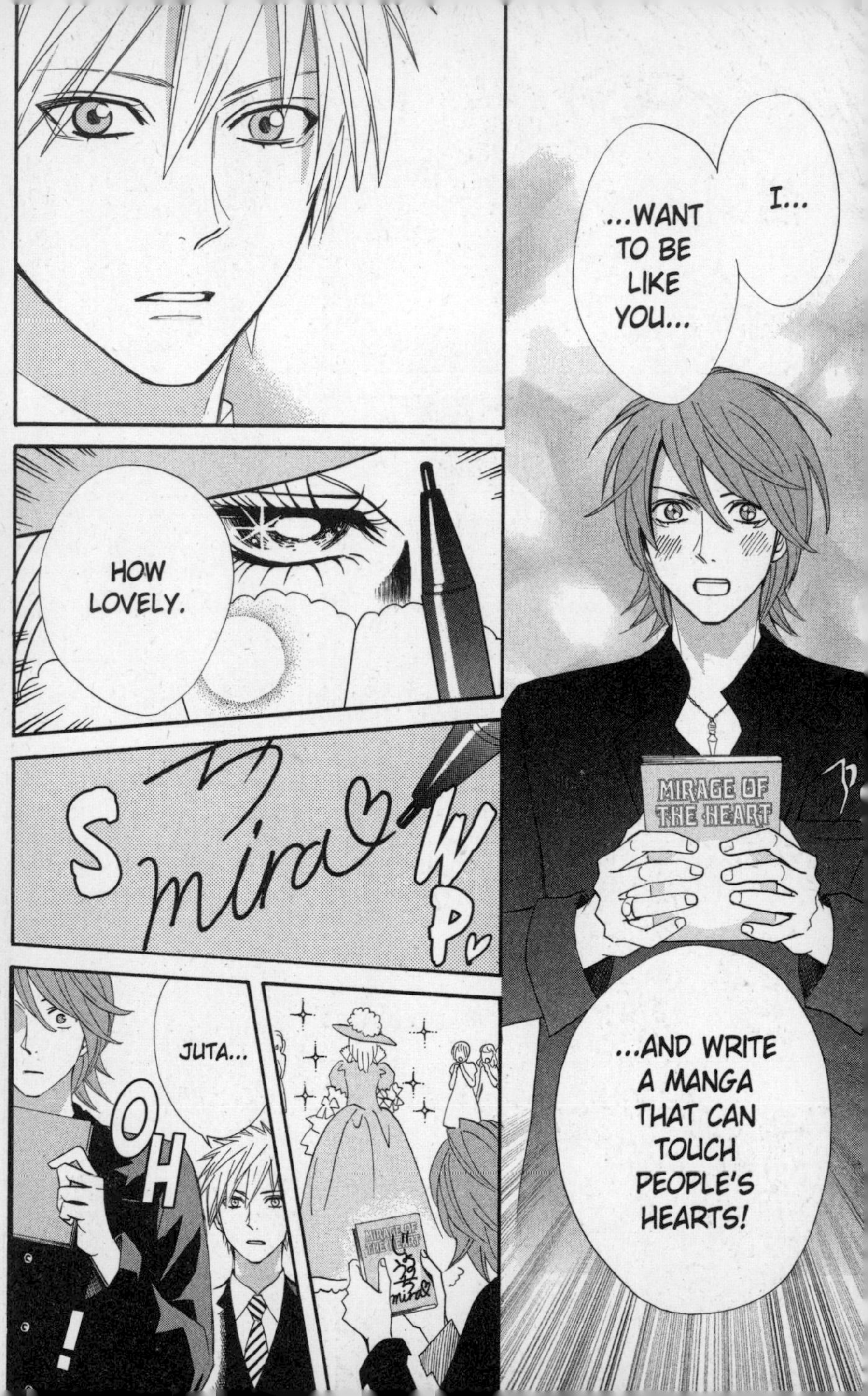
I...
...WANT TO BE LIKE YOU...
MIRAGE OF THE HEART
...AND WRITE A MANGA THAT CAN TOUCH PEOPLE'S HEARTS!
HOW LOVELY.
mira♡
SWP♡
MIRAGE OF THE HEART
JUTA...
OH!

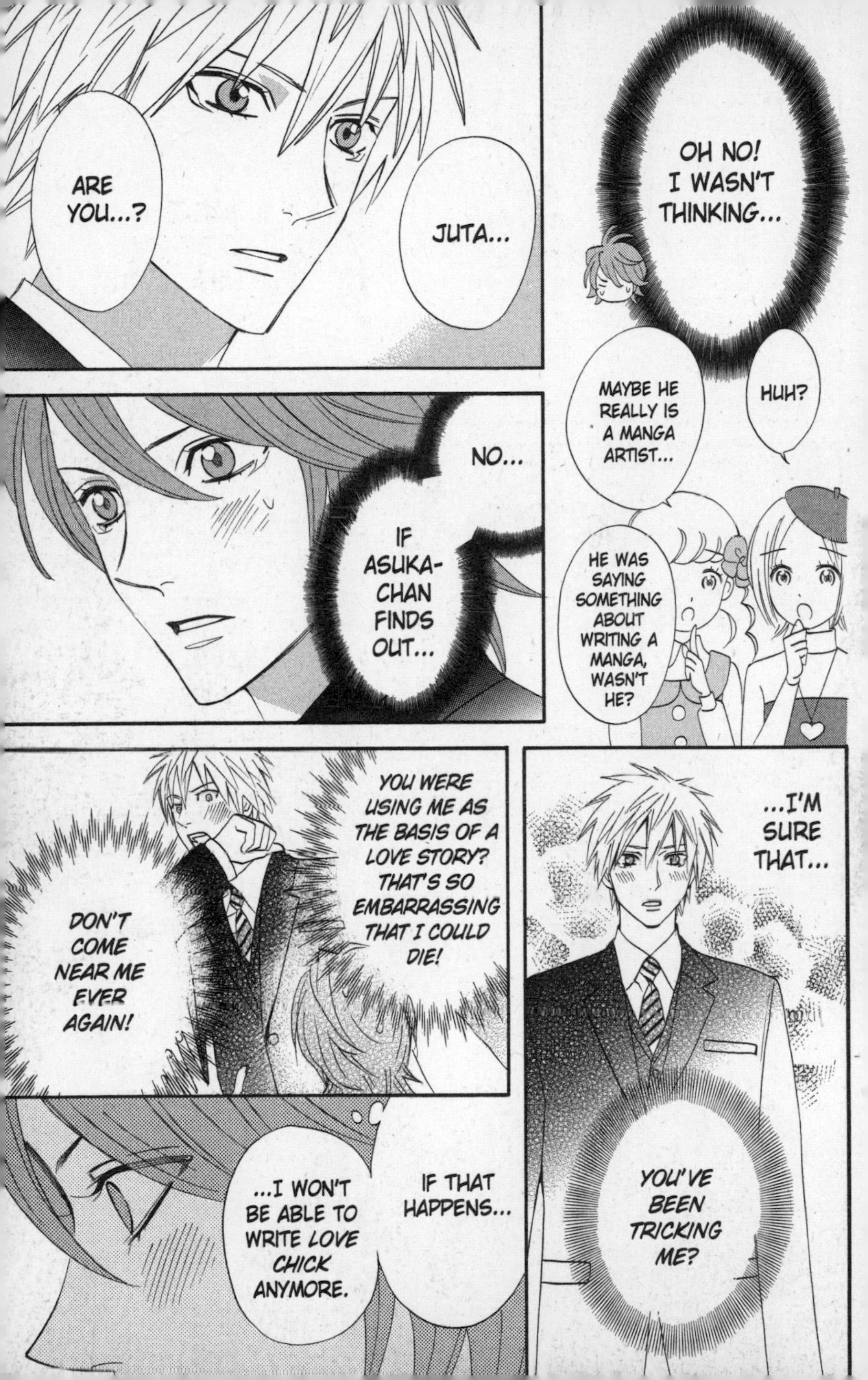
OH NO! I WASN'T THINKING...
HUH?
MAYBE HE REALLY IS A MANGA ARTIST...
HE WAS SAYING SOMETHING ABOUT WRITING A MANGA, WASN'T HE?
JUTA...
ARE YOU...?
NO...
IF ASUKA-CHAN FINDS OUT...
...I'M SURE THAT...
YOU'VE BEEN TRICKING ME?
YOU WERE USING ME AS THE BASIS OF A LOVE STORY? THAT'S SO EMBARRASSING THAT I COULD DIE!
DON'T COME NEAR ME EVER AGAIN!
IF THAT HAPPENS...
...I WON'T BE ABLE TO WRITE *LOVE CHICK* ANYMORE.

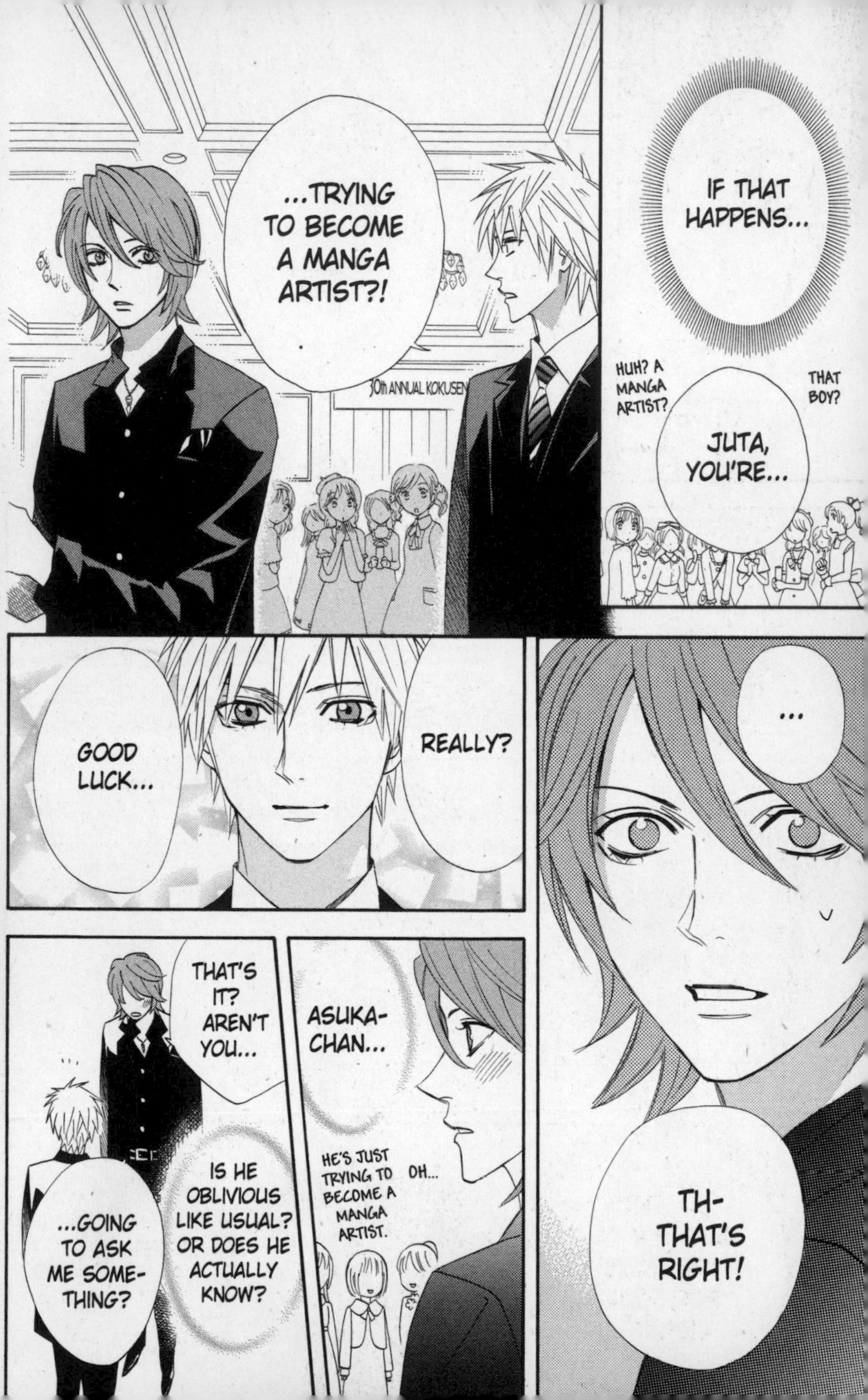
IF THAT HAPPENS...
THAT BOY?
HUH? A MANGA ARTIST?
JUTA, YOU'RE...
...TRYING TO BECOME A MANGA ARTIST?!
30th ANNUAL KOKUSEN
...
TH-THAT'S RIGHT!
REALLY?
GOOD LUCK...
ASUKA-CHAN...
OH...
HE'S JUST TRYING TO BECOME A MANGA ARTIST.
THAT'S IT? AREN'T YOU...
IS HE OBLIVIOUS LIKE USUAL? OR DOES HE ACTUALLY KNOW?
...
...GOING TO ASK ME SOMETHING?

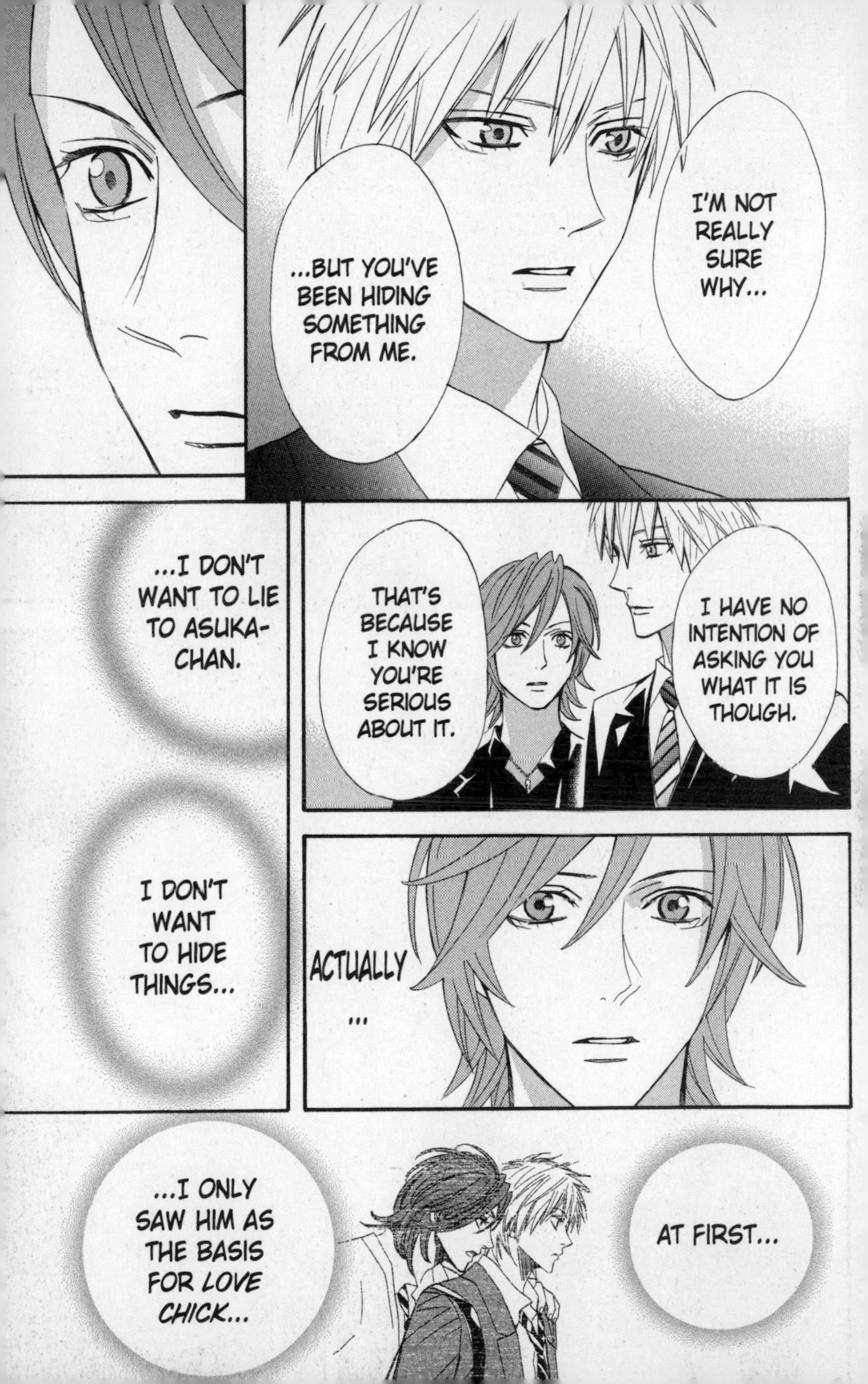
I'M NOT REALLY SURE WHY...
...BUT YOU'VE BEEN HIDING SOMETHING FROM ME.
I HAVE NO INTENTION OF ASKING YOU WHAT IT IS THOUGH.
THAT'S BECAUSE I KNOW YOU'RE SERIOUS ABOUT IT.
ACTUALLY...
...I DON'T WANT TO LIE TO ASUKA-CHAN.
I DON'T WANT TO HIDE THINGS...
AT FIRST...
...I ONLY SAW HIM AS THE BASIS FOR *LOVE CHICK*...

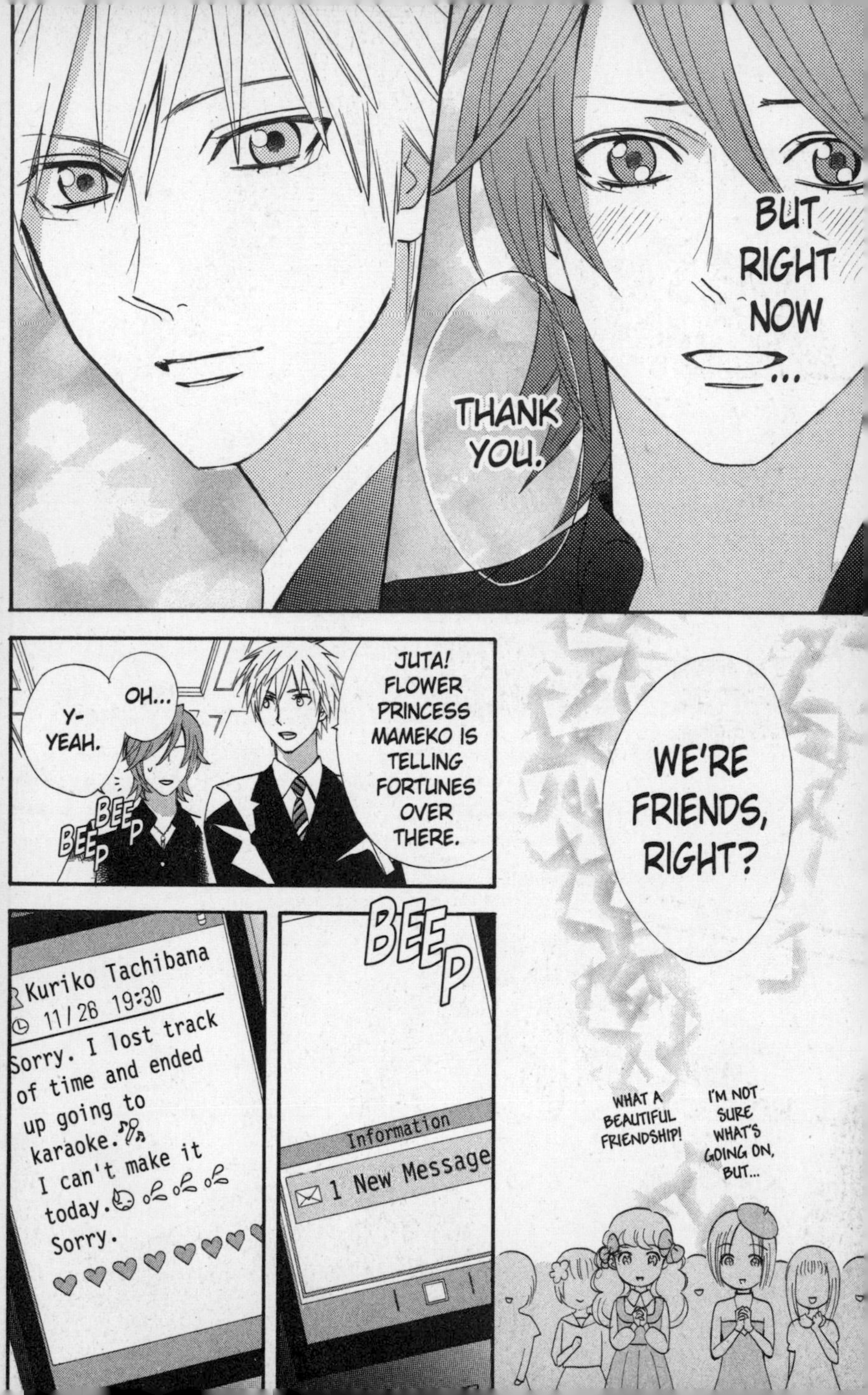
BUT RIGHT NOW...
THANK YOU.
WE'RE FRIENDS, RIGHT?
I'M NOT SURE WHAT'S GOING ON, BUT...
WHAT A BEAUTIFUL FRIENDSHIP!
JUTA! FLOWER PRINCESS MAMEKO IS TELLING FORTUNES OVER THERE.
OH...
Y-YEAH.
BEEP BEEP
BEEP
Information
1 New Message
Kuriko Tachibana
11/26 19:30
Sorry. I lost track of time and ended up going to karaoke.
I can't make it today.
Sorry.

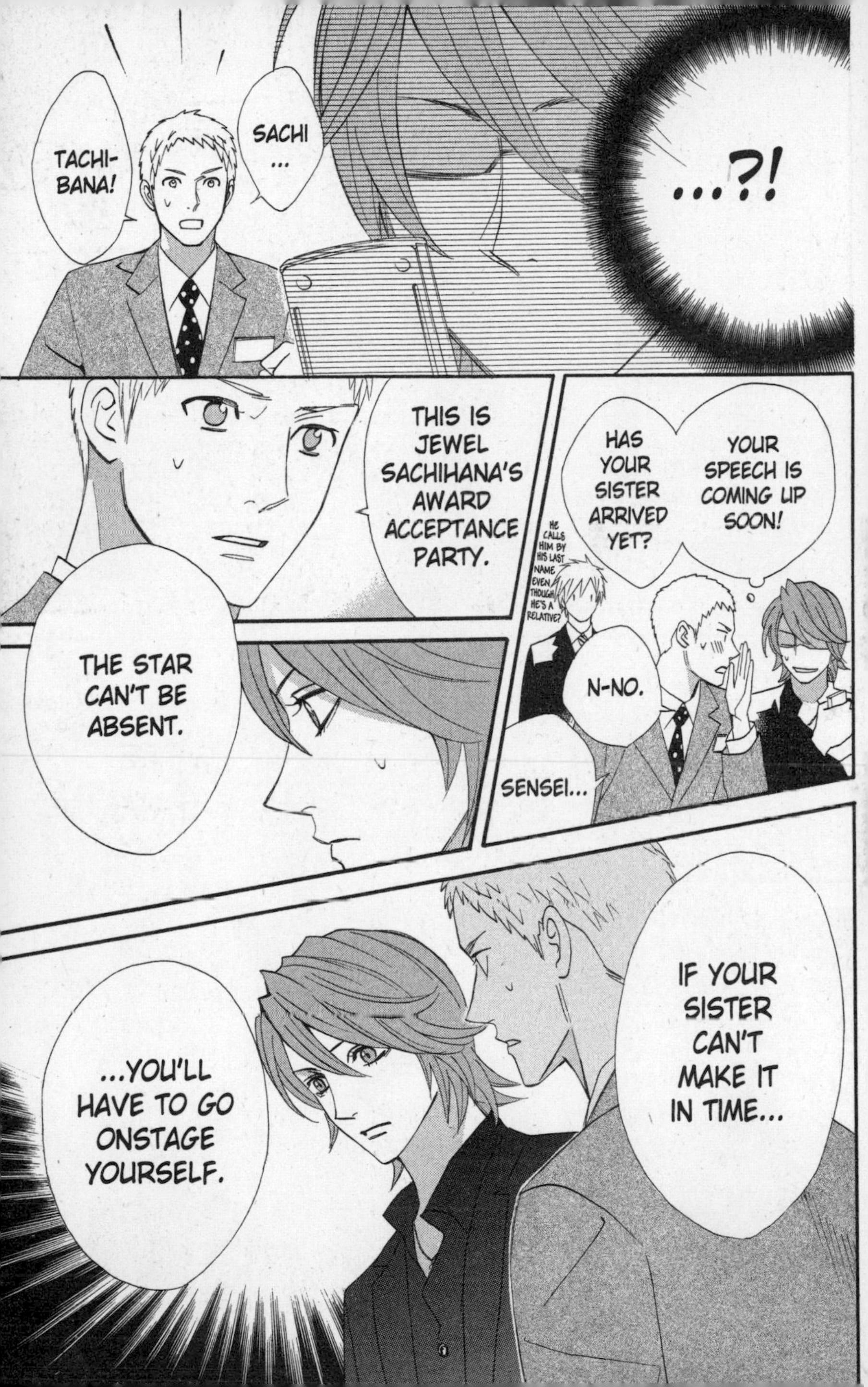
...?!
SACHI ...
TACHI-BANA!
YOUR SPEECH IS COMING UP SOON!
HAS YOUR SISTER ARRIVED YET?
HE CALLS HIM BY HIS LAST NAME EVEN THOUGH HE'S A RELATIVE?
N-NO.
SENSEI...
THIS IS JEWEL SACHIHANA'S AWARD ACCEPTANCE PARTY.
THE STAR CAN'T BE ABSENT.
IF YOUR SISTER CAN'T MAKE IT IN TIME...
...YOU'LL HAVE TO GO ONSTAGE YOURSELF.

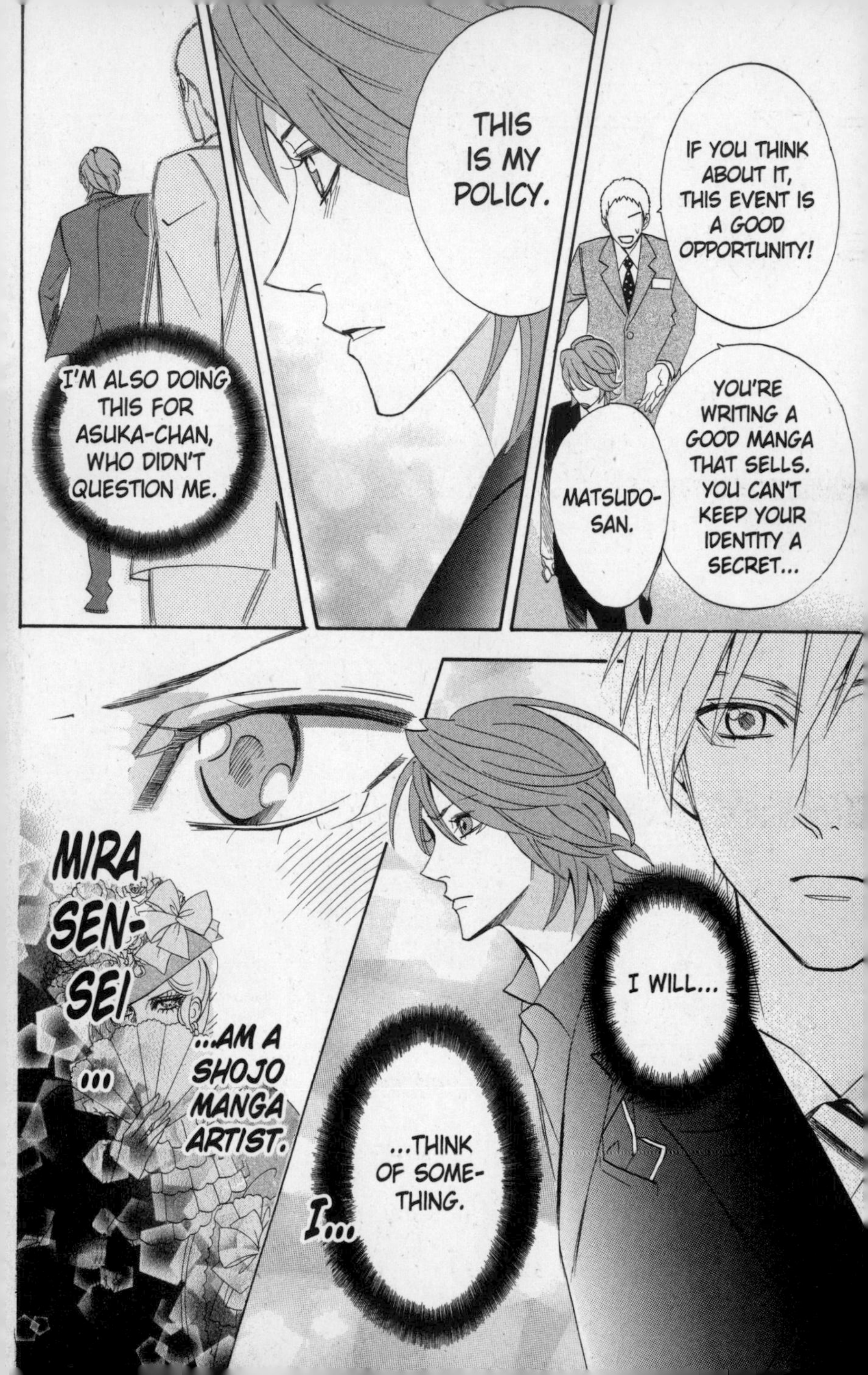
IF YOU THINK ABOUT IT, THIS EVENT IS A GOOD OPPORTUNITY!
YOU'RE WRITING A GOOD MANGA THAT SELLS. YOU CAN'T KEEP YOUR IDENTITY A SECRET...
MATSUDO-SAN.
THIS IS MY POLICY.
I'M ALSO DOING THIS FOR ASUKA-CHAN, WHO DIDN'T QUESTION ME.
I WILL...
...THINK OF SOME-THING.
I...
MIRA SEN-SEI...
...AM A SHOJO MANGA ARTIST.

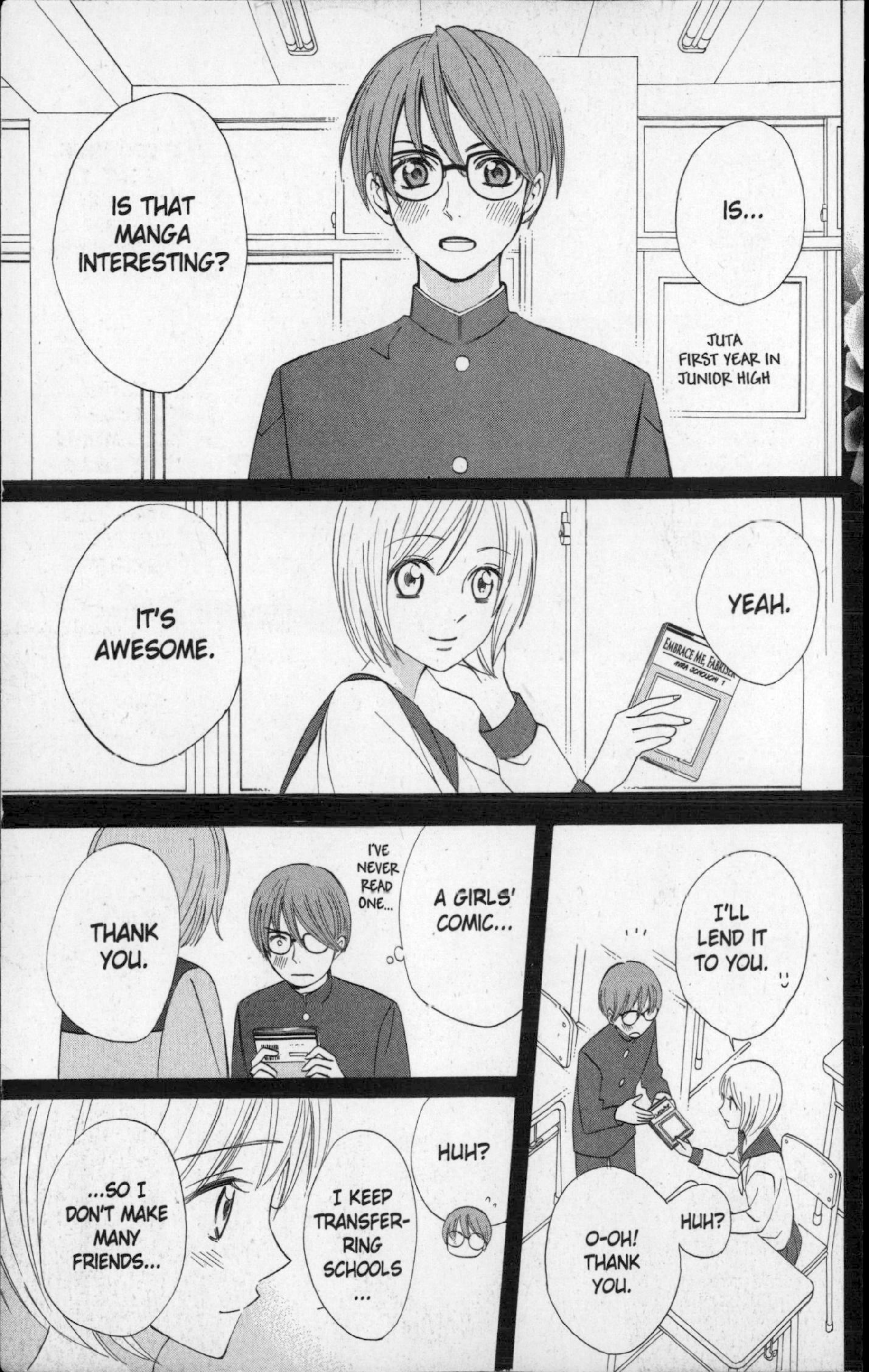
IS...
IS THAT MANGA INTERESTING?
JUTA FIRST YEAR IN JUNIOR HIGH
YEAH.
IT'S AWESOME.
I'LL LEND IT TO YOU.
HUH?
O-OH! THANK YOU.
A GIRLS' COMIC...
I'VE NEVER READ ONE...
THANK YOU.
HUH?
I KEEP TRANSFER-RING SCHOOLS ...
...SO I DON'T MAKE MANY FRIENDS...

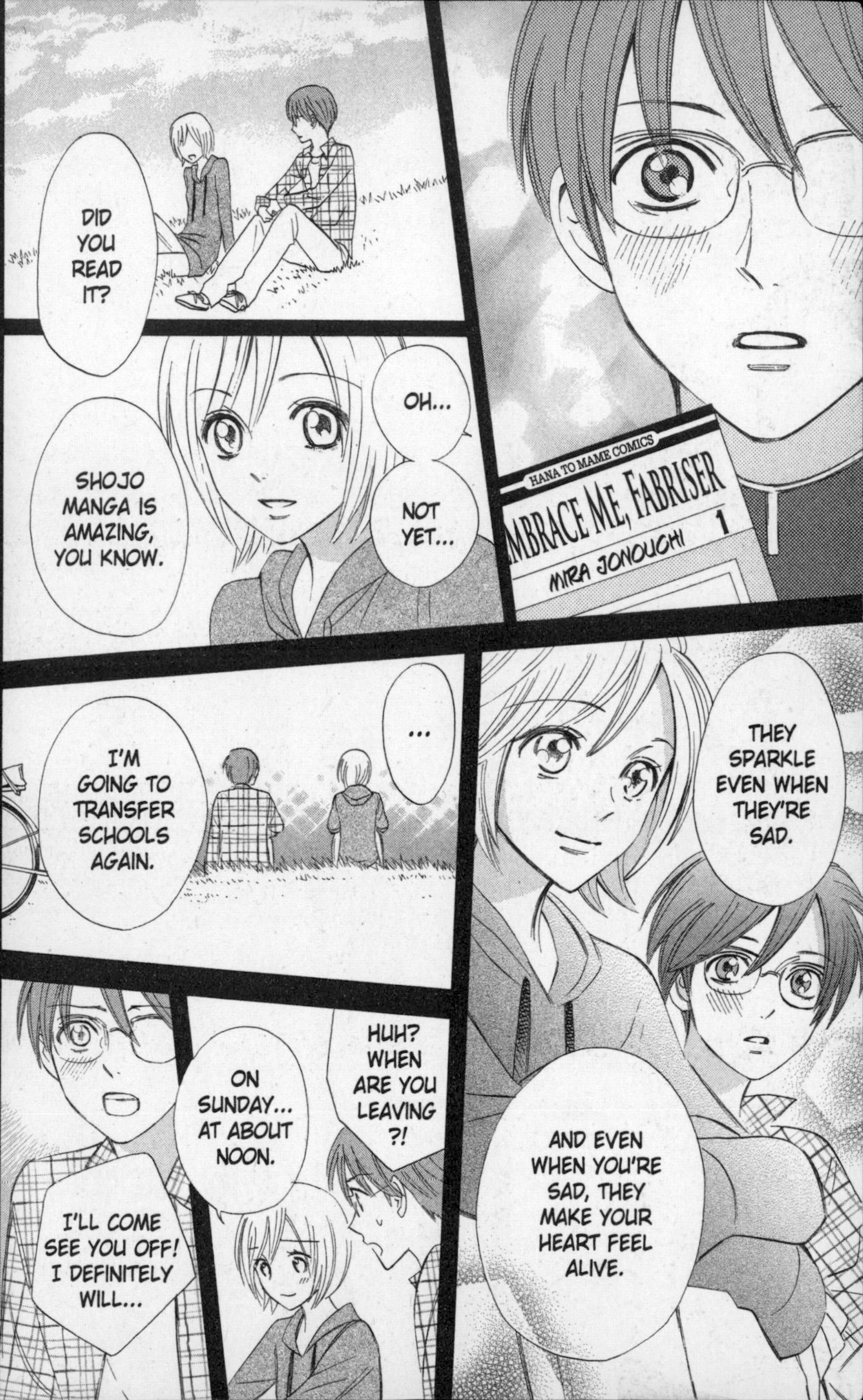
HANA TO MAME COMICS
MBRACE ME, FABRISER
1
MIRA JONOUCHI
DID YOU READ IT?
OH...
NOT YET...
SHOJO MANGA IS AMAZING, YOU KNOW.
THEY SPARKLE EVEN WHEN THEY'RE SAD.
AND EVEN WHEN YOU'RE SAD, THEY MAKE YOUR HEART FEEL ALIVE.
...
I'M GOING TO TRANSFER SCHOOLS AGAIN.
HUH? WHEN ARE YOU LEAVING ?!
ON SUNDAY... AT ABOUT NOON.
I'LL COME SEE YOU OFF! I DEFINITELY WILL...

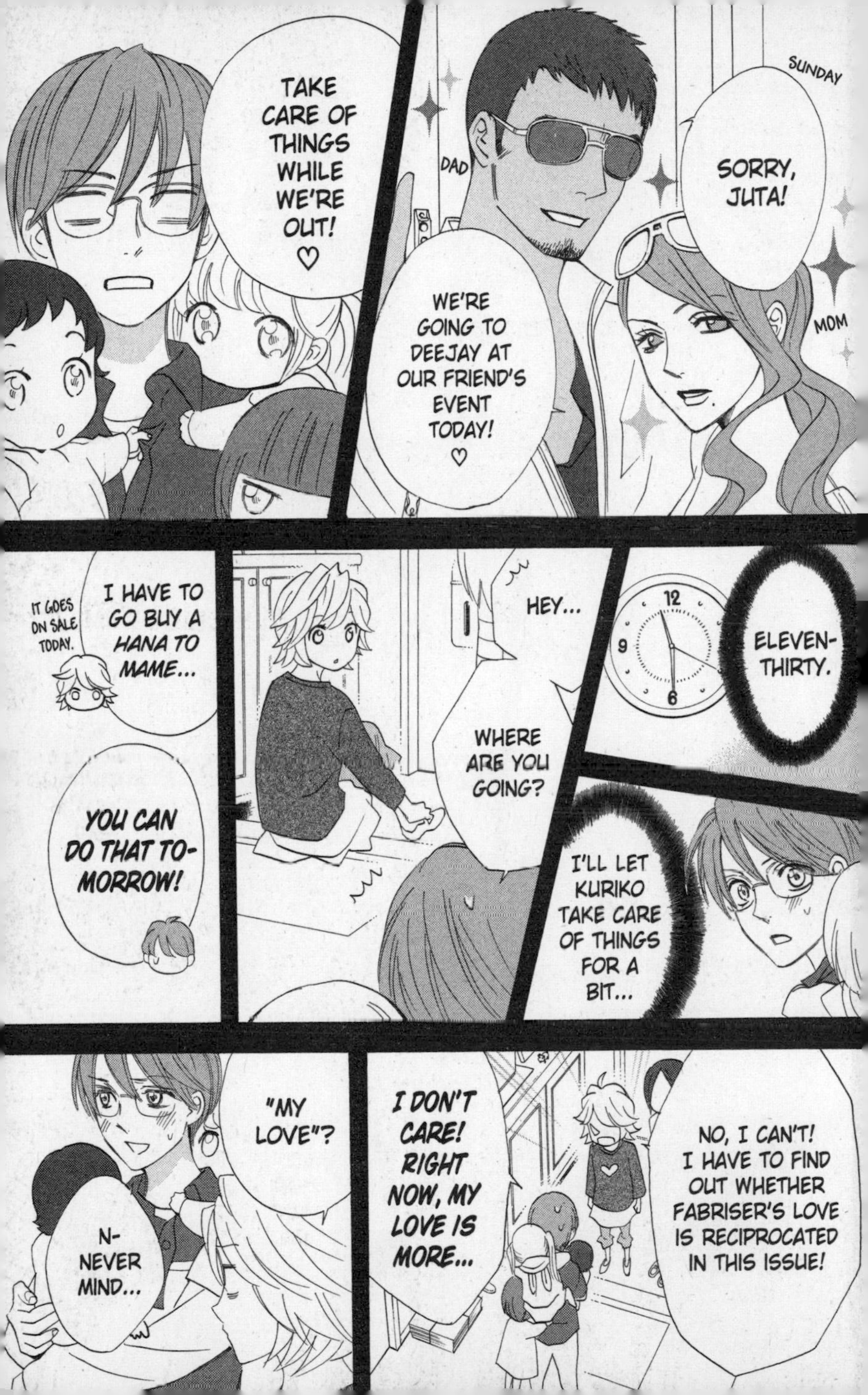
SUNDAY
SORRY, JUTA!
MOM
DAD
WE'RE GOING TO DEEJAY AT OUR FRIEND'S EVENT TODAY! ♡
TAKE CARE OF THINGS WHILE WE'RE OUT! ♡
ELEVEN-THIRTY.
I'LL LET KURIKO TAKE CARE OF THINGS FOR A BIT...
HEY...
WHERE ARE YOU GOING?
I HAVE TO GO BUY A *HANA TO MAME*...
IT GOES ON SALE TODAY.
YOU CAN DO THAT TO-MORROW!
NO, I CAN'T! I HAVE TO FIND OUT WHETHER FABRISER'S LOVE IS RECIPROCATED IN THIS ISSUE!
I DON'T CARE! RIGHT NOW, MY LOVE IS MORE...
"MY LOVE"?
N-NEVER MIND...

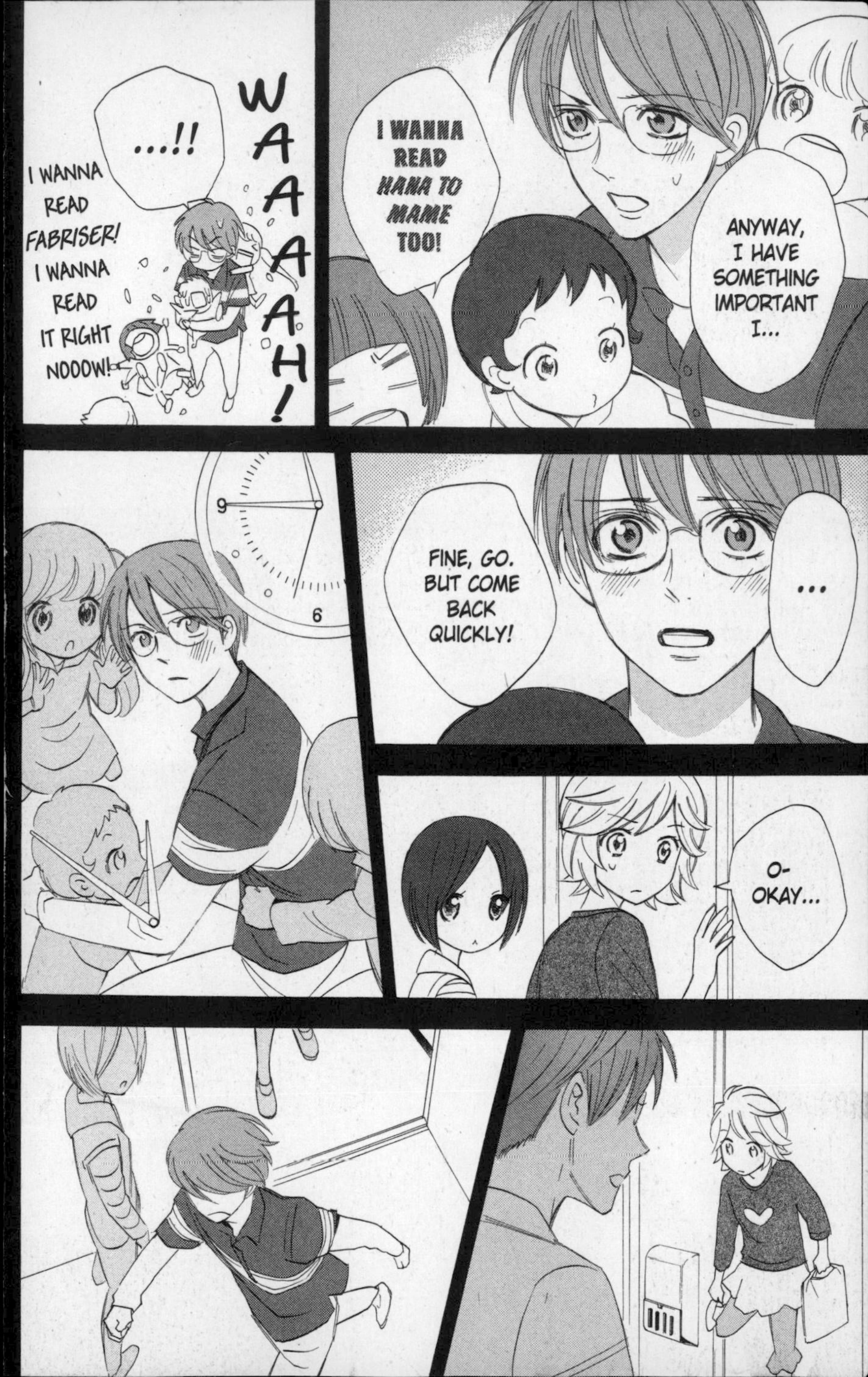
ANYWAY, I HAVE SOMETHING IMPORTANT I...
I WANNA READ HANA TO MAME TOO!
WAAAAH!
...!!
I WANNA READ FABRISER! I WANNA READ IT RIGHT NOOOW!
...
FINE, GO. BUT COME BACK QUICKLY!
O-OKAY...

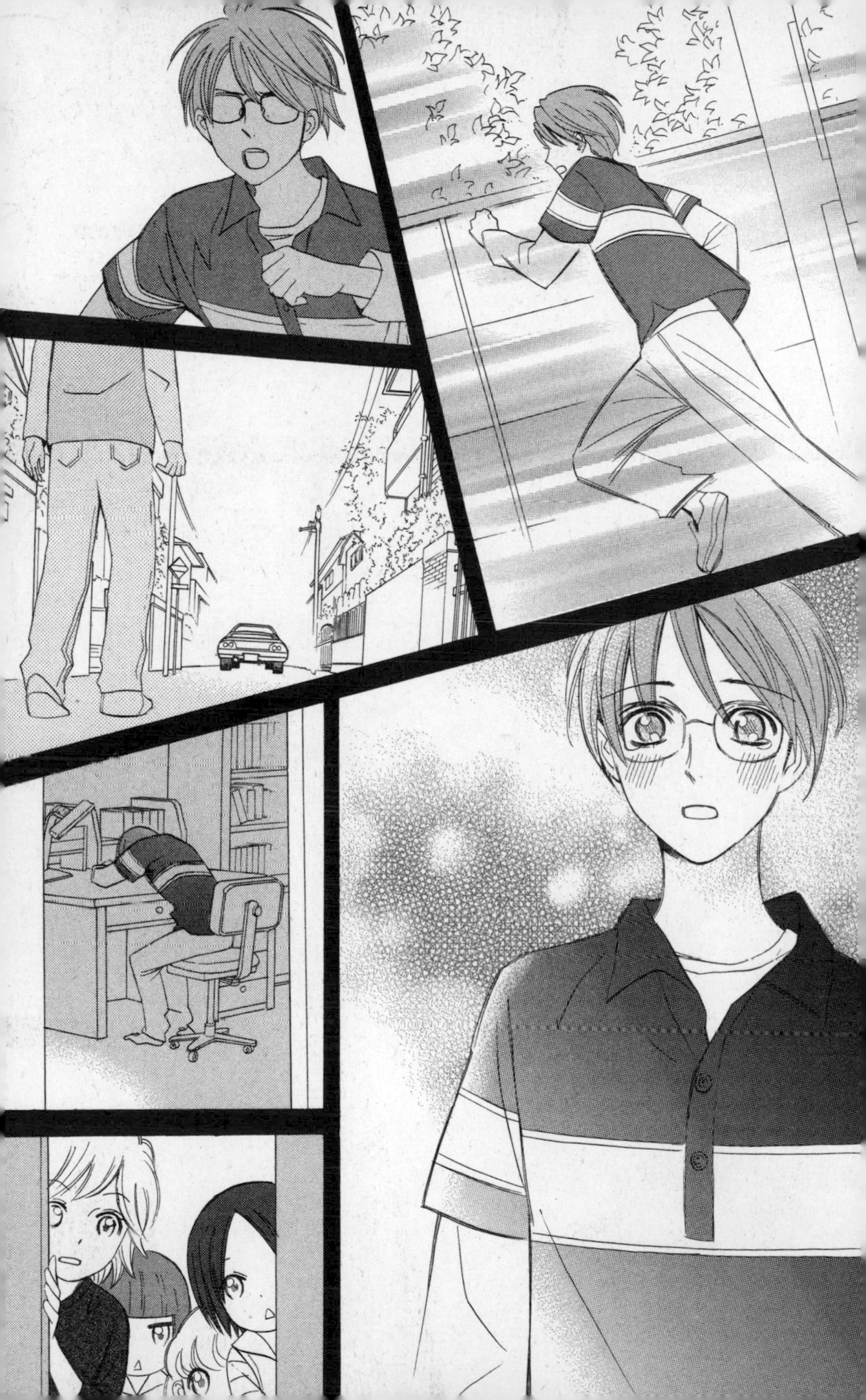

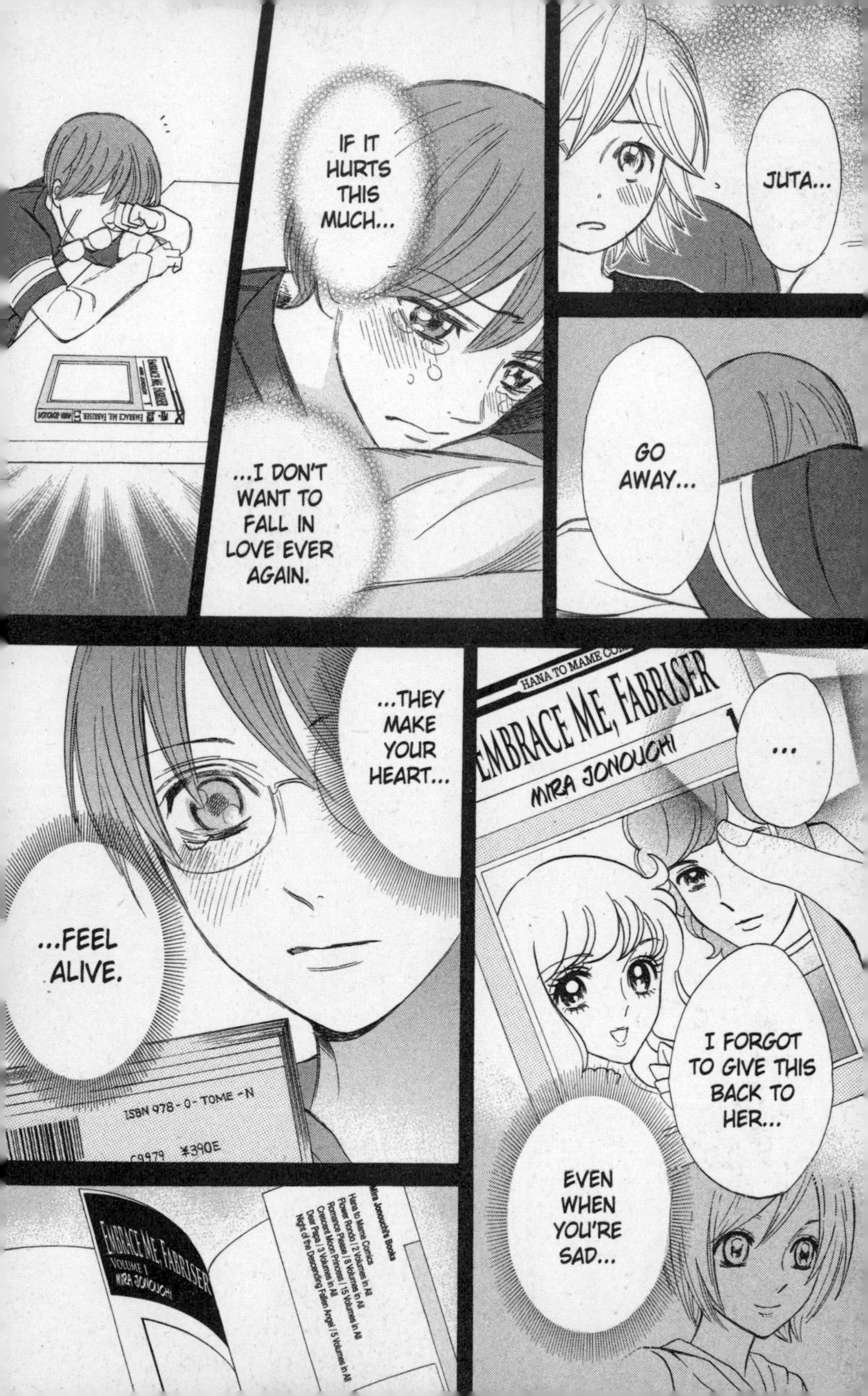
JUTA...
GO AWAY...
IF IT HURTS THIS MUCH...
...I DON'T WANT TO FALL IN LOVE EVER AGAIN.
EMBRACE ME, FABRISER
MIRA JONOUCHI
EMBRACE ME, FABRISER
MIRA JONOUCHI
...
I FORGOT TO GIVE THIS BACK TO HER...
EVEN WHEN YOU'RE SAD...
...THEY MAKE YOUR HEART...
...FEEL ALIVE.
ISBN 978-0-TOME-N
C9979 ¥390E
EMBRACE ME, FABRISER
VOLUME 1
MIRA JONOUCHI
Mira Jonouchi's Books
Hana to Mame Comics
Flower Rondo | 2 Volumes in All
Romance Please | 8 Volumes in All
Crescent Moon Princess | 15 Volumes in All
Dear Papa | 3 Volumes in All
Night of the Descending Fallen Angel | 5 Volumes in All

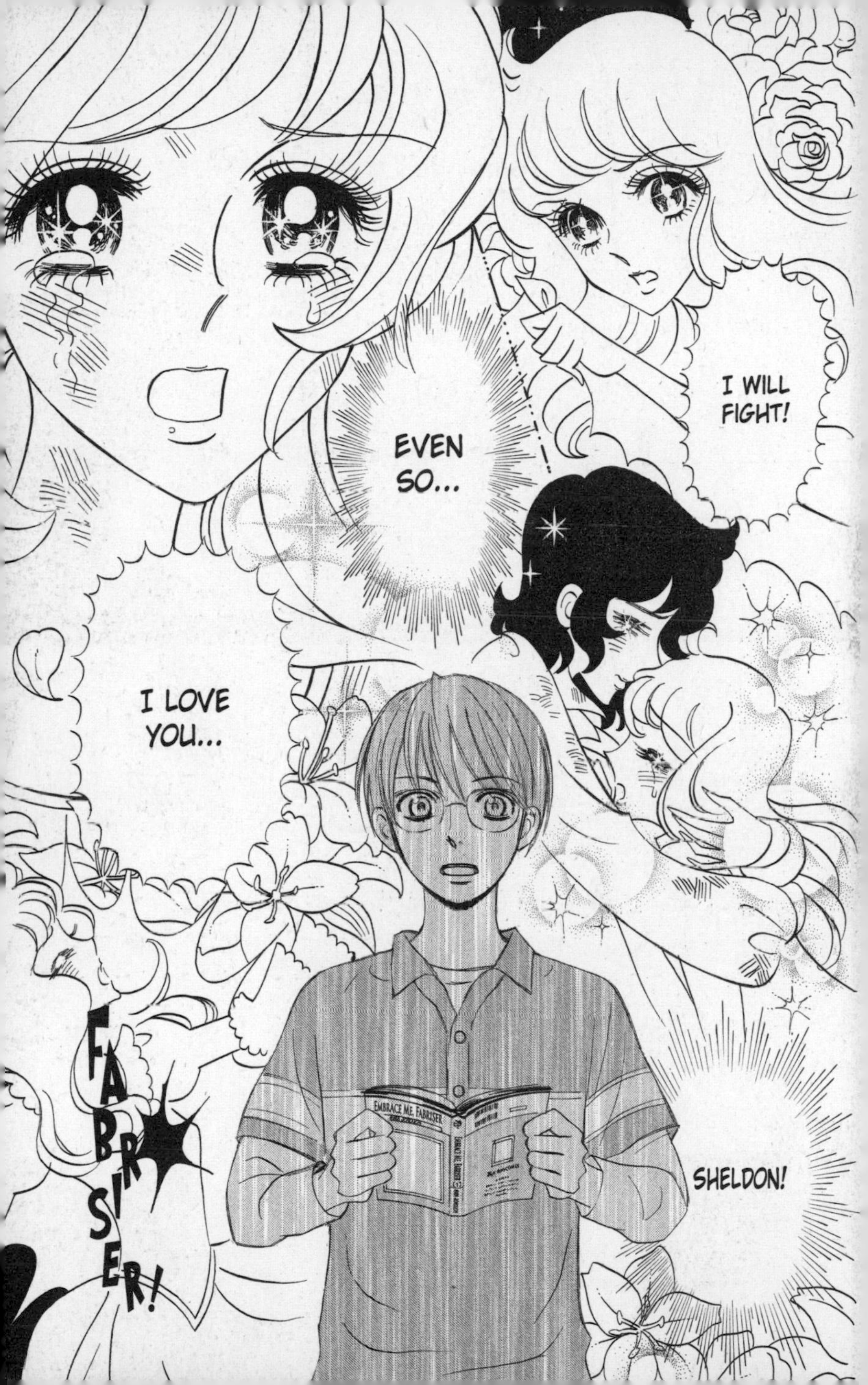
I WILL FIGHT!
EVEN SO...
I LOVE YOU...
EMBRACE ME, FABRISER
SHELDON!
FABRISER!

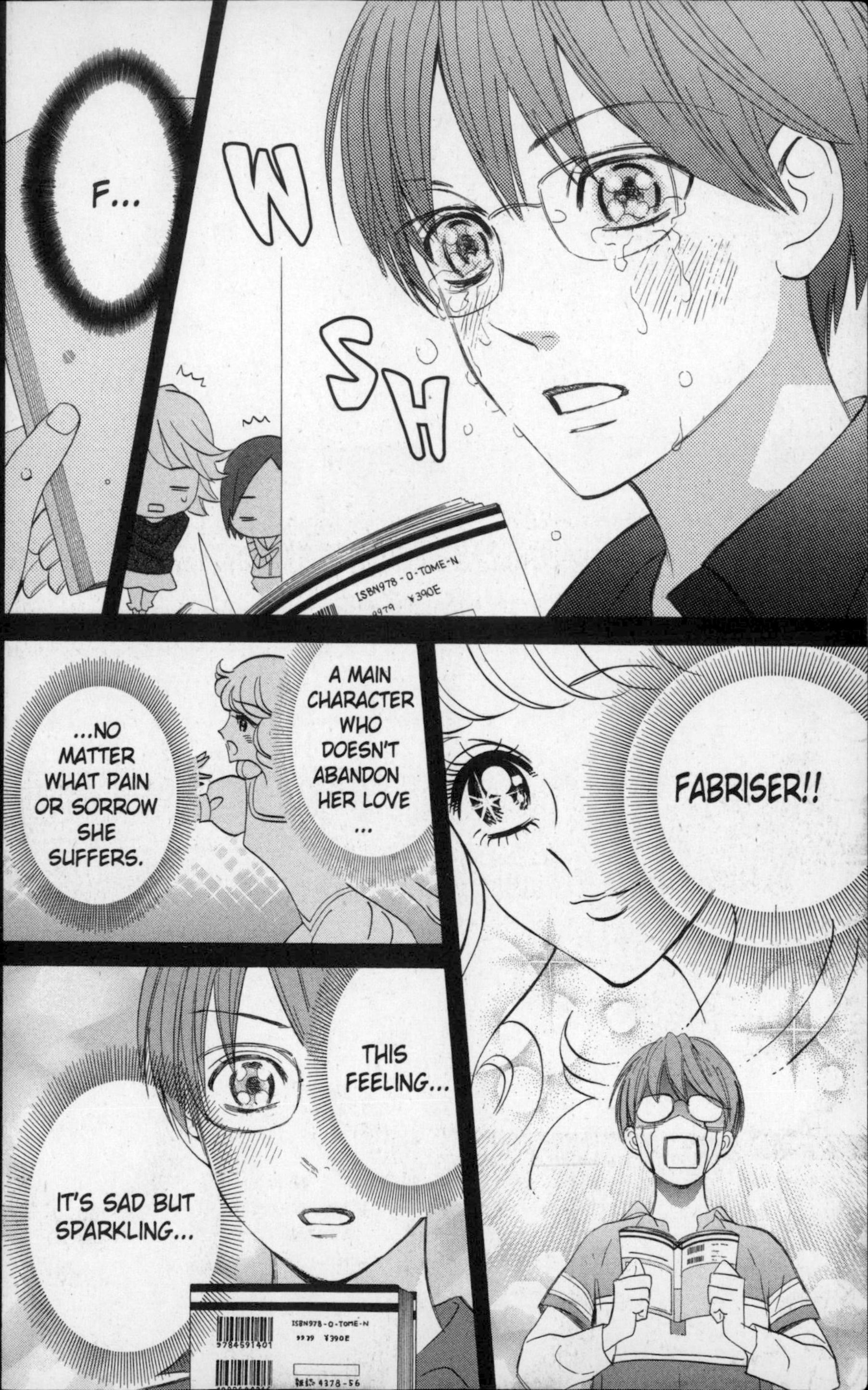

WSH
F...
ISBN978-O-TOME-N
¥390E
FABRISER!!
A MAIN CHARACTER WHO DOESN'T ABANDON HER LOVE ...
...NO MATTER WHAT PAIN OR SORROW SHE SUFFERS.
THIS FEELING...
IT'S SAD BUT SPARKLING...
ISBN978-O-TOME-N
¥390E

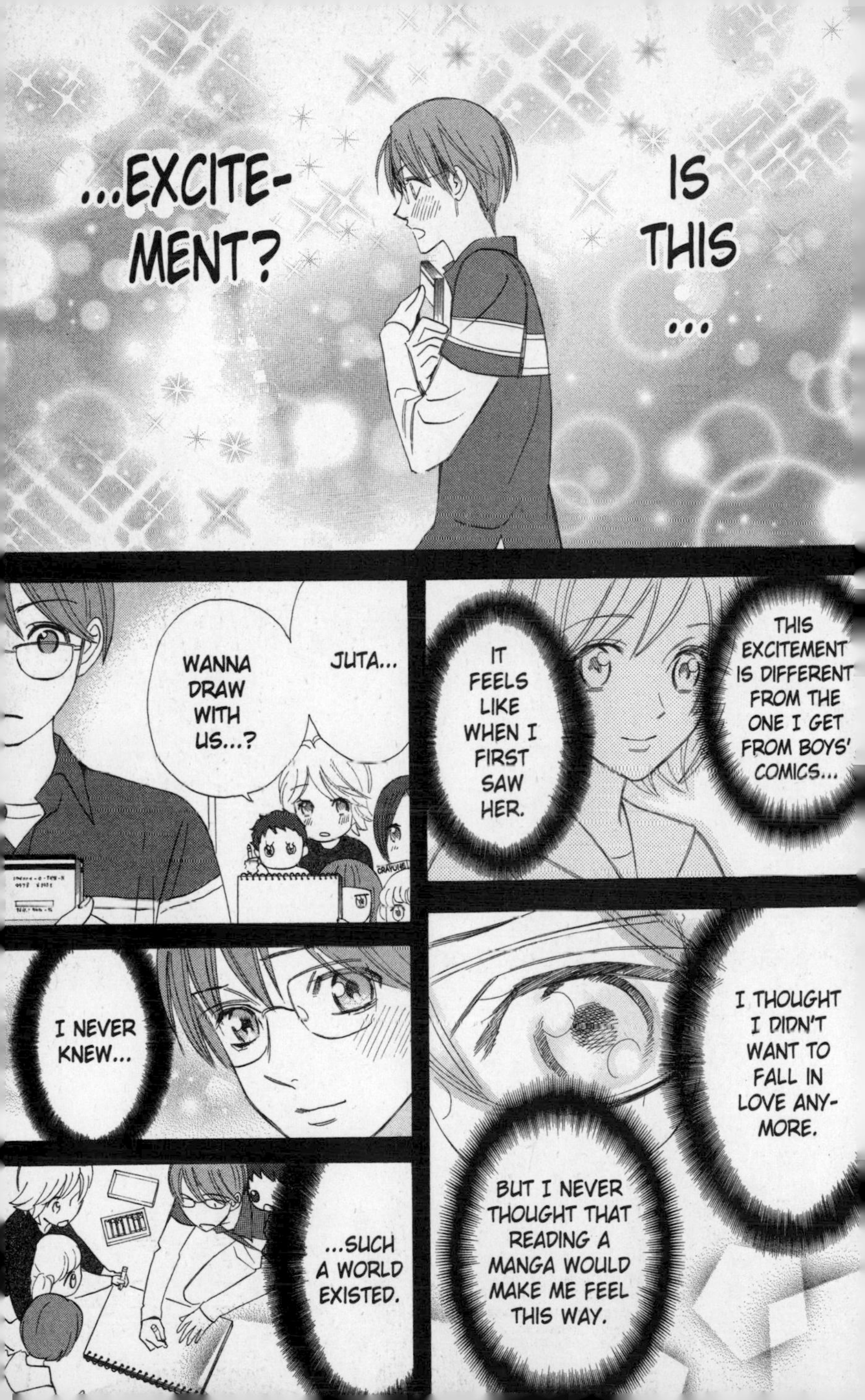
IS THIS ...
...EXCITE-MENT?
THIS EXCITEMENT IS DIFFERENT FROM THE ONE I GET FROM BOYS' COMICS...
IT FEELS LIKE WHEN I FIRST SAW HER.
JUTA...
WANNA DRAW WITH US...?
I THOUGHT I DIDN'T WANT TO FALL IN LOVE ANY-MORE.
BUT I NEVER THOUGHT THAT READING A MANGA WOULD MAKE ME FEEL THIS WAY.
I NEVER KNEW...
...SUCH A WORLD EXISTED.

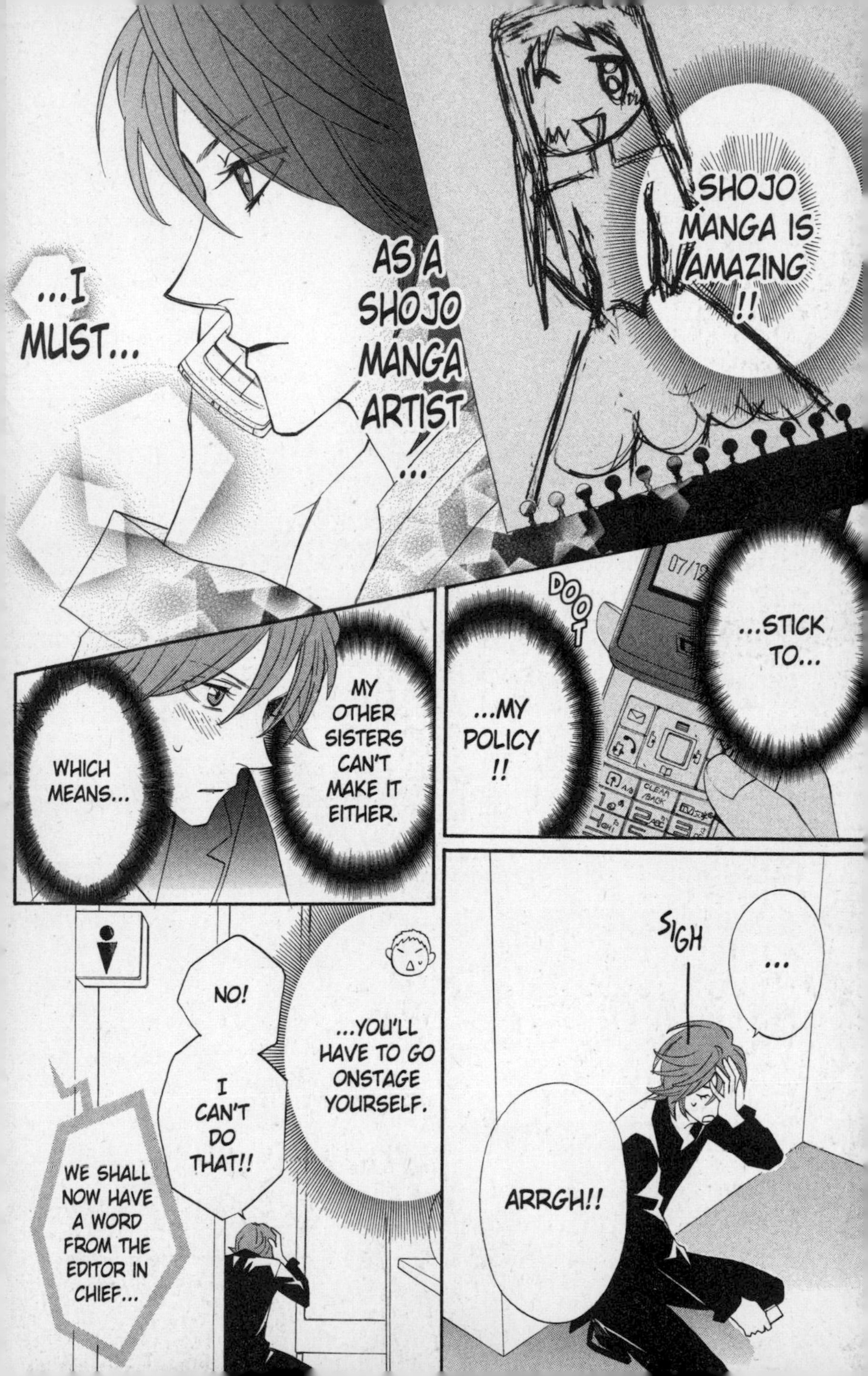
SHOJO MANGA IS AMAZING!!
AS A SHOJO MANGA ARTIST...
...I MUST...
...STICK TO...
DOOT
...MY POLICY!!
MY OTHER SISTERS CAN'T MAKE IT EITHER.
WHICH MEANS...
...
SIGH
ARRGH!!
...YOU'LL HAVE TO GO ONSTAGE YOURSELF.
NO!
I CAN'T DO THAT!!
WE SHALL NOW HAVE A WORD FROM THE EDITOR IN CHIEF...

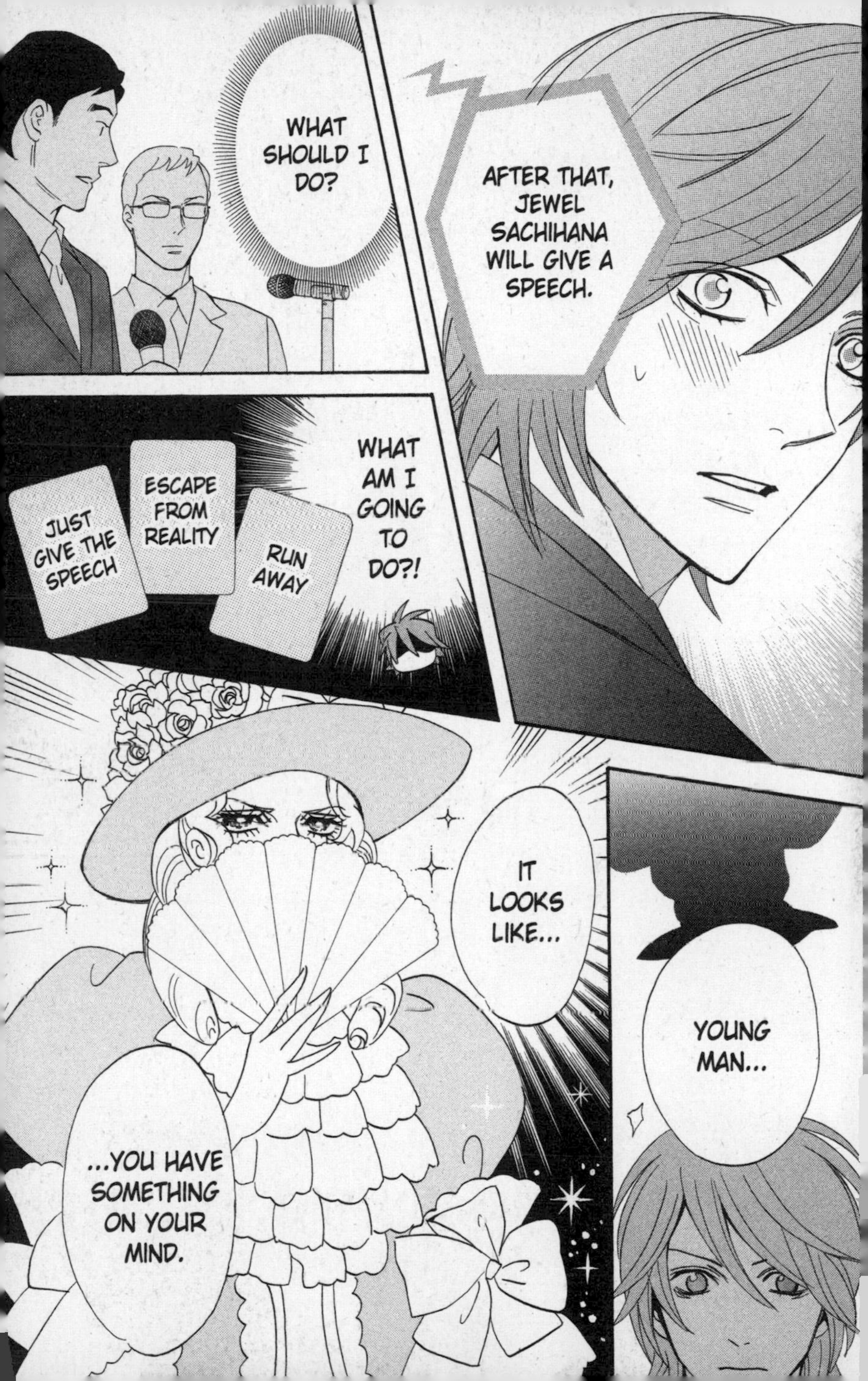
AFTER THAT, JEWEL SACHIHANA WILL GIVE A SPEECH.
WHAT SHOULD I DO?
WHAT AM I GOING TO DO?!
RUN AWAY
ESCAPE FROM REALITY
JUST GIVE THE SPEECH
YOUNG MAN...
IT LOOKS LIKE...
...YOU HAVE SOMETHING ON YOUR MIND.

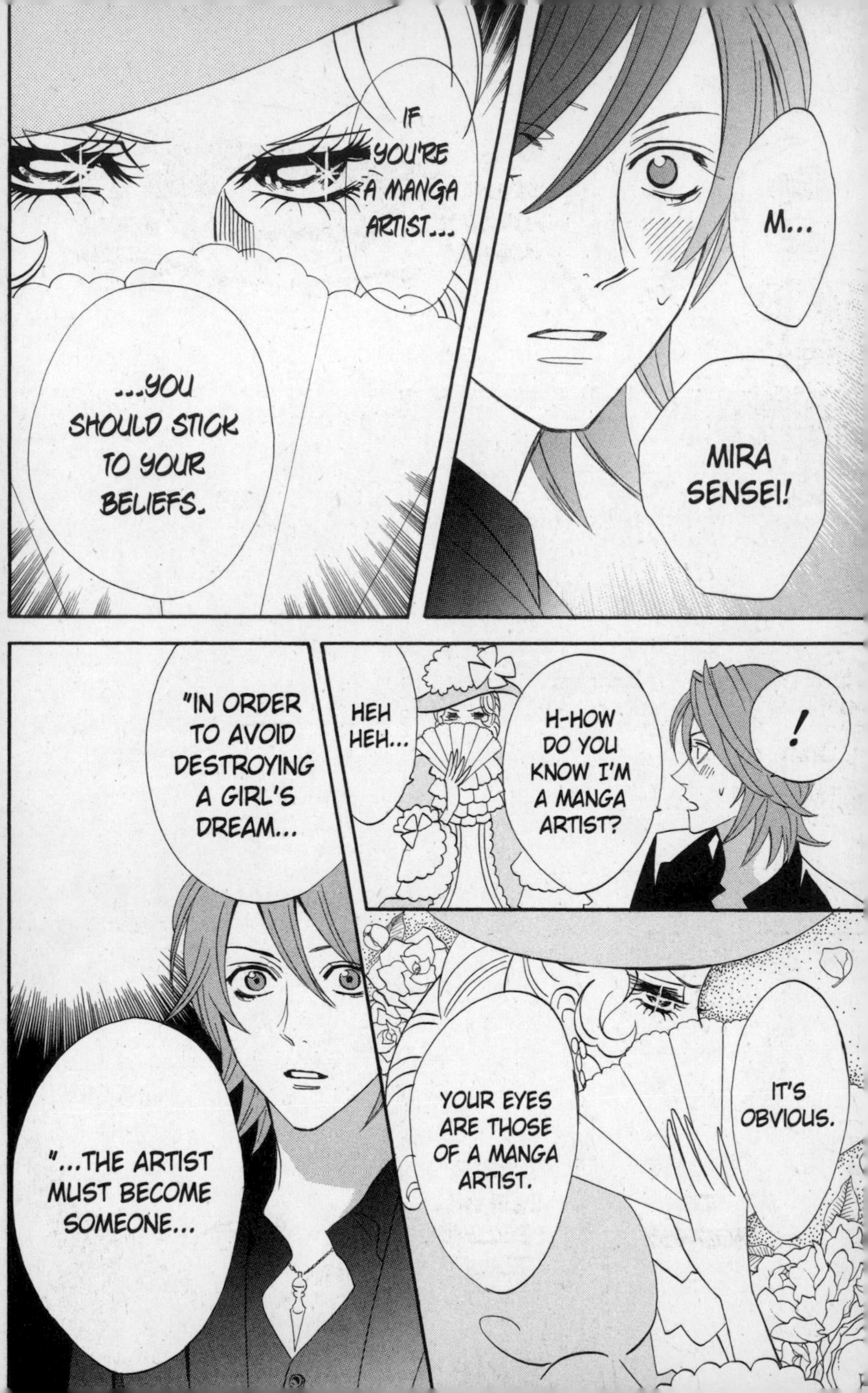
M...
MIRA SENSEI!
IF YOU'RE A MANGA ARTIST...
...YOU SHOULD STICK TO YOUR BELIEFS.
!
H-HOW DO YOU KNOW I'M A MANGA ARTIST?
HEH HEH...
IT'S OBVIOUS.
YOUR EYES ARE THOSE OF A MANGA ARTIST.
"IN ORDER TO AVOID DESTROYING A GIRL'S DREAM...
"...THE ARTIST MUST BECOME SOMEONE...

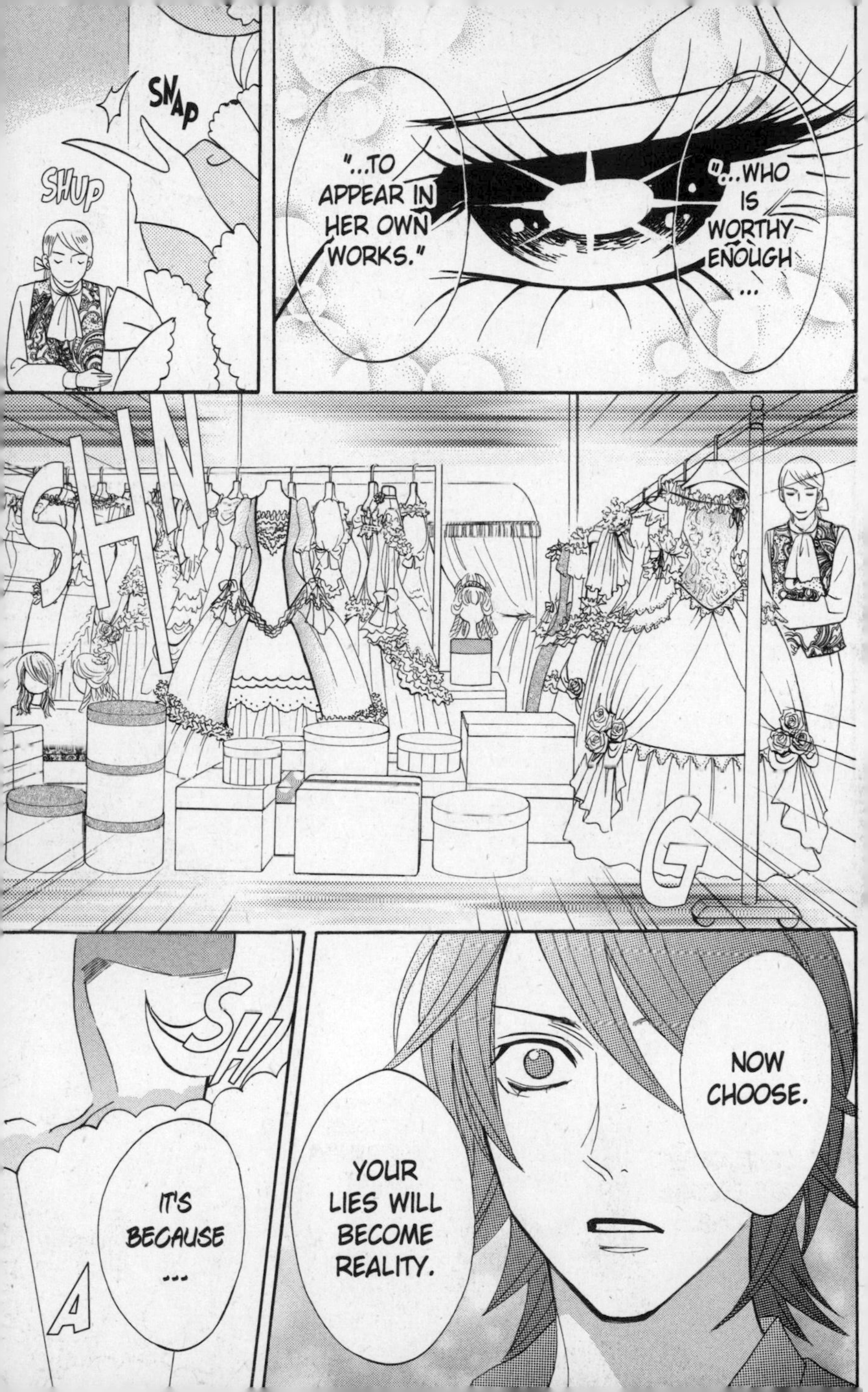
"...WHO IS WORTHY ENOUGH ...
"...TO APPEAR IN HER OWN WORKS."
SNAP
SHUP
SHIN
G
NOW CHOOSE.
YOUR LIES WILL BECOME REALITY.
SH
IT'S BECAUSE ...
A

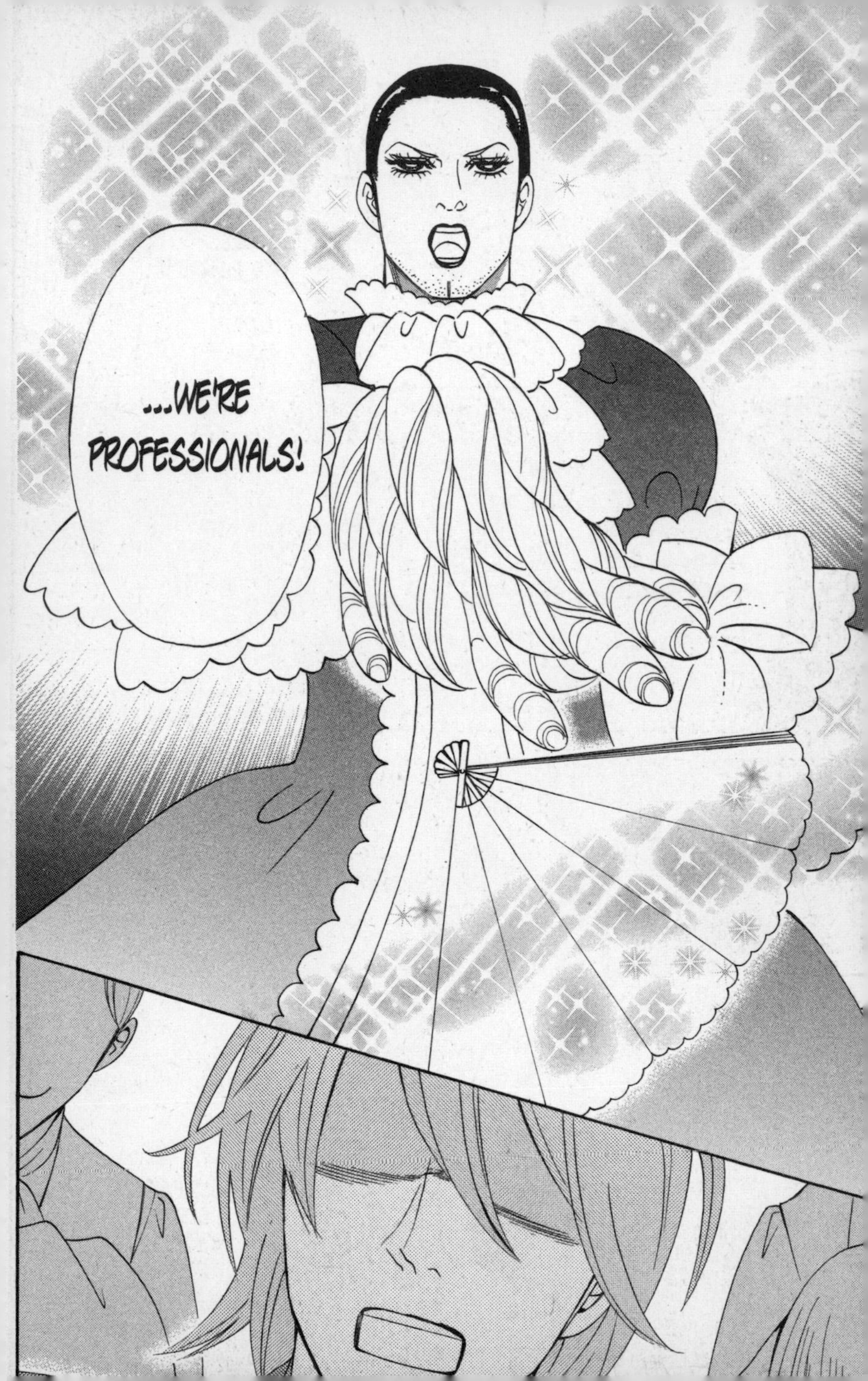
...WE'RE PROFESSIONALS!

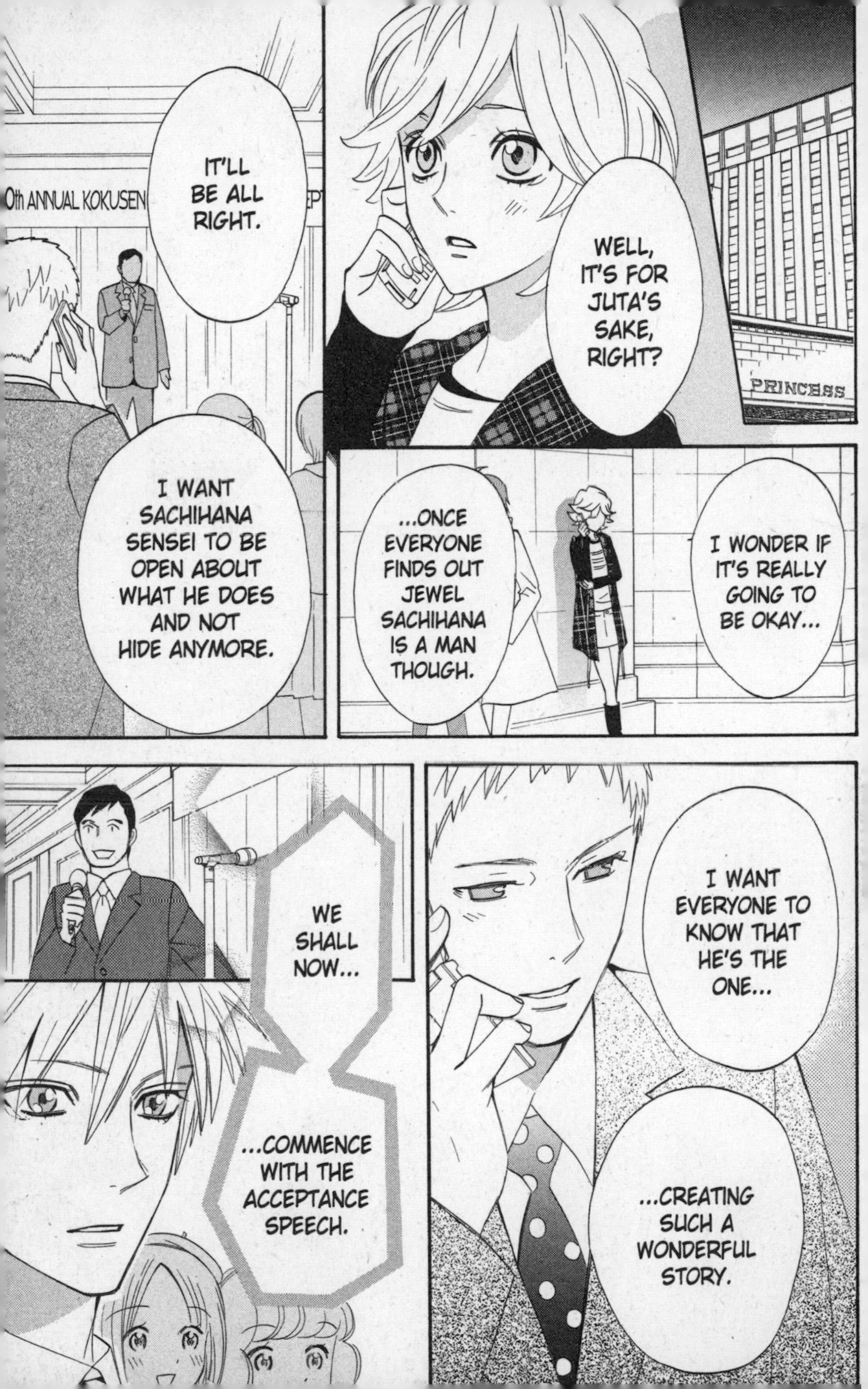

PRINCESS
WELL, IT'S FOR JUTA'S SAKE, RIGHT?
I WONDER IF IT'S REALLY GOING TO BE OKAY...
...ONCE EVERYONE FINDS OUT JEWEL SACHIHANA IS A MAN THOUGH.
0th ANNUAL KOKUSEN
IT'LL BE ALL RIGHT.
I WANT SACHIHANA SENSEI TO BE OPEN ABOUT WHAT HE DOES AND NOT HIDE ANYMORE.
I WANT EVERYONE TO KNOW THAT HE'S THE ONE...
...CREATING SUCH A WONDERFUL STORY.
WE SHALL NOW...
...COMMENCE WITH THE ACCEPTANCE SPEECH.

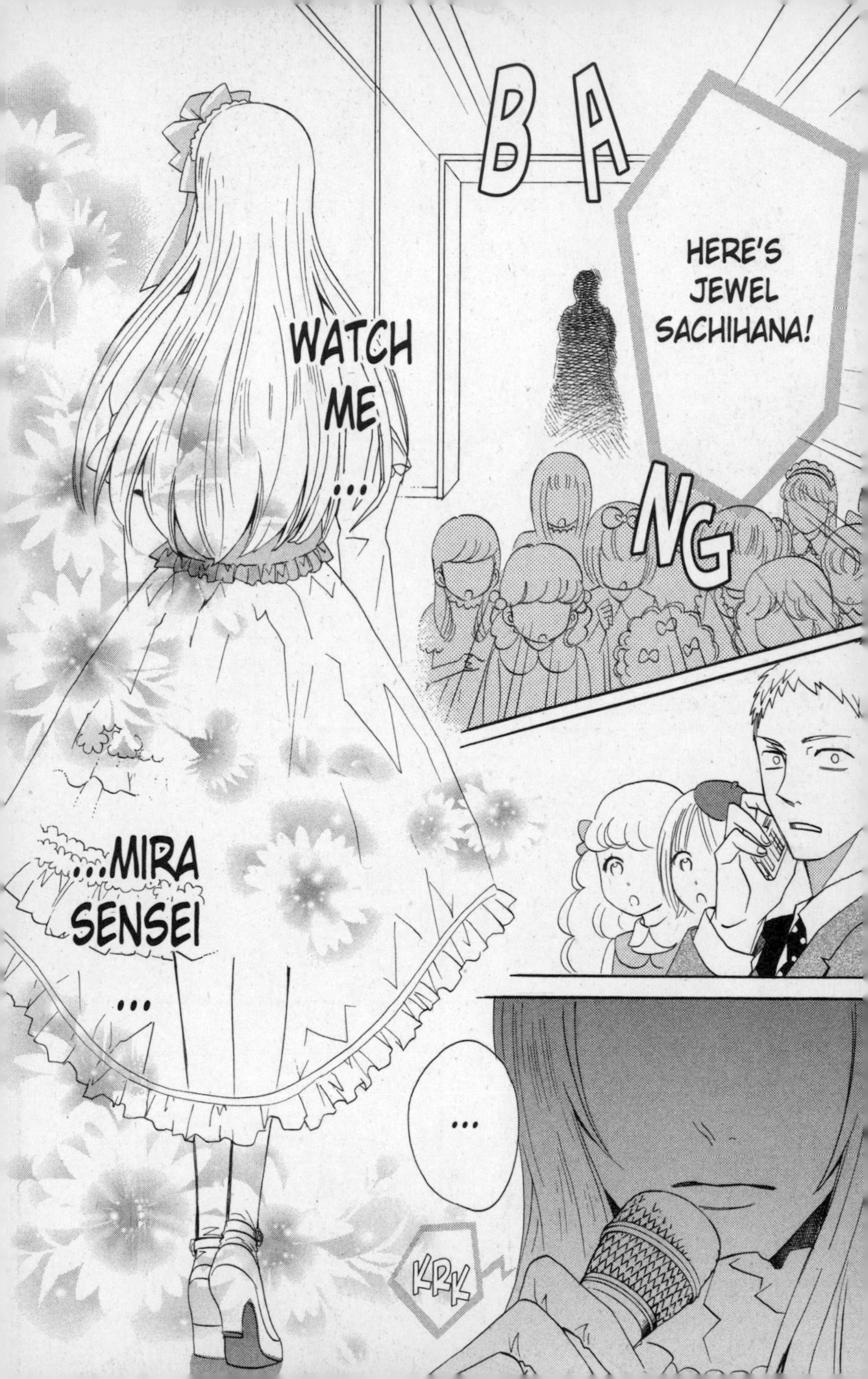
BA
NG
HERE'S JEWEL SACHIHANA!
...
KRK
WATCH ME ...
...MIRA SENSEI ...

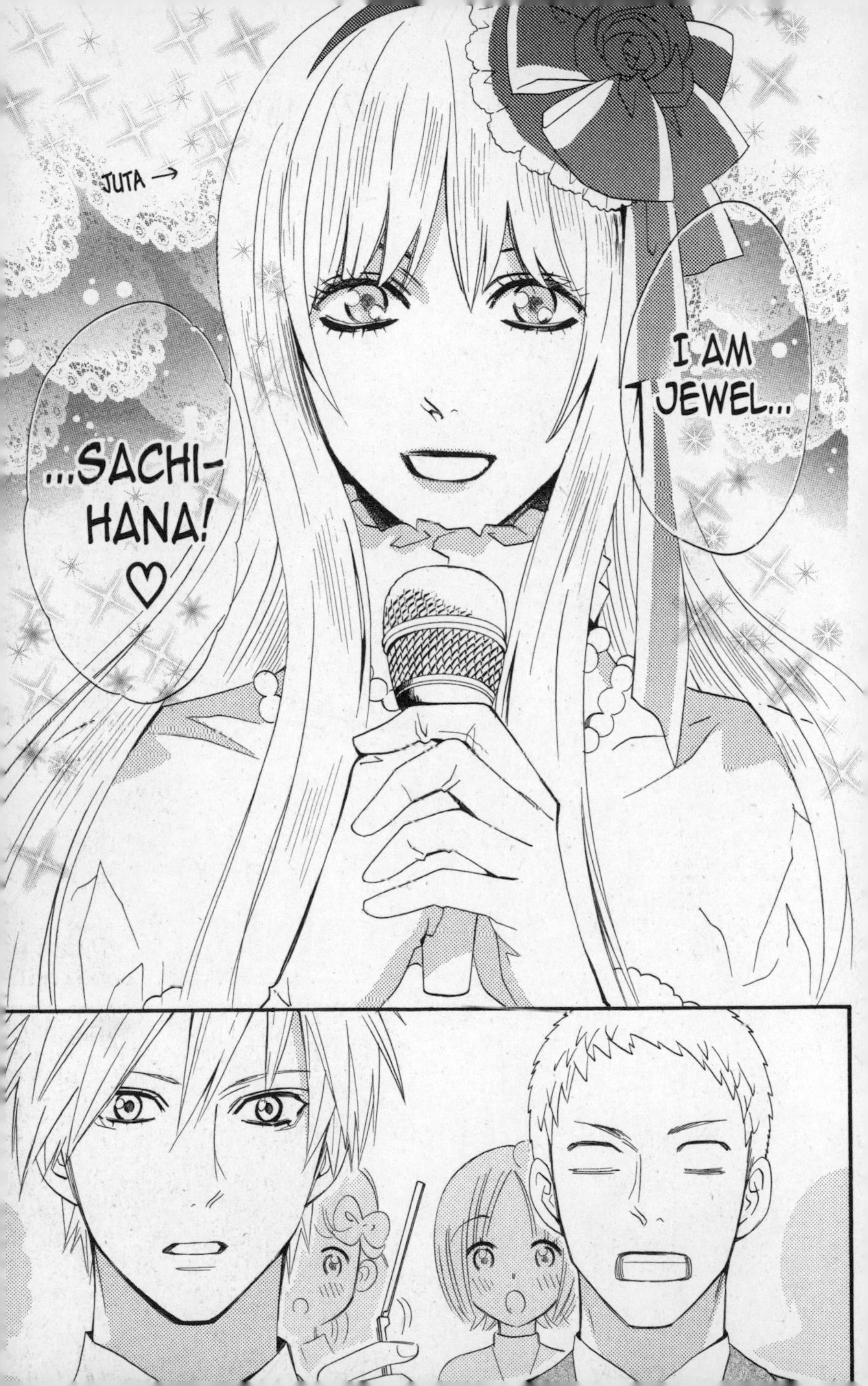
I AM JEWEL...
...SACHI-HANA! ♡
JUTA →

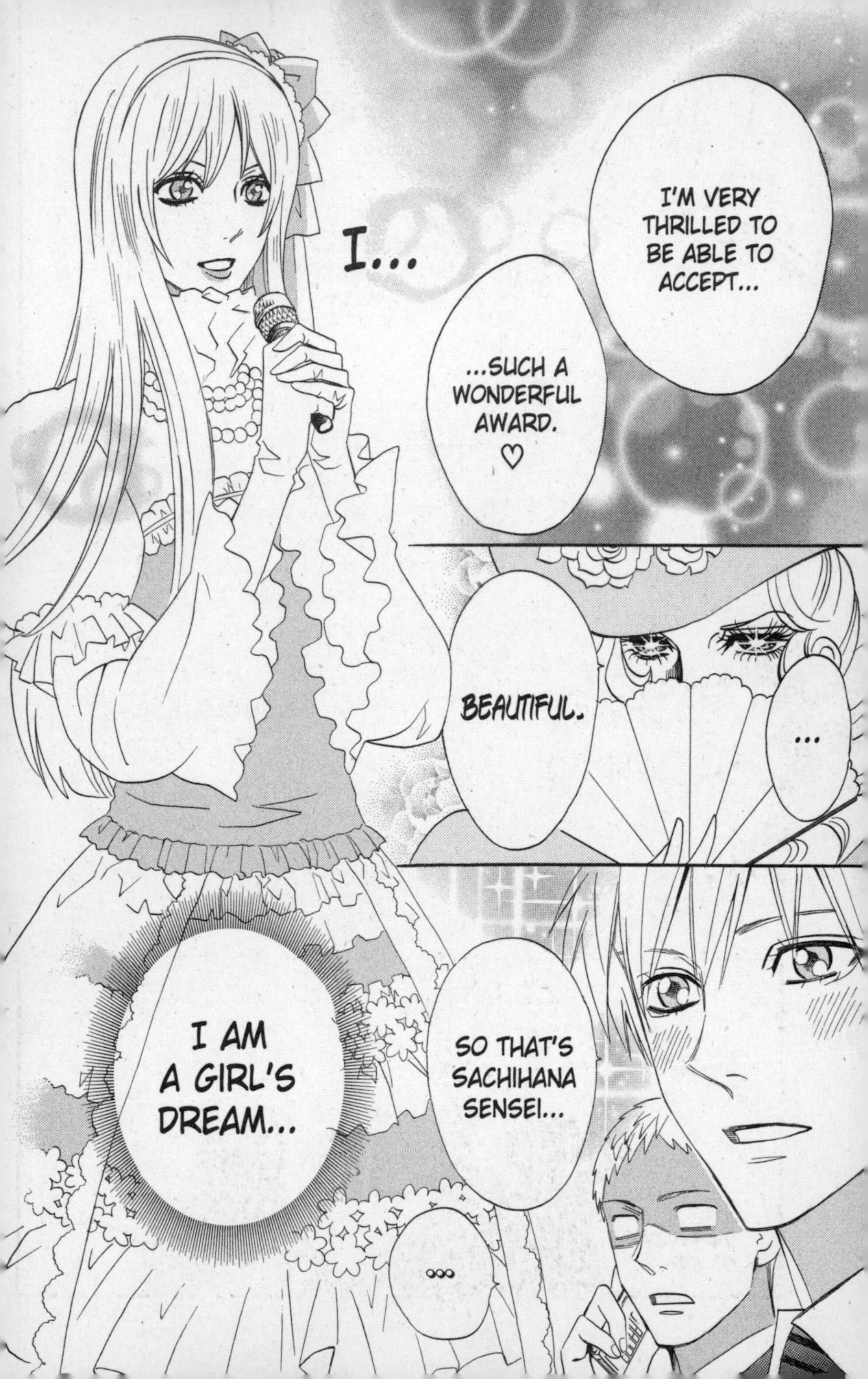

I...
I'M VERY THRILLED TO BE ABLE TO ACCEPT...
...SUCH A WONDERFUL AWARD. ♡
...
BEAUTIFUL.
SO THAT'S SACHIHANA SENSEI...
...
I AM A GIRL'S DREAM...

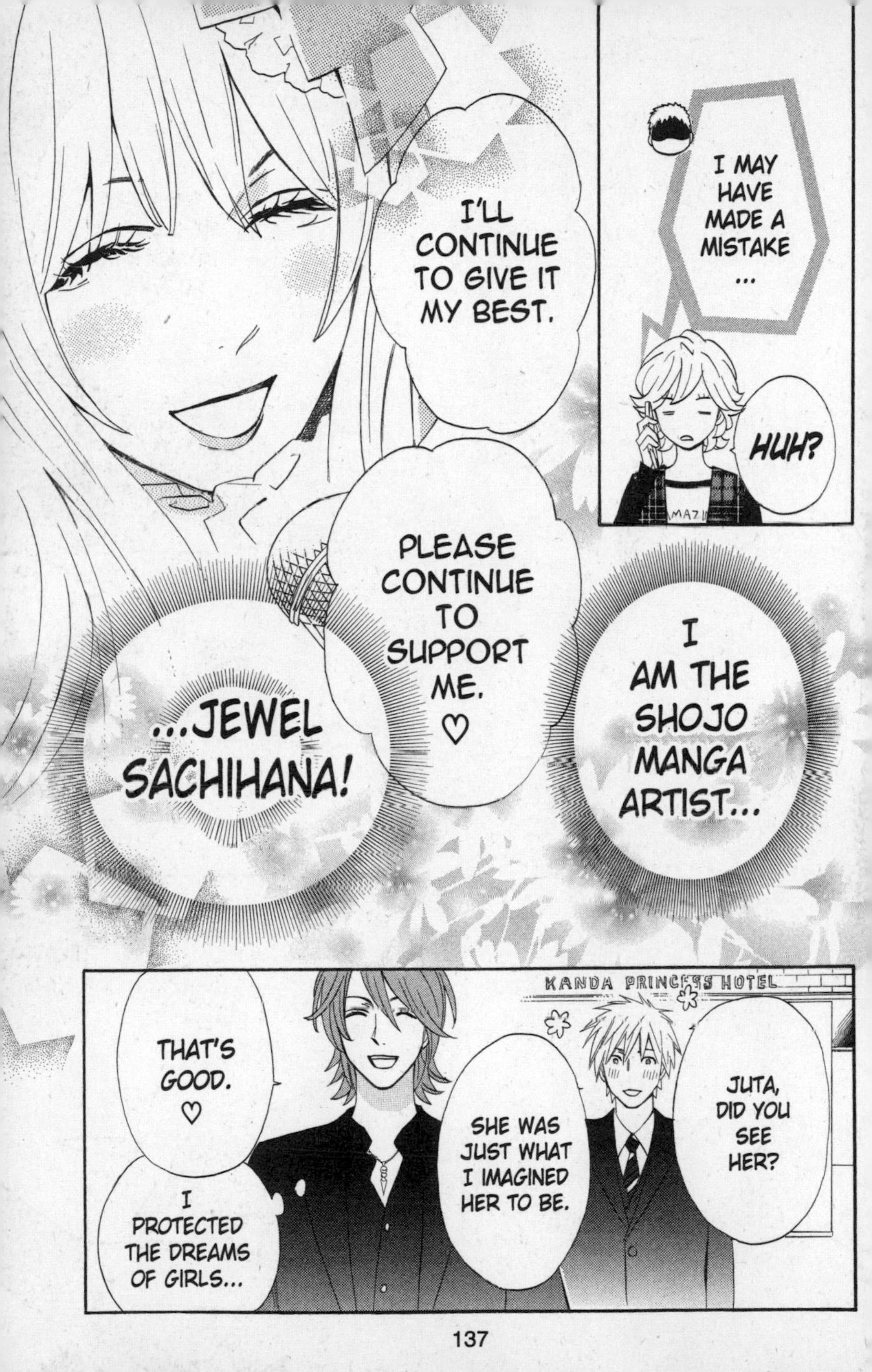
I AM THE SHOJO MANGA ARTIST...
...JEWEL SACHIHANA!
I'LL CONTINUE TO GIVE IT MY BEST.
PLEASE CONTINUE TO SUPPORT ME. ♡
I MAY HAVE MADE A MISTAKE...
HUH?
KANDA PRINCESS HOTEL
JUTA, DID YOU SEE HER?
SHE WAS JUST WHAT I IMAGINED HER TO BE.
THAT'S GOOD. ♡
I PROTECTED THE DREAMS OF GIRLS...

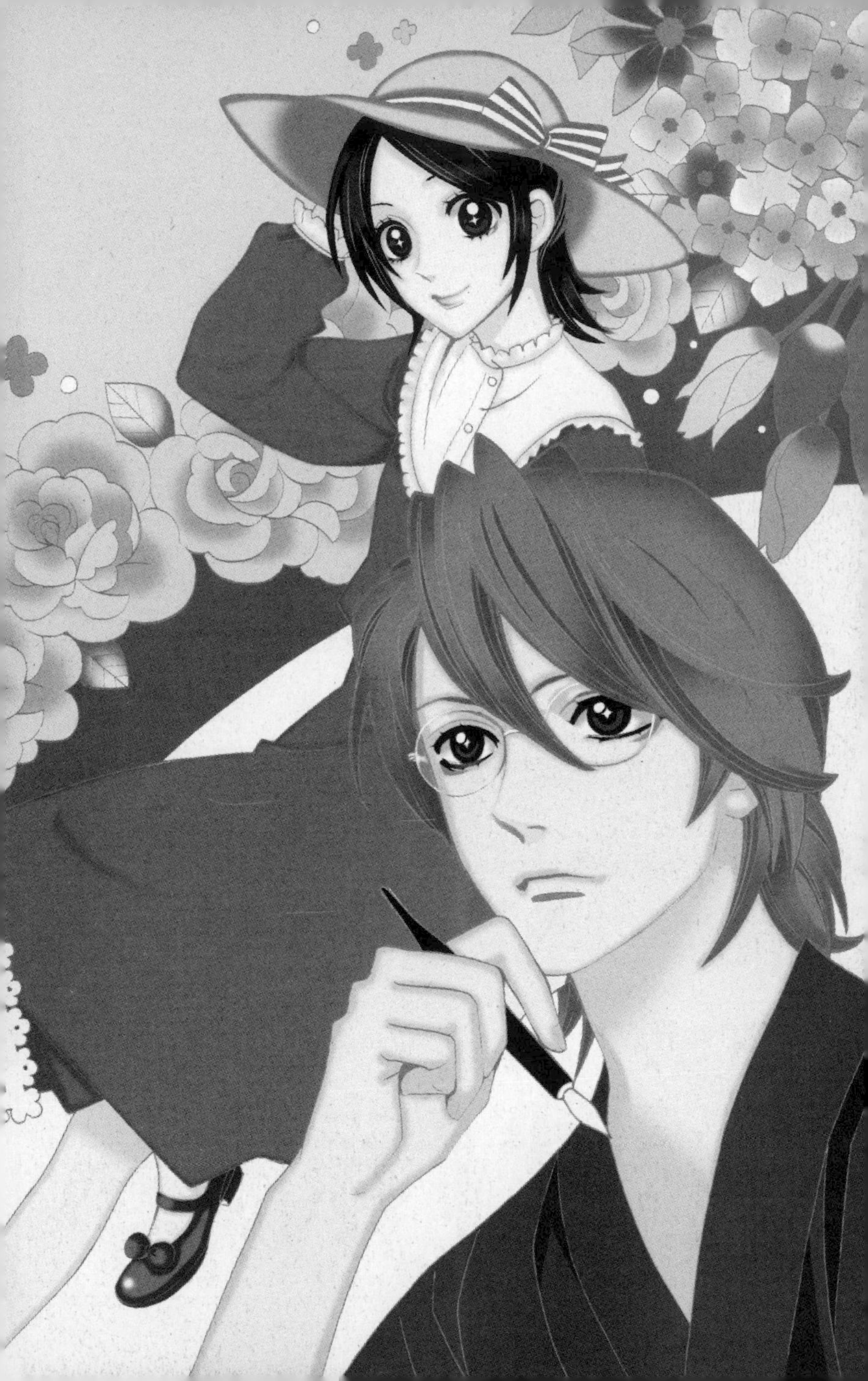

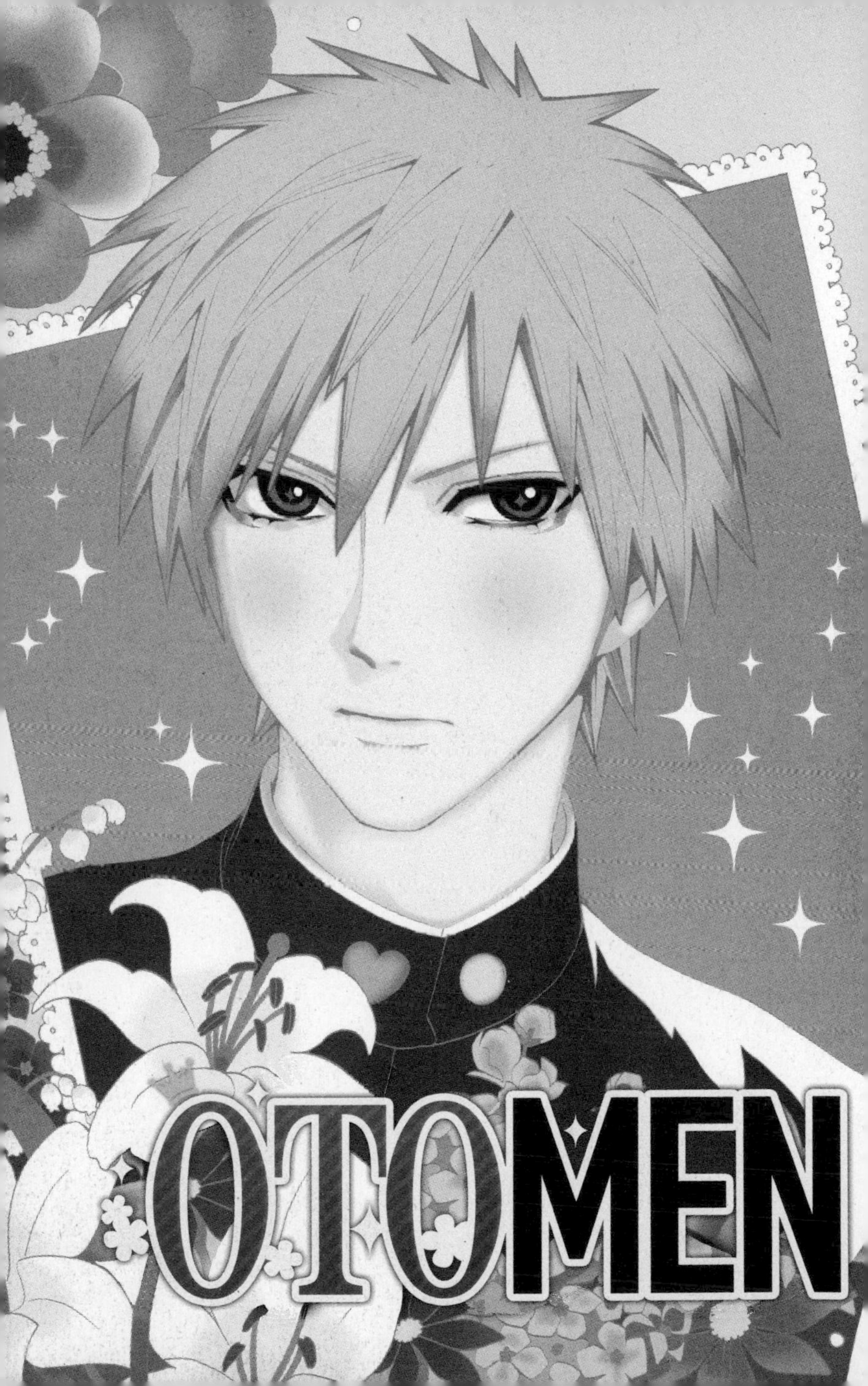
OTOMEN

OTOMEN

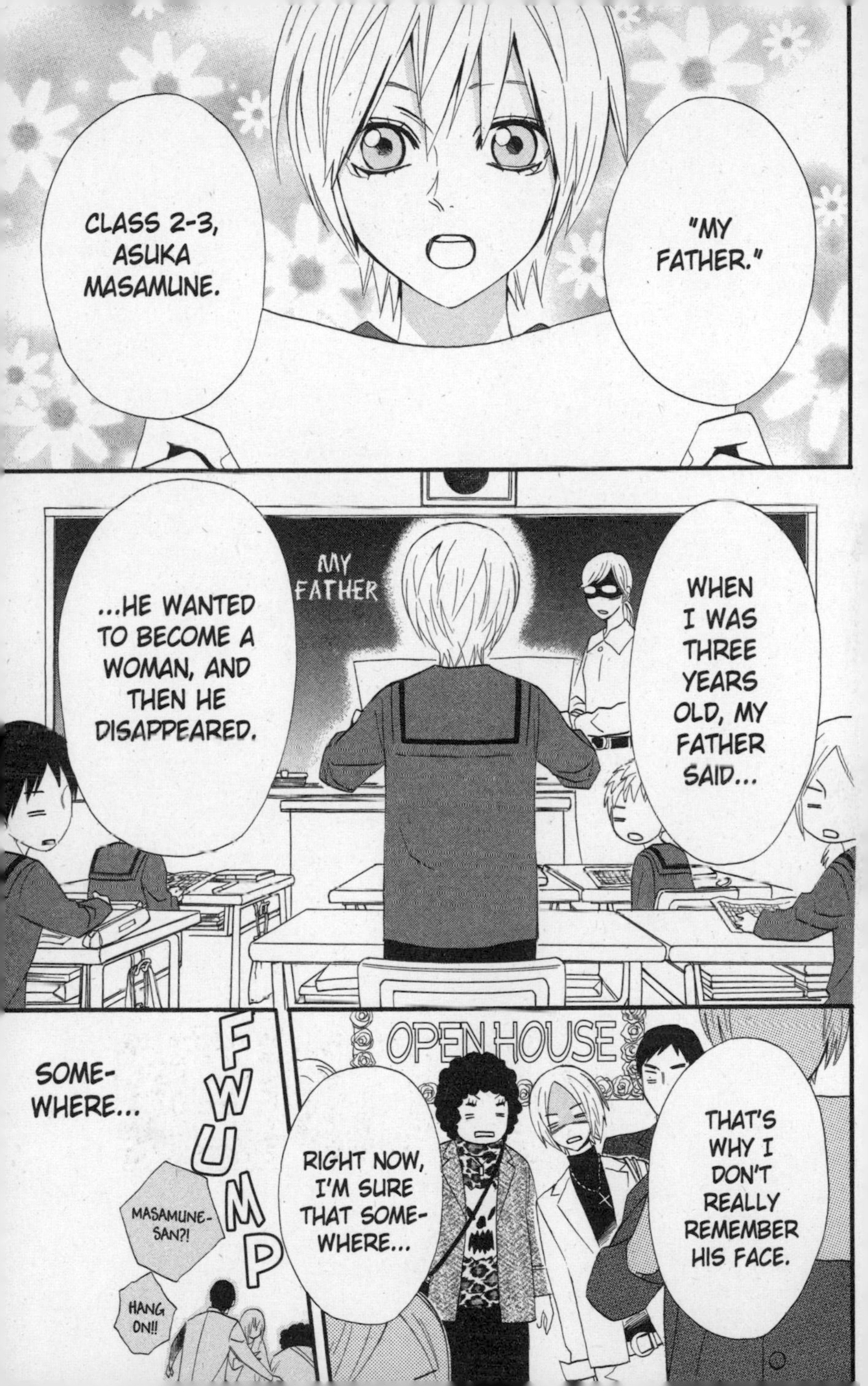
"MY FATHER."
CLASS 2-3, ASUKA MASAMUNE.
WHEN I WAS THREE YEARS OLD, MY FATHER SAID...
MY FATHER
...HE WANTED TO BECOME A WOMAN, AND THEN HE DISAPPEARED.
THAT'S WHY I DON'T REALLY REMEMBER HIS FACE.
OPEN HOUSE
RIGHT NOW, I'M SURE THAT SOME-WHERE...
FWUMP
SOME-WHERE...
MASAMUNE-SAN?!
HANG ON!!

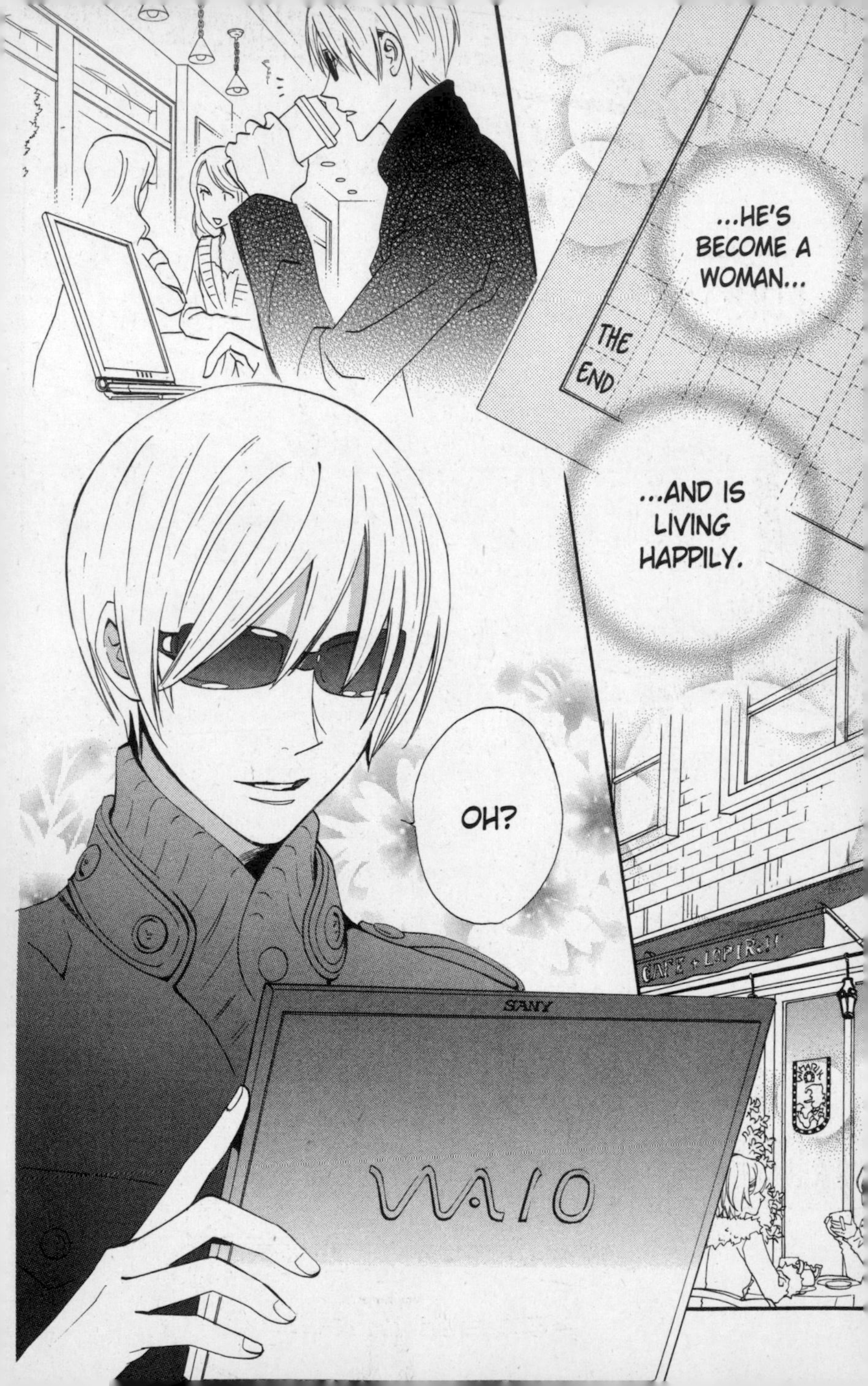
...HE'S BECOME A WOMAN...
THE END
...AND IS LIVING HAPPILY.
OH?
SANY
VAIO

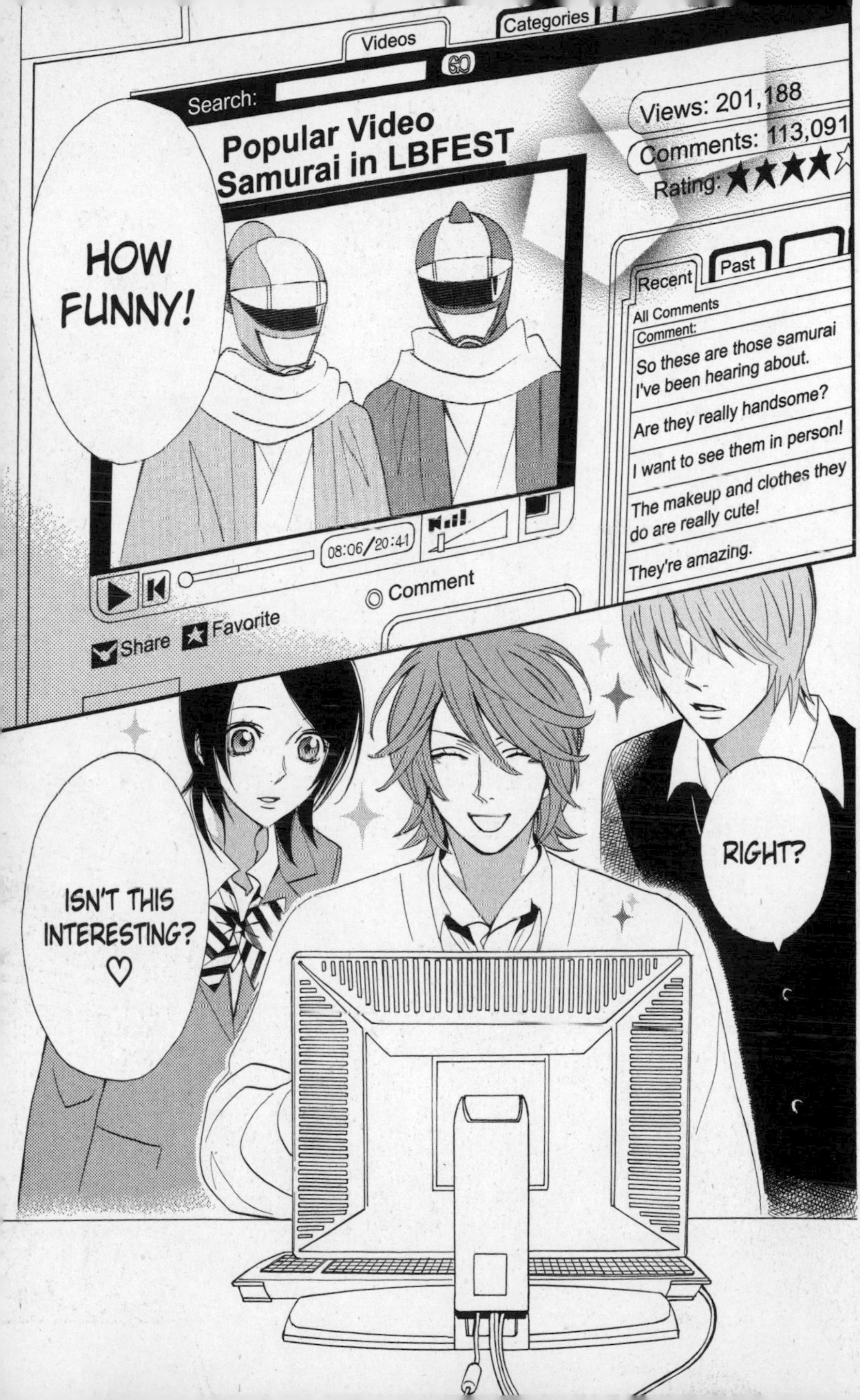
Categories
Videos
Search:
GO
Popular Video
Samurai in LBFEST
Views: 201,188
Comments: 113,091
Rating: ★★★★☆
Past
Recent
All Comments
Comment:
So these are those samurai I've been hearing about.
Are they really handsome?
I want to see them in person!
The makeup and clothes they do are really cute!
They're amazing.
08:06/20:41
Comment
Share
Favorite
HOW FUNNY!
RIGHT?
ISN'T THIS INTERESTING? ♡

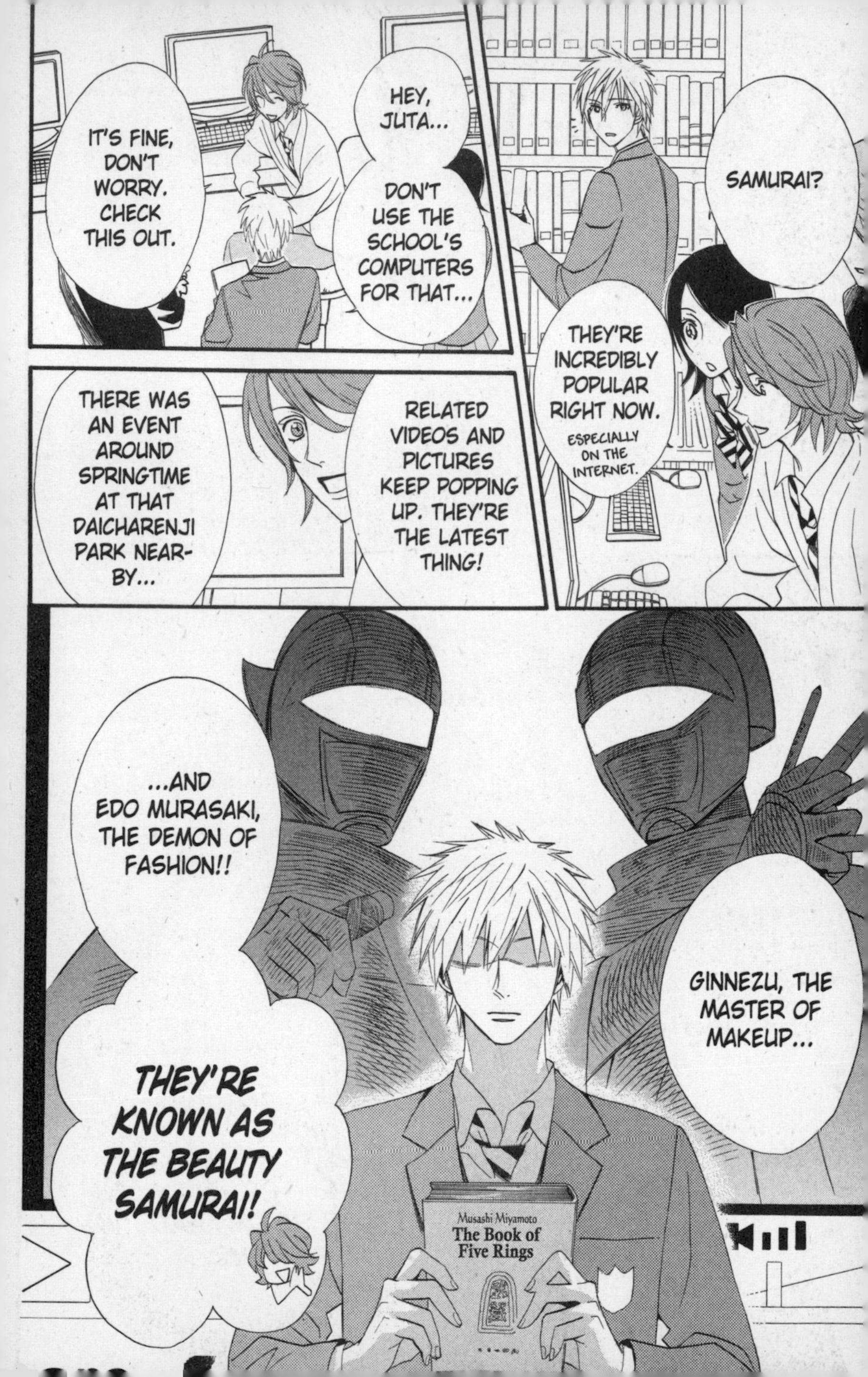
SAMURAI?
THEY'RE INCREDIBLY POPULAR RIGHT NOW.
ESPECIALLY ON THE INTERNET.
HEY, JUTA... DON'T USE THE SCHOOL'S COMPUTERS FOR THAT...
IT'S FINE, DON'T WORRY. CHECK THIS OUT.
RELATED VIDEOS AND PICTURES KEEP POPPING UP. THEY'RE THE LATEST THING!
THERE WAS AN EVENT AROUND SPRINGTIME AT THAT DAICHARENJI PARK NEAR-BY...
GINNEZU, THE MASTER OF MAKEUP...
...AND EDO MURASAKI, THE DEMON OF FASHION!!
THEY'RE KNOWN AS THE BEAUTY SAMURAI!
Musashi Miyamoto
The Book of Five Rings

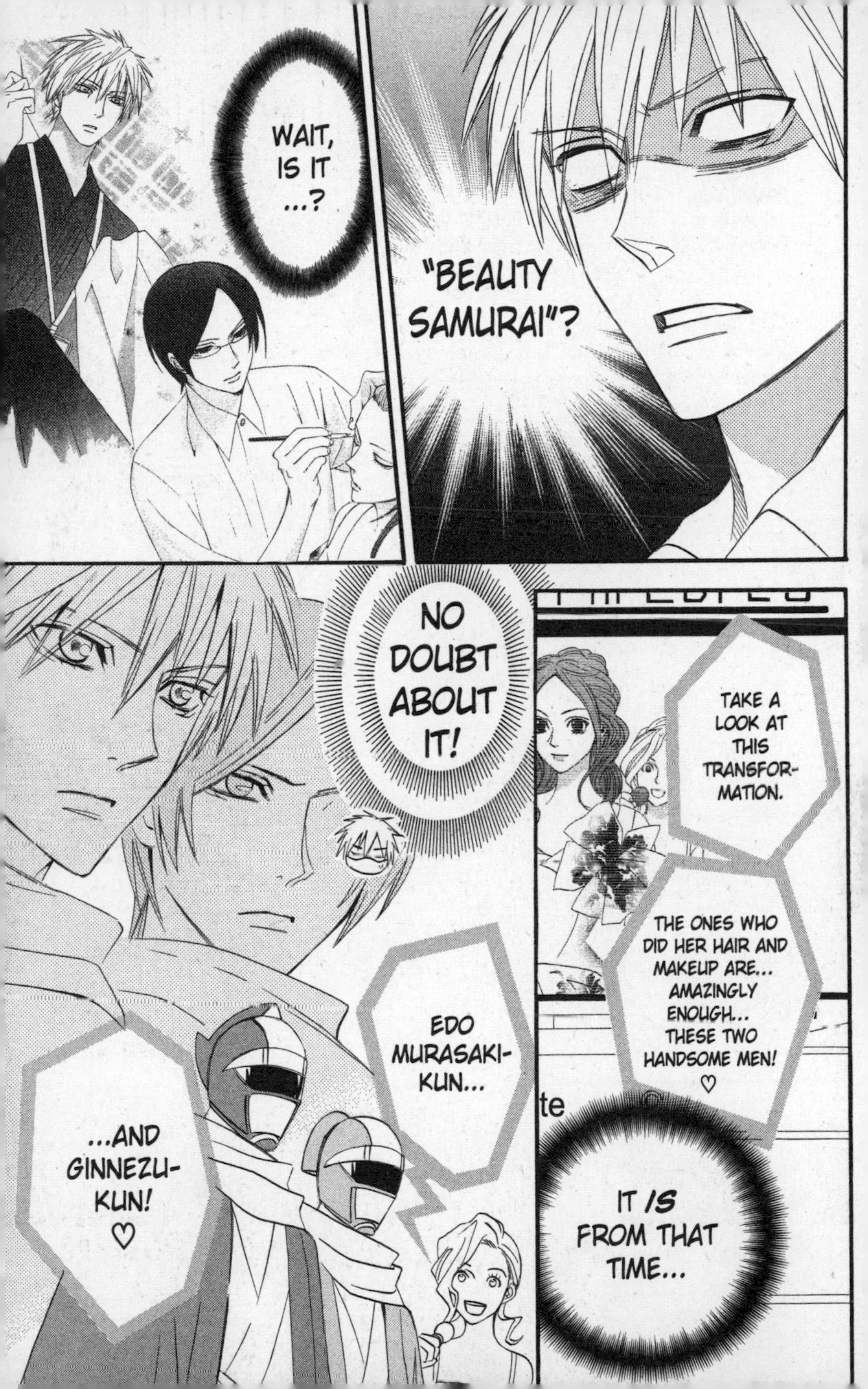
"BEAUTY SAMURAI"?
WAIT, IS IT ...?
TAKE A LOOK AT THIS TRANSFORMATION.
THE ONES WHO DID HER HAIR AND MAKEUP ARE... AMAZINGLY ENOUGH... THESE TWO HANDSOME MEN! ♡
te
IT *IS* FROM THAT TIME...
NO DOUBT ABOUT IT!
EDO MURASAKI-KUN...
...AND GINNEZU-KUN! ♡

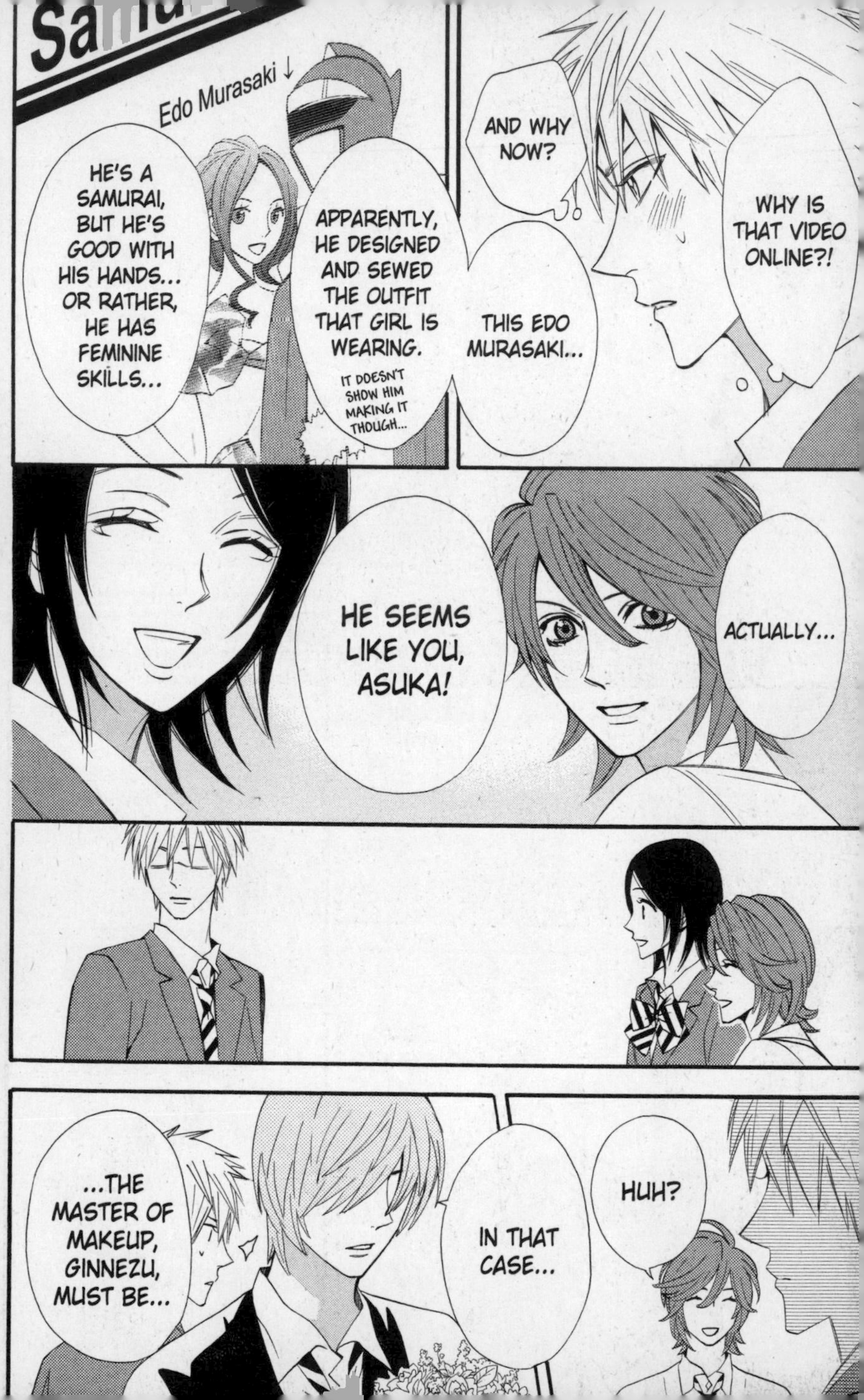
WHY IS THAT VIDEO ONLINE?!
AND WHY NOW?
THIS EDO MURASAKI...
Edo Murasaki ↓
APPARENTLY, HE DESIGNED AND SEWED THE OUTFIT THAT GIRL IS WEARING.
IT DOESN'T SHOW HIM MAKING IT THOUGH...
HE'S A SAMURAI, BUT HE'S GOOD WITH HIS HANDS... OR RATHER, HE HAS FEMININE SKILLS...
ACTUALLY...
HE SEEMS LIKE YOU, ASUKA!
HUH?
IN THAT CASE...
...THE MASTER OF MAKEUP, GINNEZU, MUST BE...

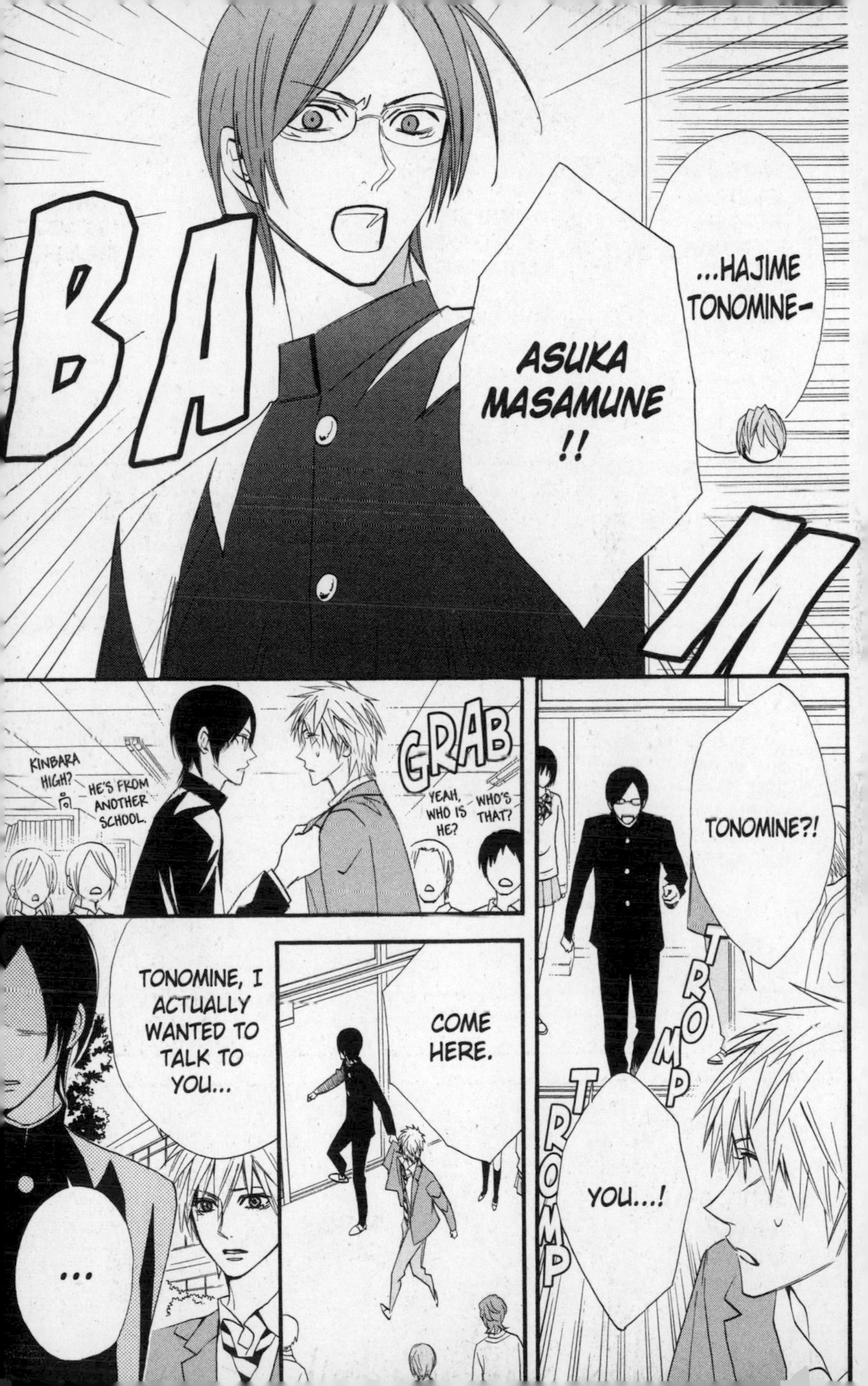
BAM
...HAJIME TONOMINE-
ASUKA MASAMUNE !!
TONOMINE?!
TROMP TROMP
YOU...!
GRAB
WHO'S THAT?
YEAH, WHO IS HE?
HE'S FROM ANOTHER SCHOOL.
KINBARA HIGH?
COME HERE.
TONOMINE, I ACTUALLY WANTED TO TALK TO YOU...
...

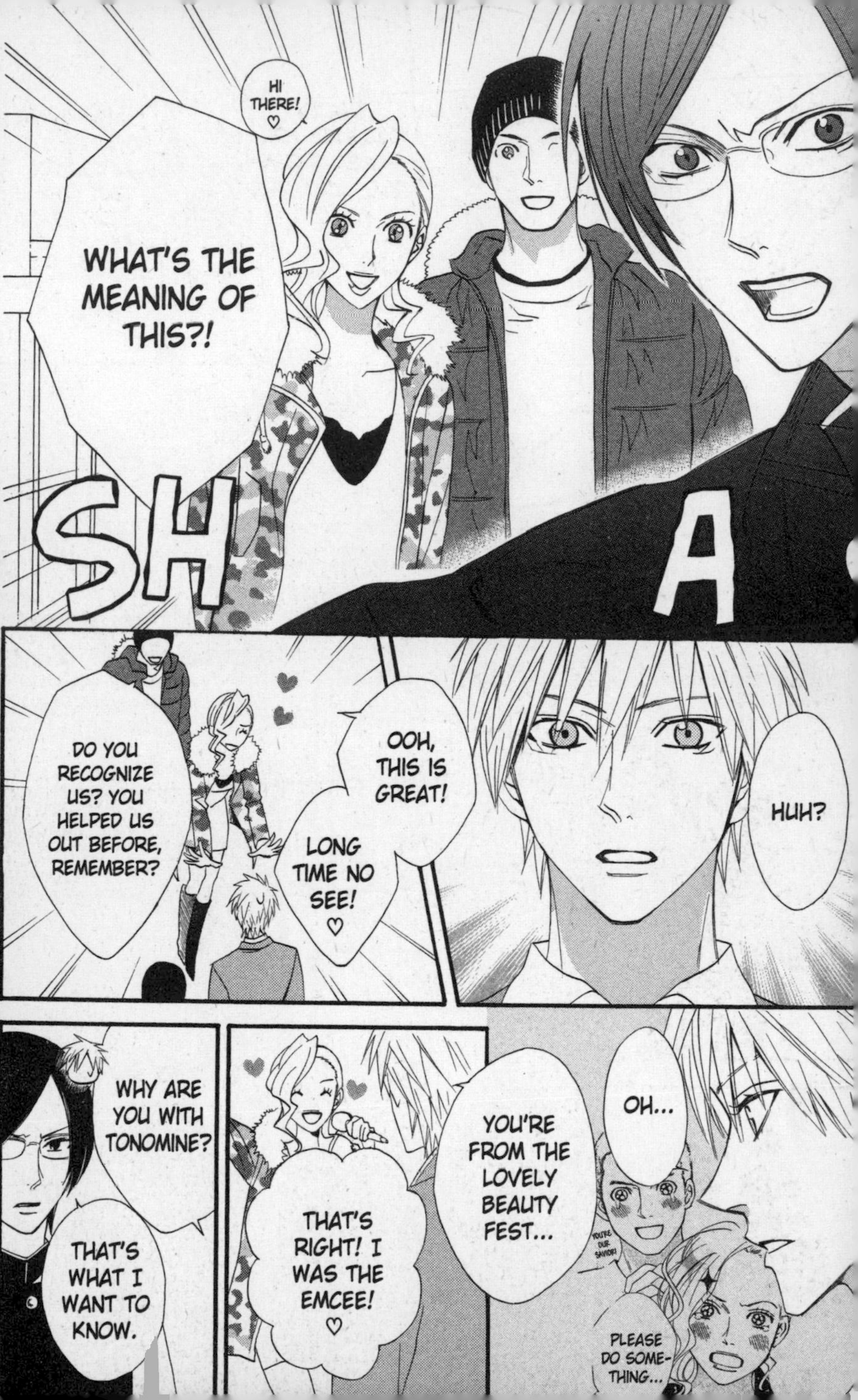
HI THERE! ♡
WHAT'S THE MEANING OF THIS?!
SHA
HUH?
OOH, THIS IS GREAT!
LONG TIME NO SEE! ♡
DO YOU RECOGNIZE US? YOU HELPED US OUT BEFORE, REMEMBER?
OH...
YOU'RE FROM THE LOVELY BEAUTY FEST...
YOU'RE OUR SAVIOR!
PLEASE DO SOME-THING...
THAT'S RIGHT! I WAS THE EMCEE! ♡
WHY ARE YOU WITH TONOMINE?
THAT'S WHAT I WANT TO KNOW.

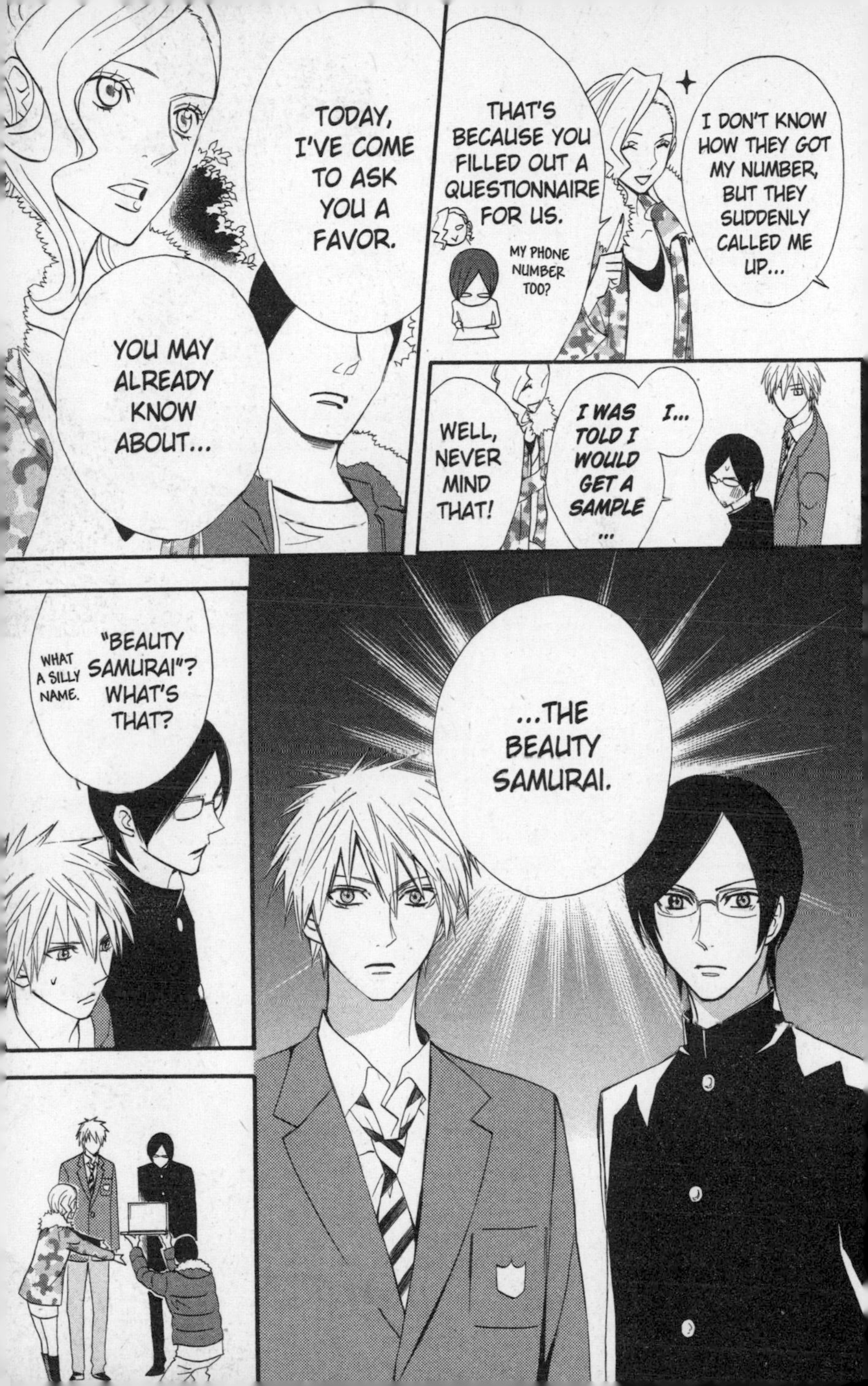
I DON'T KNOW HOW THEY GOT MY NUMBER, BUT THEY SUDDENLY CALLED ME UP...
THAT'S BECAUSE YOU FILLED OUT A QUESTIONNAIRE FOR US.
MY PHONE NUMBER TOO?
I... I WAS TOLD I WOULD GET A SAMPLE...
WELL, NEVER MIND THAT!
TODAY, I'VE COME TO ASK YOU A FAVOR.
YOU MAY ALREADY KNOW ABOUT...
...THE BEAUTY SAMURAI.
"BEAUTY SAMURAI"? WHAT'S THAT?
WHAT A SILLY NAME.

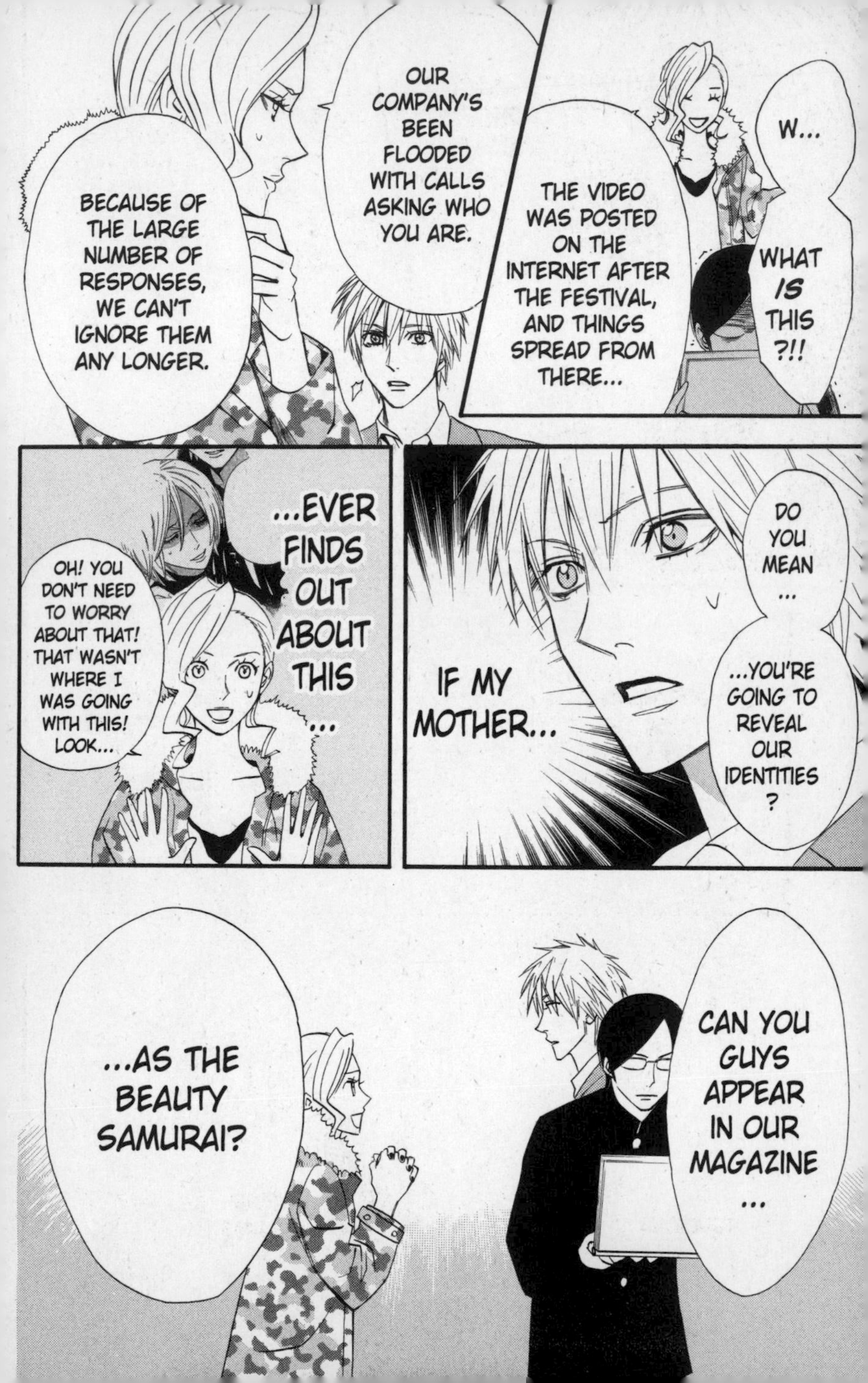
W... WHAT *IS* THIS?!!
THE VIDEO WAS POSTED ON THE INTERNET AFTER THE FESTIVAL, AND THINGS SPREAD FROM THERE...
OUR COMPANY'S BEEN FLOODED WITH CALLS ASKING WHO YOU ARE.
BECAUSE OF THE LARGE NUMBER OF RESPONSES, WE CAN'T IGNORE THEM ANY LONGER.
DO YOU MEAN...
...YOU'RE GOING TO REVEAL OUR IDENTITIES?
IF MY MOTHER...
...EVER FINDS OUT ABOUT THIS...
OH! YOU DON'T NEED TO WORRY ABOUT THAT! THAT WASN'T WHERE I WAS GOING WITH THIS! LOOK...
CAN YOU GUYS APPEAR IN OUR MAGAZINE...
...AS THE BEAUTY SAMURAI?

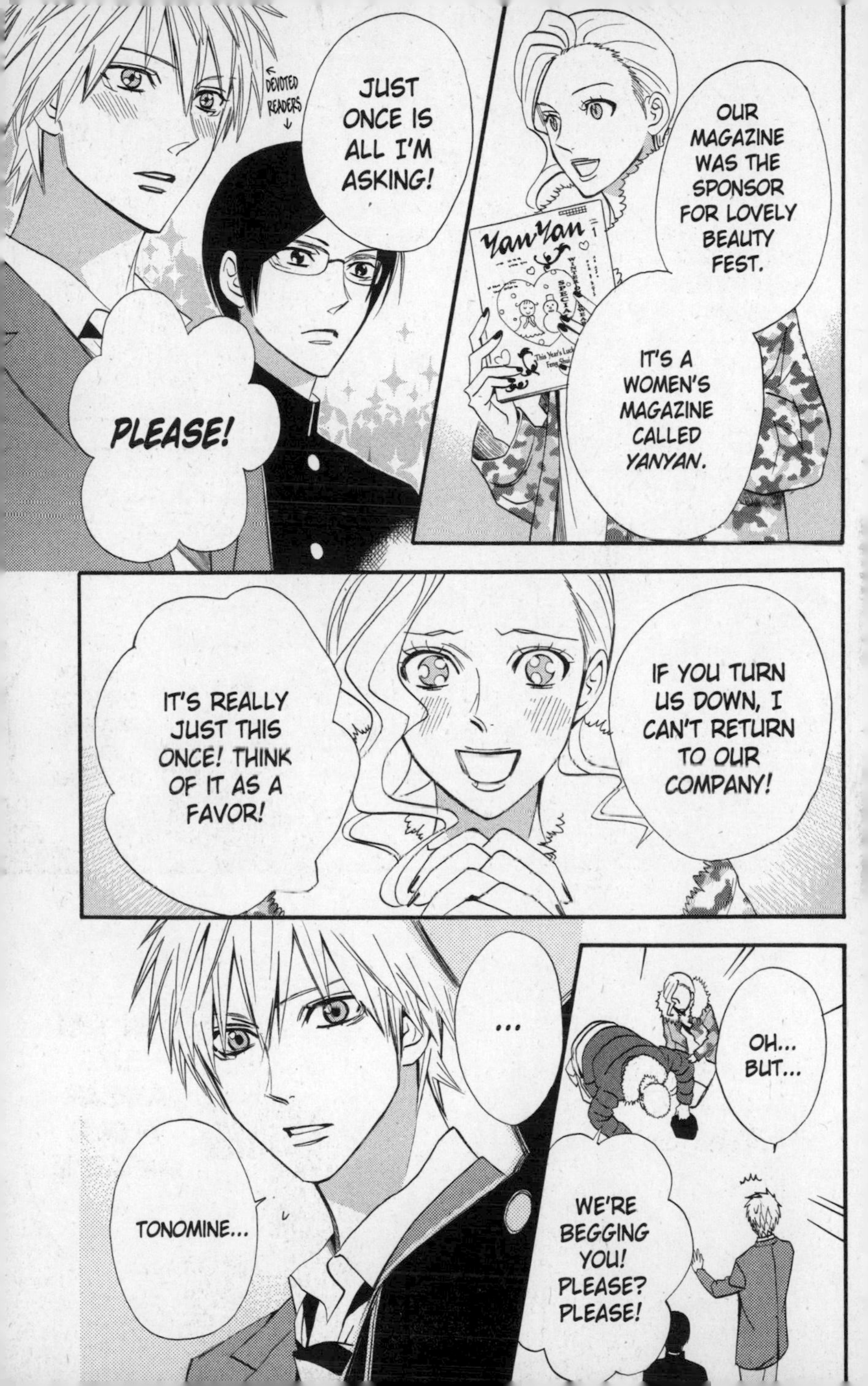
OUR MAGAZINE WAS THE SPONSOR FOR LOVELY BEAUTY FEST.
YanYan
IT'S A WOMEN'S MAGAZINE CALLED *YANYAN*.
JUST ONCE IS ALL I'M ASKING!
← DEVOTED READERS ↓
PLEASE!
IF YOU TURN US DOWN, I CAN'T RETURN TO OUR COMPANY!
IT'S REALLY JUST THIS ONCE! THINK OF IT AS A FAVOR!
OH... BUT...
WE'RE BEGGING YOU! PLEASE? PLEASE!
...
TONOMINE...

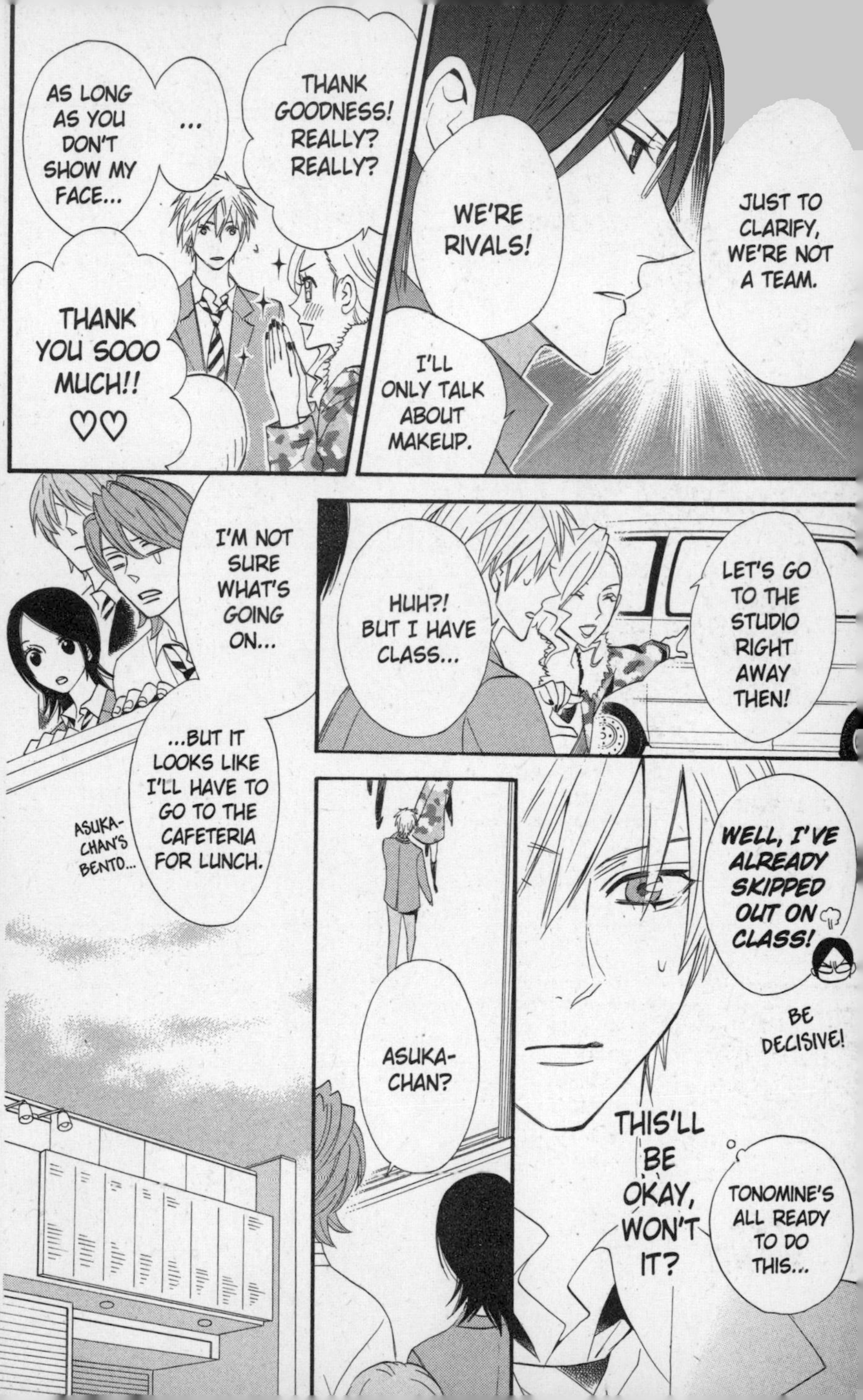
JUST TO CLARIFY, WE'RE NOT A TEAM.
WE'RE RIVALS!
I'LL ONLY TALK ABOUT MAKEUP.
THANK GOODNESS! REALLY? REALLY?
...
AS LONG AS YOU DON'T SHOW MY FACE...
THANK YOU SOOO MUCH!! ♡♡
LET'S GO TO THE STUDIO RIGHT AWAY THEN!
HUH?! BUT I HAVE CLASS...
WELL, I'VE ALREADY SKIPPED OUT ON CLASS!
BE DECISIVE!
TONOMINE'S ALL READY TO DO THIS...
THIS'LL BE OKAY, WON'T IT?
ASUKA-CHAN?
I'M NOT SURE WHAT'S GOING ON...
...BUT IT LOOKS LIKE I'LL HAVE TO GO TO THE CAFETERIA FOR LUNCH.
ASUKA-CHAN'S BENTO...

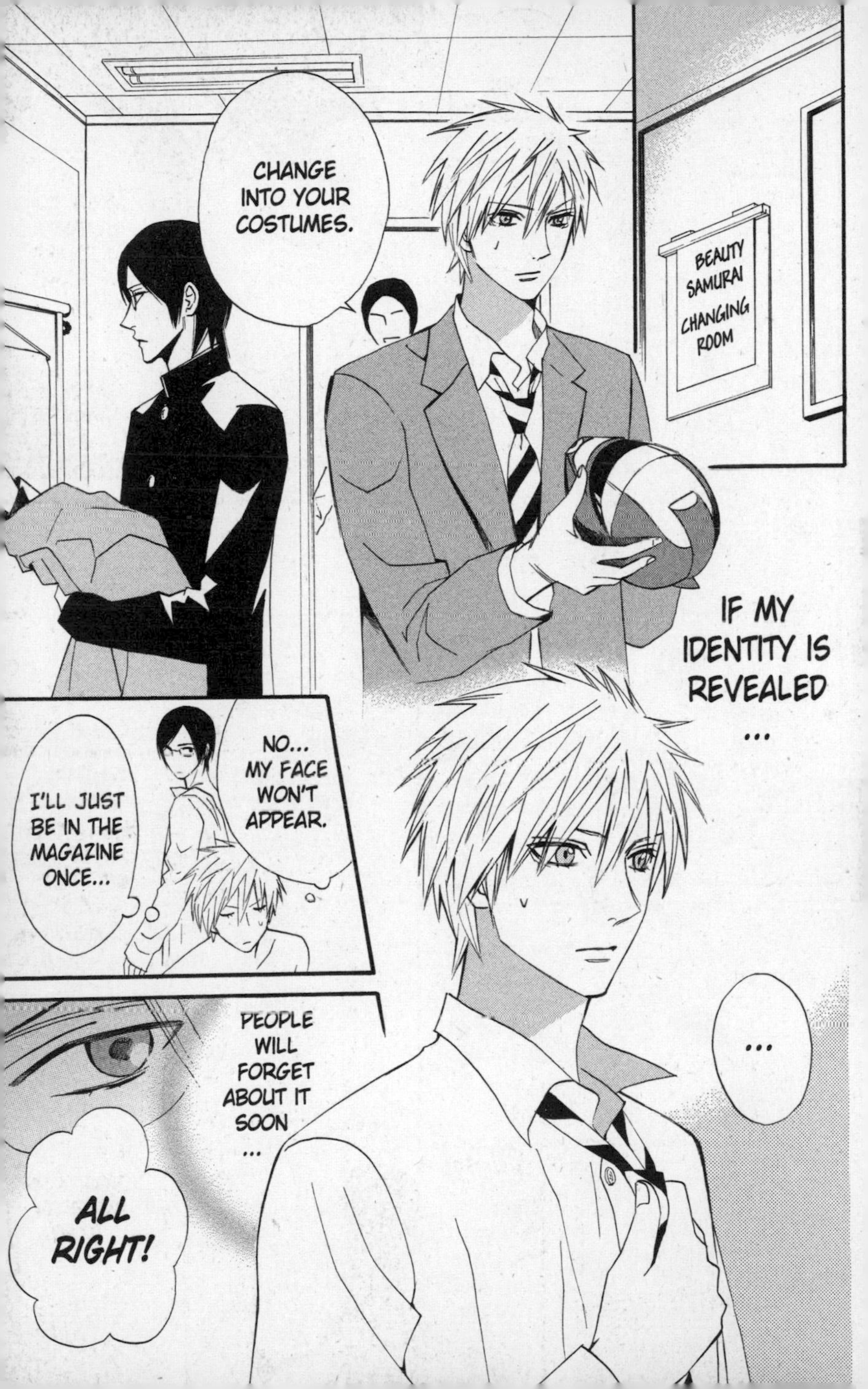
CHANGE INTO YOUR COSTUMES.
BEAUTY SAMURAI CHANGING ROOM
IF MY IDENTITY IS REVEALED ...
...
NO... MY FACE WON'T APPEAR.
I'LL JUST BE IN THE MAGAZINE ONCE...
PEOPLE WILL FORGET ABOUT IT SOON ...
ALL RIGHT!

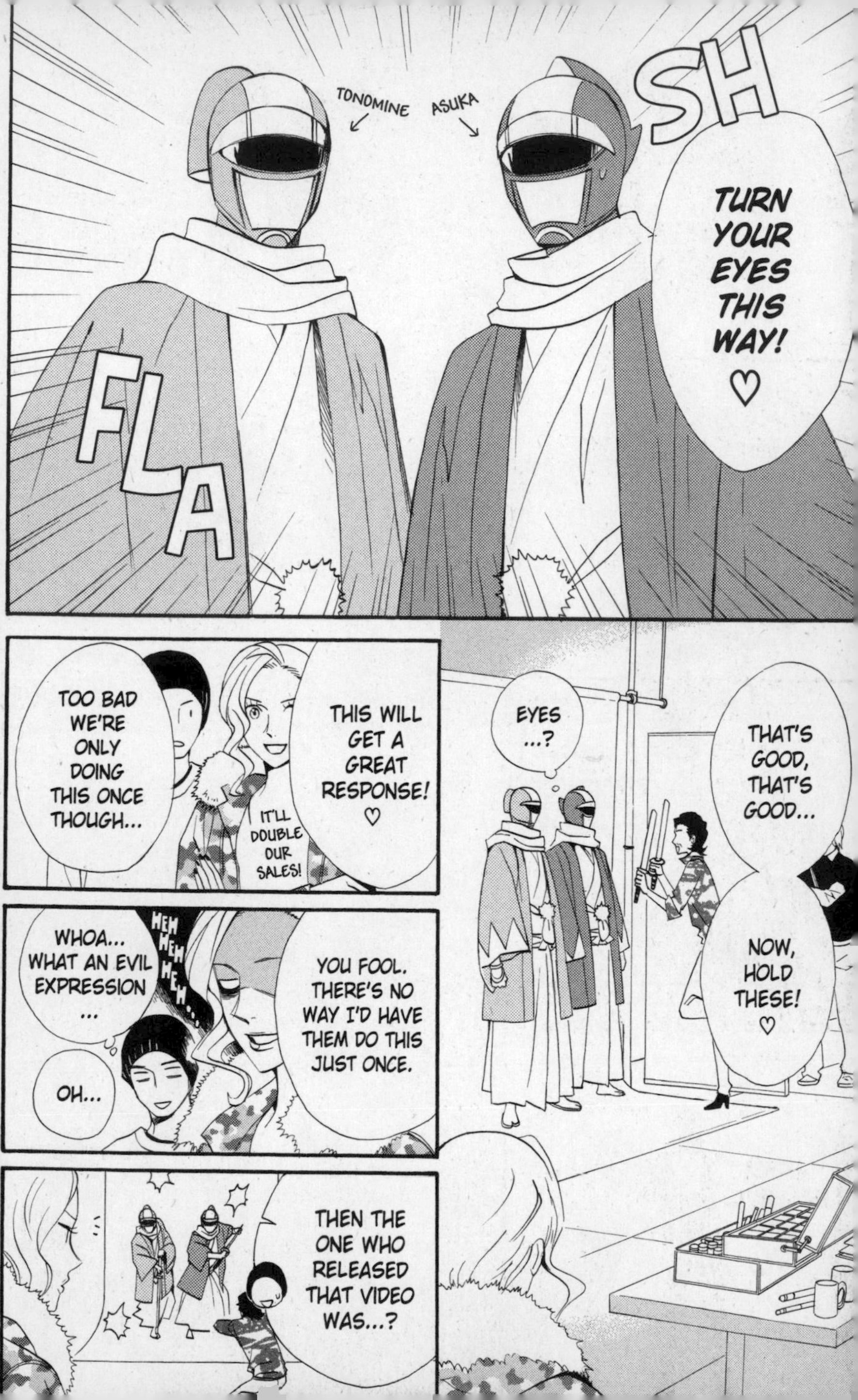
SH
TURN YOUR EYES THIS WAY! ♡
ASUKA
TONOMINE
FLA
THAT'S GOOD, THAT'S GOOD...
NOW, HOLD THESE! ♡
EYES ...?
THIS WILL GET A GREAT RESPONSE! ♡
IT'LL DOUBLE OUR SALES!
TOO BAD WE'RE ONLY DOING THIS ONCE THOUGH...
YOU FOOL. THERE'S NO WAY I'D HAVE THEM DO THIS JUST ONCE.
HEH HEH HEH...
WHOA... WHAT AN EVIL EXPRESSION ...
OH...
THEN THE ONE WHO RELEASED THAT VIDEO WAS...?

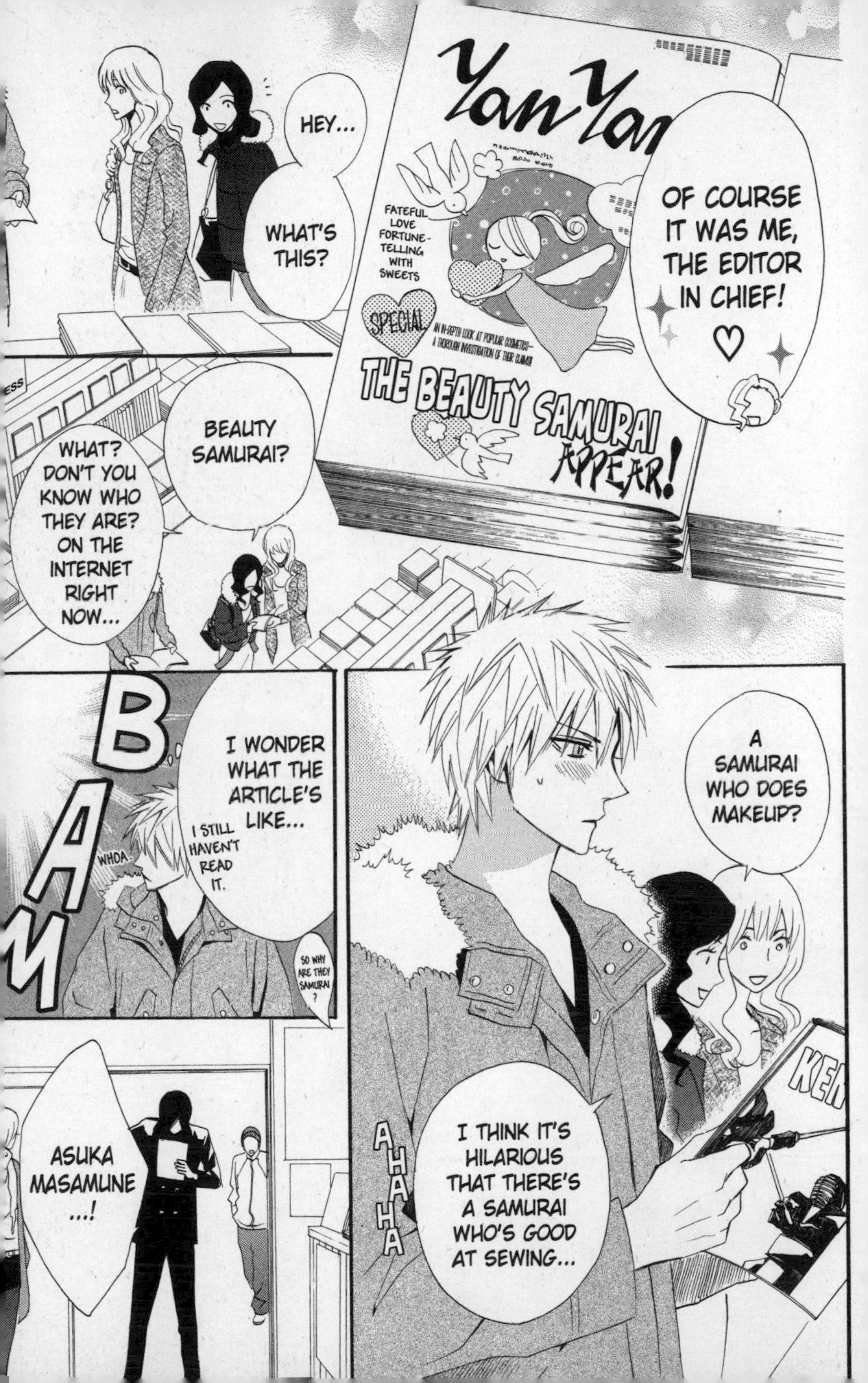
FATEFUL LOVE FORTUNE-TELLING WITH SWEETS
SPECIAL
AN IN-DEPTH LOOK AT POPULAR COSMETICS— A THOROUGH INVESTIGATION OF THEIR CLAIMS!
THE BEAUTY SAMURAI APPEAR!
OF COURSE IT WAS ME, THE EDITOR IN CHIEF! ♡
HEY...
WHAT'S THIS?
BEAUTY SAMURAI?
WHAT? DON'T YOU KNOW WHO THEY ARE? ON THE INTERNET RIGHT NOW...
A SAMURAI WHO DOES MAKEUP?
I THINK IT'S HILARIOUS THAT THERE'S A SAMURAI WHO'S GOOD AT SEWING...
AHAHA
I WONDER WHAT THE ARTICLE'S LIKE...
I STILL HAVEN'T READ IT.
WHOA.
BAM
SO WHY ARE THEY SAMURAI?
ASUKA MASAMUNE ...!

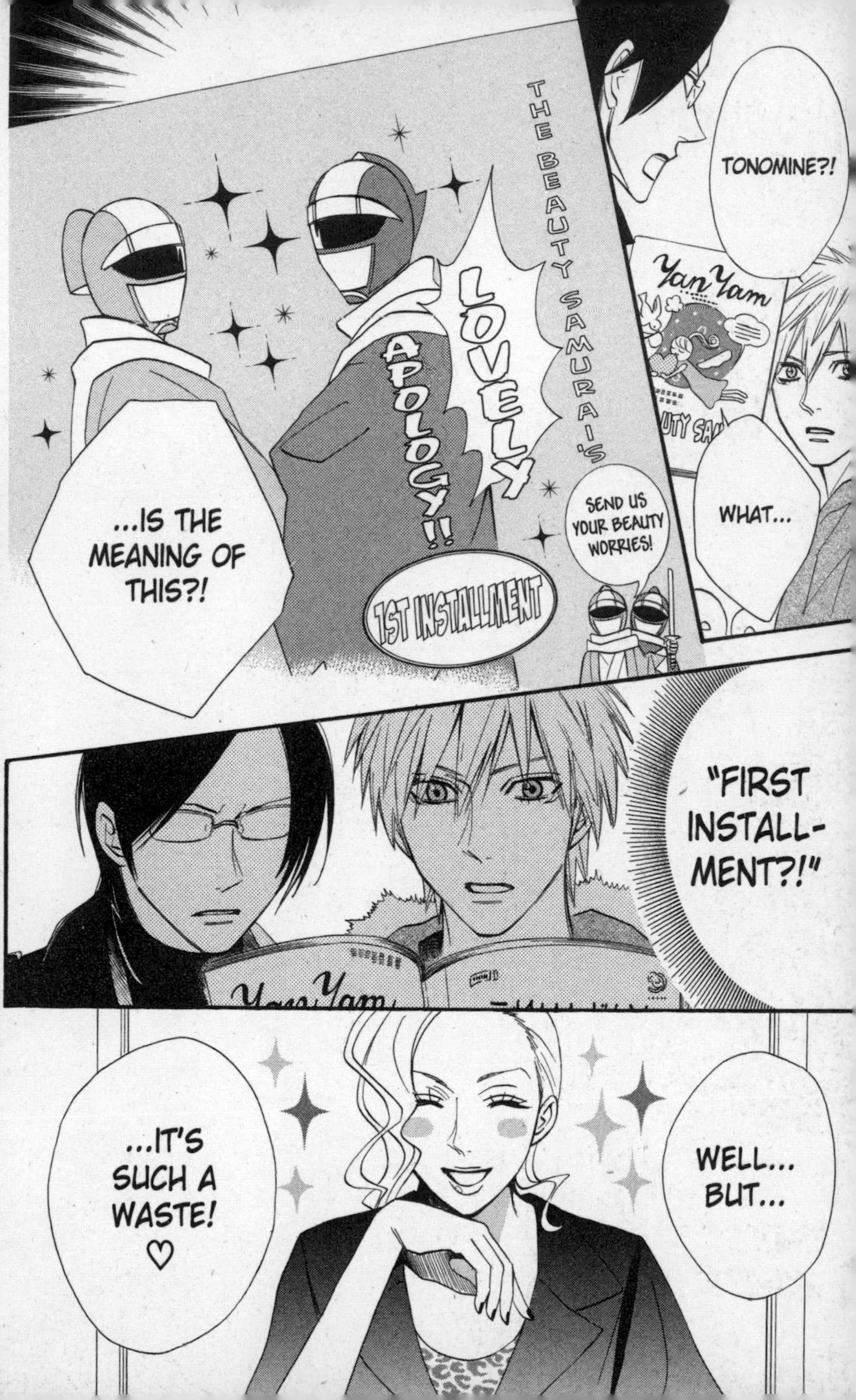
TONOMINE?!
WHAT...
THE BEAUTY SAMURAI'S LOVELY APOLOGY!!
1ST INSTALLMENT
SEND US YOUR BEAUTY WORRIES!
...IS THE MEANING OF THIS?!
"FIRST INSTALL-MENT?!"
WELL... BUT...
...IT'S SUCH A WASTE! ♡

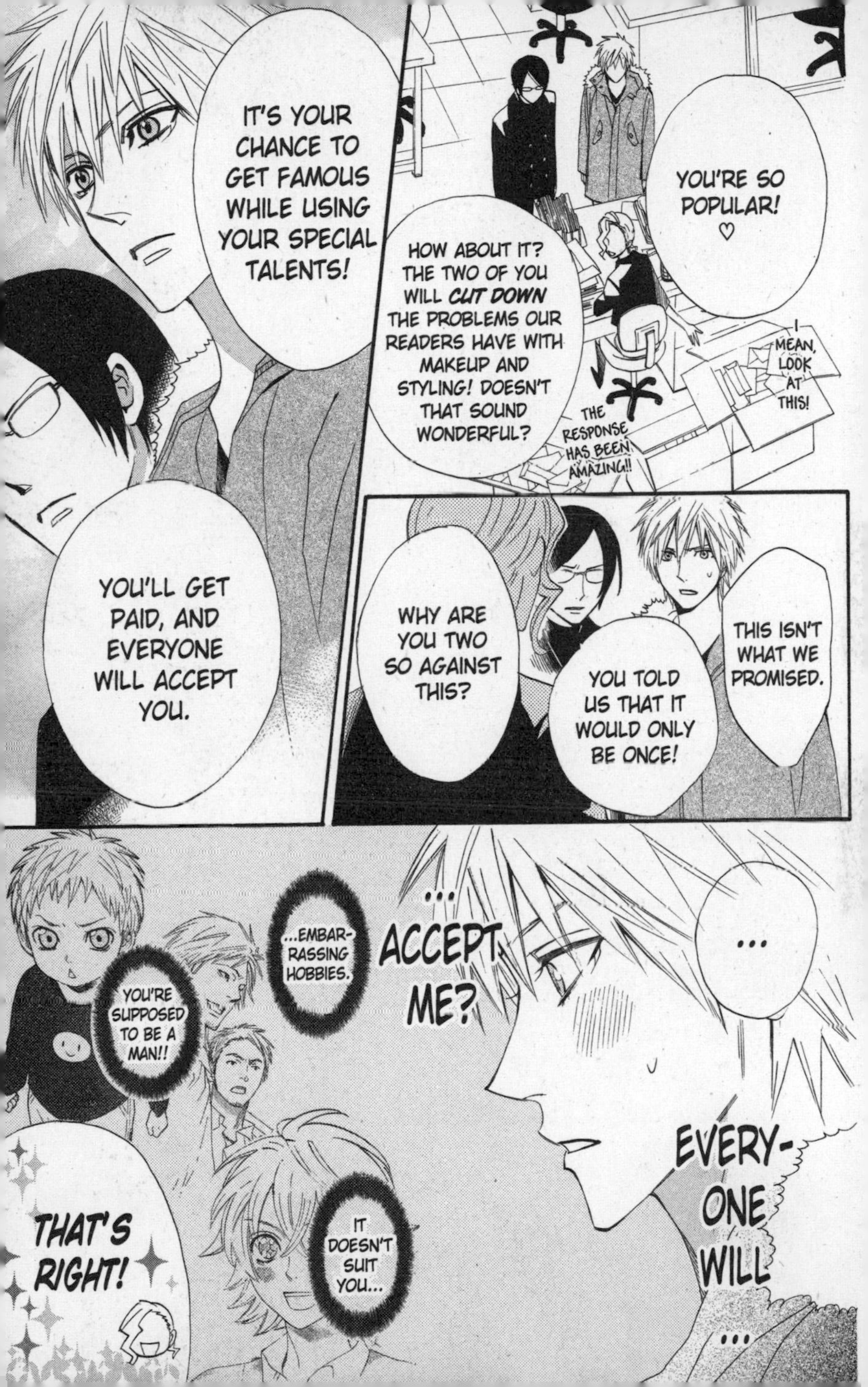
YOU'RE SO POPULAR! ♡
I MEAN, LOOK AT THIS!
THE RESPONSE HAS BEEN AMAZING!!
HOW ABOUT IT? THE TWO OF YOU WILL CUT DOWN THE PROBLEMS OUR READERS HAVE WITH MAKEUP AND STYLING! DOESN'T THAT SOUND WONDERFUL?
THIS ISN'T WHAT WE PROMISED.
YOU TOLD US THAT IT WOULD ONLY BE ONCE!
WHY ARE YOU TWO SO AGAINST THIS?
IT'S YOUR CHANCE TO GET FAMOUS WHILE USING YOUR SPECIAL TALENTS!
YOU'LL GET PAID, AND EVERYONE WILL ACCEPT YOU.
...
EVERY-ONE WILL ...
... ACCEPT ME?
...EMBAR-RASSING HOBBIES.
YOU'RE SUPPOSED TO BE A MAN!!
IT DOESN'T SUIT YOU...
THAT'S RIGHT!

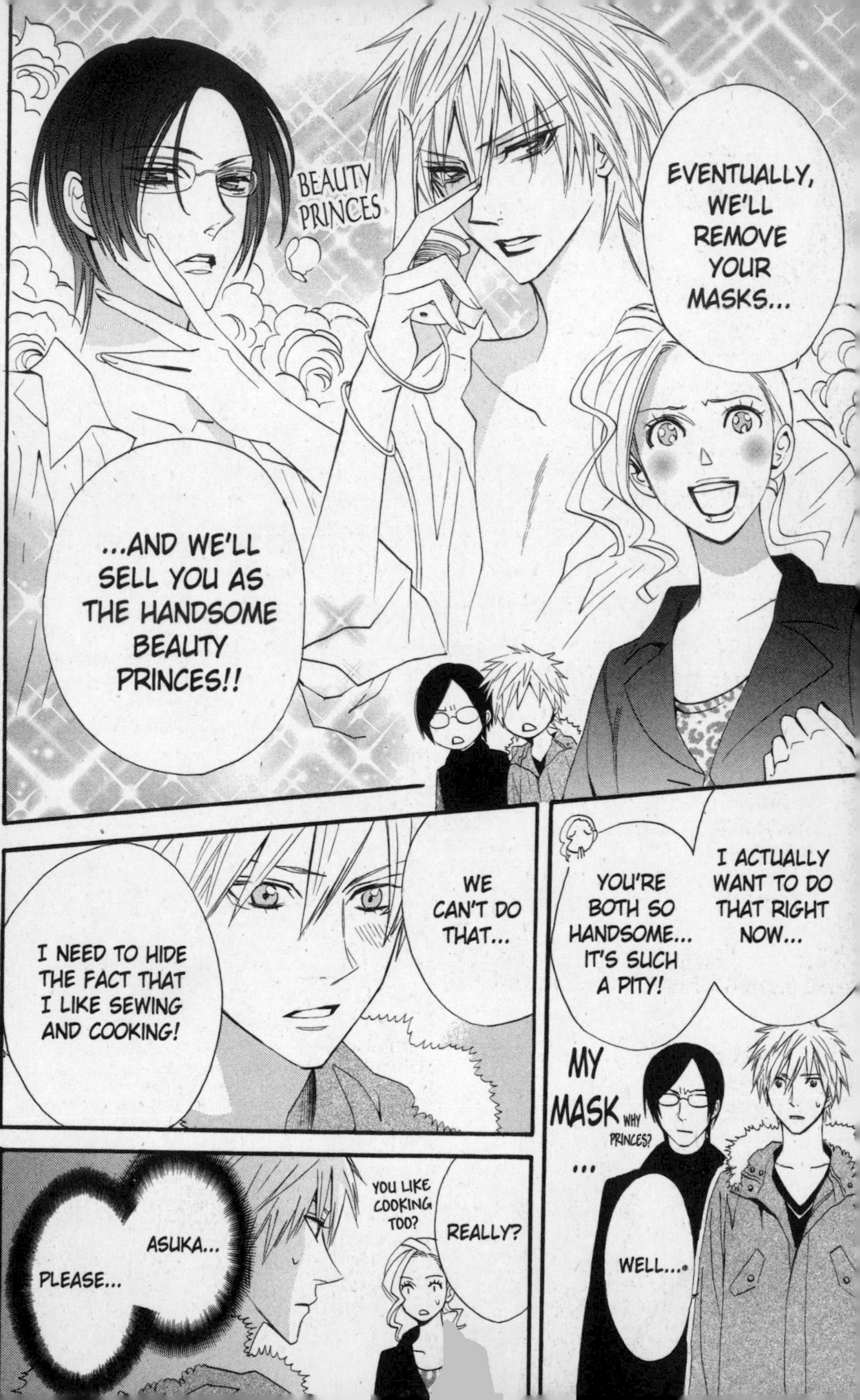
EVENTUALLY, WE'LL REMOVE YOUR MASKS...
BEAUTY PRINCES
...AND WE'LL SELL YOU AS THE HANDSOME BEAUTY PRINCES!!
I ACTUALLY WANT TO DO THAT RIGHT NOW...
YOU'RE BOTH SO HANDSOME... IT'S SUCH A PITY!
MY MASK...
WHY PRINCES?
WELL...
WE CAN'T DO THAT...
I NEED TO HIDE THE FACT THAT I LIKE SEWING AND COOKING!
REALLY?
YOU LIKE COOKING TOO?
ASUKA...
PLEASE...

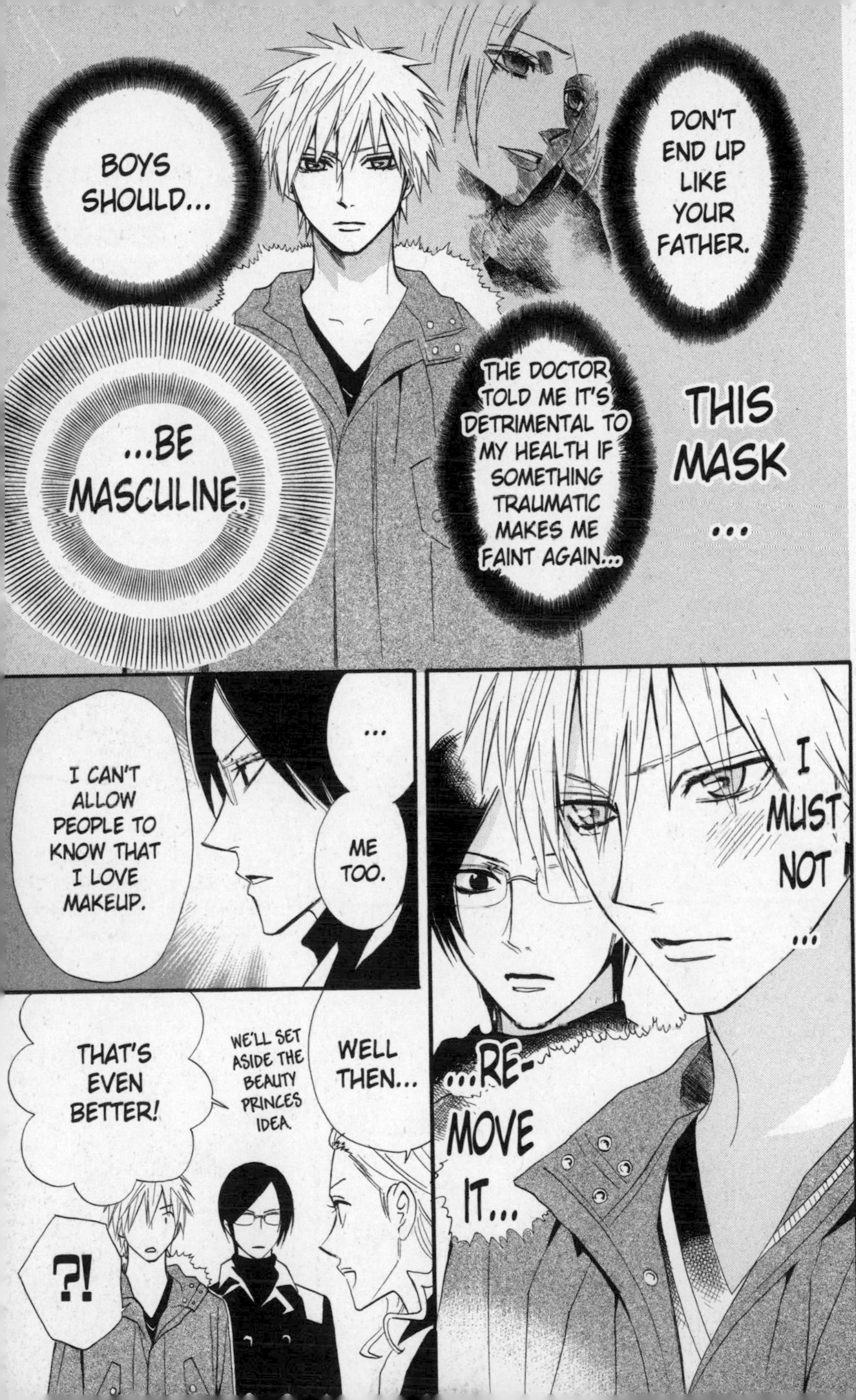
DON'T END UP LIKE YOUR FATHER.
BOYS SHOULD...
THIS MASK...
THE DOCTOR TOLD ME IT'S DETRIMENTAL TO MY HEALTH IF SOMETHING TRAUMATIC MAKES ME FAINT AGAIN...
...BE MASCULINE.
I MUST NOT...
...RE-MOVE IT...
...
I CAN'T ALLOW PEOPLE TO KNOW THAT I LOVE MAKEUP.
ME TOO.
WELL THEN...
WE'LL SET ASIDE THE BEAUTY PRINCES IDEA.
THAT'S EVEN BETTER!
?!

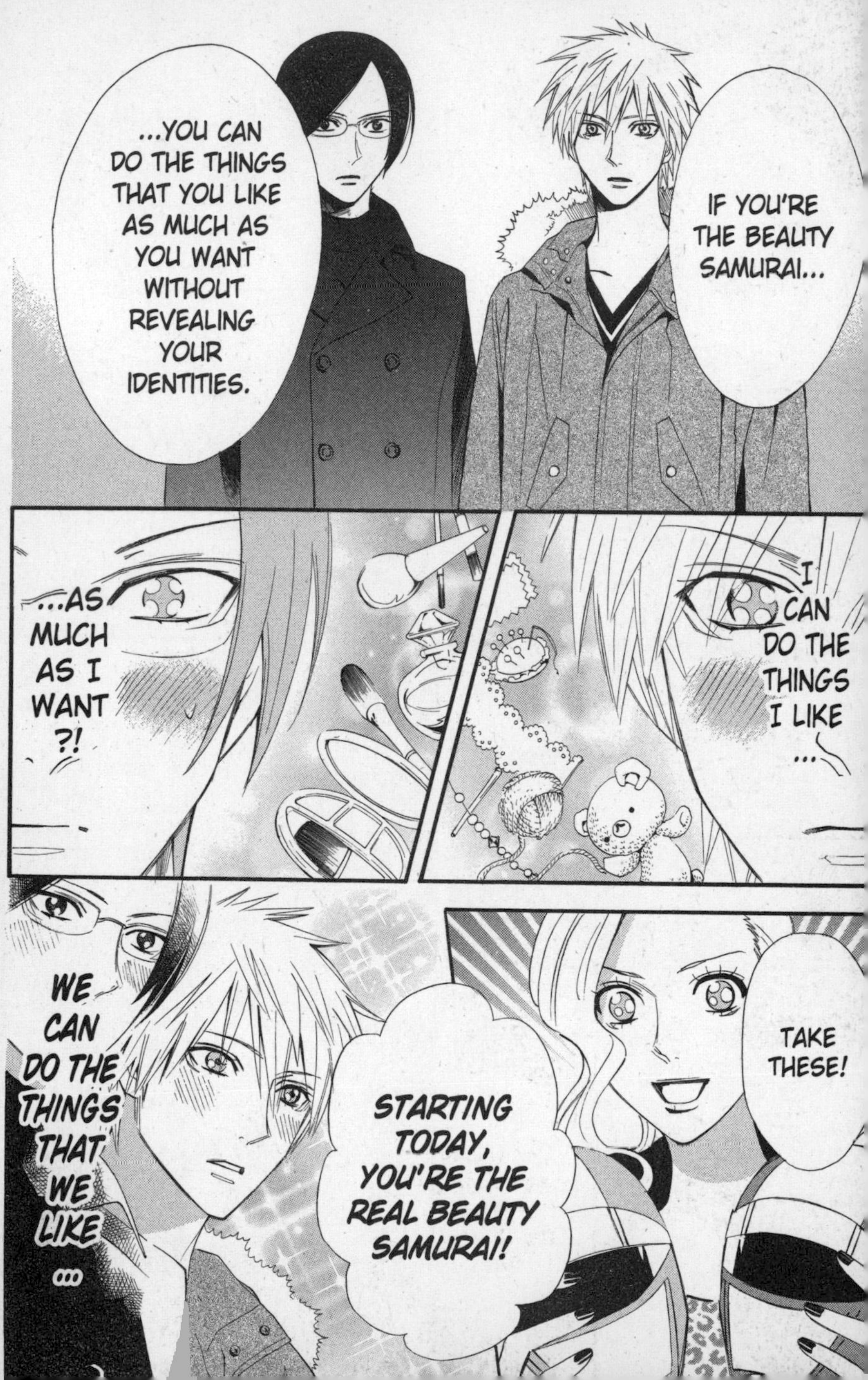
IF YOU'RE THE BEAUTY SAMURAI...
...YOU CAN DO THE THINGS THAT YOU LIKE AS MUCH AS YOU WANT WITHOUT REVEALING YOUR IDENTITIES.
I CAN DO THE THINGS I LIKE ...
...AS MUCH AS I WANT ?!
TAKE THESE!
STARTING TODAY, YOU'RE THE REAL BEAUTY SAMURAI!
WE CAN DO THE THINGS THAT WE LIKE ...

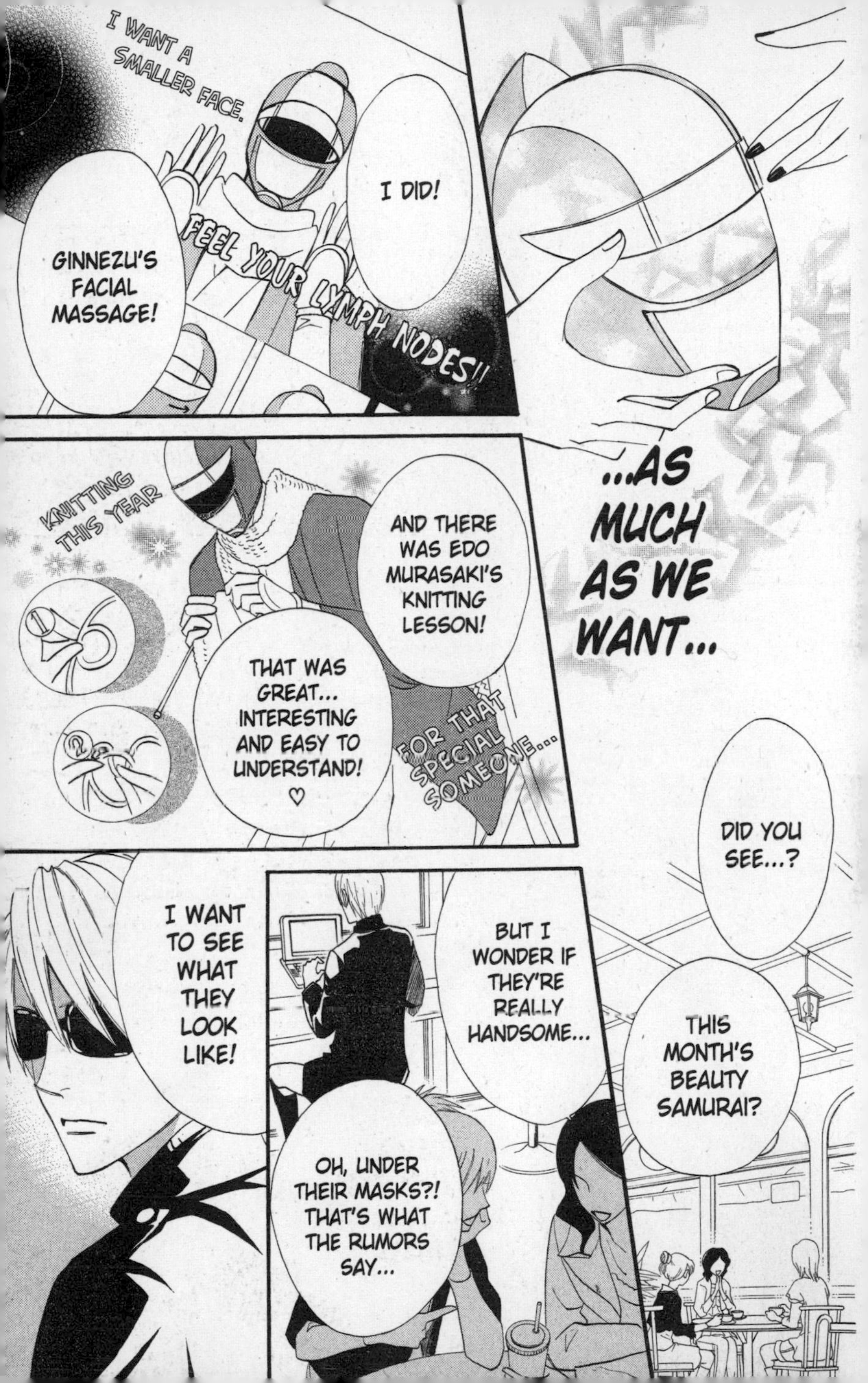
I DID!
I WANT A SMALLER FACE.
FEEL YOUR LYMPH NODES!!
GINNEZU'S FACIAL MASSAGE!
...AS MUCH AS WE WANT...
AND THERE WAS EDO MURASAKI'S KNITTING LESSON!
KNITTING THIS YEAR
FOR THAT SPECIAL SOMEONE...
THAT WAS GREAT... INTERESTING AND EASY TO UNDERSTAND! ♡
DID YOU SEE...?
THIS MONTH'S BEAUTY SAMURAI?
BUT I WONDER IF THEY'RE REALLY HANDSOME...
OH, UNDER THEIR MASKS?! THAT'S WHAT THE RUMORS SAY...
I WANT TO SEE WHAT THEY LOOK LIKE!

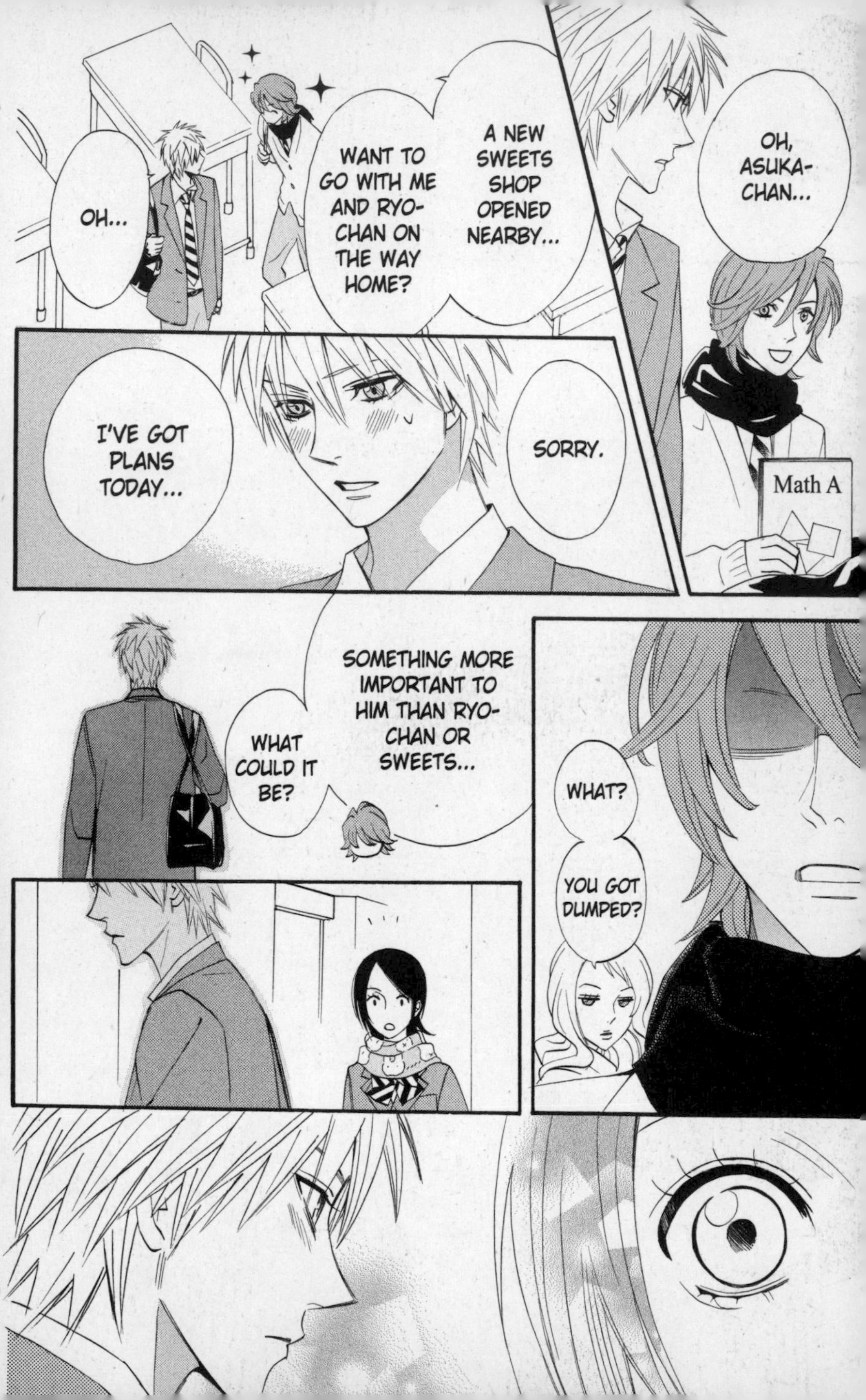
OH, ASUKA-CHAN...
Math A
A NEW SWEETS SHOP OPENED NEARBY...
WANT TO GO WITH ME AND RYO-CHAN ON THE WAY HOME?
OH...
SORRY.
I'VE GOT PLANS TODAY...
WHAT?
YOU GOT DUMPED?
SOMETHING MORE IMPORTANT TO HIM THAN RYO-CHAN OR SWEETS...
WHAT COULD IT BE?

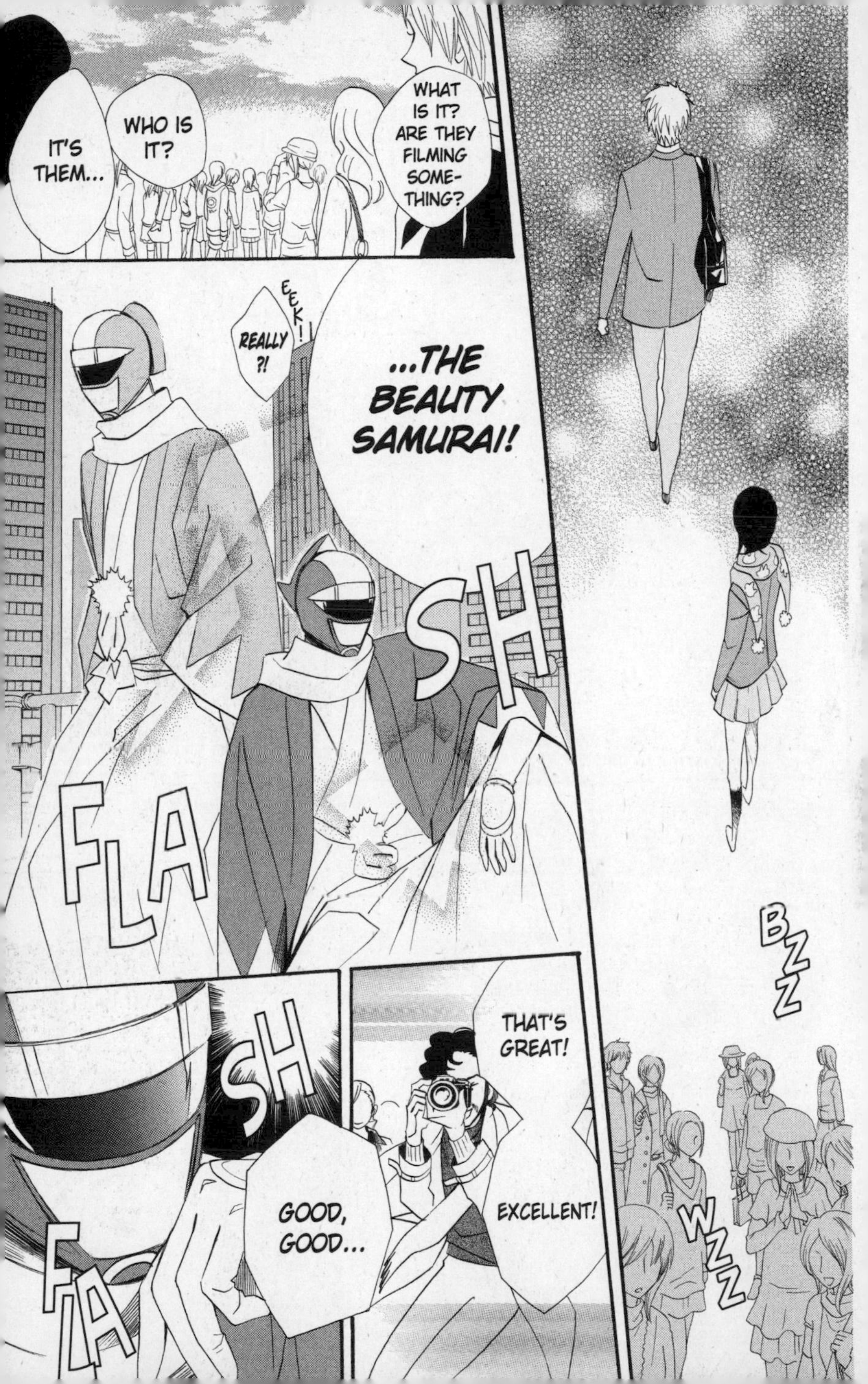
BZZ
WZZ
WHAT IS IT? ARE THEY FILMING SOMETHING?
WHO IS IT?
IT'S THEM...
...THE BEAUTY SAMURAI!
EEK!
REALLY?!
SH
FLA
THAT'S GREAT!
EXCELLENT!
GOOD, GOOD...
SH
FLA

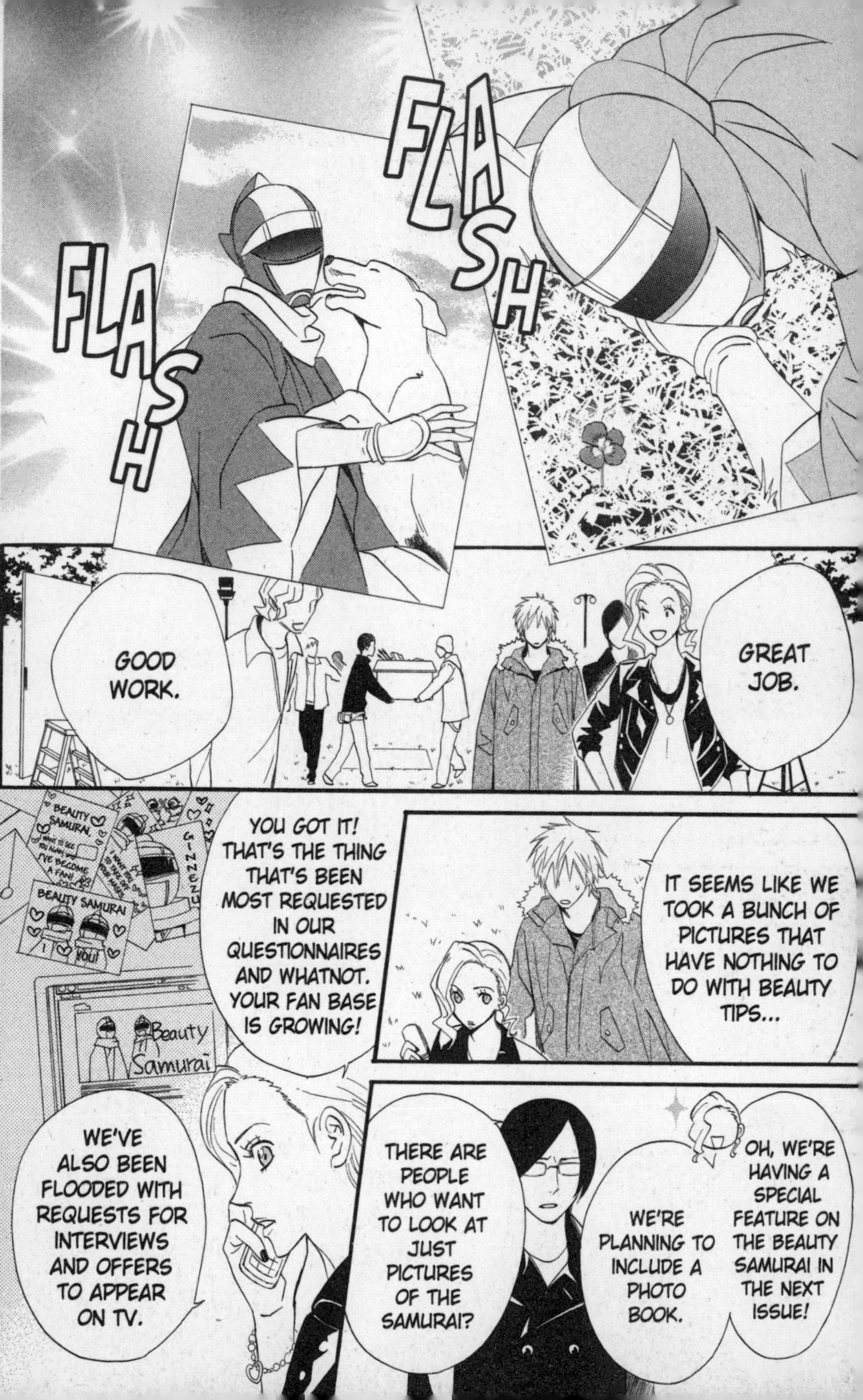
FLASH
FLASH
GREAT JOB.
GOOD WORK.
IT SEEMS LIKE WE TOOK A BUNCH OF PICTURES THAT HAVE NOTHING TO DO WITH BEAUTY TIPS...
YOU GOT IT! THAT'S THE THING THAT'S BEEN MOST REQUESTED IN OUR QUESTIONNAIRES AND WHATNOT. YOUR FAN BASE IS GROWING!
BEAUTY SAMURAI,
I'VE BECOME A FAN!
BEAUTY SAMURAI
I ♡ YOU!
Beauty Samurai
OH, WE'RE HAVING A SPECIAL FEATURE ON THE BEAUTY SAMURAI IN THE NEXT ISSUE!
WE'RE PLANNING TO INCLUDE A PHOTO BOOK.
THERE ARE PEOPLE WHO WANT TO LOOK AT JUST PICTURES OF THE SAMURAI?
WE'VE ALSO BEEN FLOODED WITH REQUESTS FOR INTERVIEWS AND OFFERS TO APPEAR ON TV.

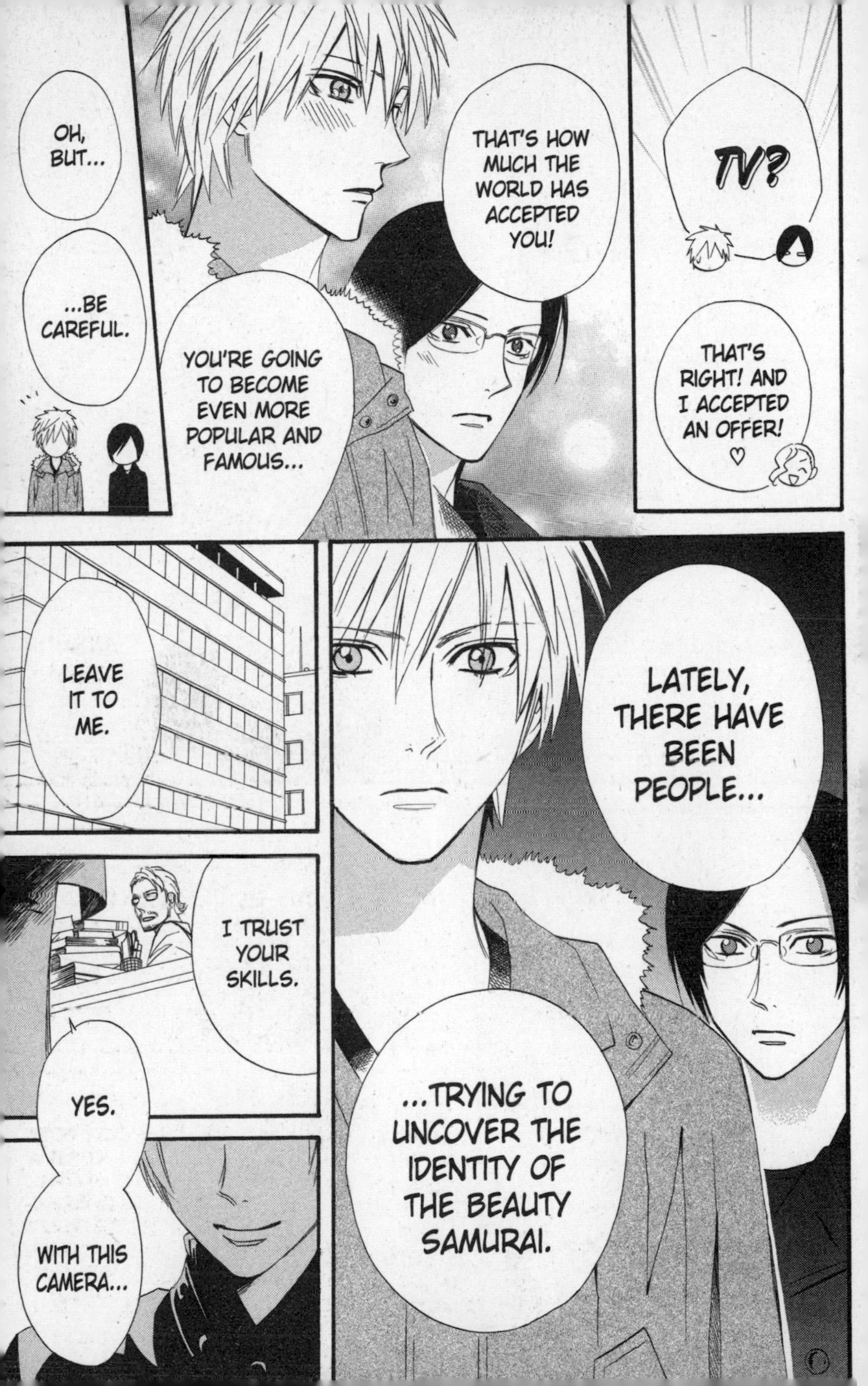
TV?
THAT'S RIGHT! AND I ACCEPTED AN OFFER! ♡
THAT'S HOW MUCH THE WORLD HAS ACCEPTED YOU!
YOU'RE GOING TO BECOME EVEN MORE POPULAR AND FAMOUS...
OH, BUT...
...BE CAREFUL.
LATELY, THERE HAVE BEEN PEOPLE...
...TRYING TO UNCOVER THE IDENTITY OF THE BEAUTY SAMURAI.
LEAVE IT TO ME.
I TRUST YOUR SKILLS.
YES.
WITH THIS CAMERA...

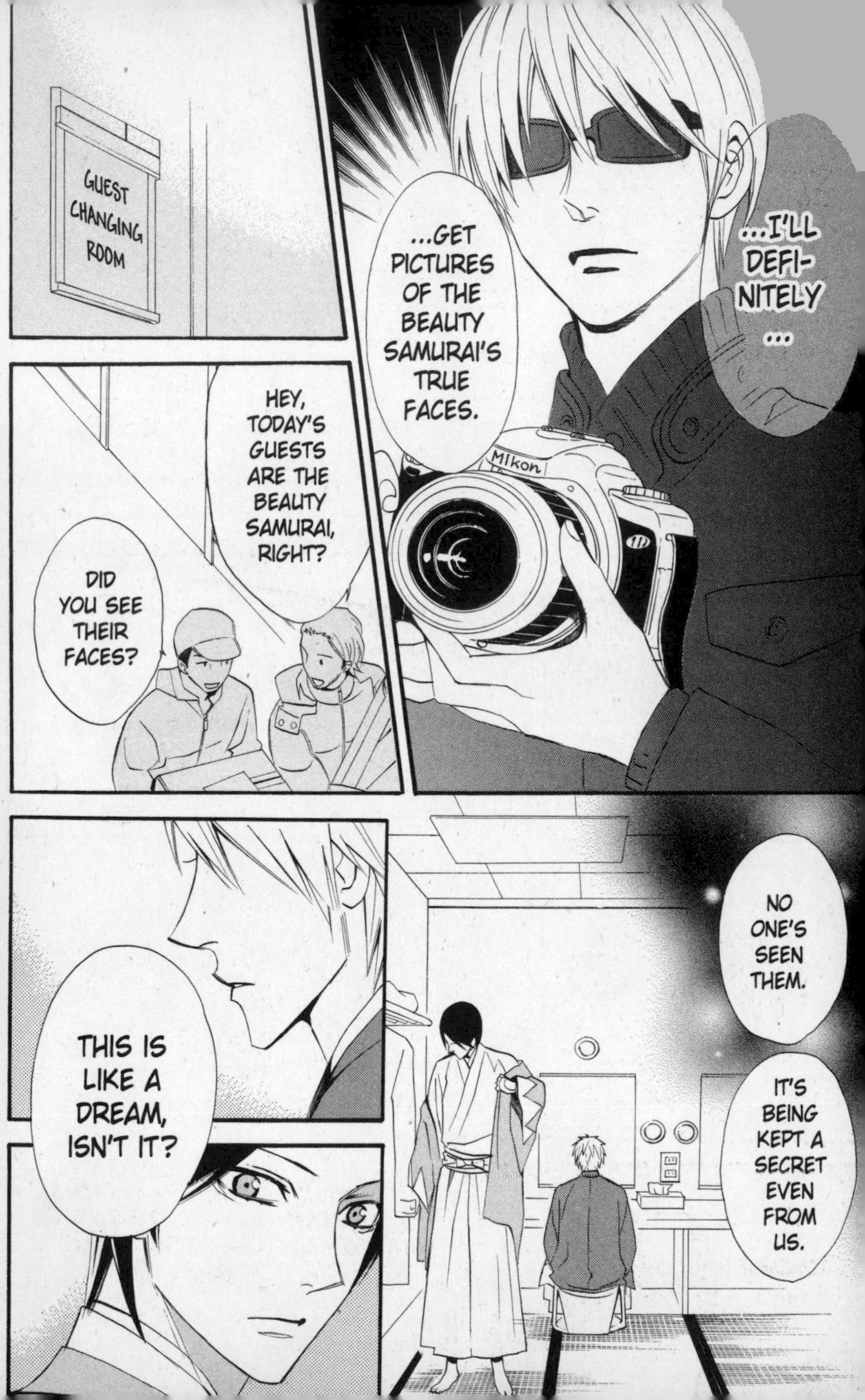
...I'LL DEFINITELY...
...GET PICTURES OF THE BEAUTY SAMURAI'S TRUE FACES.
Mikon
GUEST CHANGING ROOM
HEY, TODAY'S GUESTS ARE THE BEAUTY SAMURAI, RIGHT?
DID YOU SEE THEIR FACES?
NO ONE'S SEEN THEM.
IT'S BEING KEPT A SECRET EVEN FROM US.
THIS IS LIKE A DREAM, ISN'T IT?

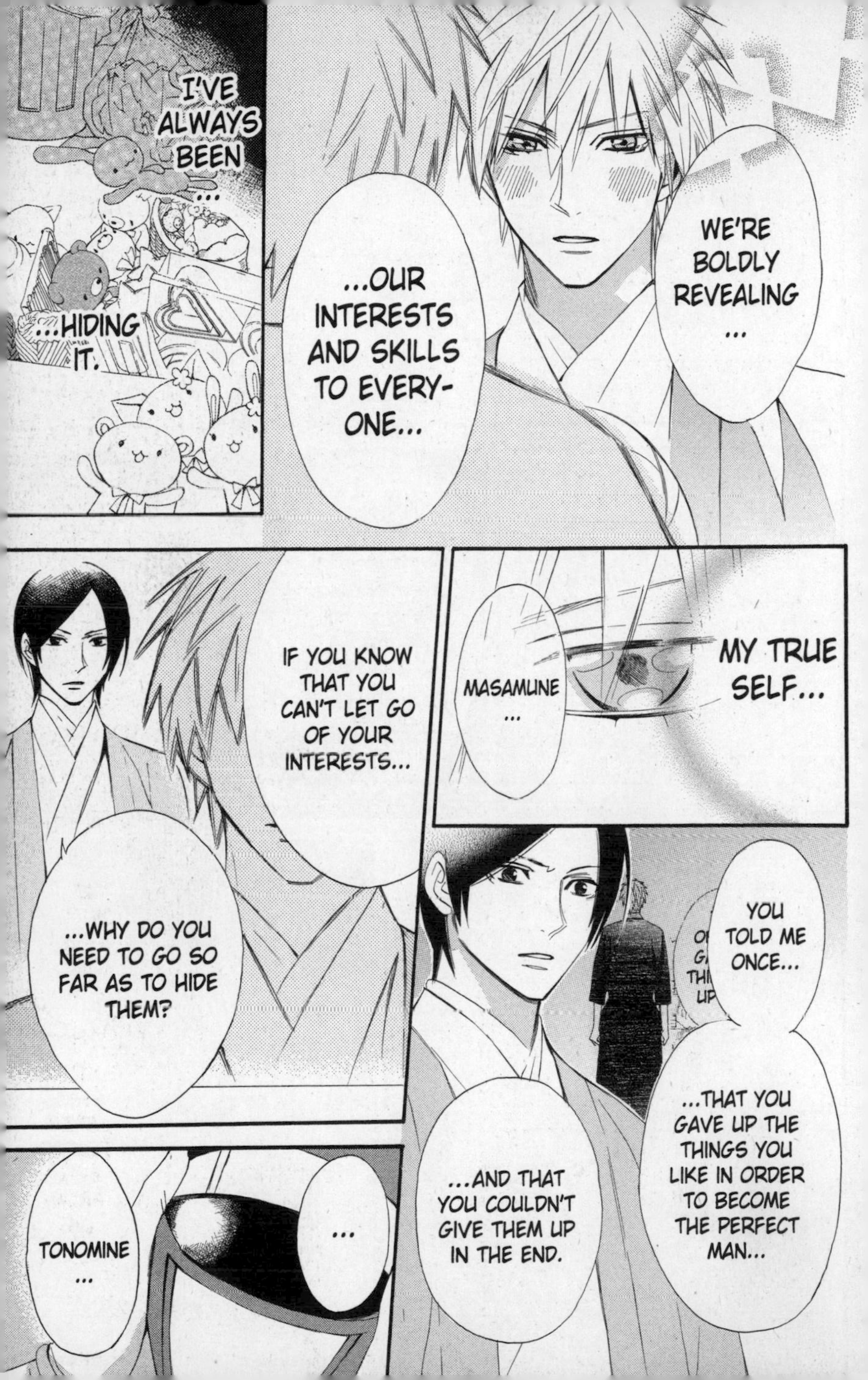
WE'RE BOLDLY REVEALING ...
...OUR INTERESTS AND SKILLS TO EVERY-ONE...
I'VE ALWAYS BEEN ...
...HIDING IT.
MY TRUE SELF...
MASAMUNE ...
IF YOU KNOW THAT YOU CAN'T LET GO OF YOUR INTERESTS...
...WHY DO YOU NEED TO GO SO FAR AS TO HIDE THEM?
YOU TOLD ME ONCE...
...THAT YOU GAVE UP THE THINGS YOU LIKE IN ORDER TO BECOME THE PERFECT MAN...
...AND THAT YOU COULDN'T GIVE THEM UP IN THE END.
...
TONOMINE ...

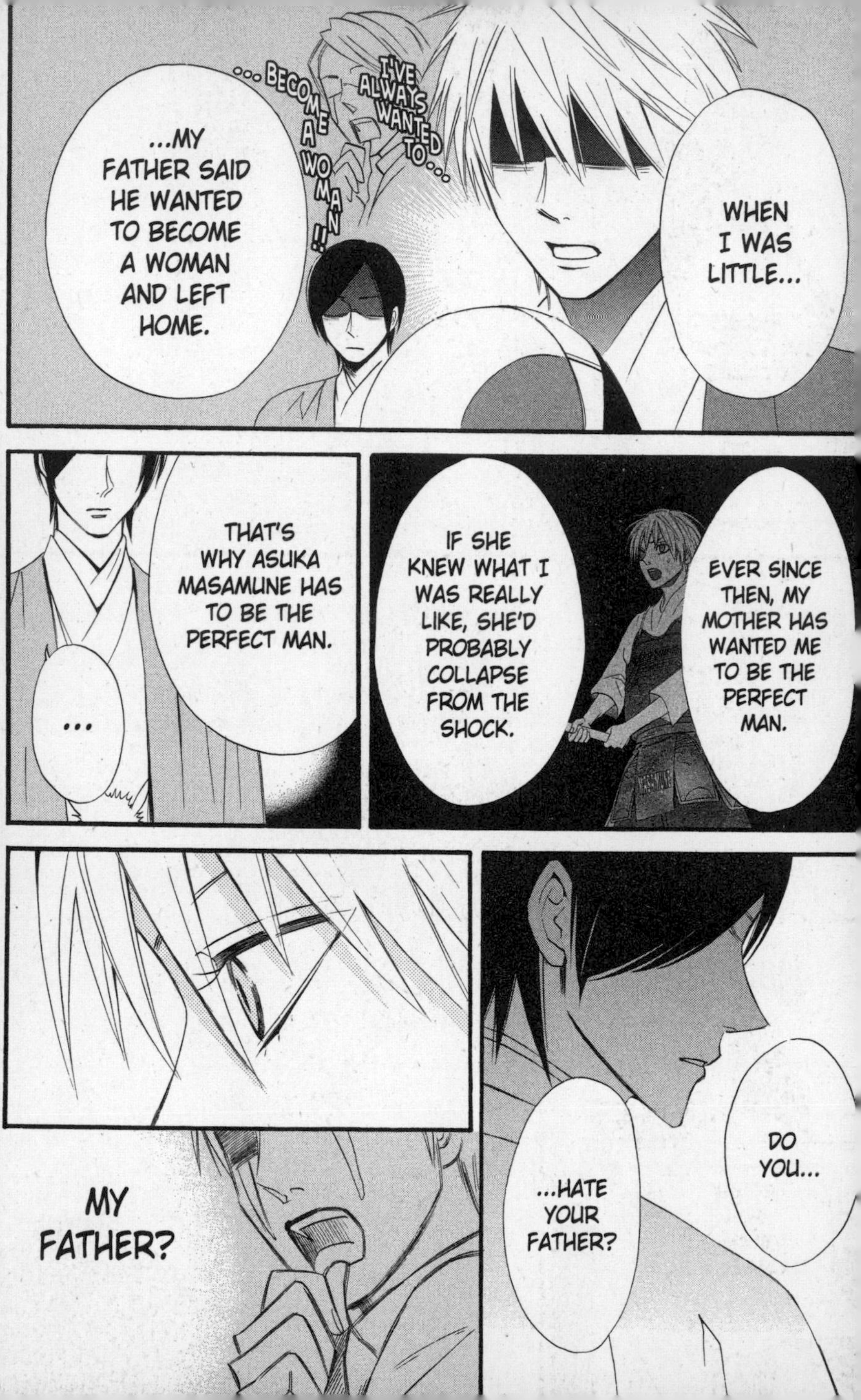
WHEN I WAS LITTLE...
I'VE ALWAYS WANTED TO...
...BECOME A WOMAN!!
...MY FATHER SAID HE WANTED TO BECOME A WOMAN AND LEFT HOME.
EVER SINCE THEN, MY MOTHER HAS WANTED ME TO BE THE PERFECT MAN.
IF SHE KNEW WHAT I WAS REALLY LIKE, SHE'D PROBABLY COLLAPSE FROM THE SHOCK.
THAT'S WHY ASUKA MASAMUNE HAS TO BE THE PERFECT MAN.
...
DO YOU...
...HATE YOUR FATHER?
MY FATHER?

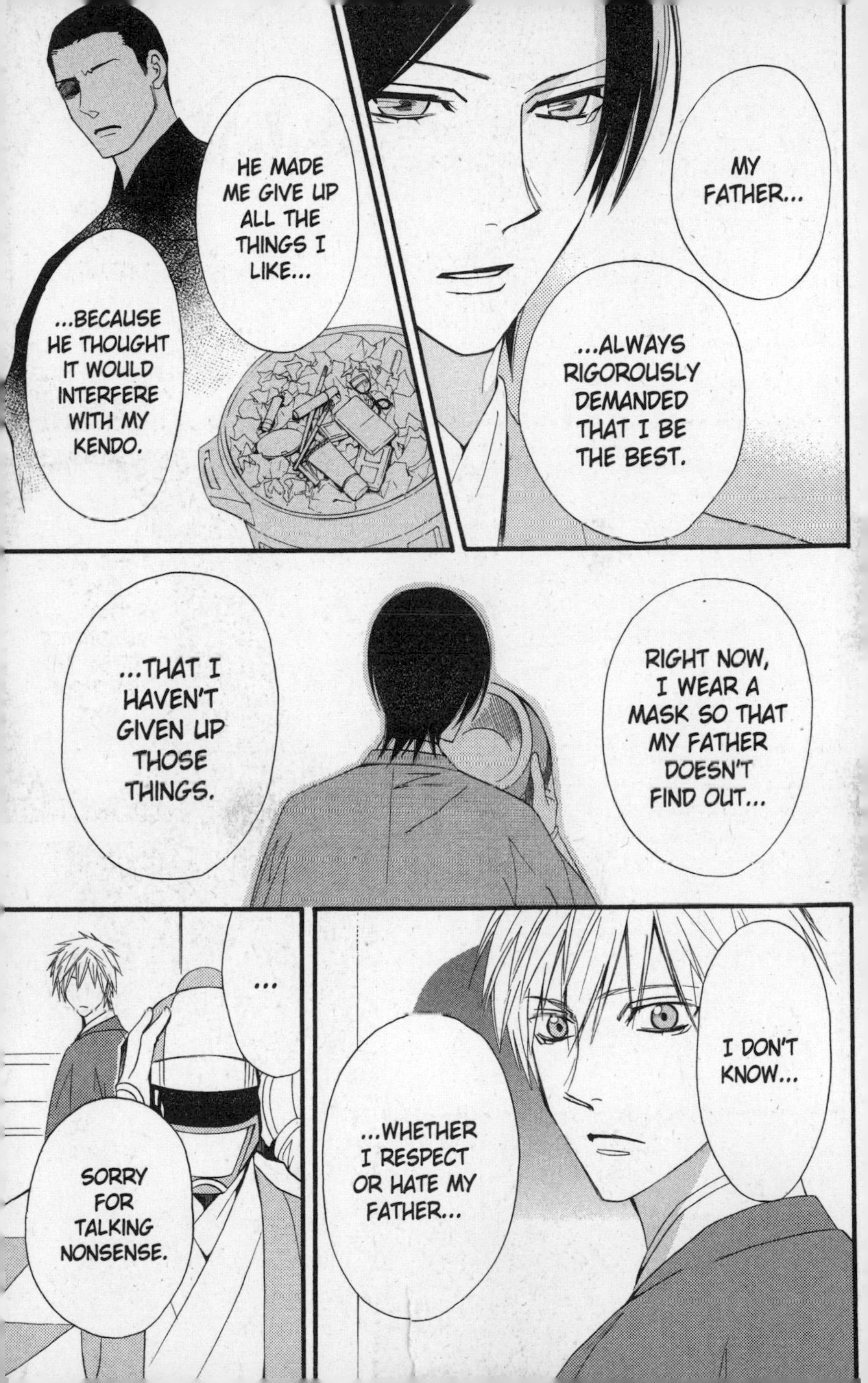
MY FATHER...
...ALWAYS RIGOROUSLY DEMANDED THAT I BE THE BEST.
HE MADE ME GIVE UP ALL THE THINGS I LIKE...
...BECAUSE HE THOUGHT IT WOULD INTERFERE WITH MY KENDO.
RIGHT NOW, I WEAR A MASK SO THAT MY FATHER DOESN'T FIND OUT...
...THAT I HAVEN'T GIVEN UP THOSE THINGS.
I DON'T KNOW...
...WHETHER I RESPECT OR HATE MY FATHER...
...
SORRY FOR TALKING NONSENSE.

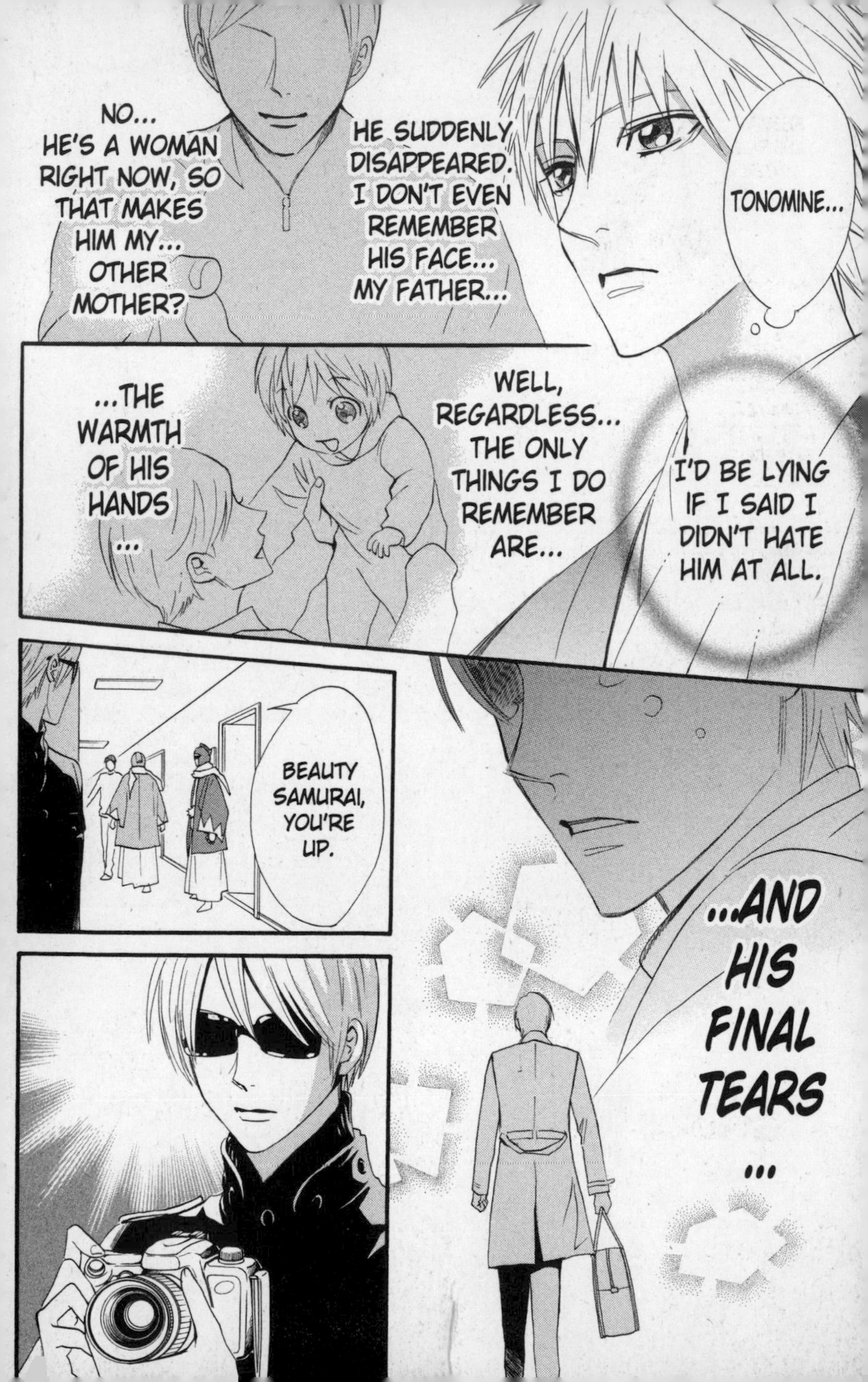
TONOMINE...
HE SUDDENLY DISAPPEARED. I DON'T EVEN REMEMBER HIS FACE... MY FATHER...
NO... HE'S A WOMAN RIGHT NOW, SO THAT MAKES HIM MY... OTHER MOTHER?
I'D BE LYING IF I SAID I DIDN'T HATE HIM AT ALL.
WELL, REGARDLESS... THE ONLY THINGS I DO REMEMBER ARE...
...THE WARMTH OF HIS HANDS ...
...AND HIS FINAL TEARS ...
BEAUTY SAMURAI, YOU'RE UP.

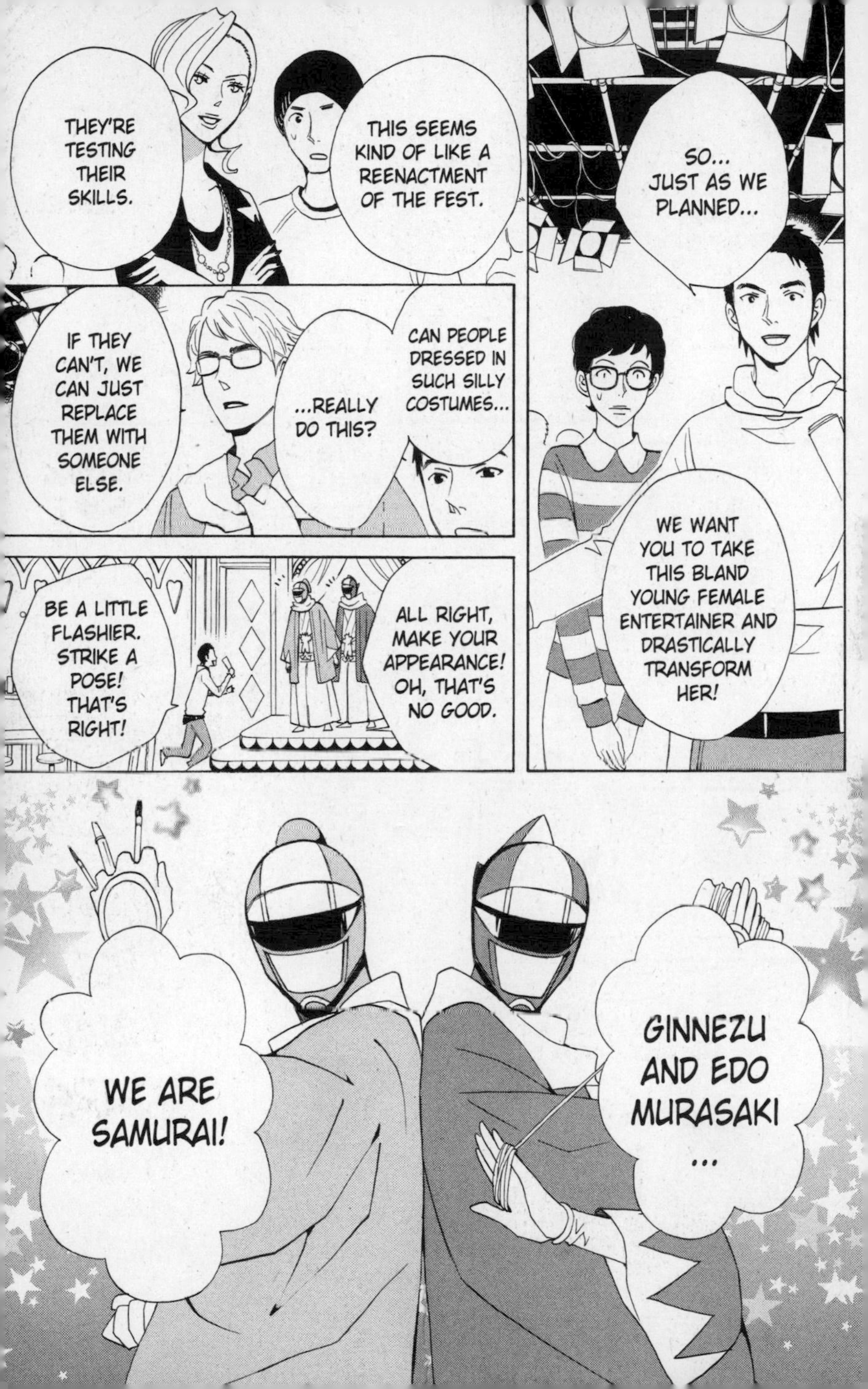

SO... JUST AS WE PLANNED...
WE WANT YOU TO TAKE THIS BLAND YOUNG FEMALE ENTERTAINER AND DRASTICALLY TRANSFORM HER!
THIS SEEMS KIND OF LIKE A REENACTMENT OF THE FEST.
THEY'RE TESTING THEIR SKILLS.
CAN PEOPLE DRESSED IN SUCH SILLY COSTUMES...
...REALLY DO THIS?
IF THEY CAN'T, WE CAN JUST REPLACE THEM WITH SOMEONE ELSE.
ALL RIGHT, MAKE YOUR APPEARANCE! OH, THAT'S NO GOOD.
BE A LITTLE FLASHIER. STRIKE A POSE! THAT'S RIGHT!
GINNEZU AND EDO MURASAKI ...
WE ARE SAMURAI!

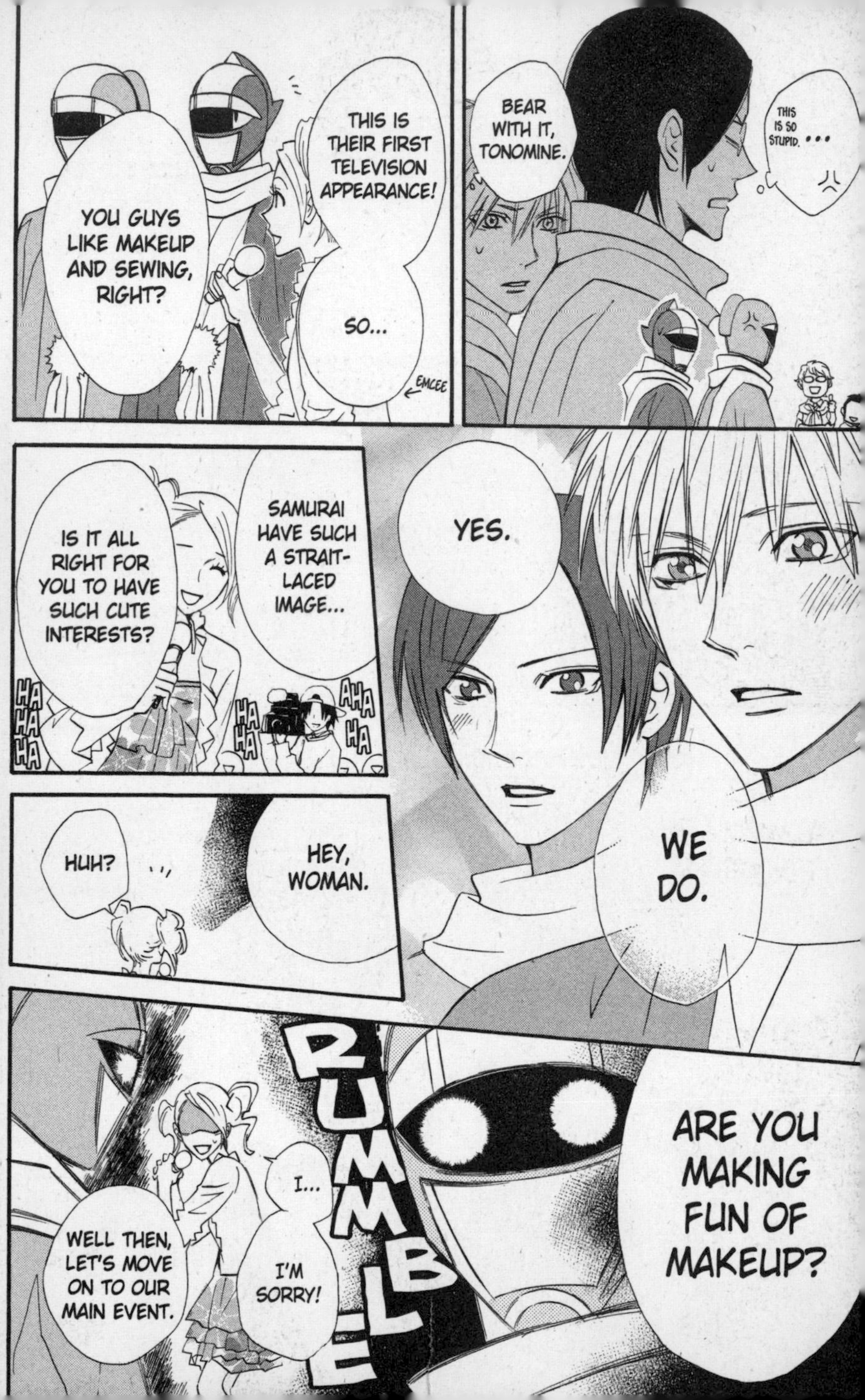
THIS IS SO STUPID. ...
BEAR WITH IT, TONOMINE.
THIS IS THEIR FIRST TELEVISION APPEARANCE!
SO...
YOU GUYS LIKE MAKEUP AND SEWING, RIGHT?
EMCEE
YES.
WE DO.
SAMURAI HAVE SUCH A STRAIT-LACED IMAGE...
IS IT ALL RIGHT FOR YOU TO HAVE SUCH CUTE INTERESTS?
AHA HA HA
HA HA
HA HA HA HA
HEY, WOMAN.
HUH?
ARE YOU MAKING FUN OF MAKEUP?
RUMBLE
I...
I'M SORRY!
WELL THEN, LET'S MOVE ON TO OUR MAIN EVENT.

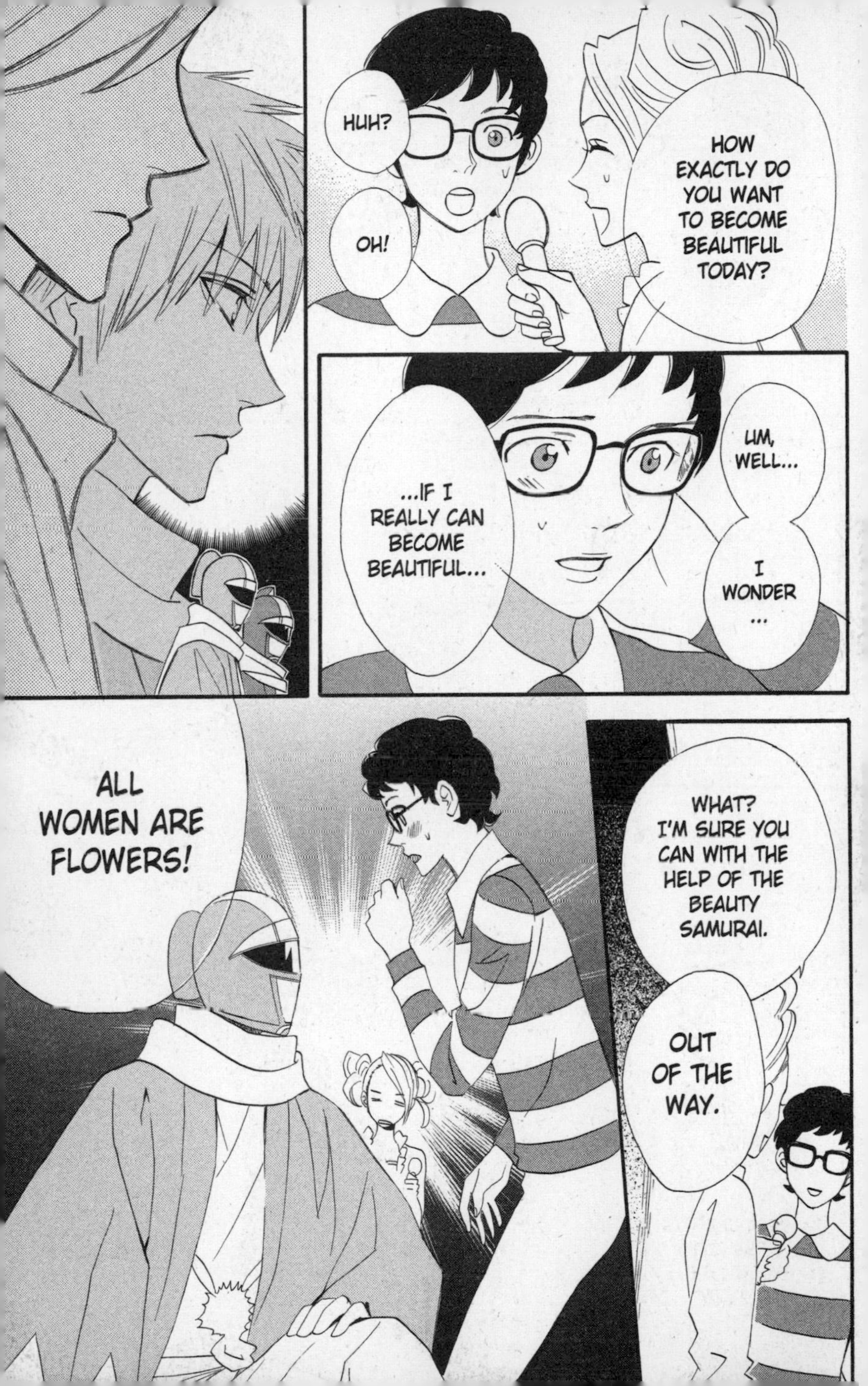
HOW EXACTLY DO YOU WANT TO BECOME BEAUTIFUL TODAY?
HUH?
OH!
UM, WELL...
I WONDER...
...IF I REALLY CAN BECOME BEAUTIFUL...
WHAT? I'M SURE YOU CAN WITH THE HELP OF THE BEAUTY SAMURAI.
OUT OF THE WAY.
ALL WOMEN ARE FLOWERS!

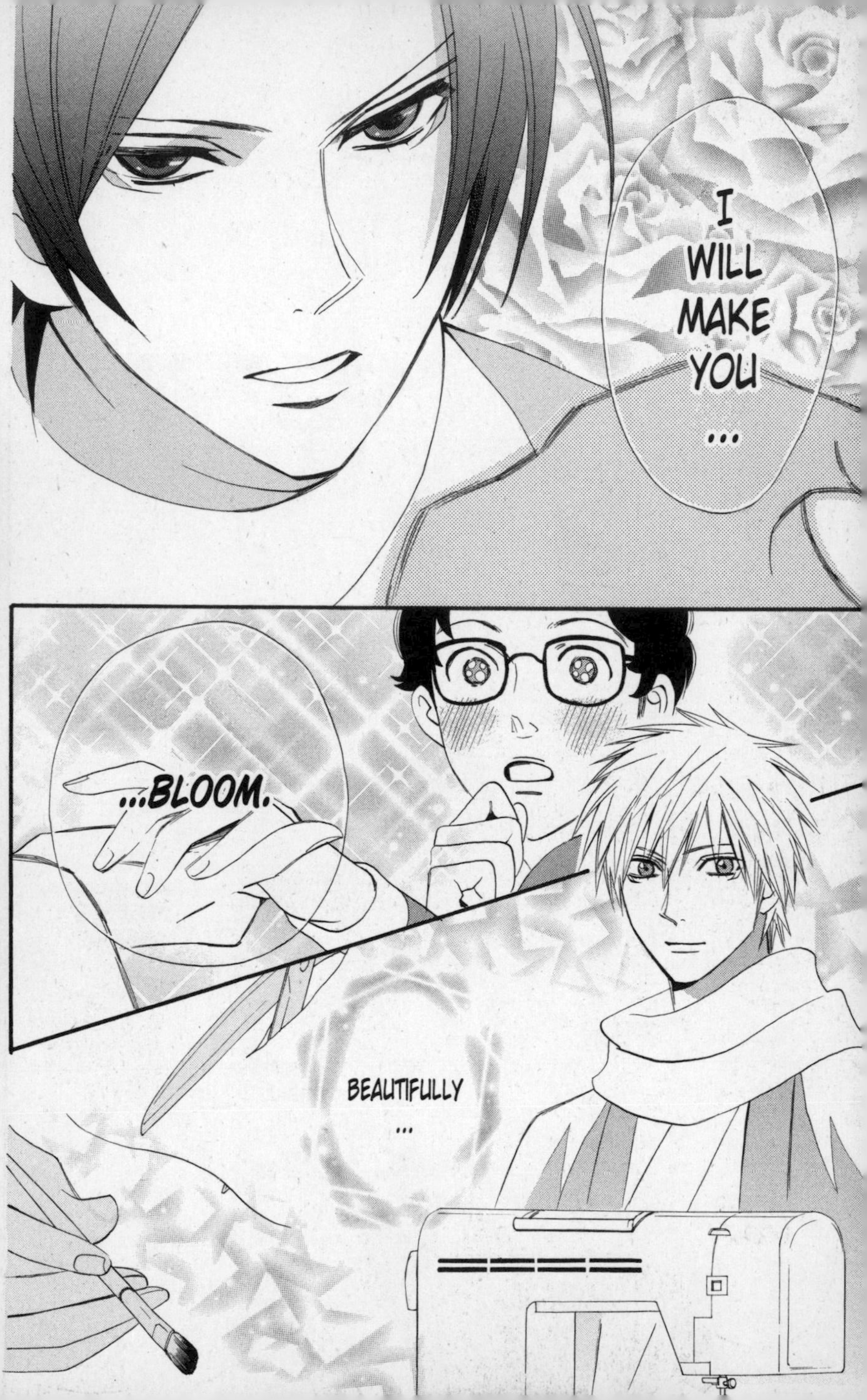
I WILL MAKE YOU ...
...BLOOM.
BEAUTIFULLY ...

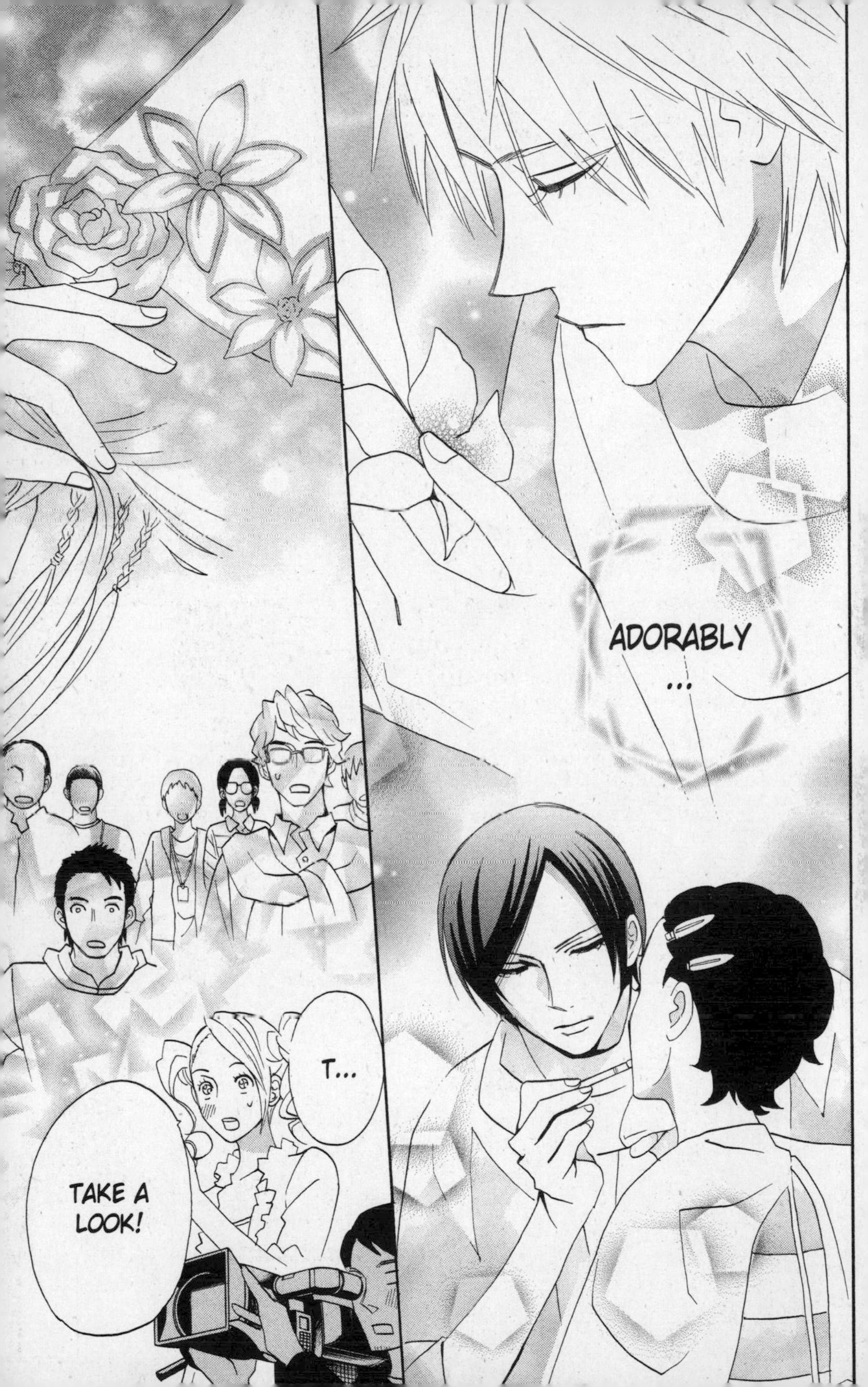
ADORABLY
...
T...
TAKE A LOOK!

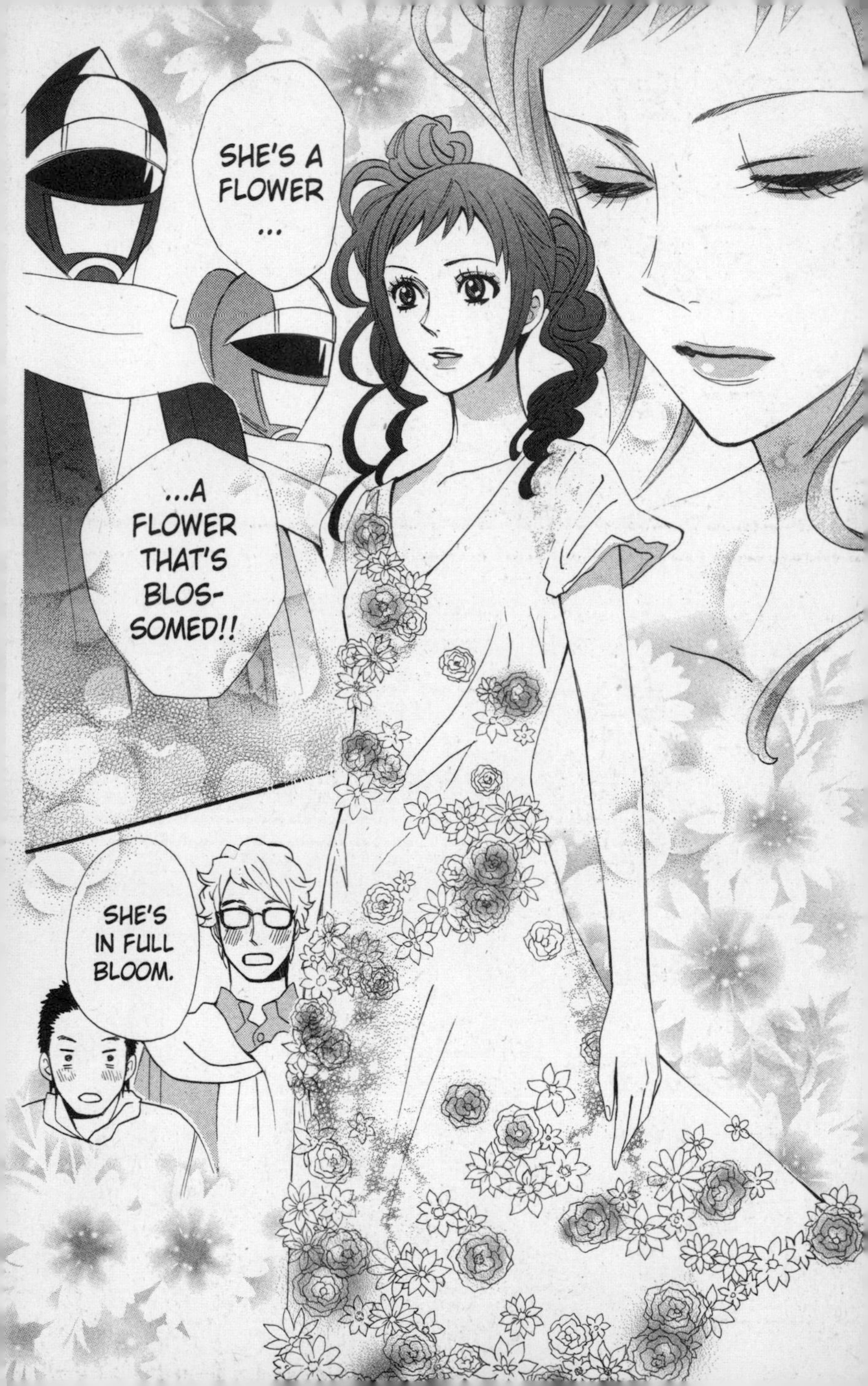
SHE'S A FLOWER ...
...A FLOWER THAT'S BLOS-SOMED!!
SHE'S IN FULL BLOOM.

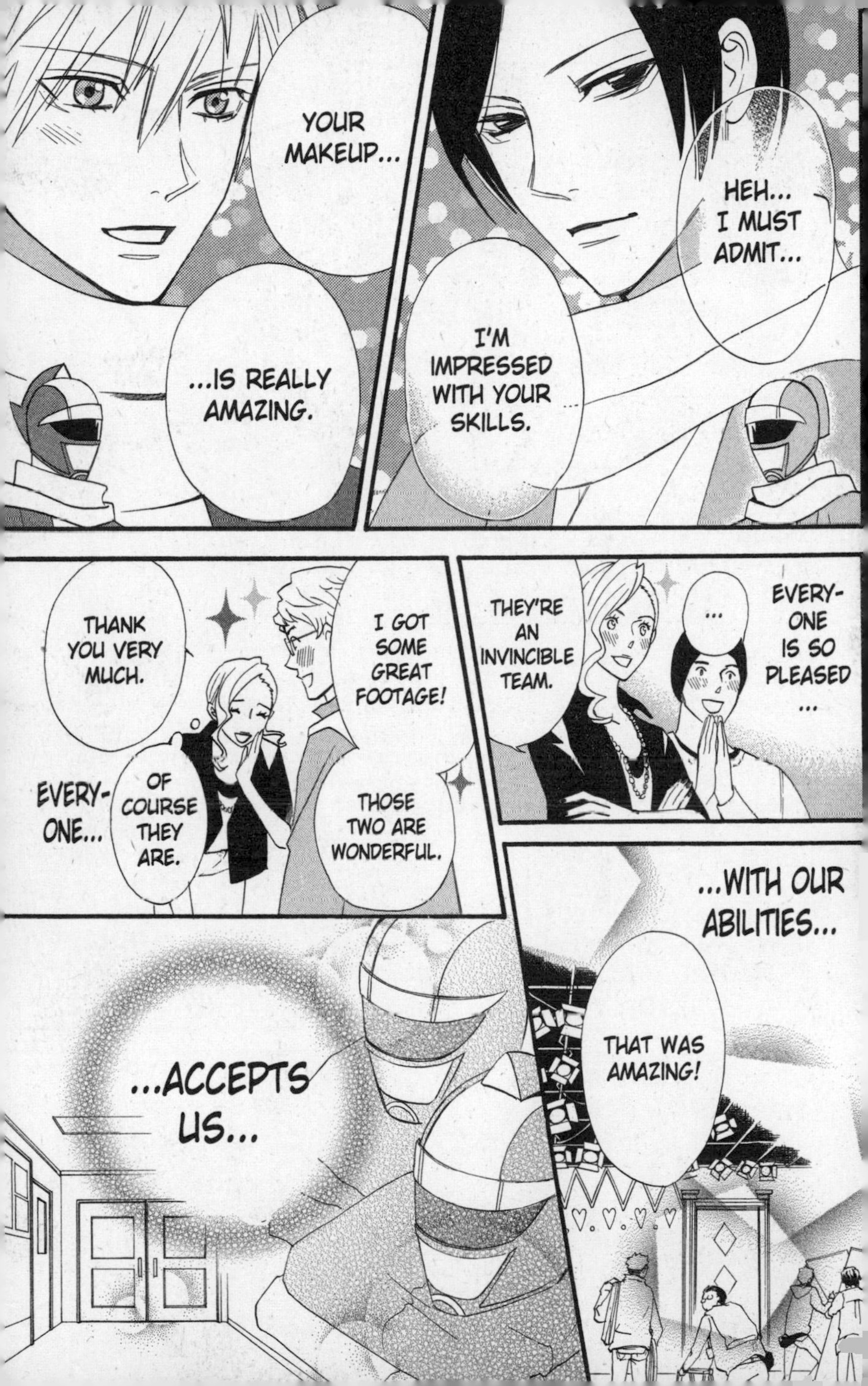
HEH... I MUST ADMIT...
I'M IMPRESSED WITH YOUR SKILLS.
YOUR MAKEUP...
...IS REALLY AMAZING.
EVERY-ONE IS SO PLEASED...
...
THEY'RE AN INVINCIBLE TEAM.
I GOT SOME GREAT FOOTAGE!
THOSE TWO ARE WONDERFUL.
THANK YOU VERY MUCH.
OF COURSE THEY ARE.
EVERY-ONE...
...WITH OUR ABILITIES...
THAT WAS AMAZING!
...ACCEPTS US...

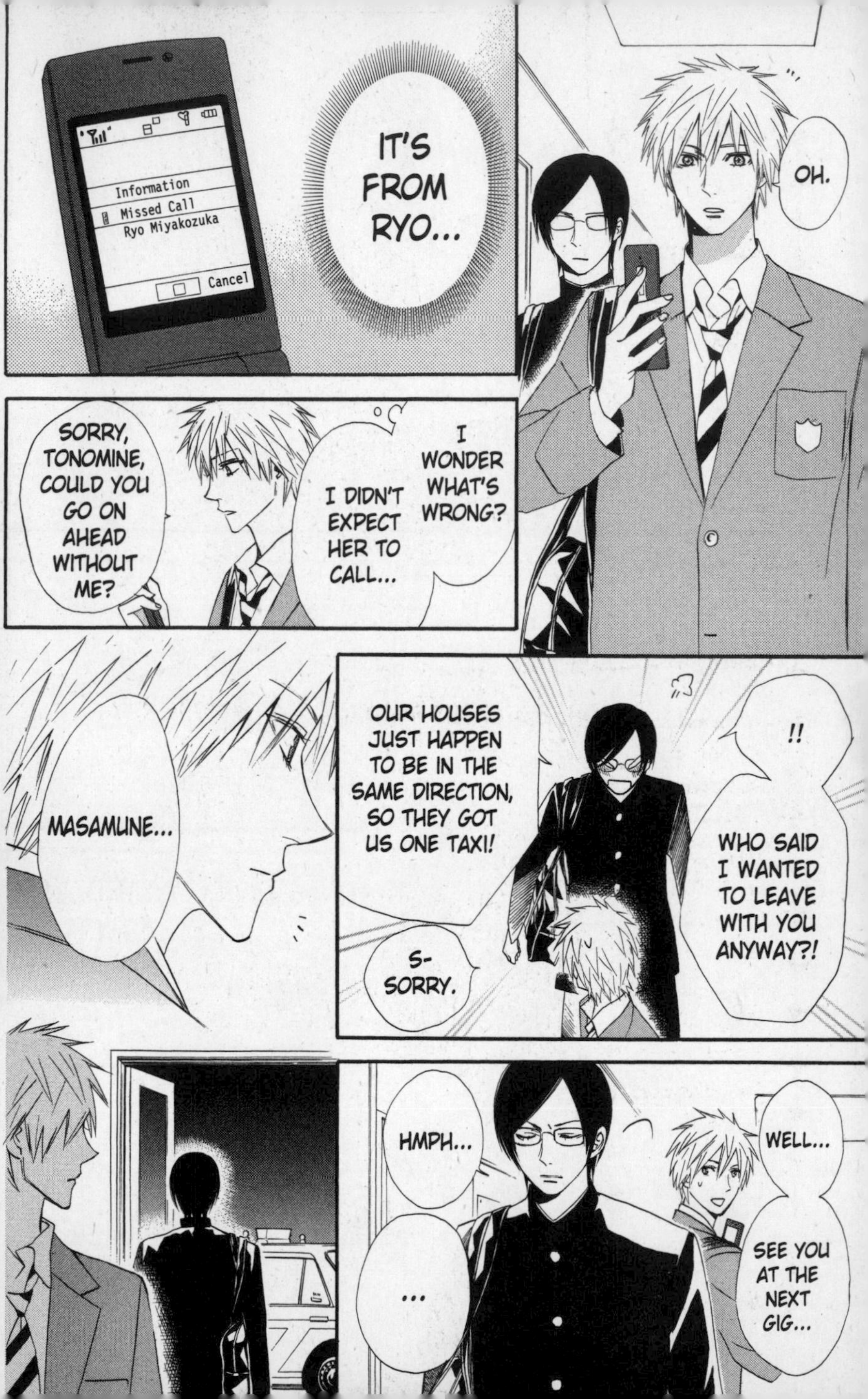
OH.
IT'S FROM RYO...
Information
Missed Call
Ryo Miyakozuka
Cancel
I WONDER WHAT'S WRONG?
I DIDN'T EXPECT HER TO CALL...
SORRY, TONOMINE, COULD YOU GO ON AHEAD WITHOUT ME?
!!
OUR HOUSES JUST HAPPEN TO BE IN THE SAME DIRECTION, SO THEY GOT US ONE TAXI!
WHO SAID I WANTED TO LEAVE WITH YOU ANYWAY?!
S-SORRY.
MASAMUNE...
WELL...
SEE YOU AT THE NEXT GIG...
HMPH...
...

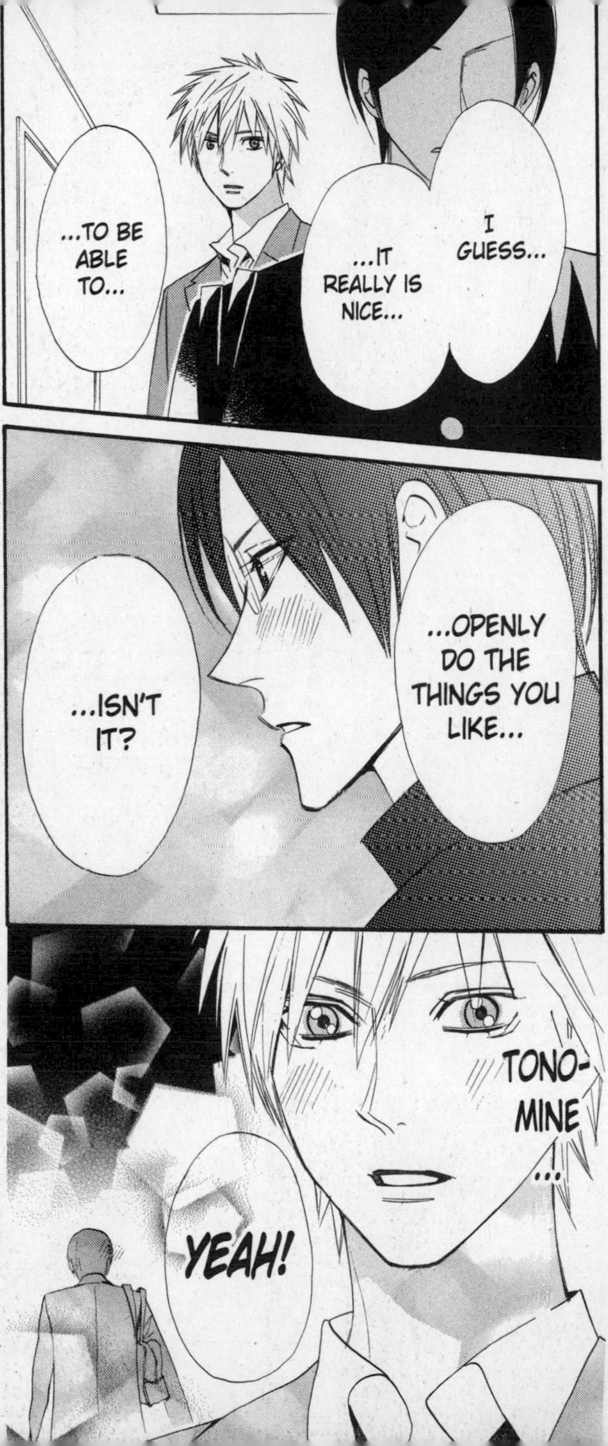
I GUESS...
...IT REALLY IS NICE...
...TO BE ABLE TO...
...OPENLY DO THE THINGS YOU LIKE...
...ISN'T IT?
TONO-MINE...
YEAH!

Production Assistance:

Shimada-san
Takowa-san
Kawashima-san
Kuwana-san
Tanaka-san
Nishizawa-san
Yone-san
Nakazawa-san
Sakurai-san

Special Thanks:

Abe-san
Abewo
All My Readers

If you have any thoughts or opinions, please send them to:

Aya Kanno
c/o Otomen Editor
P.O. Box 77010
San Francisco, CA
94107

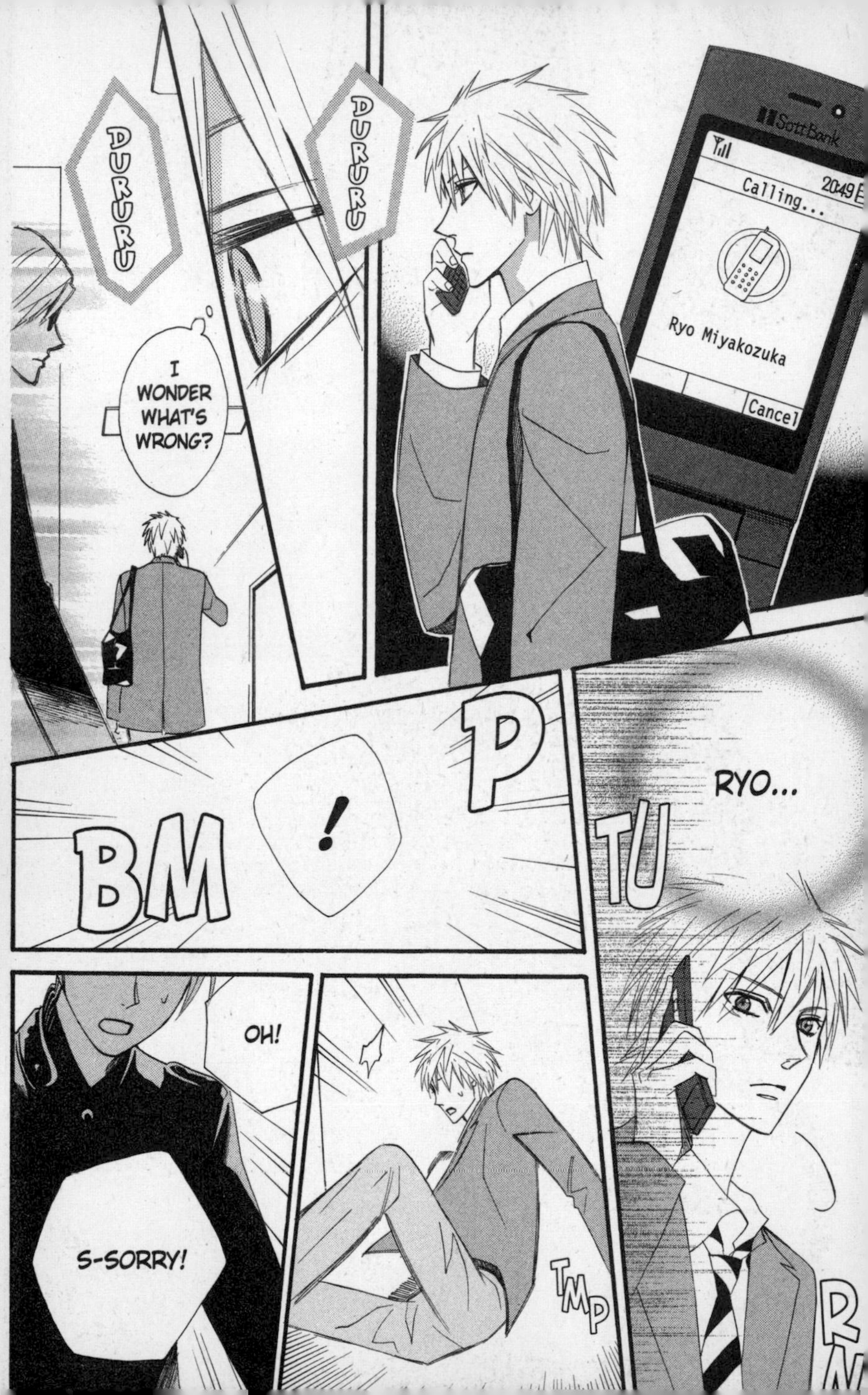
Calling...
Ryo Miyakozuka
Cancel
DURURU
DURURU
I WONDER WHAT'S WRONG?
RYO...
TU
RRN
P
!
BM
TMP
OH!
S-SORRY!

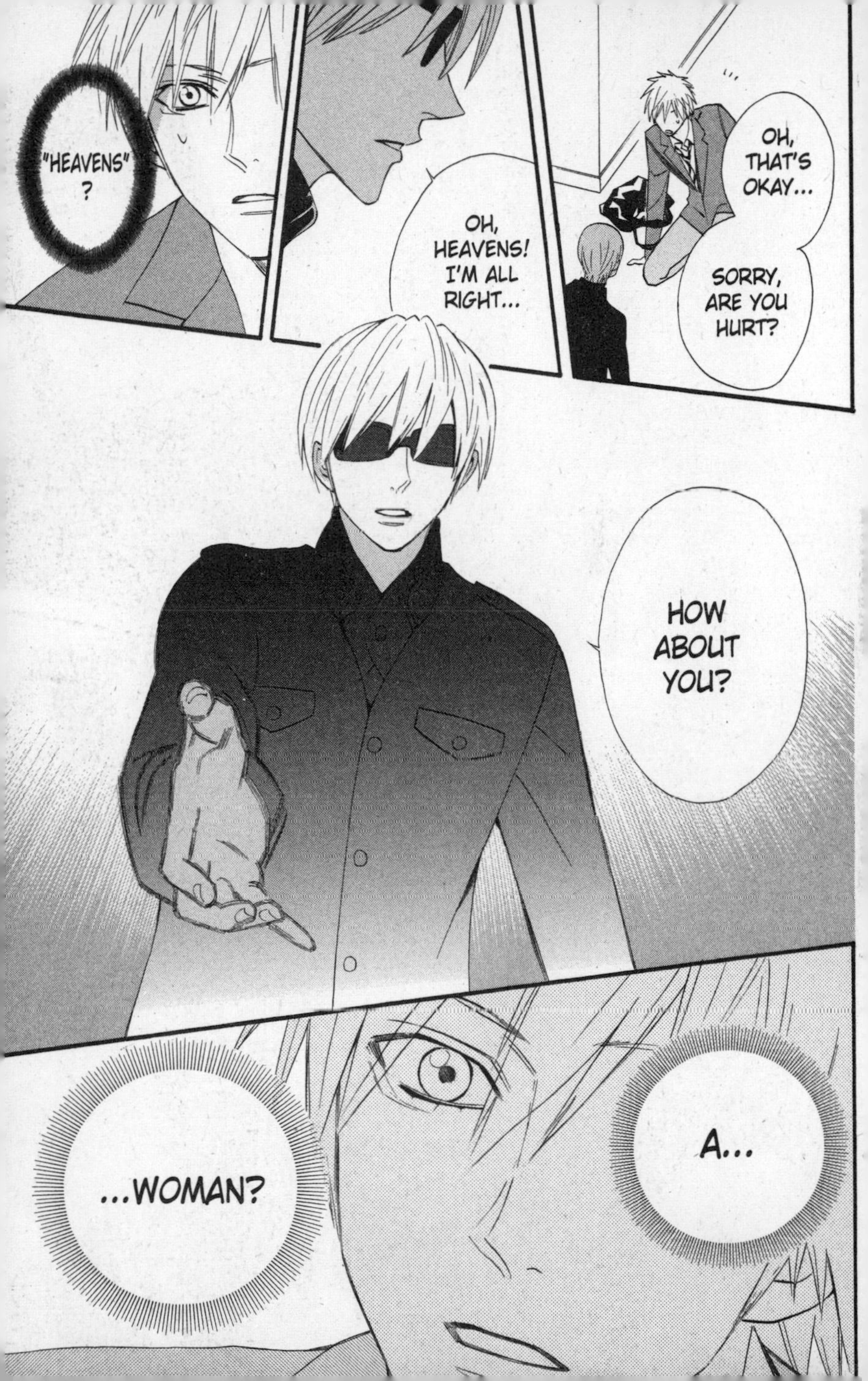
OH, THAT'S OKAY...
SORRY, ARE YOU HURT?
OH, HEAVENS! I'M ALL RIGHT...
"HEAVENS" ?
HOW ABOUT YOU?
A...
...WOMAN?

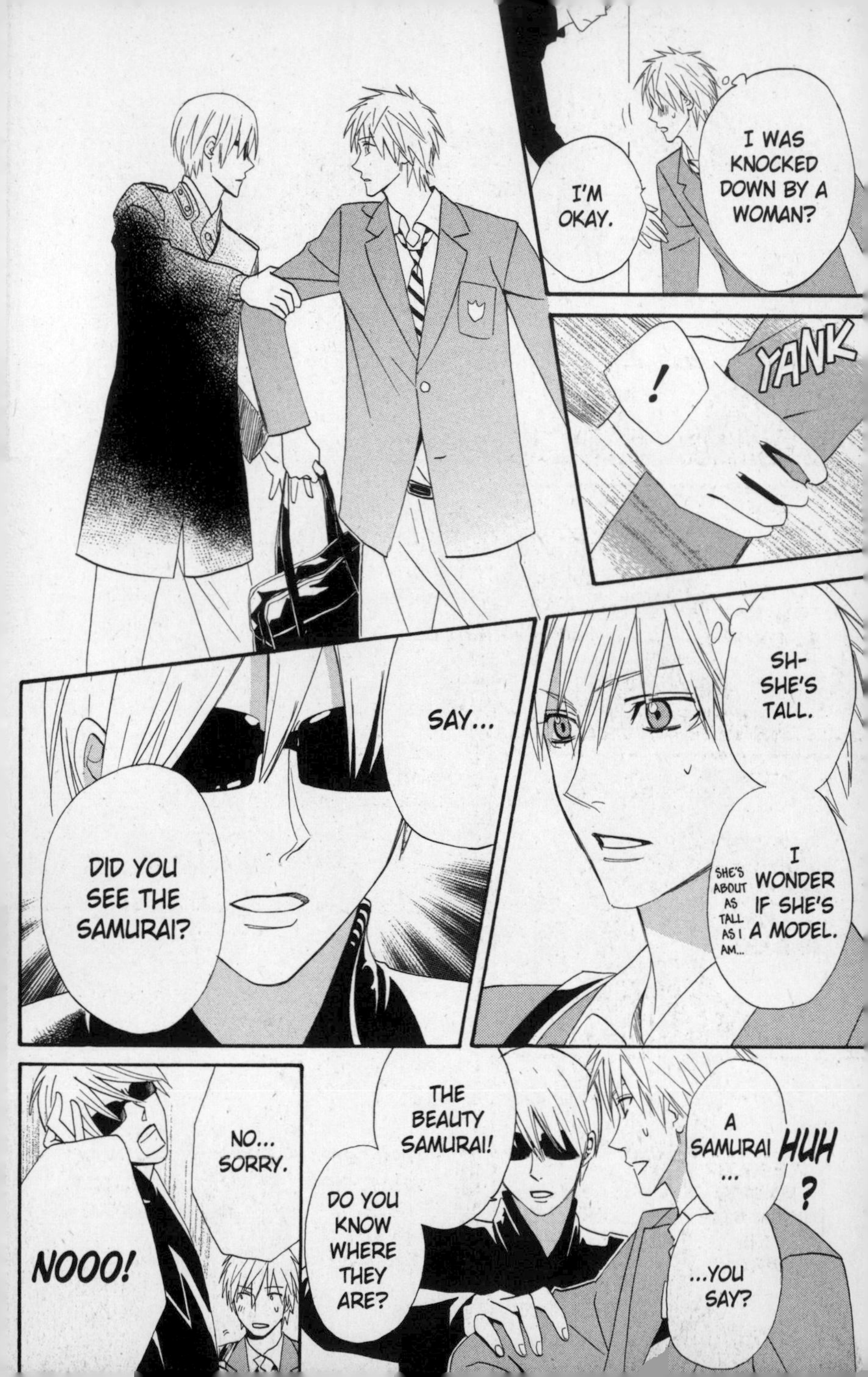
I WAS KNOCKED DOWN BY A WOMAN?
I'M OKAY.
!
YANK
SH-SHE'S TALL.
I WONDER IF SHE'S A MODEL.
SHE'S ABOUT AS TALL AS I AM...
SAY...
DID YOU SEE THE SAMURAI?
A SAMURAI ...
HUH?
...YOU SAY?
THE BEAUTY SAMURAI!
DO YOU KNOW WHERE THEY ARE?
NO... SORRY.
NOOO!

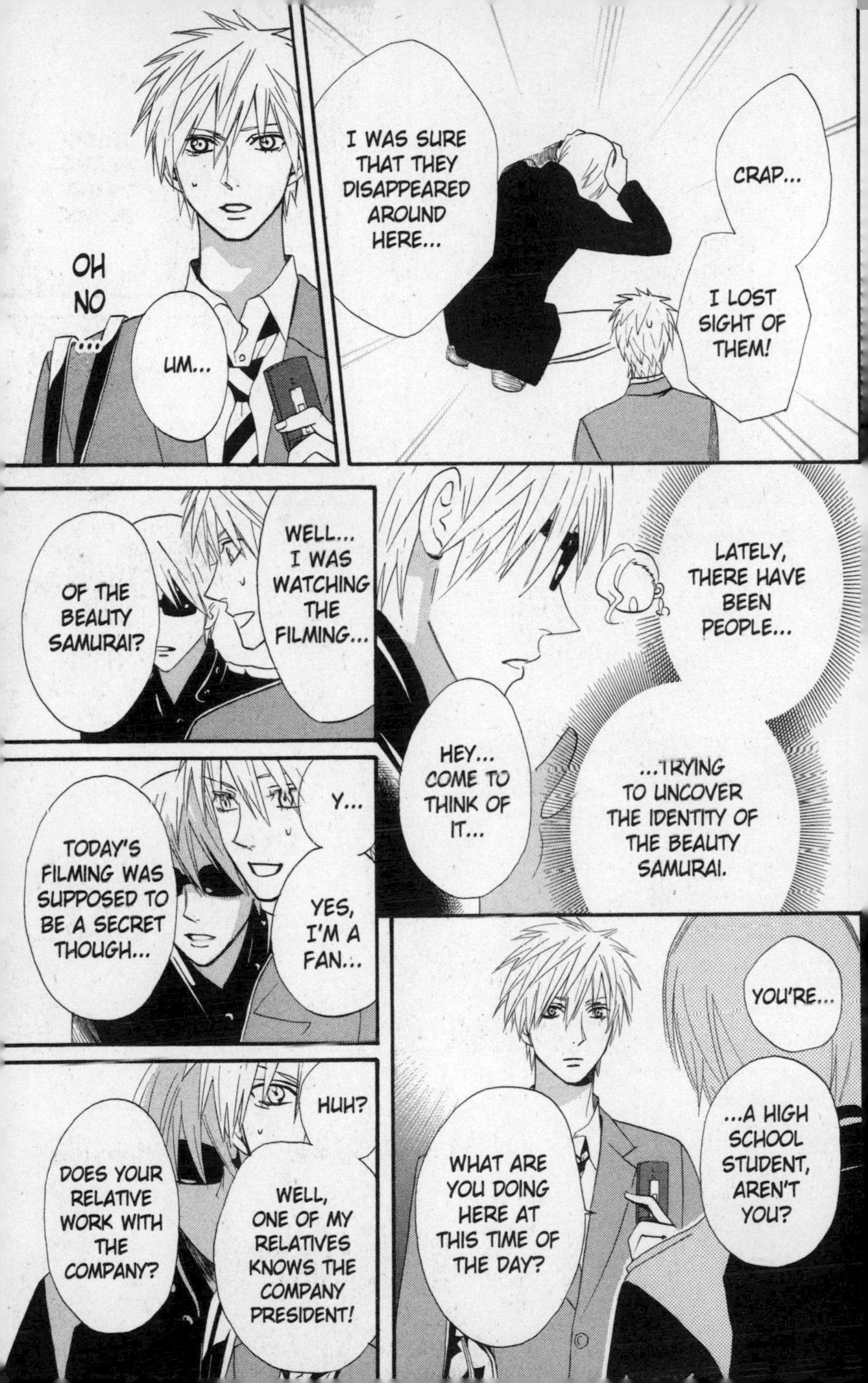
CRAP...
I LOST SIGHT OF THEM!
I WAS SURE THAT THEY DISAPPEARED AROUND HERE...
UM...
OH NO ...
LATELY, THERE HAVE BEEN PEOPLE...
...TRYING TO UNCOVER THE IDENTITY OF THE BEAUTY SAMURAI.
HEY... COME TO THINK OF IT...
YOU'RE...
...A HIGH SCHOOL STUDENT, AREN'T YOU?
WHAT ARE YOU DOING HERE AT THIS TIME OF THE DAY?
WELL... I WAS WATCHING THE FILMING...
OF THE BEAUTY SAMURAI?
Y...
YES, I'M A FAN...
TODAY'S FILMING WAS SUPPOSED TO BE A SECRET THOUGH...
HUH?
WELL, ONE OF MY RELATIVES KNOWS THE COMPANY PRESIDENT!
DOES YOUR RELATIVE WORK WITH THE COMPANY?

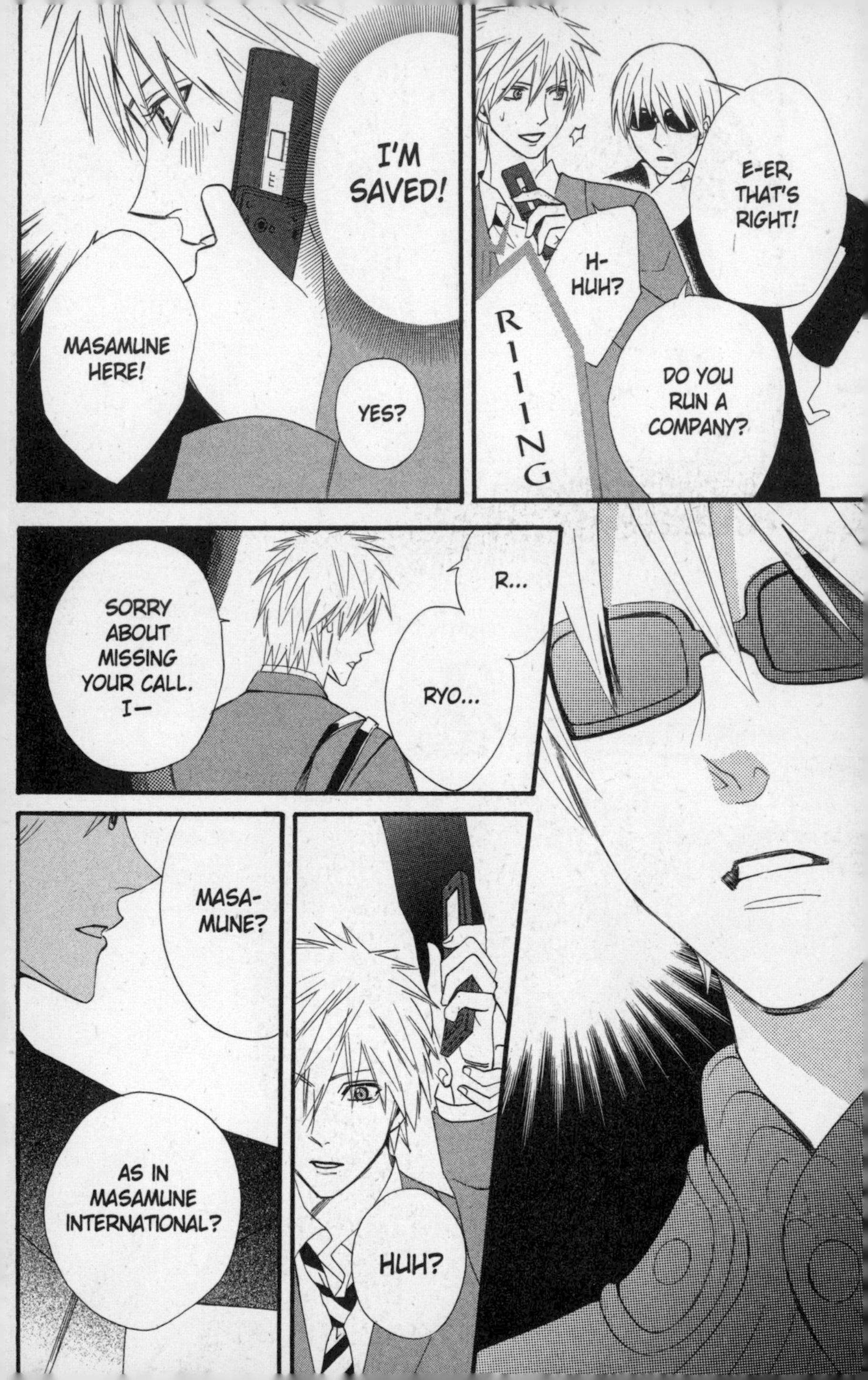
E-ER, THAT'S RIGHT!
DO YOU RUN A COMPANY?
H-HUH?
RIIING
I'M SAVED!
MASAMUNE HERE!
YES?
R...
RYO...
SORRY ABOUT MISSING YOUR CALL. I—
HUH?
MASA-MUNE?
AS IN MASAMUNE INTERNATIONAL?

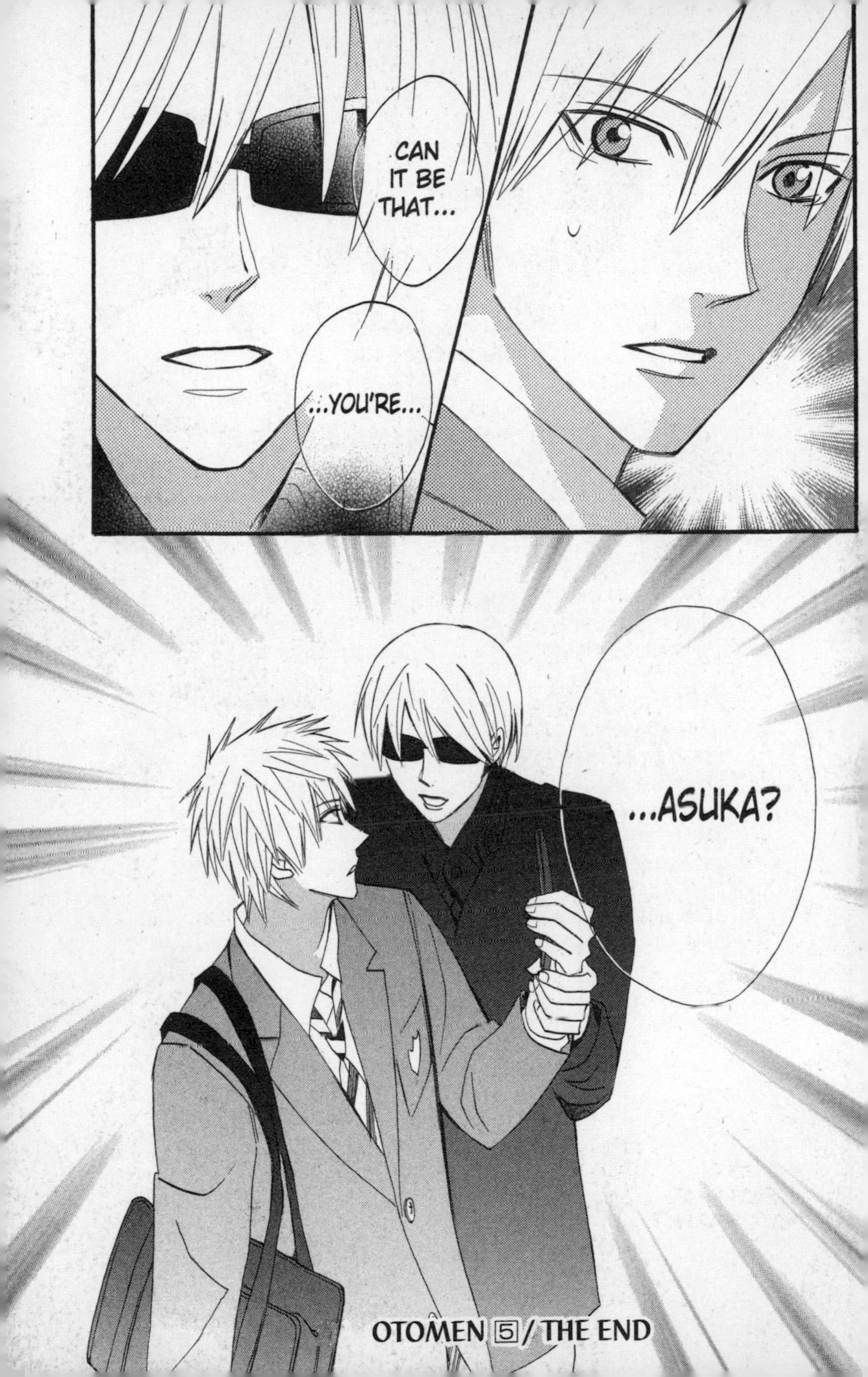
CAN IT BE THAT...
...YOU'RE...
...ASUKA?
OTOMEN 5 / THE END

Confused by some of the terms, but too MANLY to ask for help?

Here are some **cultural notes** to assist you!

ḣONORIFICS

Chan – an informal honorific used to address children and females. *Chan* can also be used toward animals, lovers, intimate friends and people whom one has known since childhood.

Kun – an informal honorific used primarily toward males. It can be used by people of more senior status addressing those junior to them or by anyone addressing boys or young men. Like *chan*, *kun* is often added to nicknames to emphasize friendship or intimacy.

San – the most common honorific title. It is used to address people outside one's immediate family and close circle of friends.

Sensei – honorific title used to address teachers as well as professionals such as doctors, lawyers and artists.

Sama – honorific used to address persons much higher in rank than oneself.

NOTES

Page 5 | Hana to Mame
The name *Hana to Mame* (Flowers and Beans) is a play on the real shojo manga
magazine *Hana to Yume* (Flowers and Dreams) published by Hakusensha.

Page 5 | Tsun-sama
Juta makes this word up by combining *tsundere* and *ore-sama*. *Tsundere* describes
a character who is *tsuntsun* (cold or irritable) and later becomes *deredere*
(affectionate or sentimental). *Ore-sama* describes a pompous and arrogant person,
as it combines *ore* (me) with the honorific *sama*.

Page 22, panel 1 | Yakisoba
Panfried noodles often sold at festivals in Japan.

Page 22, panel 3 | Takoyaki
Dough balls with pieces of octopus in them. They are made using a hot plate and are
often sold at Japanese festivals. *Tako* means "octopus" in Japanese.

Page 22, panel 5 | Butler Café
A themed café where the servers dress up as butlers and treat the customers
as masters.

Page 49, panel 3 | Bento
A bento is a lunch box that may contain rice, meat, pickles and an assortment of
side dishes. Sometimes the food is arranged in such a way as to resemble objects
like animals, flowers, leaves, and so forth. A *Shokado bento* comes in a special lunch
box that is split into four parts.

Aya Kanno was born in Tokyo, Japan.
She is the creator of *Soul Rescue* and *Blank Slate*
(originally published as *Akusaga* in Japan's
BetsuHana magazine). Her latest work, *Otomen*,
is currently being serialized in *BetsuHana*.

OTOMEN
Vol. 5
Shojo Beat Edition

Story and Art by | **AYA KANNO**

Translation & Adaptation | **JN Productions**
Touch-up Art & Lettering | **Mark McMurray**
Design | **Fawn Lau**
Editor | **Amy Yu**

VP, Production | **Alvin Lu**
VP, Sales & Product Marketing | **Gonzalo Ferreyra**
VP, Creative | **Linda Espinosa**
Publisher | **Hyoe Narita**

Otomen by Aya Kanno © Aya Kanno 2008
All rights reserved. First published in Japan in 2008 by HAKUSENSHA, Inc., Tokyo.
English language translation rights arranged with HAKUSENSHA, Inc., Tokyo.

The rights of the author(s) of the work(s) in this publication to be so identified
have been asserted in accordance with the Copyright, Designs and Patents Act 1988.
A CIP catalogue record for this book is available from the British Library.

Printed in the U.S.A.

Published by VIZ Media, LLC
P.O. Box 77010
San Francisco, CA 94107

10 9 8 7 6 5 4 3 2 1
First printing, February 2010

PARENTAL ADVISORY
OTOMEN is rated T for Teen and is recommended
for ages 13 and up. This volume contains
suggestive themes.
ratings.viz.com

www.viz.com

www.shojobeat.com

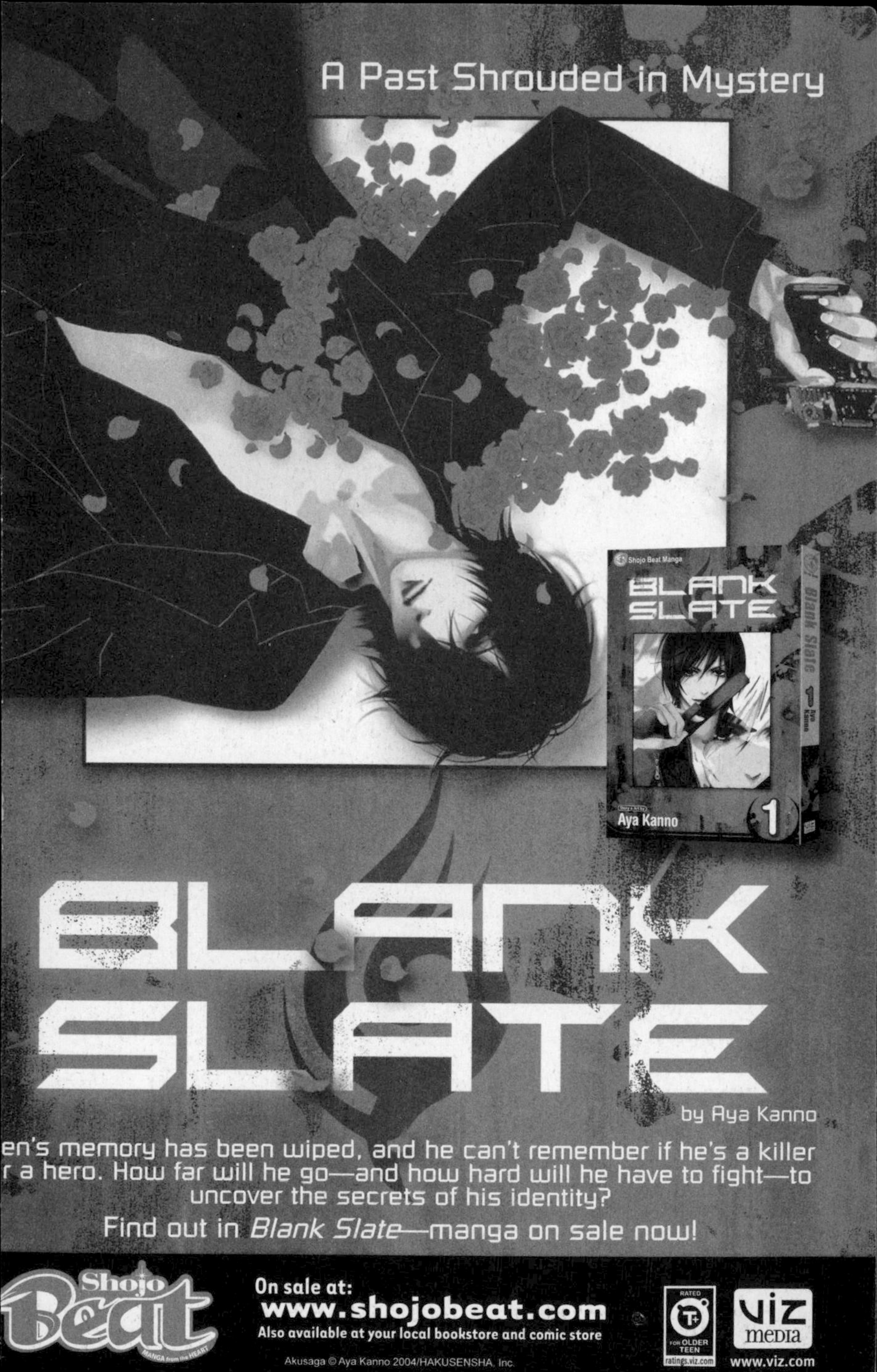
A Past Shrouded in Mystery
Shojo Beat Manga
BLANK SLATE
Blank Slate
1
Aya Kanno
Story & Art by
Aya Kanno
1
BLANK SLATE
by Aya Kanno
en's memory has been wiped, and he can't remember if he's a killer
r a hero. How far will he go—and how hard will he have to fight—to
uncover the secrets of his identity?
Find out in Blank Slate—manga on sale now!
Shojo Beat
MANGA from the HEART
On sale at:
www.shojobeat.com
Also available at your local bookstore and comic store
Akusaga © Aya Kanno 2004/HAKUSENSHA, Inc.
RATED
T+
FOR OLDER TEEN
ratings.viz.com
viz media
www.viz.com

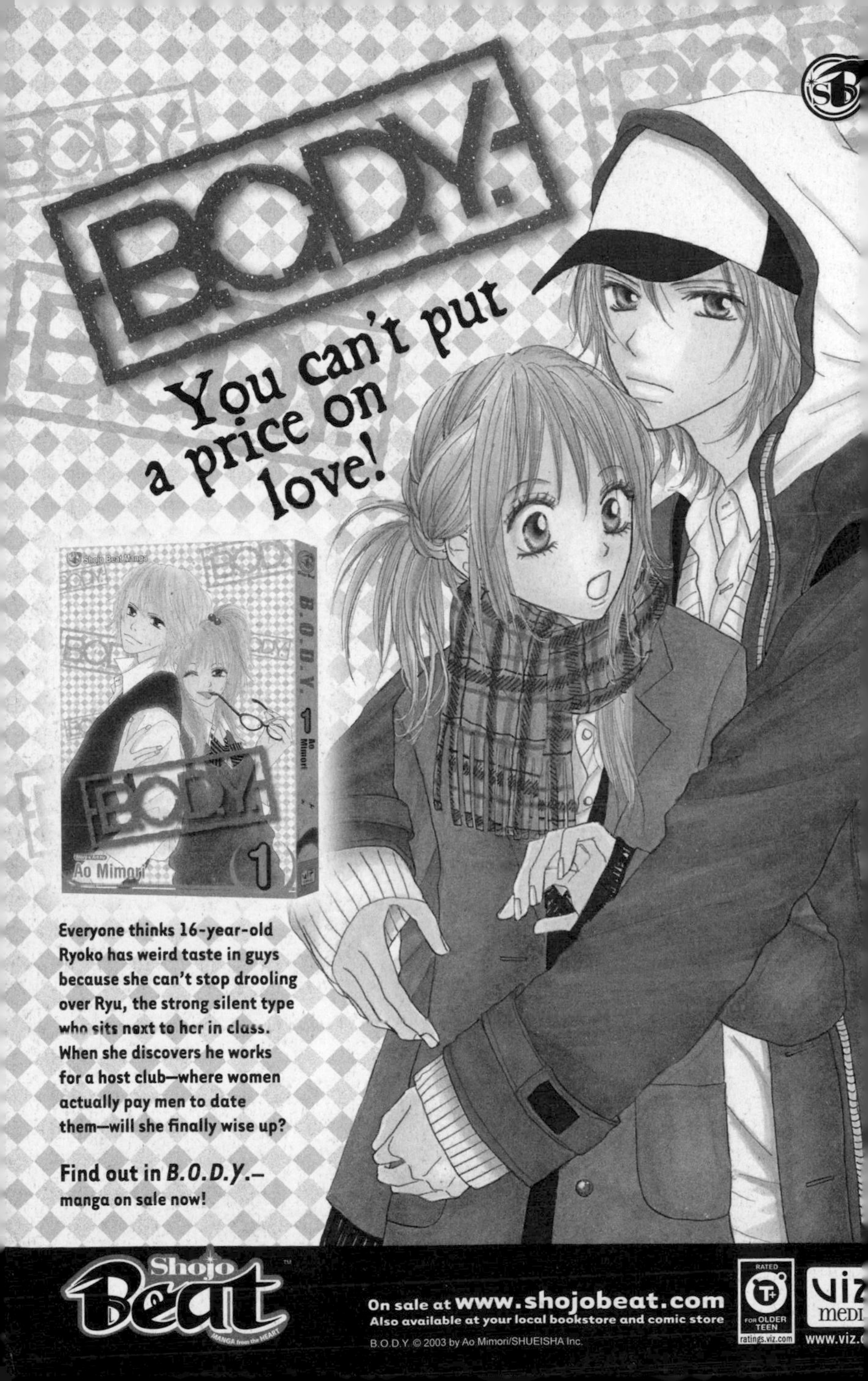
B.O.D.Y.
You can't put a price on love!
Shojo Beat Manga
B.O.D.Y.
1
Ao Mimori
Everyone thinks 16-year-old Ryoko has weird taste in guys because she can't stop drooling over Ryu, the strong silent type who sits next to her in class. When she discovers he works for a host club—where women actually pay men to date them—will she finally wise up?
Find out in *B.O.D.Y.*—manga on sale now!
Shojo Beat
MANGA from the HEART
On sale at www.shojobeat.com
Also available at your local bookstore and comic store
B.O.D.Y. © 2003 by Ao Mimori/SHUEISHA Inc.
RATED T+ FOR OLDER TEEN
ratings.viz.com